The First Step on the Longer Path

Becoming an ESL Teacher

MARY ASHWORTH

Pippin Publishing Limited

Poems on pages 7 and 8 are reproduced from *Common
Threads*, a book of prose and poetry by English as a second
language students at Hugh John Macdonald School in
Winnipeg, Manitoba. Used by permission.

Edited by Dyanne Rivers
Designed by John Zehethofer
Printed and bound by The Alger Press Limited

Canadian Cataloguing in Publication Data

Ashworth, Mary
    The first step on the longer path

(The Pippin teacher's library ; 5)
Includes bibliographical references.
ISBN 0-88751-054-X

1. English language — Study and teaching as a second
language (Elementary).* 2. English language — Study
and teaching as a second language (Secondary).*
I. Title. II. Series.

PE1128.A2A75 1992   428'.007   C92-093530-3

ISBN 0-88751-054-X

10   9   8   7   6   5   4   3   2   1

CONTENTS

To Margaret and David

Acknowledgments

I would like to thank Jonathan Lovat Dickson and Lee Gunderson for their support and encouragement, and Sally Clinton, Sylvia Helmer, Ken Reeder and Patricia Wakefield for their comments and advice. The responsibility for the content is, of course, mine.

INTRODUCTION

By sea, land and air, children have been part of this century's exodus of thousands upon thousands of economic, political and religious refugees who have left the familiar sights, smells and sounds of their homelands for what is new, different and often frightening.

> When I went to school on my first day,
> Teachers talked to me in English.
> I didn't understand nothing.
> I went to the wrong washroom.
> I didn't know how to say "Hi."
>
> Mao Ching

The inability to understand and communicate with other people can be devastating as the functioning individual, whether adult or child, suddenly loses contact with what is most precious — other human beings.

> I went to school
> And the teacher's talk
> Made me feel strange.
>
> Chung Tang

It is within the power of both teacher and child to alleviate the fear and restore communication. As the days pass, as they work together, understanding grows, confidence returns and teacher and child meet in a new relationship.

But now
I feel nothing
Can be unhappy
And strange.

My Linh Tran

Most teachers working in English-speaking countries will, at some time during their careers, meet children for whom English is a second language. These teachers may or may not have received training in teaching English as a second language to non-English-speaking children. At the same time, while administrators and consultants may not actually work with ESL (English as a second language) children, they should be in a position to help those who do. Therefore, this book is intended for student teachers, teachers, administrators and consultants.

My purpose is to present some practical ideas based on good theory for teaching English as a second language to children from kindergarten to grade 12 and to point teachers, administrators and consultants in the direction of further ideas.

To keep the book short and easy to read, every option open to teachers of ESL is not explored. The focus is on selecting activities that have proved effective and can be put into practice by classroom teachers, particularly by those who have non-ESL as well as ESL children in their classes. Many of the activities can be used equally well with non-ESL and ESL children. Those interested in further reading may find that the bibliography contains some helpful suggestions.

Because no two teaching situations are identical, it is up to you, the reader, to determine where to place your focus. May I suggest that you keep the following questions in mind as you read the book:

What are the needs of the students in *my* class?

What are *my* needs?

What difficulties do I face?

How can I overcome them?

I begin by looking at the students themselves, then go on to explain how language works and how children learn a second language. The chapter on assessment and programs takes care of some of the administrative aspects of ESL. The remainder of the book deals with teaching practices: spoken language, reading, writing, language and content, lesson and unit planning, including using audio-visual aids, and, last, communities, conflict and classrooms. It is not necessary to read the book sequentially.

I am retired! The days when I gave formal lectures on ESL methodology are behind me. I shall not, I hope, lecture to you, but rather make suggestions that you may wish to try.

No matter where the children come from nor in which country they settle, the words written by Alexander Israel Wittenberg in *The Prime Imperative* must constantly engage every teacher: "In a free society, the very best education must be accessible to every child. In addition, this education must measure up against the best education that is or has been available anywhere."

This book is just a first step for those who see the need to walk the longer path to achieving full expertise in the teaching of English as a second language to children.

. . . .

LEARNING

ABOUT STUDENTS

The more you know about the ESL students in your class, the more you can help them. In addition to getting the usual information — name, age, address, country of origin, date of entry, status, etc. — you may find it helpful to pose, perhaps through an interpreter, some of the following questions. The questions you choose to ask will depend, to some degree, on the student's age. The information obtained should be kept on file.

What languages are spoken in the home?

This information will enable you to match the student to a buddy who speaks the same language and, if necessary, find interpreters and translators. Because languages differ in their patterns of sound, structure, use and writing systems, a knowledge of these differences will also make you sympathetic to the initial problems the student may have with learning English.

When did the student speak his first word in the home language? How well does the student now speak the home language compared with other children of the same age?

If the student seems to be slow in acquiring English, the fact that he was slow in acquiring the home language *may* suggest a learning problem. Conversely, above average command of the home language *may* suggest a gifted student.

What is the composition of the family circle? Who is the primary caregiver? What responsibilities does the student have within the home? What group experiences has the student had within the home or the community?

Because the home is the most important factor determining a child's degree of success in school, the more you know about the home the better. You may be able to determine whether behavior expected at home differs substantially from behavior expected at school. Some secondary school students may be living on their own and may need advice about various concerns.

What is the attitude of the home towards learning English and towards maintaining the home language?

In planning a student's program, it is helpful to know how much support the home will give the child in both acquiring the new language and maintaining the first language — an important element in the student's further academic progress.

How well does the student read and write her native language? How well does she express ideas in that language? How well does the student handle mathematical concepts? How well does she compare with other students in the homeland?

Past performance in school can often be an indicator of future performance. Children who cannot respond well to questions asked in English are sometimes erroneously labeled "slow." When they have acquired adequate English vocabulary and structure, which may take five years, many will perform as well as, if not better than, they did in their homeland.

Has the student's schooling been interrupted? If so, why and for how long?

A student's current difficulties in school may have nothing to do with intelligence, but a lot to do with lack of opportunity to get a good education.

What subjects did the student study in his homeland?

The student may be more knowledgeable than his peers in some subjects and less knowledgeable in others, requiring a booster program to fill in the gaps.

Does the student have any medical problems, such as hearing or sight impairments, epilepsy or head injuries, that might affect academic progress?

If physical problems can be treated, a student's chances for success increase.

How does the student feel about starting life in a new country? Did the student undergo trauma or culture shock sufficient to affect her emotional well-being or capacity for learning?

Emotional factors do affect learning, including language learning. It is therefore not enough to pay attention only to ESL students' linguistic needs; their emotional needs must be addressed also.

Is the student an immigrant? A refugee? An international student? A second-generation immigrant? A native child?

While immigrant parents usually decided to leave their homeland voluntarily, refugees left fearing for their lives. International students have been sent away from home, perhaps for the first time, to get a better education. The parents of second-generation ESL students often believe that it is the home's responsibility to ensure that the child gets a good foundation in his ancestral language and culture, and that it is the school's responsibility to teach the child English. A native child may bring a growing sense of pride in his own language and culture and this should be fostered. These differences in background influence a student's orientation to school.

Conclude the interview by making sure you can pronounce the new student's name correctly. In some cultures, the name is an integral part of the child's identity. You should therefore not anglicize it to make it easier to pronounce, nor should you give the child an English name unless the parents request one. Both parents and child will appreciate your efforts to use the child's given name and, if you can find someone to teach you, speak a few phrases in the child's language such as, "Hello," "Goodbye," and "See you tomorrow."

It may also prove useful to gather information about a student's parents.

— When and why did they move from their homeland to an English-speaking country?

— What expectations do they have for their son or daughter?
— What expectations do the parents have for themselves in terms of employment and further education or training?
— What assistance do the parents need to help them settle into their new homeland?
— What level of schooling did the parents reach? Where did they obtain their education?
— What is the breadwinner's present occupation? Is this what she or he was trained for?
— Do the parents realize that speaking, reading and writing the home language help their child learn English and progress academically?
— Are the parents aware that they are entitled to services offered by the school and the community that will help them learn English and become part of the community?

You may not be able to gather all this information in a single interview but, as you build trust, you and the parents will be more open with each other.

Orientation

It's a good idea to conduct the student and parents on a tour of the school, showing them various facilities such as the office, lunchroom, playground, washrooms and classrooms the student will attend. In addition, both student and parents should meet an authority figure (the principal or vice-principal), school nurse or counselor, and one or more teachers who will have prime responsibility for the student.

It's also helpful to set up the child with a buddy, first a student who speaks the same language, later a monolingual English-speaking student.

Invite the parents to visit the school and watch a class in action. If the school is not able to supply one, suggest that they bring an interpreter to explain what is happening and why.

If the parents have difficulty understanding English, ask them to supply the name, address and phone number of an English-speaking friend who can be contacted if an emergency arises.

Try to anticipate the student's and parents' needs and provide answers whenever possible.

Culture

Children bring to school the culture of the home and this reflects the culture of the ethnic community they are part of. Cultural differences can cause misunderstandings among people of any age. Students who feel their culture is valued and understood by the school and the larger community tend to do better in school than those who feel it is rejected. The major cultural differences that affect children are:

— Child-rearing practices.
— Teaching and learning styles.
— Educational opportunities and expectations.
— Value systems.

Here are some suggestions you can use to find out about other cultures:

— Find someone from the ethnic community you are interested in who will spend time answering your questions.
— Seek help from teachers and counselors who have had experience with students from particular homelands and from social workers in the community who deal with newcomers. The school or community library is often a good source of books about specific countries or cultures.
— Keep a journal so that next year you may help other teachers and also reassess your own procedures in light of your new understanding.

If you're able to meet someone from the ethnic community you're interested in, you might ask the following questions:

How do gestures vary?

We send hidden messages through gestures. A gesture wrongly interpreted can cause misunderstanding and embarrassment.

How do children dress for school in the home country? What aspects of dress have religious significance?

Teachers can help ESL students avoid ridicule by explaining to other children the significance of, for example, a turban, and by according different dress customs the respect they deserve.

What foods are taboo? What foods have, in the past, constituted the main diet? What foods in the host country are probably unknown to the family?

Some ESL students are laughed at when they open their lunch bags. Not only can teachers support them by discussing foods of other countries with the class, but they can also sometimes help the family make the transition to new foods and new ways of marketing foods.

What games do the children play in the native country? With whom do they play? Is play valued?

In some cultures, play is not regarded as essential to a child's growth and development. Therefore, some parents see games, puppets and field trips as a waste of time, believing that school should consist of reading, writing and arithmetic only. Teachers can help parents reassess the value of play. If you invite the ESL student to teach classmates games from his homeland, it will help build his sense of belonging.

What duties are children expected to perform in the home? Are boys and girls treated differently? What is the relationship between children and adults?

Men are still the dominant sex in some cultures where boys are not expected to help around the home and may have more freedom than girls. Some boys — and their fathers — may need help adjusting to a woman teacher. At the same time, girls from these cultures may seem somewhat withdrawn because women are discouraged from speaking out in public.

How do child-rearing practices differ? How do teaching and learning styles differ between schools in the native country and the host country?

Parents are children's first teachers. This means that children's learning styles are formed according to the customs and beliefs of the culture in which they grow up. If your teaching style is very different from the child's learning style, she may be confused and frustrated.

What values are considered important in the native country? For instance, is punctuality considered a virtue?

Values are transmitted from adults to children and from children to children. ESL children experience severe tension when the values of the home are at odds with those of the school. Teachers who understand the differences can often help ease the trauma that arises.

What major festivals may require the children to be kept home from school?

Most schools still observe Christian festivals, but more and more children come from homes that subscribe to one of the other great religions with its own special feast days. The children's absence on such days should be accepted. Children and parents are delighted when a festival from their culture is given respect and recognition by the school.

What expectations do ESL parents have of schools? What aspirations do they have for their children?

Parents' aspirations for their children can be too high or too low and are often built on their own youthful experiences in their homeland or on hearsay about the host country. To be supportive of their children and realistic about their futures, parents must understand the school's goals and philosophy, its programs and options.

Cross-Cultural Counseling

Many ESL students have been uprooted from places and people they hold dear. They may not have been consulted about leaving their homeland and they may have suffered some painful and frightening experiences. Counselors who are both bilingual and bicultural can help them work through the trauma. If this kind of counseling is not available, you can work wonders with a little TLC (tender loving care), but be sure you know how to express it in a way that won't be misunderstood. For example, a friendly pat on the head is not acceptable in some cultures. As the weeks pass, ensure that the student is growing in self-esteem through encouragement received from her teachers and peers.

Educational systems vary. Counselors or teachers may have to explain to both parents and students, not just once, but on a number of occasions, how the new system varies from that in their homeland. Watch for signs of stress in the student. These may be manifested by withdrawal or acting out.

Age Groups

PRESCHOOLERS AND THE EARLY GRADES

Approaches to child-rearing and socializing children vary from culture to culture. These affect routines, patterns of interaction, customs, behavioral expectations, rewards and punishments. If what goes on in the home differs greatly from what goes on at school, the child will be confused and upset. The more you know about child-rearing in other cultures, the more you will be able to adapt your ways somewhat to those of the child, especially in the early days. In time, the child will adapt to the new ways.

MIDDLE GRADES

Teaching and learning styles also vary from culture to culture. Some employ question-and-answer, some use observation and practice, some discourage argument and discussion, some place the responsibility for learning on the student, and some require the student to memorize the text and repeat it back. By the time they reach the middle grades, students are already conditioned to particular teaching and learning styles. The more you can find out about your ESL students' educational backgrounds, the more you can help them adjust to their new learning environment.

SENIOR GRADES

It takes five to seven years for ESL students to master sufficient academic English to compete on equal terms with their peers. All students require a high level of proficiency in spoken and written English if they are to succeed in post-secondary institutions and enter skilled or professional employment. Generally speaking, however, ESL teenagers do not have five to seven years before they reach the age for entering post-secondary institutions. Therefore, they are often under a great deal of pressure to learn English quickly. Try to understand their aspirations, but help them be realistic. Check local colleges for ESL courses they can attend after leaving high school.

The School

The school is the first community ESL students will encounter. Their first impressions will affect the way they feel about their peers, their teachers and the nation they are now part of. Because the school is a microcosm of the world outside, they may meet both acceptance and rejection. From time to time, teachers and administrators need to check their own attitudes and practices:

— How well are non-English speaking students received in your school?
— Does multiculturalism or cultural pluralism mean more than food and dances? If so, what?
— Does the talk in the staffroom include racist jokes? Do comments indicate some deep-seated prejudice? Or are students with different linguistic and cultural backgrounds accepted and, if so, how is this demonstrated to the student body?
— Are notices to parents translated into other languages if more than 10 students speak that language?
— Do teachers resent having classes that have a mix of non-ESL and ESL students who speak different languages, are different ages, and come from different educational backgrounds? If so, why?
— What assistance do teachers receive from the administration to help them help non-English speaking students? What additional help should they receive?

Guiding Principles

Let's sum up this chapter with some basic principles that, if put into practice, can help students master English and adjust to a new culture:

— ESL students' first language and culture should be supplemented, not supplanted, by the second language and culture.
— The experiences and skills ESL students bring with them are the foundation for future learning and should be used.
— While ESL students may acquire social skills in English in a year or two, it may take them five to seven years to acquire proficiency in academic English. Schools must make a long-term commitment to supporting them.
— The more ESL students interact with English-speaking students, the faster and better they will learn English and adjust to the new culture. Integration — with support — into the social and academic life of the school should begin as soon as ESL students are ready to meet their peers.
— Schools and minority parents must work together for the good of the children.

. . . .

HOW LANGUAGE WORKS

Language is an emotional topic. While habits of eating and dress may change over a period of years, behaviors connected with language, learned during the formative pre-school years, remain part of every individual's deep-down identity. Children can be easily hurt if their mother tongue is denigrated in any way. ESL students must therefore be encouraged to add English to their linguistic repertoire, which may already include more than one language, while maintaining and improving their skills in their first language. At the same time, some students whose mother tongue is English speak a dialect sufficiently different from that spoken in the schools that it causes problems. These children may need to add standard English to their repertoire while maintaining their home dialect.

Teachers can provide valuable help to children struggling to master English if they know how language, particularly the English language, works and if they are aware of the theories that explain how children learn and acquire a second language. These theories will be reviewed in the next chapter.

A sound knowledge of the workings of the English language benefits teachers in the many ways. First, it is difficult for teachers to teach what they do not know. A teacher working with ESL students of any age needs at least an elementary understanding of the rules of English as they relate to the various systems: sounds, words, sentences and meaning.

Further, some older students will have studied English grammar in their homeland and will expect their teacher's knowledge to be as good as, if not better than, their own. And, as problems in structure, use and usage arise and need correction, particularly in the upper grades, a common terminology to describe the components of English and their functions makes explanation easier.

A language is a complex system of systems. The teacher's competence in English will enable him to tell when a student has made an error and, if an explanation is warranted, his knowledge of the underlying structure — grammar — of English will enable him to explain the nature of the error and present an acceptable model. Further, teachers who take pleasure in knowing how English works in various situations for various purposes usually end up using it to better advantage themselves.

It is impossible in a chapter of this length to do justice to the great body of knowledge that linguists around the world have built up, particularly in this century, about the fascinating phenomenon that separates humankind from animals — language. I'll begin with some general statements about language, then look at some important aspects of English, particularly those that are either vital to the mastery of English or seem to cause problems for ESL students. Teachers who wish to augment this rather sketchy overview of how English works will find some useful resources listed in the bibliography.

Facts about Language

There are no primitive languages.

Every language can satisfy the psychological, emotional and social needs of its speakers. Therefore, no ESL student speaks a primitive language, no matter what part of the world she comes from.

No language is linguistically superior to any other.

In this century, English has become an important world language. In the 16th century, Spanish and Portuguese predominated. In the 21st century, Chinese may become a major world language. If this happens, it will be because China has assumed an important place in the community of nations, not because the Chinese language is inherently superior.

All the languages and dialects spoken by ESL students should be respected, but children and their parents should recognize the importance of mastering standard English if it is the medium of instruction in schools, colleges and universities in the country where they now reside.

Languages change, often by creating new words, to meet the scientific and technological demands of the modern world.

Some ESL students will have words in their own language for present-day scientific and technological concepts and will merely need to be given the English word. Others may need to learn both the concept and the English word.

All languages allow speakers to create new utterances, but these utterances must stay within the rules established over the centuries by speakers of a particular language.

ESL students will have to learn the rules that govern English. Some of these will be similar to those in their first language while others will differ considerably.

No language is wholly regular. There are exceptions to the rules of all languages.

ESL students may complain about the many irregularities in English but, if they search, they will also find irregularities in their first language. Irregularity is something they will have to put up with!

Purposes for Which ESL Students Use Language

Like children whose first language is English, ESL students assume roles — son or daughter, friend, student, consumer, worker — that vary with their age. Each role has some language specific to it. Within the school, for example, students meet a variety of people whose positions require them to use different levels of formality in spoken and written English. Students might interact with other students, the classroom teacher, the principal, a counselor, teacher's aide, the custodian, school nurse and other teachers. In addition, ESL students interact with a variety of people in different situations in the community and in the workplace and will need to use different levels of formality in these places.

At school, ESL students study a variety of subjects, such as math, music, physics, English literature and biology. Each has a vocabulary and structures that are particular to it and must be mastered.

ESL students need language to get help, to collect and record facts, to express their emotions, to think with and to interact socially.

By watching one or two English-speaking students closely, teachers can become aware of the variety of purposes for which children use language and the variety of language they use. To become integrated into the school and community, ESL students must master this same variety of language for many of the same purposes.

The Structure of Language

Before this century's revolution in the study of linguistics, grammars were prescriptive. In other words, they told people what they ought to say. Today grammars are descriptive, telling people what actually is said in different situations. The notion of what is or is not "correct" English lies not in the structure of the language but in the users of the language and in the situation.

Grammar refers to the rules of the language. Every speaker of English knows, mostly unconsciously, the rules of English — how to make questions, how to indicate plurality, which verb form to use after another, etc. This is referred to as a speaker's "competence." What a speaker does with this knowledge, what he actually says or writes, is referred to as his "performance." A speaker's competence is usually superior to his performance. In other words, most people, in everyday practice, don't use all the knowledge they have of the language and how it works.

Students learning English must master some of the rules governing the sound system, the word system, the structure of sentences and how to extract meaning if they are to compete on equal terms with their peers. The more rules they master (the greater their competence), the more native-like their English will be (the better their performance). This does not mean, however, they should be formally taught each rule. They'll pick up many of the rules if they are exposed to English in situations that have meaning and interest for them.

One way of looking at language is to divide it into levels or components, remembering that these levels or components are interrelated. For example:

A meaning can be expressed in many forms: How much is that item? What does it cost? What does it sell for? Similarly a form can have more than one meaning: They are entertaining women.

Another way of dividing language into levels is

Certain structures can be used in a number of situations. For example, structures that deal with cause and effect can be used in various school subjects such as science and home economics. Conversely, the use to which language is to be put helps determine the structure that should be used. For example, refusing an invitation politely or rudely requires different structures.

A third model tends to see language as consisting of layers, much like the stories in a house, with phonology in the basement and semantics in the attic. In fact, there is much overlap and interplay among the levels. Language is a system of interdependent systems, which, while they may be looked at separately, cannot exist without each other.

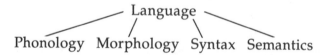

PHONOLOGY

Phonology is the study of speech sounds.

Phonemes

A phoneme is the smallest speech sound that makes a difference in meaning. For example, /b/ and /p/ are phonemes because "bin" and "pin" have different meanings determined by the initial sound of each word. The symbols for phonemes are written between slashes to distinguish them from letters. Not all English phonemes are found in other languages.

There are 24 consonant phonemes and about 15 vowel phonemes in English, all represented by the 26 letters of the alphabet. The number of vowel phonemes varies according to the dialect of the speaker. For example, a Scot, a Newfoundlander and an Alabaman each use some different vowel phonemes, which, when combined with different intonation patterns, causes them to sound different from each other.

Here are the International Phonetic Alphabet symbols representing the 24 consonant phonemes.

/p/	pin	/s/	sip
/b/	bin	/z/	zip
/t/	tin	/ʃ/	ship
/d/	din	/ʒ/	vision
/k/	kill	/m/	mine
/g/	gill	/n/	nine
/tʃ/	chill	/ŋ/	king
/dʒ/	Jill	/w/	will
/f/	fine	/h/	hill
/v/	vine	/j/	yet
/θ/	thigh	/l/	Lil
/ð/	thy	/r/	rill

And these are the International Phonetic Alphabet symbols representing the 15 most frequently used vowel phonemes.

Front Vowels		Back Vowels	
/i/	beat	/ɑ/	bought
/ɪ/	bit	/ɔ/	law
/eɪ/	bait	/əʊ/	boat
/ɛ/	bet	/ʊ/	pull
/æ/	bat	/u/	pool
Central Vowels		Diphthongs	
/ə/	sofa	/aʊ/	bough
/ʌ/	butt	/aɪ/	buy
		/ɔɪ/	boy

Phonemes are differentiated by the point and manner of articulation. The points of articulation can be seen in this diagram.

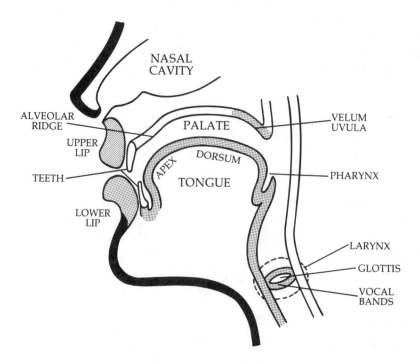

The manner of articulation may be:

— Voiced or voiceless: Try saying /f/ as in "fine" and /v/ as in "vine," placing your fingers on your larynx so you can feel the difference. When you say "fine," your vocal chords remain still, while they vibrate when you say "vine."

— Stop or continuant: Say "stop" and try to make the /p/ carry on. Then say "bun" and make the /n/ carry on. The first is a stop, the second a continuant.

— Nasal or oral: Most sounds come out through the mouth but in /m/, /n/ and /ŋ/, the air is directed through the nose. To check, make one of the three sounds and pinch your nose.

— Created by friction: Called fricatives, these consonant sounds (e.g., /f/, /s/ and /h/) are heard when air is forced between two vocal organs, such as the lips, tongue or teeth, that are held close together to create friction.

Vowels sounds are voiced and made by opening the jaw wide or by closing it and moving the tongue to the front or back of the mouth. To see how this works, stand in front of a mirror and say aloud only the vowels in the following words in the order listed. Watch what happens to your jaw, your tongue and your lips.

/i/	beat	/ɑʊ/	bought
/ɪ/	bit	/ɔ/	law
/eɪ/	bait	/əʊ/	boat
/ɛ/	bet	/ʊ/	pull
/æ/	bat	/u/	pool

To learn how and where the consonant sounds are made, stand in front of a mirror and say aloud the words listed with the consonant phonemes on page 25, watching what occurs at the points of articulation.

English permits certain sequences of phonemes, but not others. For example, words can begin with /str/ but not /stl/, with /pr/ but not /pm/. Some languages permit sequences not permitted in English.

Phonemes that seem to cause ESL students the most trouble are /θ/ as in "thigh" and /ð/ as in "thy," /l/ as in "Lil" and /r/ as in "rill," /f/ as in "fine" and /v/ as in "vine," /ʒ/ as in "vision," /tʃ/ as in "chill" and /dʒ/ as in "Jill."

Intonation, Stress and Pauses

Speakers of English also send messages to their listeners by means of intonation, stress, and pauses.

Three levels of pitch or intonation — rising, falling and steady — can be combined to send certain messages.

A statement is signalled by a steady pitch ending with a rising, then falling, pitch:

Joan is here.

A question that begins with an interrogative word (who, when, why, where, how) is signalled by a steady pitch ending with a rising, then falling, pitch:

When is Joan coming?

A question that begins with an auxiliary verb ends on a rising pitch:

Is Joan coming?

A question expressed in statement form also ends on a rising pitch:

Joan is here?

A change in the normal intonation pattern can draw the attention of the listener to some feature of concern to the speaker, or it can be just plain confusing!

In English sentences, we stress the content words (nouns, verbs, adjectives and adverbs). Function words (conjunctions, prepositions, articles and auxiliary verbs) are usually un-stressed. Let's look, for example, at Tennyson's lines:

/   /   /
Break, break, break,
      /   /   /
On thy cold grey stones, O Sea!

Although each line has three stresses, the first line contains three syllables and the second line seven — the unimportant words are swallowed.

It's interesting to note that the English stress system can be used to create humor as in: Where did the Lone Ranger take his garbage? To the dump, to the dump, to the dump!

The meaning of a sentence can also be changed by stressing one word and making it louder and higher in pitch. Try saying the following sentence a number of times, increasing the loud-ness and raising the pitch of one word each time. Consider the change that occurs in the meaning:

NATURALLY he'd like some cake.
Naturally HE'D like some cake.
Naturally he'd LIKE some cake.
Naturally he'd like SOME cake.
Naturally he'd like some CAKE.

Changing the tempo of a sentence can also create emphasis. While speed of speech suggests urgency, a pause may be a call for deliberation. Pauses usually mark the boundaries of im-portant elements, such as clauses and sometimes phrases, in a spoken sentence.

The best way to learn about the music of the English language is to listen to the way speakers use it to get things done, make a point or express an emotion. Perhaps this anecdote about Mark Twain expresses best what is meant by the "music" of English. Apparently, he cut himself shaving and uttered a string of curses. When his wife, attempting to shame him, repeated his oaths word-for-word, Twain replied, "You've got the words, my dear, but not the music!"

MORPHOLOGY

Morphology is the study of the structure of words. Morphemes are the smallest *meaningful* elements into which words can be broken down.

Syllables

Morphemes are not the same as syllables, which often have no meaning. For example, "unhappiness" can be broken down into three morphemes — "un" (a prefix signaling a negative), "happi" (the root word) and "ness" (a suffix signaling that the word is a noun) — and four syllables — "un-hap-pi-ness" — where each syllable must contain a vowel. The second and third syllables have no meaning. For this reason, keep in mind that word analysis rather than syllabication exercises is more likely to produce understanding in young readers.

Prefixes

A prefix is placed before a root word and can alter the meaning. For example, "in" and "un" produce the opposite meaning (e.g., active — inactive, happy — unhappy) and "re" can mean do it again (e.g., read — reread). Most spellers contain lists of prefixes and their meanings.

Suffixes

Suffixes are placed after a root word. Derivational suffixes change the grammatical category of a word. For example, adding "ly" to "happy" (happily) changes an adjective to an adverb, adding "ness" to "happy" (happiness) changes an adjective to a noun, and adding "al" to "music" (musical) changes a noun to an adjective.

Inflectional suffixes, on the other hand, make changes within the grammatical category. For example, an inflectional suffix may change a present tense verb to the past tense (e.g., walk — walked), a singular noun to plural (e.g., boy — boys), or make comparisons within the adjective category (e.g., big — bigger).

Compound Words

Compound words are formed by combining two root words (e.g., black + berry = blackberry: a berry that is black). In this instance, the word that results is the sum of its parts, but this is not always the case. For example, "blacklist" refers not to a list that is black but to a list of people who are to be boycotted.

Pronunciation

Some morphemes that, when written, appear the same are not always pronounced the same way. The best examples are the past tense and the plural markers. Listen to the endings as you say the following words aloud:

Past Tense	Plural
stopped /t/	ducks /s/
robbed /d/	eggs /z/
batted /ɪd/	churches /ɪz/

Vocabulary

An ever-expanding vocabulary is central to mastering English. ESL students must either pick up or be taught words in the following categories. A few examples are given in each category, but ESL students' needs will be different depending on their age and, therefore, grade level, as well as their previous knowledge of English:

— Personal: Personal pronouns, body parts, clothing, emotions, kinship terms.
— Getting help: Requests, apologies, thanks.
— Everyday: Colors, days of the week, months, money, weather, numbers, telling time, the alphabet.
— Around school: Classroom, office, nurse, gym, counselor, sports.
— Subject matter: Arithmetic, social studies, home economics, art.

- Relationships: Up and down, near and far, because, however.
- Concepts: Space, time, weight, nuclear fission.
- Instructional words and commands: Take out, write, read, turn to page..., bring, stop, begin.
- Around the community: Bus, community center, store, police officer
- Around home: Food, rooms, apartment, house.

Vocabulary can also be classified into the following word groups:

- By root word: e.g., happy: happiness, happily.
- By key word and associated words: e.g., water: ocean, river, rain, drink, tap.
- By subject matter: e.g., arithmetic: add, subtract, divide, multiply.
- By part of speech: e.g., nouns: box, book, desk, hat.
- By language function: e.g., requests, refusals, invitations.
- By similarity or opposition: e.g., big — large, big — small.
- By theme: e.g., pollution, conservation.
- By concept: e.g., space, time.
- By topic: e.g., computer, United Nations.
- By rhyme: e.g., sing — ring

Knowing what a word means involves experiencing it and using it many times in different contexts in both spoken and written language.

Dictionaries

Dictionaries provide information about pronunciation and meaning. For many beginning students, however, using an English dictionary creates more problems than it solves. A student looks up one word, is given three or four more, none of which she understands and must therefore look up, and the process goes on. A bilingual dictionary in English and the student's own language can be helpful, but should not become a crutch.

Dictionaries can also be an aid to spelling provided the student understands that different letters or combinations of letters can produce identical sounds (e.g., /f/ in phonics and fish). While children often complain that English spelling is irregular, it is, in fact, remarkably regular considering the way oral language changes in time while spelling is frozen in print. Exposure to written English and friendly correction will, eventually, enable the student to spell even the most problematic English words!

If students can break down new words into meaningful elements (morphemes), they will be able to attack new material without constantly referring to a dictionary. The rules and patterns of English spelling can be found in any speller.

SYNTAX

Syntax is the study of the arrangement of words in sentences so as to arrive at meaning.

We face an immediate problem, however, in trying to identify a sentence. Is it the expression of a complete thought? "A dog" can express a complete thought but it would not be considered a sentence. Must a sentence have a subject and a predicate; that is, must the predicate say something about the subject (topic)? But what is the topic in "It's snowing," or "John gave Bill three hundred dollars"? Or is a sentence a group of words that falls between a capital letter and a period? There are reputedly more than 200 definitions of a sentence, but that does not seem to prevent native speakers of English from recognizing and feeling comfortable with some basic word arrangements.

Sentence Patterns

As a general rule, basic sentences in English follow the pattern of Subject-Verb-Object (S-V-O). Some languages don't follow this pattern but instead use S-O-V.

A sentence can be looked at as consisting of a series of slots.

N=Noun V=Verb LV=Linking Verb Adj=Adjective
N1=First Noun N2=Second Noun N3=Third Noun

Wasps sting. N1 V
John loves Amy. N1 V N2
Amy is my cousin. N1 LV N1
Amy is beautiful. N1 LV Adj
Amy told the children a story. N1 V N2 N3

They elected Rosemary leader. N1 V N2 N2
They painted the house gray. N1 V N2 Adj

New sentences can be created by simply inserting different words into the slots as in the following examples.

N1   V   N2
John loves   Amy.
Bill loves   Amy.
Bill kissed Amy.
Bill kissed Lulubelle.

Confusion can arise when it is not clear into which slot certain words fit. Take, for example, the sentence, "He gave her dog biscuits." Did he give biscuits to her dog or did he give dog biscuits to her?

Jokes often use this confusion between slots to produce humor. (e.g., How do you make a Venetian blind? Stick your fingers in his eyes).

A fun way to learn how English works is to examine jokes that use language rather than situations to produce humor.

Word Order

Some elements in a sentence are fixed, while others can be moved. Let's look, for example, at the sentence, "The tabby cat caught the rat early one morning." While "tabby" must precede "cat," the phrase "early one morning" can be moved to the beginning of the sentence. However, it can't be placed between "tabby" and "cat."

Try moving the adjectives preceding "balls" in this sentence: All my 10 brand new big red rubber balls were stolen.

Word arrangements that are permissible in English may not be permissible in another language and vice versa. For example, adjectives follow, rather than precede, nouns in some languages.

Content and Function Words

Content words are nouns, verbs, adjectives and adverbs, while prepositions, conjunctions, auxiliary verbs and articles are function words.

If content words are replaced by nonsense words, a sentence will still *sound* like English. Consider, for example, this famous nonsense rhyme from Lewis Carroll's *Through the Looking Glass:*

'Twas brillig and the slithy toves
Did gyre and gimble in the wabe...

It might be rewritten as:

'Twas [afternoon] and the [happy children]
Did [jump] and [dance] in the [leaves]...

If, on the other hand, the function words are replaced by nonsense words, it is difficult to derive any meaning at all from the verse.

['Bsmit] afternoon [ront fram] happy children
[Mot] jump [ront] dance [gop fram] leaves.

The foregoing makes it clear that students who are taught only to name objects are a long way from mastering English. They must also have a grasp of the function words essential to expressing relationships.

Phrases and Clauses

Phrases do not contain a verb and usually expand the head-word. They can come before or after the headword.

All the new	students	in the classroom
Phrase	Headword	Phrase

Unlike phrases, clauses contain a verb. Coordinate clauses have equal status: that is, each is a principal clause and can stand alone. For example, in the sentence, "John read a book and Bill watched television," both "John read a book" and "Bill watched television" are principal clauses that could stand on their own as sentences. They are joined by the coordinate conjunction "and."

Subordinate clauses, on the other hand, cannot stand alone. In the sentence, "John was reading a book when Bill arrived," for example, "John was reading a book" is the principal clause while "when Bill arrived" is a subordinate clause. In this case, the subordinate clause cannot stand as a sentence on its own. Subordinate clauses are introduced by subordinators such as the subordinate conjunctions "when" and "if" or the pronouns "who," "that" and "which."

Sentences can be made up of principal and subordinate clauses:

Simple sentences contain one principal clause (e.g., John read a book). Compound sentences contain two or more principal clauses (e.g., John read a book and Bill watched television). Complex sentences contain a principal clause and one or more subordinate clauses (e.g., John, who was feeling tired, read a book). Compound-complex sentences contain two or more principal clauses and one or more subordinate clauses (e.g., John, who was feeling tired, read a book and Bill watched television).

When students have learned to combine thought elements into complex sentences, they are able to express various nuances of meaning.

Transformations

A simple sentence such as "John read a book" can be transformed into a question, a negative statement or a negative question. This is important because most conversations depend, to some extent, on questions and answers. The example, "John read a book," might be transformed into a question by saying, "Did John read the book?" The same statement can be transformed into a negative statement by saying, "John didn't read the book," and a negative question by saying, "Didn't John read the book?"

A statement in the active voice can be transformed into a statement in the passive voice. For example, "John read the book," can be transformed into the passive, "The book was read (by John)."

While the meaning of these two sentences is the same, use of the passive can change the emphasis and, if necessary, remove reference to the doer of the action, a useful device at times.

Verb Forms

Verbs can indicate whether an act is complete, in progress, occurred yesterday, is going on now, or will occur tomorrow. In addition, they can also denote whether the act was a single event or one of a series, and suggest what might or should happen. Some verb forms can follow others, but some cannot.

It's worth noting that some English verb forms don't have the same use or meaning in other languages.

The following list sets out the most commonly used verb forms. To use these comfortably, it's vital to know the various forms of the verbs "to be" and "to have."

Simple present	John reads his book.
Present continuous	John is reading his book.
Present perfect	John has read his book.
Present perfect continuous	John has been reading his book.
Simple past	John read his book.
Past continuous	John was reading his book.
Past perfect	John has read his book.
Past perfect continuous	John had been reading his book.
Simple future	John will read his book.
Alternative future	John is going to read his book.
Future continuous	John will be reading his book.
Future perfect	John will have read his book.
Future perfect continuous	John will have been reading his book.
Present conditional	If John had the time, he would read a book.
Past conditional	If John had had the time, he would have read a book.
Future conditional	If John has the time, he will read a book.

It will take most ESL students some years to master the English verb system, but for those going on to higher education accomplishing this is very important.

Modals

Some auxiliaries, known as modals, can be used to indicate the mood of the speaker (e.g., "I will" suggests a determination not found in "I might...," "I must...," suggests action will probably follow, whereas "I ought to..." is indecisive). The modals are "can — could," "will — would," "may — might," "shall — should — ought to," and "must."

Because modal auxiliaries do not exist in all languages, some ESL students find the system difficult to learn. Nevertheless, the nuances of meaning distinguished by modals make it vital that they be learned.

Articles

Unlike English, not all languages use the articles "a," "an," and "the."

"A" and "an" are used before a singular noun that has not previously been specified (e.g., I have a banana), while "the" is used before a noun that has been specified (e.g., The banana is in my lunch box). "An" is used before nouns beginning with a vowel (e.g., I have an orange).

If the noun is plural, it is preceded by a word like "some" or "many" when unspecified, but by "the" when specified (e.g., I have some oranges. The oranges are in my lunch box). There are also occasions when no article is used (e.g., I like oranges).

SEMANTICS

Semantics is the study of meaning in language. Meaning cannot be extracted only by looking up words in a dictionary or analyzing the structure of a sentence. Past experiences and present context play a part in defining meaning. Students need a lot of exposure to the English language in meaningful and interesting situations where objects, gestures, facial expressions and events all play a part in giving meaning to words.

Words

Every word or morpheme has a meaning agreed upon by most people. This is its denotation or reference; that is, what's found by looking it up in the dictionary. However, a word's reference does not comprise its total meaning. When words are strung together in a context or situation, both speaker and listener, because of their varied experiences, may draw different meanings — connotation or sense — from them. For example, "home" is defined as "dwelling place, fixed residence of family or household" in the dictionary. This is its reference. However, teacher and students may have had very different experiences of home and these will affect the meaning, or sense, they bring to the word.

Words that are similar, though rarely identical, in meaning are synonyms while antonyms are opposite in meaning.

Sentences

The meaning of sentences can be changed by the way they are said, what has gone before, the person to whom they are said and the context in which they are said.

Idioms

The meaning of sentences such as, "He's pulling your leg," or "She let the cat out of the bag," cannot be discovered by looking up each word in the dictionary. Rather, the meaning must be experienced in context or explained.

Discourse and Text

In the past, linguistic analysis focused on the sentence, but recently much attention has been paid to the way sentences work together in sequence to produce what is called "discourse" or "text." Extended meaning is not conveyed by a single sentence, but by a series of utterances that combine to produce a coherent stretch of language such as a conversation or an essay. While "discourse" is used by some to refer to spoken language and "text" to written language, this dichotomy is not standard among linguists. Both terms are used by some to refer to either spoken or written language.

Different types of discourse and text, such as conversation, interviews, speeches, articles, essays and stories (sometimes referred to as "discourse tasks"), when analyzed, are shown to have their own structures and rituals. In a conversation there are, for example, acceptable ways of taking turns, changing the topic and concluding. An essay requires an opening statement, various paragraphs that expand on the statement, and a summary. Students who ignore the structure and rituals of discourse and text as used by competent native speakers and writers of English may have difficulty integrating both socially and academically, or, conversely, may experience difficulty following or comprehending some of the more demanding forms of text or discourse such as subject-matter textbooks, mathematics word problems or formal addresses.

FORMALITY

Different situations require different levels of formality in both spoken and written language. Using informal language in a very formal situation or vice versa marks the speaker or writer as different and can create an uncomfortable situation.

ENGLISH FOR SPECIAL PURPOSES

Different professions such as science, law, religion, medicine, journalism, sport, broadcasting and advertising use language in ways that can baffle ESL students when they first encounter it. Only exposure and explanation over time can help students unravel English used for special purposes.

DIALECTS

Throughout the world, people speak many varieties of English in which pronunciation, vocabulary and certain aspects of grammar identify the speaker as coming from a particular region or social background. Unfortunately, there is a social stigma attached to some dialects, while others are difficult to understand. Just as some students must learn English as a second language, so it is advisable for some students who speak a non-standard English dialect to add standard English to their speech repertoire.

HOW A SECOND LANGUAGE
IS ACQUIRED AND TAUGHT

W hile there are certainly similarities between the way young children up to the age of six learn English as their first language at home and older students (six to 18 years old) learn English as their second language in school, there are also some distinct differences.

— Young children learning English as their first language do not know another language; ESL students do.
— Young children do not know how to read and write; some ESL students do, but in another language.
— Young children are highly motivated to learn their first language because they need to get things done; not all ESL students are highly motivated to learn English because they already have a language and know how to use it.
— Because young children are surrounded by English all day, there is high input; some ESL students hear English for only five hours a day at school.
— Young children learn concepts and language simultaneously; ESL students have already learned many concepts, some of which may differ from those of English-speaking students (e.g., the way the color band breaks down).
— Young children are immature mentally, emotionally and socially; ESL students, depending on their age, may have reached higher levels of maturity before starting to learn English.

- Young children have many years ahead of them in which to master English; ESL students, particularly teenagers, have a very few years in which to master English in order, for example, to attend a post-secondary institution.
- While young children and ESL students soon master conversational skills in their first language, the rules that govern the conduct of conversations from culture to culture may not always be transferable.
- When English-speaking children begin school, they already have a storehouse of structures and vocabulary they can use in reading and writing; ESL children have these in their first language but not in English.
- When young children are learning English as their first language, parents and other adults pay more attention to the content of what they say than to the form in which it is said; teachers, however, seem to pay more attention to how an ESL student structures a sentence than to what is said.
- Young children usually get immediate complimentary feedback from their parents when they attempt to speak English; ESL students may be ridiculed or have to wait some time before being complimented.

On the other hand, some of the similarities are:

- Both groups need to hear English modeled by adults and their peers in a variety of situations. In other words, they need plenty of comprehensible input.
- Imitation plays a role in acquiring both a first and second language.
- Both groups of children need to try out language, test it, receive feedback and try again.
- Both groups learn better when adult language is adapted to their ability to comprehend.
- Both learn faster when language and content are combined.

Theories of Second Language Acquisition

There is no shortage of theories explaining how children learn or acquire a second language. While some of these are out-of-date, they have provided the seed for methods of teaching ESL that are still practiced to some degree today.

AUDIO-LINGUAL HABIT THEORY

The behaviorists, led by B.F. Skinner, said that learning a second language involved learning a new set of language habits and that practice — drill — was the way to learn these. They believed that performance (what the speaker can say in the language) precedes competence (what the speaker knows about the rules of the language). This theory is now largely outmoded.

During its heyday, however, this theory resulted in a plethora of drills. Though some of these were meaningful to students, many meant little or nothing. While there is certainly a need for students to practice what they are learning, this can be achieved in ways other than merely parroting what the teacher says.

COGNITIVE-CODE THEORY

The cognitivists, led by linguist Noam Chomsky and psychologist Jerome Bruner, point to people's ability to create new utterances that could never be drilled into them. As a result, they believe that second language learning involves both a conscious understanding of how the second language works and the conscious application of the mind to the creation of meaningful utterances. Emphasis is on communication or communicative competence.

Teachers should therefore ensure that real communication takes place. Students should be encouraged to talk about what is important to them, consciously applying the rules of language as they create utterances.

ACQUISITION VERSUS LEARNING

Stephen Krashen differentiates between the *acquisition* of and *learning* a second language. In his view, acquisition is a process somewhat similar to the way young children become fluent in their first language. The process is largely unconscious as ESL children "pick up" aspects of the second language with no formal training.

Learning a second language, on the other hand, is a conscious process whereby rules are taught, learned and applied.

Older ESL students will use learning as a strategy more than younger students, but all ESL students will *acquire* more language than they *learn*, provided they are exposed to sufficient language that is interesting, relevant and comprehensible. Teachers should ensure that there are opportunities for both language acquisition and learning during the school day.

MONITOR HYPOTHESIS

Stephen Krashen also believes that some older ESL students monitor their own performance, provided they are conscious of some of the rules. Students who over-correct themselves can become self-conscious, hesitant to speak because they are focusing on form. On the other hand, students who under-correct themselves can be difficult to understand because they are focusing on content and garbling the form. The optimal situation occurs when students pay some attention to both form and content. Teachers can help students do this by showing them strategies they might employ and by explaining when it is appropriate to monitor their language.

NATURAL ORDER HYPOTHESIS

Research has shown that children learning English as their first language acquire some grammatical rules before others (e.g., the ability to form plurals is mastered before the ability to change a sentence from the active to the passive voice). While there appears to be a degree of predictability to the order in which ESL students master some grammatical rules, it is not identical to the order in which first language learners master them. Keep in mind that the need to use a specific grammatical rule or structure will override any theory of order established by research. Because this need is based on age, aims and the particulars of a given situation, a grammatical syllabus will never meet the needs of all students.

Teachers need to know how to teach specific grammatical items when the need arises and should not base language teaching on a sequence of items selected by someone who does not know the students.

Stephen Krashen says that the acquisition of English by ESL students seems to depend on sufficient exposure to English in situations that are interesting, relevant and comprehensible. In other words, the language must be suitable to the learner's age, experiences and aims. It must also be comprehensible, something that is often achieved with the assistance of visual aids, gestures and facial expressions. New structures and vocabulary will be acquired as meaning becomes clear to students.

While input cannot be grammatically structured because the focus is on meaning (content) not form, the language can be simplified. There must be enough exposure to the language that the learner has something — building blocks — to work with but is not overwhelmed to the point where she becomes frustrated and closes her mind to the never-ending incomprehensible flow of the second language. In an ideal situation, the student's anxiety level must be low. Both teachers and students must remember that fluency does not occur immediately, but develops over months and years as it is acquired rather than taught.

Making meaning clear is a task that faces all teachers, whether they are working with ESL or non-ESL students. The chapter titled Language and Content suggests ways this can be done in regular classrooms. Students will need strategies for seeking help and indicating that they do not understand — ways of managing the discussion so that meaning becomes clear to them.

AFFECTIVE FILTER HYPOTHESIS

Children who are anxious, tense, lacking in self-confidence or unmotivated are not good learners of anything, including a second language. Stephen Krashen suggests that it is as if an "affective filter" has been placed between the language they are hearing and their minds. If anxiety is high, the filter does not allow much meaningful language to pass through. If learners do not receive meaningful messages, it is difficult for them to produce them. A vital component of effective language learning is interaction between speakers of English as a first and second language.

It is very important that the classroom and playground be accepting, friendly, supportive places, and that ESL students receive counseling for other problems they may face, such as the trauma of being uprooted, their parents' employment difficulties, racist comments and pressure to succeed.

THE SILENT PERIOD

In order to "perform," all learners must listen to English to increase their competence, their conscious and unconscious understanding of the rules of the language. While some children may attempt speech within a few days of arriving in the English-speaking school, others may say nothing for weeks. Nevertheless, if they are exposed to English, the phonological, morphological and syntactical rules will be taking shape in their heads.

Children will speak when they are ready. They should not be embarrassed by demands that they speak before they are ready. They need time to build their confidence through encouragement and support. One way to do this is to speak to them as if they are replying, as if communication is, in fact, taking place. If children are forced to speak English too soon, they may fall back on the rules of their first language rather than try to work with the rules of English.

OTHER FACTORS AFFECTING SECOND LANGUAGE ACQUISITION

Age

One outdated theory held that, at puberty, children lost the ability to learn a second language. While young children, because of their greater facial plasticity, master the sounds of English like native speakers, teenagers have an advantage in that they are more mature and know how to learn. They will therefore consciously adopt strategies that will help them learn more structures and more vocabulary faster than young children. Young children, however, have more time in which to learn English than teenagers, who are often under pressure from their families to learn quickly so they can, for example, attend a post-secondary institution. The resulting anxiety can slow down the learning process.

A student's age should not predetermine the teacher's assessment of his potential for success or failure. Research has shown that teachers' expectations affect students' achievements. With ESL students, a positive attitude is very important and expectations must be neither too high nor too low.

The length of time students have lived in an English-speaking country can also affect achievement. A longer period of residence usually means there has been more time for input, resulting in greater fluency, but this is not always true. If students have had no access to English outside the classroom or if their anxiety levels are high, they may still be struggling after five years in the country, regardless of their age.

Some ESL students may have been slow (language-delayed) in acquiring their first language. If this can be established as fact, it may, in some cases, account for the slow acquisition of English. Great care must be taken, however, not to label a child a slow learner just because speech is hesitant. More time may be all that is needed to acquire the necessary level of competence to perform better.

Simplifying Language

When parents talk to young babies, they usually simplify their language. For beginning ESL students, teachers need to simplify their language initially, but they should neither distort the language nor shout. ESL students need to hear acceptable English modeled by teachers and peers.

Simplifying instructions to ESL students does not mean using baby talk. Visual aids, for example, can do much to bridge the gap between language and meaning.

The Good Language Learner

The good language learner exhibits certain traits. She is ready to take risks in trying to use English, is motivated to learn English, searches for meaning, is ready to acculturate but respects and maintains her first language and culture, is emotionally stable and has a low anxiety level, is self-confident, monitors her own performance, seeks help when it is needed, develops strategies for both language learning and academic learning, and comes from a supportive home.

Some ESL students will need to learn strategies that will turn them from poor or indifferent learners into good learners. It may be necessary for teachers to teach these strategies consciously.

Bilingualism

Bilingualism in English and any other language is an advantage. Research has shown that, academically, bilingual children do as well as, if not better than, monolingual children. The fact that they speak two languages provides two channels for information to enter and leave the brain. Bilingual children are often found to be more flexible in their thinking and more creative than monolingual children. They also have access to the wisdom of their elders and may have greater career opportunities.

Parents can help maintain bilingualism in children by talking to them in their first language at home, a situation that is preferable to talking to them in broken English. Young children can be helped to learn to read in English if their parents read to them in their first language — it is, after all, the process that is being taught, not the specifics of the English language system.

Parents' efforts to help children maintain their first language should be supported by the school. For example, books in languages spoken by ESL students should be available in the library.

Interlanguage

Interlanguage represents the steps between knowing no English and knowing everything, or nearly everything! It takes time and effort to learn a new language. There is a risk that some ESL students may "freeze" their second language learning at a level where they think they have picked up enough to do whatever it is they want at the time. Later, when doors to post-secondary institutions are closed to them because their English is too poor for them to be accepted into the course of their choice or business opportunities pass them by, they may regret that they did not persevere. It takes about two years for students to master social English and five to seven years to master academic English — the English of abstract thought.

Teachers must encourage students to persist in their efforts to master English with near-native proficiency.

Setting

Language *acquisition* occurs in many settings: on the playground, walking to and from school, on the sports field, in a friend's home, in the store, and at a recreation center.

Language *learning*, however, is more likely to take place in the classroom or during one-on-one consultations between teacher and student.

Teachers can provide new ESL students with buddies who will help get them involved in a variety of activities. ESL students should be helped to see that the school is trying to supplement, not supplant, their first language and culture.

Methods of Teaching a Second Language

There is little doubt that teaching helps students learn and acquire a second language, especially when it is combined with content teaching, provides plenty of interesting, relevant, comprehensible input, does not raise the anxiety level and provides strategies for further learning of both language and content.

Based on theories of second language acquisition that have arisen over the years, various teaching methods have been practiced. Although some of these methods are no longer in vogue, each still has something to say to classroom teachers.

AUDIO-LINGUALISM

Audio-lingualism, largely outdated now, is based on the work of behavioral psychologists and structural grammar. Learning a second language is regarded as a process of learning a new set of language habits, and drills are considered an integral part of this process. As students listen and repeat, they are conditioned to respond correctly to oral and written stimuli. It doesn't matter if they consciously understand the rule that governs their response because audio-linguists believe that performance precedes competence. The first language is not used in the classroom.

Audio-lingual lessons usually follow a set order:

— The new material (e.g., a new sentence pattern) is presented.
— Through drill, the new material is memorized.

— It is manipulated (e.g., transformed into a question).
— Then, in theory, it is applied in situations outside the classroom.

While drills have fallen into disfavor as a teaching method, they do not necessarily have to be boring and meaningless. Students need opportunities to practice the language they require for daily communication. With a little imagination, teachers can find ways of providing practice without imposing boredom.

COGNITIVE-CODE APPROACH

This approach emerged from the work of cognitivists and transformational-generative grammarians, who believe language is governed by rules, at least some of which should be learned consciously. Hence the term "cognitive" in the title, the "code" being the target language. The emphasis is on communication, which requires students to produce meaningful sentences. Rote memorization is avoided and using the first language is considered acceptable. Advocates of this approach believe that competence precedes performance.

Students are not parrots. They have brains, which they can use to understand consciously how a language works. Teachers can provide opportunities for them to create new, meaningful utterances.

THE SILENT WAY

This method was developed by Caleb Gattegno who placed responsibility for learning on the learner. Teachers model the word, phrase or sentence to be learned just once. Avoiding repetition requires students to concentrate and develop strategies for language learning. It is, of course, the teacher who is silent, not the students, who are expected to create utterances using the material presented and, in this way, develop independence. The teacher provides support and encouragement as well as the initial language model.

This method is based on the theory that, while teachers teach a second language, students will not necessarily learn it unless the responsibility for doing so rests with them.

In the mid-1960s, James Asher developed the total physical response method, in which beginning students remain silent while demonstrating physically their comprehension of commands such as, "Stand up and walk to the door." The verb is central to this method, which emphasizes meaning over form. The grammar and vocabulary selected are relevant to the classroom situation and the age of the students.

As students gain confidence and understanding, they take over the teacher's role and give the commands themselves, producing new combinations. The anxiety level should be low. Subsequently, other teaching methods requiring students to engage in more normal conversation are used.

Some students require more time than others to produce a new language orally. When this method is used, teachers can discern whether students have understood what has been said, while giving them time to gain confidence before they speak.

THE NATURAL APPROACH

This approach was developed by Tracy Terrell and Stephen Krashen. The teacher uses only the target language to provide input for students to acquire. The students, however, may speak in either their first or second language. As the aim is communication, errors in the second language are not corrected unless they impede communication. While some formal work with grammar may be included, the aim is to encourage the students to talk about matters that concern them, including problem-solving.

Learning a language means communicating in a new way and this requires meaningful, relevant input and an opportunity to discuss meaningful, relevant topics.

LANGUAGE AND CONTENT

In his book, *Language and Content*, Bernard Mohan points out, "It is absurd to ignore the role of content in the language class, just as it is absurd to ignore the role of language as the medium of learning in the content class." Language teaching and learning are inextricably interwoven with content teaching and learning. As this approach is of particular importance to all classroom teachers who have one or more ESL students in their class, the chapter titled Language and Content has been devoted to explaining both its concepts and application.

THE ROLE OF GRAMMAR

Administrators are often concerned that ESL students do not appear to be learning enough grammar! Learning English grammar, however, does not necessarily mean that ESL students can use it creatively in a variety of situations. As in other learning, a rule is learned best at the moment it is needed. Students who monitor their own language output carefully may well seek understanding of the rules more frequently than those who simply let the words flow. Teachers have a responsibility to correct errors that impede communication. As the need arises, these can be corrected with the whole class, a small group or an individual. It is unlikely that teaching a long list of grammatical items with no regard for the students' previous knowledge of English or their immediate needs will result in much language acquisition.

. . . .

ASSESSMENT AND PROGRAMS

Sensitive and appropriate assessment techniques combined with placement in a suitable program are critical to ensuring that ESL students have the opportunity to become successful learners.

Assessment of ESL Students

To ensure that their placement and progress are in line with their aims and abilities, ESL students may need to undergo regular assessment at predetermined intervals. This assessment may take place in a district center or in the school and, while some tests may be administered to groups of students, others may require one-on-one testing.

ASSESSMENT FOR INITIAL PLACEMENT

A student's initial placement will depend on the criteria established by the school for its ESL program(s), but as far as possible students should be placed with others of their own age group.

The initial interview described in the first chapter will already have elicited some valuable information. Provided the student can respond to questions such as, "What is your name?" and "How old are you?" it is worth continuing with further tests of English ability in the areas of listening, speaking, reading and writing.

Some schools make up their own tests, while others use standardized tests. There are, however, drawbacks to using standardized tests. The results may be entered on the student's record card, leading to a situation where, for example, it may appear to another teacher at a later date that a 14-year-old boy was reading at a grade two level. The fact that he was a beginning ESL student at the time the test was administered may be overlooked. In addition, some students may perform badly on standardized tests because either they don't understand the instructions or the tests are culture-bound.

Some schools deal with this problem by modifying standardized tests — giving the students more time, omitting certain items, substituting words or phrases to make comprehension easier, and so on. These modifications destroy the reliability and validity of the test so that the norms no longer apply. Many schools prefer to use teacher-created tests that help sort students according to criteria that fit their particular ESL and regular programs.

A student's ability in subject matter can be assessed by evaluating her previous school records in terms of the system she is entering and having a bilingual counselor talk to her to find out what she has previously studied and, if the textbooks used in the homeland are available, asking her to indicate the point she has reached. Math computation skills can be checked by a test, provided it contains no problems that require a knowledge of English.

Young children should not be subjected to any formal tests.

Conversation

It is useful to begin with a conversation in a relaxed atmosphere. It should not appear to the student that this is a test. By asking increasingly complex questions that require increasingly complex answers, the student can be pushed to the limits of his English ability. The questions should cover matters the student is familiar with, such as travel to the new country, present living conditions, previous education and family. Students, too, should be encouraged to ask questions of the interviewer about the new school.

Listening

A listening test can begin with a few simple commands to see if the student can carry them out before going to a more formal test. Then the student can be asked to listen to a story and retell it, or teenagers can listen to some classroom instructions and material and make notes, an important and advanced skill.

Speaking

The conversation and listening tests will already have revealed the student's ability to pronounce English so as to be understood and use the prosodic features acceptably — provided she is prepared to speak! As noted in the previous chapter, some students prefer to remain silent for various reasons. This should not be interpreted to mean that the student knows no English or is stupid. The situation may have engendered fear that resulted in silence and time may show that she actually knows considerable English and is very bright.

Reading

The student can be asked to read orally and silently from a variety of texts and answer some questions to establish an approximate level. If standardized tests are used, they should be interpreted with great caution. Because the student is not fluent in English, these tests show how much more he must learn in order to achieve at grade level. They say nothing, however, about his intelligence or potential.

Writing

The student can be asked to write about herself or a topic of interest that may have come up during the early conversation. The composition may reveal problems of organization as well as syntactical errors.

REVIEW OF INITIAL PLACEMENT

There is always the possibility that the initial placement was wrong because it was based on a faulty test, faulty assessment results, faulty interpretation of the results or on a poor performance by the student because of fear and anxiety. During the days and weeks that follow the initial placement, the teacher's observation of the student will either confirm that the placement is right or point to a different placement. A review should be mandatory after six weeks.

Whether students are placed in an ESL class or center or in a regular program with ESL support, it is essential for all teachers to monitor their progress and meet regularly to see what more can be done to help them learn English, cope with the subject matter and integrate into the life of the school.

DIAGNOSTIC TESTING

Like some non-ESL students, some ESL students have learning difficulties. However, it is not always easy to determine whether the problem is the result of a learning disability or a lack of facility in English.

The results of IQ tests administered to students who have been learning English for less than two years are, in most instances, useless. IQ tests are normed on subjects for whom English is the first language and whose background reflects the cultural content and types of questions asked. Further, if the psychologist interpreting the results does not know the student tested is not a native English-speaker who has been in the country a relatively short time, the student may be labeled a slow learner. This label may be difficult to shake off.

For at least the first two years, observation of students by experienced teachers is preferable to the administration of standardized tests, unless those interpreting the tests are trained in cross-cultural testing, or the test given uses the student's first language. Even when this is the case, there may be problems if the test is simply a translation of an English test with all the English cultural content intact.

TRANSITION TO THE REGULAR PROGRAM

The time at which a student is ready to transfer from the ESL to a regular program depends on a number of factors, not the least of which is the attitude of the teachers in whose classrooms she may be placed. If teachers are not prepared to welcome and work with the ESL student, the transition may be a disaster. Other factors to be considered include whether the subject matter of the course requires a low or high use of English. For example, physical education requires low use — a student can copy other children and soon master the commands — while social studies, with its lectures and textbooks, requires high use. If the student has some background in the subject area, she is more likely to meet success (e.g., she may have studied math, but not necessarily the history of her adopted country). The level reached by the student in the subject matter in her previous education as well as her personality — see The Good Language Learner in the preceding chapter — are also factors to be considered.

The decision to place the student in the mainstream should be made at a conference of the ESL teacher, regular classroom teachers and the counselor. Some examples of the student's work should be available. A decision made at this conference should not be considered irrevocable. It may be necessary for the student to return to the ESL teacher for help and reassurance for some weeks before she becomes fully independent.

MONITORING PROGRESS IN THE REGULAR PROGRAM

A file of the student's work should be kept so that, over time, his progress can be measured by comparing his early and later efforts. The teacher's observations are an extremely important part of the monitoring process. In the months immediately following the student's entrance into the mainstream, the results of classroom tests that employ a lot of English should not be accepted as a true indication of the student's ability. As facility in English increases, the student's potential will probably prove to be higher.

COUNSELING

Immediately after the decision about the student's program has been made, the parents should be informed. They need to understand what the program is and where it will lead. This information is best communicated in the parents' own language. Every effort should be made to keep in touch with them, perhaps by bilingual cross-cultural workers or bilingual volunteers. The student should also have access to these bilingual aides so that she can ask questions or express concerns.

Programs for ESL Students

While there is a variety of programs, each with its own objectives and formats, they fall into four basic categories: self-contained programs; withdrawal programs; transitional programs; and mainstreaming.

Each program has distinct advantages and disadvantages. Schools or districts take a number of factors into consideration when choosing one or more of the programs:

— Their own philosophy regarding the education of ESL students.
— The number of ESL students to be served and whether they are clustered in a few schools or dispersed throughout the system across a wide geographic area.
— The availability of space for the class or classes.
— The funding available.
— The ease or difficulty of transporting ESL students to other schools.
— Ministry or department of education regulations.

SELF-CONTAINED PROGRAMS

All the students in these programs are ESL, usually at the beginning stages of mastering English. While the students stay together in one room for much of the day, there are a number of organizational variations.

Full-Day Reception Classes

In this situation, the ESL teacher is responsible for the total program. As students become more proficient in English they are time-tabled into regular subject classes where they have some chance of success. Students are on individualized programs for some weeks, during which time their ability in English and in other subject areas is assessed. The teacher's role is not only to teach English and prepare the students to enter the mainstream, but also to help them adjust to the new culture.

Advantages: The reception class enables students to receive intensive English language training from a specialist ESL teacher who understands their linguistic, cultural, social and emotional needs.

Disadvantages: Unless some attempt is made to integrate ESL students with their peers, the class can become a ghetto where the students have no model except their teacher. Recent language learning theories suggest that segregating ESL students may hinder rather than help their progress by denying them access to the natural language environment of the rest of the school.

Half-Day Reception Classes

Students spend half the school day in an ESL class and half in a regular class. The ESL teacher may work with children in kindergarten to grade three in the morning and those in grade four to six in the afternoon or whatever grouping seems best. Sometimes children travel by bus or taxi from their own school to attend an ESL class at another school for half the day.

Advantages: Students have an opportunity not only to receive intensive English-language training, but also to meet and mingle with their peers in a normal school situation for half the day. In school districts where numbers do not warrant the employment of a full-time ESL teacher, a part-time teacher can be hired.

Disadvantages: In schools with rotating student timetables, the half-day program can disrupt the continuity of subject-matter courses for the student. Students who must travel to another school for the ESL program may lose instructional time in the regular program and may not form an attachment to their home school.

Bilingual Programs

In bilingual programs, the children have a common first language, such as Cantonese or Spanish, which is also spoken by the teacher or teacher's aide or both. In some bilingual programs, the students' first language is used for only as long as it takes them to achieve basic fluency in English. In others, the aim is to help students become fluent and literate in both languages.

Advantages: In a bilingual program students are never at a loss for meaning. They can continue to study subject matter in their first language while gaining mastery of the second language. This means they don't have to mark time academically while learning English. Research suggests that bilingualism assists cognitive development.

Disadvantages: Some students may use the first language as a crutch and not take seriously the task of learning English. Sometimes segregating students of one language, particularly if they are members of a visible minority, can draw attention to the fact that they are "different," which can lead to increased prejudice and racism.

WITHDRAWAL OR PULL-OUT PROGRAMS

In these programs, ESL students are enrolled in regular classes with English-speaking children of the same age and are withdrawn or pulled out for varying periods for language instruction and orientation.

Withdrawal programs have many advantages. Students get the benefit of periods of intensive English-language training while simultaneously being part of everyday school life. The withdrawal program can provide students with a period of relaxation away from the pressure of the regular classroom, where achieving success is difficult, as well as an opportunity to ask questions about aspects of school life.

On the other hand, some students, already in a state of shock over the move to a new land, find it difficult to cope emotionally and psychologically with being integrated into a new school system. They may need more time with one teacher than the withdrawal system can offer. Each of the withdrawal programs described here can be abused if it is required to service too many students.

English Language or Learning Center

An ELC has a permanent location within the school. It acts as a reception center for new students, assessing their facility in English and some subject areas. Center staff make the initial placement and program decisions in consultation with other teachers. The ELC provides support for students of various ages at various levels of English language development on an individual or small-group basis. It also provides support for regular teachers who have ESL students in their classes and often becomes the focal point for multicultural activities in the school.

Itinerant ESL Teachers

In some districts where there aren't enough ESL students in any one school to set up a program, an itinerant ESL teacher travels from school to school withdrawing students for varying periods.

Tutorials

ESL students may be withdrawn from class to work one-on-one with a regular teacher, a teacher's aide, a volunteer, or another student under a "buddy system."

TRANSITIONAL PROGRAMS

Transitional programs help students make the move into the mainstream by concentrating on a particular need.

Transitional Subject-Matter Classes

Transitional subject-matter classes are primarily for secondary school students who are beyond the beginning level of English and are almost, but not quite, ready to enter the mainstream. In a transitional class, the content parallels, as far as possible, the content in the regular class, but the language is modified and methods that enhance understanding are used. These classes are sometimes team-taught by ESL and content teachers. Some schools award credits for students who achieve success in transitional classes.

Advantages: Students have an opportunity to learn both language and content simultaneously and experience success. This may be denied them in a regular class where the new vocabulary, complex syntax and the fast rate of the teacher's delivery combine to make understanding difficult. The possibility of obtaining credits provides a stimulus for students to enroll and work hard in the transitional class.

Disadvantages: If credits are not given, students resent taking transitional courses and will therefore prefer to enroll in a regular course and risk failure. If the class is not team-taught, students may face an ESL teacher who does not know the content or a content teacher who does not know how to teach a second language.

Vocational Pre-Employment Programs

Not all ESL students want to pursue academic studies. The efforts of many may be directed towards obtaining work. Vocational or pre-employment programs may, by giving these students facility in English and some work skills, make it possible for students to go directly into gainful employment or take further training at a vocational training institution.

Advantages: Students who go through these programs may be in a position to claim that they have local job experience if the course entails on-site training. Students may also have made some useful contacts and learned how to look for and obtain a job as well as how and where to obtain further training.

Disadvantages: Sometimes these programs are used as dumping grounds for students who really need further language training, a booster program or help in a special education class. In addition, if real-life experience is not provided, the content can remain at a very theoretical level.

Academic Booster Programs

Academic booster programs are designed for students who experience difficulty in their academic studies as a result of interrupted or limited educational backgrounds. The emphasis is usually placed on developing skills in oral and written English, particularly reading, and in mathematics.

Advantages: Students can build on the skills and knowledge they bring with them and do not have to experience the failure and frustration that occurs when they must attempt to bridge an academic gap on their own. Regular teachers are relieved of the responsibility of trying to bring one or more students up to grade level while coping with normal teaching activities.

Disadvantages: Students in booster programs, as in any special education program, can find themselves labeled "slow learners." In fact, they may not be slow at all, merely disadvantaged by their previous educational opportunities.

Special Education and ESL

Apart from the need to master English, some ESL students have learning problems that may be caused by cognitive, emotional or social factors. In an atmosphere of tender loving care, they require a program that incorporates English language training along with concept and skills development at a level and pace suited to their various abilities, backgrounds and goals.

Advantages: These students often need considerably more care than can be given in either a regular or an ESL classroom. They need the kind of help and support that a specialist in both ESL and special education can provide to a small group. As a result of this program, some students who might otherwise have dropped out of school may, in time, be integrated into the mainstream.

Disadvantages: Failure to diagnose ESL students' learning problems accurately can result in students being incorrectly placed in special education classes or spending too long in the program or both. If the teacher is not trained in special education and ESL, the students may suffer through a series of dull, meaningless exercises that teach them nothing except to hate school.

Preschool Programs

Preschool or kindergarten programs help prepare young non-English speaking children for school by teaching them English along with the routines that are part of school life. Day-care programs can also do much to prepare the ESL child for school.

Advantages: A child who enters school speaking no English is at a social, emotional and academic disadvantage in a regular classroom. Preschool ESL programs can not only help minimize this disadvantage but also, by encouraging children to become bilingual, maximize their potential.

Disadvantages: Poor language development programs can result when preschool children are taught by inadequately trained teachers or day-care workers. Parents can be given the wrong impression regarding the contribution they can make to their child's cognitive development if their language is denigrated and English is held up as being the only essential.

MAINSTREAMING

Many of the programs outlined previously involve a degree of mainstreaming at some time. There are, however, two mainstreaming programs that should be described separately.

Mainstream Support Program

Once the decision to place an ESL student in the mainstream has been made, support should be provided. A student should continue to have access to the ESL teacher for perhaps as long as three months or be given the opportunity to return to the ESL class when the going gets too rough in the regular class. The ESL teacher might observe the student in the regular classroom, then consult with the regular teacher to discover the skills he lacks and how these might be strengthened and the course modified.

Advantages: Entering the mainstream requires students to move from *learning* to *using* the new language. Most ESL students are anxious to join their peers in regular classrooms and they see their entry into the mainstream as an indication of success in learning the second language. Additional support will keep their motivation high.

Disadvantages: If ESL students enter the mainstream too early or under the wrong conditions (e.g., if there's no support or the teacher is hostile), the results can be devastating. They will see themselves as failures and as unwanted, emotions that have negative effects on their self-confidence and motivation and, hence, on their ability to learn.

Immersion Programs

In some school districts that receive a very small number of non-English speaking students or in districts where ESL students are dispersed over a wide area, it may not be possible to employ an ESL teacher to run a special program and ESL students must therefore spend all day in a regular class.

Advantages: ESL students have access to a number of English-speaking models. They are constantly challenged to try and make sense of the language they hear in the context of the regular classroom. They cannot wait to be taught but must formulate and test their own hypotheses about how English works. The presence of ESL students can enrich the classroom atmosphere by promoting cross-cultural and cross-linguistic understanding.

Disadvantages: For some students, the challenge of learning the new language on their own, coming so soon after being uprooted, is simply too much, particularly if the teacher and class are not sympathetic to and understanding of the difficulties facing the newcomers. In addition to mastering the new language, ESL students may be under considerable pressure to keep up with their peers academically. Fear of failure, fear of ridicule and loneliness may cause some students to drop out of school.

Putting an ESL Program in Place

RECOGNIZING THE NEED FOR AN ESL PROGRAM

Indicators to watch for are teachers who are frustrated, who feel that the presence of ESL students in their classes is hampering their effectiveness, and parents of ESL students who express concern that their children are not progressing. At the same time, there may be complaints from parents of non-ESL children that ESL students are holding back other students and from employers that ESL students do not know enough English to handle the jobs for which they were hired.

Other indicators are a high dropout rate among ESL students, blaming the school's low rating on local or national tests on the presence of ESL students and a rise in the number of ESL students in the school.

Needs Analysis

The purpose of a needs analysis is to identify the potential student population for an ESL program and the needs of this population. The following descriptive and statistical data should be collected:

— The number of ESL students in the school, categorized as beginners, intermediate and advanced according to their facility in English.
— The age range of these students and the first languages they speak.
— The degree of permanent residence within this student body.
— The specific language skills these students will need to achieve success in school, in entering a post-secondary institution and in integrating into the community.
— The schools in which the students are located and their proximity to reliable transportation should they need to commute to another school.

Using the information gathered, the program planners must establish the objectives of the program and the means for reaching those objectives. Details to be planned for are:

Design

— Format.
— Scheduling of classes, groups or individuals.
— Size of classes or groups.
— Content of the program.
— Emphasis within the program.

Administration

— Budget.
— Funding.
— Selection of students.
— Hiring and supervision of teachers and teachers' aides.
— Evaluation of the program.

Instructional Concerns

— Criteria for admission to and exit from the program.
— Curriculum planning.
— Resources, human and material.

EVALUATING THE PROGRAM

The following is a standard six-point procedure for evaluating a program:

— Issues: What questions should be asked about the program?
— Information: What information should be collected in order to answer the issue questions and from whom should it be collected?
— Method: How should the information be collected? Who will design the instrument that might be used?
— Time: Over what period of time will the information be collected and analyzed?
— Analysis: How will the data be analyzed? What criteria will be used? What comparisons will be made?
— Reporting: How will the findings be reported? Who will receive the report?

LISTENING AND SPEAKING

All children want to communicate. For them, language is a means of communication, not a subject to be studied. They learn language through meaningful, purposeful interaction. Oral communication involves both listening and responding. In classrooms where no talking is the rule, the level of linguistic interaction will be low, and learning of both language and content by ESL students will be inhibited. In an article that appeared in the *TESOL Quarterly*, D. Scott Enright and Mary Lou McCloskey suggest that classrooms should be organized on the basis of purpose, previous experience and students' interests, and to promote collaboration, holism, support and variety.

This may mean moving the furniture around to make communication easier for pairs and small groups. ESL students should be placed with English-speaking students who are prepared to provide comprehensible input and support and encourage their efforts to communicate in English.

The aim of communicative language teaching is to produce communicative competence in ESL students. Communicative competence consists of four components:

Grammatical Competence: Students have control over the phonological, morphological and syntactical rules that underlie well-formed utterances. Students may not be able to state what these rules are, but they prove competence by using them correctly.

Sociolinguistic Competence: Students know when and how to use different aspects of English, such as formal and informal speech, in various social situations.

Discourse Competence: Students know how to produce an extended piece of discourse, such as a conversation, a speech or an interview, in which various sentences are connected sequentially to form a coherent and meaningful whole.

Strategic Competence: Students know how to sustain communication by using various coping and survival strategies, such as guessing, hesitating, asking for repetition and seeking clarification.

Difficulties in Developing Communicative Competence in Oral English

The purposes for which children use oral language were listed in the chapter titled How Language Works. The more fluent children are, the more likely it is that they will be able to achieve their purposes. But, as they try to become fluent in oral English, second language learners are bound to encounter difficulties. One of these will be frustration that they can't do things in their second language, such as explain, persuade and respond to what is said to them, that they are able to do in their first.

LISTENING

ESL students may not be able to process all the language they hear, with the result that they only partially understand what is said to them. Their answers may therefore sound odd and their actions may appear peculiar. Further, they may not know how to ask for clarification — and so the misunderstanding continues. It may also be necessary for some ESL students to develop longer attention spans.

SPEAKING

Poor pronunciation, strange use of stress and intonation, odd grammatical structures and inappropriate use of formal or informal speech throw up barriers between ESL students and their listeners. In addition, they may stand too close to their listeners, using the distance acceptable in their own culture but not to speakers of English.

Because body language varies from culture to culture, ESL students who can neither produce nor read body language used by the English-speaking community will have communication problems.

COMPREHENSIBLE LANGUAGE

Students must hear language that is comprehensible to them if they are to produce language that is comprehensible to others. Comprehensible language must be of interest to the students, taking into account their ages, interests, backgrounds and future goals. It must also be presented in a variety of contexts — in the classroom, on the playground, in different subject areas — so that, with the help of gestures or visual aids, they can draw meaning from what is said.

The responsibility for ensuring that the language of the classroom is comprehensible rests with teachers. If they don't accept this responsibility, ESL students' progress in achieving oral fluency will be delayed.

The Whole Language Approach

The whole language approach recognizes that listening, speaking, reading and writing are not totally separate modes of communication, but are interdependent and should, where possible, be combined in activities that develop all four skills. Because it is necessary for ESL teachers to have a clear idea of how each skill can be developed, first on its own, then in combination with the other skills, this chapter will look at listening and speaking, and the following two chapters at reading and writing. Then the chapters titled Language and Content and Lesson Planning will draw the four skills together.

Listening

LISTENING COMPREHENSION

Students go through various stages in learning to comprehend spoken English:

- They hear the "music" of the language (i.e., the intonation, stress and pauses).
- They hear individual sounds and start to recognize and internalize individual words.
- They recognize often-used phrases and sentences and know what they mean.
- They are able to hold in their memory the first part of an utterance while processing what follows.
- They hear key words and recognize that what follows is important in relationship to what has gone before.
- They can break into a flow of speech asking for clarification.

Points to Remember

- Listening is an *active* skill that involves the students in decoding, sorting, classifying and relating experiences in order to extract meaning.
- Students must listen to get meaning, not just to parrot what was said.
- Some students need to listen for longer periods than others before they are ready to respond.
- The speaker's style of delivery should be natural and the content appropriate.
- Students should grow from listening for one detail, to listening for content and inference.
- Students should be encouraged to predict and guess what may happen from what they have heard.

DEVELOPING LISTENING SKILLS

The teacher's role is to provide opportunities for ESL students to *listen* to interesting and meaningful material. Both ESL and regular classroom teachers have successfully used the following activities to develop children's listening skills.

- Provide the ESL student with a buddy who can speak the student's language. Ask the buddy to repeat quietly the essence of what is said, first in English, then in translation.
- Later, provide a monolingual English-speaking buddy who will repeat the essence of what is said using gestures and visual aids to assist meaning.

- Provide short tapes with appropriate listening material, perhaps something connected with the topic under study. Let the ESL student listen to them a number of times. Another student can help make the tapes.
- Use the language master or listening post to give the student an opportunity to listen to and repeat what he hears. Relate it to some aspect of class work or a social activity.
- Play games, such as Bingo, or organize activities in physical education that require the ESL student to listen, then perform an action.
- Teach the class songs and poems that require group performance. In this situation, the ESL student will be able to hear something many times without being singled out to perform in public.
- Teach note-taking skills, including guide words such as, "in addition," "on the other hand," "nevertheless," "however," etc.
- Students of all ages enjoy stories. Use pictures and gestures to assist comprehension as a story is read aloud. Then tape the story for the ESL student and invite her to listen and look at the pictures simultaneously. After she has listened and looked two or three times, suggest that she draw her own pictures.
- Demonstrate intonation, stress, pauses, gestures and facial expressions that speakers use to make their points. Screen a film, turning off the sound to draw attention to these actions, then turn on the sound.
- Try to ensure that ESL students hear exchanges between teacher and student, student and student, and teacher and teacher — varieties of formal and informal language spoken by people of different ages and different occupations in different situations.
- Ensure that the meaning of a lesson or lecture is clarified by using visual aids.
- Some subject areas, such as physical education and art, provide excellent opportunities for students to listen and respond by carrying out a physical act. Often a teacher or student describes orally what needs to be done and students perform with little, if any, talking.
- Oral instructions regarding an assignment may not be clear enough for ESL students. A copy of a completed

assignment, or a one-on-one explanation, may be needed. ESL students are often capable of completing an assignment once they understand what is required.

Speaking

SURVIVAL ENGLISH

For their own safety in case they get lost, beginning ESL students must learn immediately to recognize and respond to these questions: What is your name? Where do you live? What school do you go to?

TEACHING PRONUNCIATION

Age can be both an asset and a liability in mastering English pronunciation. Older students may be shy, may have lost the power of mimicry, may be more concerned with what they say than how they say it and may not have developed a good ear for languages. On the other hand, they have learned how to learn, have longer attention spans and may have already had the experience of learning another language.

Encourage students to imitate their teachers and peers. Give them opportunities to listen one-on-one to a speaker who presents a good model of spoken English and to repeat what is said, striving to match the model. Some sounds will need more practice than others. Difficult sounds should be isolated and worked on briefly, then practiced in words, phrases or sentences. Stress and intonation should also be practiced.

CORRECTING ERRORS

Because making errors is a natural and unavoidable part of second language learning, be careful not to over-correct ESL students or they may prefer to remain silent. In the early stages, correct them only when meaning is unclear or distorted. Encourage students to monitor their own speech. As they gain confidence, their speech will improve in accuracy and quantity.

While ESL students should be challenged to say more and say it better, they should not be asked to do the impossible.

Know what each student can do and move on from there. Take some time to analyze a student's problems:

- Does he have a short attention span?
- Does he have difficulty responding because he doesn't concentrate on what is said?
- Does he have difficulty with particular sounds, with word or sentence stress or intonation so that meaning is obscured?
- Does his lack of confidence prevent him from taking part in oral activities?
- Does he fail to correct himself because he doesn't monitor his performance?

Check the list of attributes described under The Good Language Learner in the chapter titled How a Second Language Is Acquired and Taught and encourage the student to learn new strategies.

CONVERSATION

Because much human interaction consists of conversation, it is important that ESL students learn how English-speaking people open, close and take turns in a conversation, interrupt without giving offense and change the topic. In addition, they need to know topics that are not acceptable in certain situations, the polite forms of address, and current idioms and slang they can use in speech with their peers but perhaps not with authority figures!

Native speakers of English know the rules governing conversation because they use them every day. Teachers who analyze the way colleagues and students get things done through proficient use of the linguistic and sociolinguistic conventions of English provide themselves with much teachable material for use with ESL students.

TEACHING VOCABULARY

- Teach words that hold the key to the topic to be taught. These might be concrete words, such as "cooking," "pan" and "stove," abstract words, such as "patriotism," "loyalty" and "rebellion," or linking words, such as "but," "on the other hand" and "alternatively."
- Teach key words from the passage to be read.

- Teach students how to get meaning from context.
- Take a field trip, perhaps down the hall to the nurse's office or into the community to the firehall. Work on trip-related vocabulary before, during and after the excursion.
- Play games such as I Spy and Bingo, using different vocabulary each time.
- Have crossword puzzles available to be worked on in pairs of ESL and non-ESL students.
- Provide a root word and invite students to make derivatives and use them in sentences.
- Make a cloze exercise from a passage the students have read. Let them fill in the blanks and then discuss the possible options.
- Suggest that students make lists of words used frequently in subject areas, such as chemistry or arithmetic, or in interest areas, such as football and rock and roll.
- Encourage the ESL student and buddy to make a dictionary of contemporary slang.
- Help the students make and keep personal dictionaries of words they need.
- Suggest that students write their own definitions of key words in various subjects.
- When a new word appears, try to use it often during the next few days.
- Group words together. See the Vocabulary section of the chapter titled How Language Works.

DEVELOPING SPEAKING SKILLS

The teacher's role is to provide opportunities for ESL students to speak. ESL students are usually highly motivated to speak, but are often afraid of meeting ridicule and failure. An accepting and encouraging classroom atmosphere is crucial to ESL students' progress in oral communication.

- Use the language master, listening post, cassette recorder or a buddy to provide the student with opportunities to hear and practice sounds she is having difficulty with.
- Ask the student to bring something from home and describe it (show and tell). Make sure he has an opportunity to practice before giving the talk.

- After an ESL student has heard an illustrated story two or three times, invite her to retell it. Provide help with the vocabulary but don't worry about the correctness of the grammar: this can come later.
- Do choral speaking or chanting in unison with the class. Poems in which a line is repeated (e.g., There was an old woman who swallowed a fly...) are particularly good for this.
- Teach songs, both familiar favorites and suitable current tunes.
- Teach finger-play games to younger children.
- Teach games that require repetition of a question and answer, such as "Do you have a ...?" and "Yes, I do," or "No, I don't."
- Encourage younger ESL children to pair up with English-speaking children, for example, to play house, make murals or find leaves and flowers in the park.
- Young ESL students will sometimes speak more freely when they are part of a puppet play. The puppet acts as a mask — the student doesn't make mistakes, the puppet does!
- Dramatize a story. Begin by giving the ESL student only a small speaking part, then, as she is able to handle it, increase her role.
- Invite small groups to engage in role playing. Let the ESL student watch and listen until he feels confident enough to play a role.
- Pair the ESL student with another student to review work previously discussed in class. Encourage the student to ask questions.
- If the non-ESL students are working in groups, put the ESL student in one where she will receive support and encouragement to talk.
- After teaching interviewing skills and acceptable questions, let the ESL student play both the part of the interviewer and that of the interviewee.
- If the class is giving oral reports, don't insist that the ESL student give one until he has practiced it and developed confidence. On the other hand, do not let lack of fluency in English become an excuse that lasts forever!
- Take time after class to let the ESL student know that you know that she is there! Often, ESL students don't

say much because they're embarrassed by their lack of English, and teachers don't ask them to perform in order to spare them embarrassment. As a result, students sometimes feel invisible. They talk more readily when they feel the teacher is sympathetic and ready to help.

— When the situation arises, give the ESL student the opportunity to display her knowledge of another language.

— Encourage students to answer questions, but give them time to think out their answers before replying. Oral fluency requires practice.

— Prepare students for both listening and speaking activities by presenting some of the vocabulary, idioms and phrases first, using visual aids and gestures to convey meaning. Remember, one learns to ski by skiing, to swim by swimming, and to talk by talking!

— ESL methodology books contain many oral language drills that require students to listen and repeat or transform a statement into a question and so forth. While it is true that practice makes perfect, opponents of drills argue that they are boring and that the student does not necessarily want — or need — to know at that precise moment what the particular drill is teaching. Practice is more meaningful if it's carried out when the need arises.

— If possible, ensure that the student goes to lunch and walks home with English speakers.

— Ensure that the ESL student is invited to join extra-curricular activities, both at school and in the community.

WORKING WITH A BUDDY

To learn social language, ESL students need to be part of various social groups and situations. A buddy can make certain that the new student isn't left out. A buddy can also help the ESL student become familiar with the school and neighborhood, and with community activities. Here are some suggestions you might give to a buddy who has volunteered to help an ESL student named Rodolfo:

— Try to put yourself in Rodolfo's shoes. Imagine what it must be like not to understand a word that is said to you, not to be able to read any directions on the street, in the school, or newspapers, magazines and books when all your life you have been able to do so.

— Try to guess what Rodolfo needs to know or do at particular moments. You can tell him the names of some objects or you can take him to the washroom, playground or gym.

— How would you feel if you had to leave all your friends behind and go to another country? We all need friends. Try to be one to Rodolfo and introduce him to your friends.

— Help Rodolfo with his school work. Show him the pages that have been assigned for reading. Discuss the assignment with him. Encourage him. Do you know how long it will take Rodolfo before his English is as good as yours? About four or five years! So he will need help from you and other students, as well as teachers, for some time to come.

— As you get to know Rodolfo, ask him to tell you about the country he came from or teach you some of his language. A whole new world may open up!

. . . .

READING

The debate over how children learn to read has spawned a variety of theories and teaching methodologies. Many are variations on four important theories known as the bottom-up approach, the top-down approach, the interactive approach and the whole language (holistic) approach.

The bottom-up approach emphasizes learning letters and sounds first, then words, sentences and paragraphs. Skills taught center around phonics, word recognition and word analysis. Basal readers are designed on the principle that children should master a series of skills in a specified order.

Advocates of the top-down approach believe that children learn to read by reading and that the meaning resides in the head of the reader, not in the print. Students are thought to *acquire* basic skills such as phonics and word recognition by reading meaningful material.

The interactive approach suggests that children use both the bottom-up and the top-down approaches to make sense of the text before them.

The whole language approach is similar to the top-down approach in that proponents argue that children learn to read by reading and don't need to be taught each skill separately. However, whole language advocates also believe that reading and writing go hand-in-hand with speaking and listening and that children should read — and write — as soon as they start school. Skills in both areas will be learned by manipulating both oral and written language in meaningful, relevant and interesting situations.

The theory a teacher adopts will determine the kinds of activities students will be asked to complete as part of the process of learning to read. In his book, *ESL Literacy Instruction*, Lee Gunderson suggests that teachers first ask themselves how students should be taught to read, then list the activities they believe will assist in this process. Their responses will indicate which theory will form the basis of their reading program.

ESL Students and Reading

Some ways of helping ESL students learn to read are more successful than others. First, however, the ways ESL children differ from non-ESL students and the particular problems they face must be considered.

AGE

Some ESL students may be too young to have acquired any degree of literacy in their first language. Others, such as teenagers, may have already had eight or nine years of schooling and be highly literate in their first language. Older students know what literacy is even though they cannot read English.

PREVIOUS SCHOOLING

Some students may already have had an education poorer than, equal to, or better than their English-speaking peers. Their literacy levels in their first language may therefore vary not only according to their age but also according to their previous school experience.

WRITING SYSTEM

Some students, while highly literate, may be used to an entirely different symbol system, such as hieroglyphics rather than letters, and may be used to reading from right to left rather than left to right.

BACKGROUND KNOWLEDGE

Reading comprehension depends to a great extent on the background knowledge students bring to the page. Students may be advanced in some subject areas and behind in others. Differences in cultural customs and values also affect the meaning the student extracts from the written page.

FIRST LANGUAGE LITERACY

In relation to their first language, students may be described as preliterate, semiliterate, literate or illiterate.

Methodologies

No single method of teaching reading will be adequate either for one ESL student or all ESL students. A combination of various approaches is advised.

SIGHT-WHOLE-WORD APPROACH (BOTTOM-UP)

Label objects in the classroom. Bring in or copy signs, such as stop signs, that students are likely to encounter in the outside world. Make sure they have time to become familiar with the shape of the word and its pronunciation. Once children have mastered the words, suggest that they put the cards in a file for later review.

PHONICS (BOTTOM-UP)

Analyze words to discover the relationship between sounds and letters. Find other examples of the relationship between sound and spelling (i.e., $/\eta/$ — the "ng" sound in words like "sing," "bring," "bang," etc.). Because some ESL students learn to decode the letters without grasping the meaning, be careful that children don't master phonics at the expense of comprehension.

DIRECTED READING APPROACH — DRA — (BOTTOM-UP)

This basic approach is used widely around the world and consists of five steps:

1. Development of background material.
2. Introduction to new and key vocabulary.
3. Guided reading.
4. Comprehension check.
5. Skills development exercises.

PSYCHOLINGUISTIC APPROACH (TOP-DOWN)

Native speakers of English are able, because of their knowledge of English syntax and semantics, to guess what follows the text they have already read. ESL students with low facility in English may have difficulty predicting either the part of speech or a word with an acceptable meaning. An examination of students' miscues will provide an indication of their knowledge of English grammar and vocabulary.

INDEPENDENT READING (TOP-DOWN)

In some schools and classes, time is set aside for sustained silent reading. ESL students should be guided to interesting reading material at their reading level or slightly above. Students who are literate in their first language but still struggling in English should be encouraged to maintain their first language skills. The librarian can order books in the ESL students' first languages, or students can be asked to bring books from home to read during some silent reading periods. In this way, their minds will be stimulated through knowledge acquired in the first language while second language reading skills are still being mastered.

STORY TIME (TOP-DOWN)

Read aloud to the students using pictures and gestures to help convey meaning. If possible, help the children follow the print.

DIRECTED READING-THINKING APPROACH — DRTA — (TOP-DOWN)

Give the children a copy of a short story and ask them to cover up all the text except the title. Ask," What do you think the story will be about? Why do you think so?" After they've struggled with their answers, have them uncover the first sentence and read it together. Then ask, "What do you think will happen next? Why do you think so?" Carry on this way, uncovering one or two sentences each time and asking the same questions. While the children are learning this process, you may find it easier to put the story on an overhead transparency. Emphasis is on meaning and understanding, which is assisted by guessing.

LANGUAGE EXPERIENCE APPROACH — LEA (INTERACTIVE)

When students' facility in English is low, invite them to tell about an experience. This works best if it's a common experience so that all may contribute. Write what they say on the chalkboard, using the children's own words as far as possible. Make changes to the language only when it is badly flawed. Read over the story a number of times, in unison and individually, identify words, add words, look at parts of words, copy it and change it. In other words, get some mileage out of it!

BASAL READER (INTERACTIVE)

Basal readers present reading skills in sequence. Use only those stories likely to interest students and those exercises that will help them master comprehension, skimming and scanning skills. Do not feel obliged to read every story and complete every exercise. Doing so is boring and unnecessary.

ORAL READING (INTERACTIVE)

If children are grouped for oral reading, do not place the ESL students in the lowest group. They need to hear the best readers in the class, the ones on whom they should model their performance. Don't ask ESL students to read aloud until they have had time to practice. No one likes looking foolish in front of others. Work on comprehension, pronunciation and word analysis during this time.

WHOLE LANGUAGE (HOLISTIC)

Choose a theme. Involve the children in listening, speaking, reading and writing activities that revolve around the theme. Introduce new vocabulary and new sentence structures by using visual aids. Work the theme long enough for the children to become familiar with both content and language, but not so long that they become bored.

Assessment

ESL students will need to be assessed to pinpoint their starting level in reading and to evaluate their progress. This can be done in a number of ways.

COMPARING WITH OTHER STUDENTS

Experienced teachers will probably be able to make a fairly sound judgment about ESL students' reading abilities by comparing them with other students they have taught, taking into account that the subject matter may be new and that ESL students have a limited English vocabulary and may have difficulty unraveling compound-complex sentences.

TEACHER-MADE TESTS

A test created by the teacher can help confirm the first impression. The test might include:

Oral Reading: To give an insight into the student's need for phonics and help with pronunciation, stress, pitch and comprehension.

Miscue Analysis: Noting mistakes in oral reading will provide an indication of how well the student is processing the language. For instance, if the passage says, "He ran home," and the student reads "He ran *to* home," she has made a sensible mistake. Although the word "to" is not in the original text, it follows the pattern of the phrase, "He ran to school." If, however, another student reads, "He ran honey," he has processed neither the sense nor the vocabulary and needs much more help than the first student. An examination of oral reading miscues can provide insight into the student's ability to process written language. Miscues usually fall into one of these categories: mispronunciation, substitution, insertion, omission, repetition, reversal, hesitation or self-correction.

Cloze: Take a piece of writing, such as a paragraph from a story or a textbook, leave the first and last sentences intact, and delete every seventh or eighth word. Ask the student to fill in the blanks or provide a choice of words for each blank. Like other assessment methods, this test provides insight into the way the student processes the language. Some answers, which may not be those found in the original text, may be good guesses and make pretty good sense. Others may show that the student doesn't yet have a sense of which slots require a particular part of speech or which words make better sense in particular situations.

Questions: Ask questions to determine whether the student has understood what he has read, can make inferences and judgments, and can apply the knowledge gained to other situations.

STANDARDIZED READING TESTS

The results of standardized reading tests given to ESL students who have been learning English for less than five years are always suspect and should never be accepted at face value. Students may have trouble with a test because they are not used to taking tests at all or to taking tests in this specific format, lack sufficient vocabulary, cannot unravel compound-complex sentences, and do not have background in the content they are asked to read.

In other words, their problems lie with format, content, vocabulary and sentence structure and can be cleared up over time. A low score does not necessarily indicate a poor reader, but rather a student who needs help in taking tests, building vocabulary, adding new sentence structures, and enlarging knowledge. What a standardized test will indicate is where the student needs help in order to achieve success as a reader.

READING LEVELS

In *ESL Literacy Instruction,* Lee Gunderson points out that, in 1946, Emmett Betts described four different reading levels that are still applied today:

Independent: High word recognition and comprehension.

Instructional: With some assistance, the student can work with the material.

Frustration: Low word recognition and comprehension, causing frustration.

Capacity: The student can comprehend 75 per cent of the material when it is read aloud by the teacher.

ESL students should not be left to flounder at the frustration level as this raises anxiety and slows the process of language acquisition.

Reading teachers usually differentiate between three different comprehension levels:

Literal Comprehension: The reader can answer questions dealing with detail at the surface level of the text.

Inferential Comprehension: The reader can make inferences from the ideas the writer presents.

Critical-Evaluative Comprehension: The reader can evaluate and make critical judgments about what she has read. These might include whether the text expresses fact or opinion or how the knowledge might be applied in different situations.

Choosing Materials

READABILITY FEATURES

A number of features affect how easy or difficult a reading passage will be for an ESL student: the number of multisyllabic words, the number of words new to the student, whether the vocabulary is concrete or abstract, the complexity of the sentences, the number and kind of figures of speech, the length of the passage, the student's familiarity with content, including cultural content, and the style.

Because readability formulas tend to count only the number of syllables, sentences and uncommon words in a passage, while omitting other important features, they are of limited value to ESL teachers. Teachers will therefore have to use their own judgment regarding the readability of a passage for a particular student based on the features listed previously and their personal knowledge of the student.

SELECTING MATERIALS

As with any children, materials for ESL students should be chosen on the basis of their interest, relevance and readability.

Picture books, picture dictionaries, newspapers, advertisements, texts from a lower grade (with the cover concealed if the student is likely to be embarrassed), basal readers, short stories from various cultures, folk tales, legends, poems, plays and big books can all be used, though some may need to be simplified. While some vocabulary can be taught before reading, words and expressions taught in context are usually understood and remembered better than those taught out of context.

Only a limited amount of bilingual material — with English on one page and another language on the facing page — is available.

Teaching Beginning Reading

Some ESL students may need to go through a readiness period in which they have time to develop some oral language ability and become familiar with the look of English print. Teachers must design reading programs for ESL students based on the students' literacy levels in their own language and in English, their respective ages and interests, and the teacher's own understanding of how reading should be taught to non-English speaking children.

ESL teachers can introduce a variety of activities to help beginning readers of English as a second language.

EXPANDING VOCABULARY

Ensure that new words are repeated orally and seen often and encourage every student to make a personal vocabulary book. Use flash cards and sentence strips for extra practice and provide practice in dictionary use. Group words according to roots, meaning and association and use visual and aural imagery to clarify meaning. Highlight key words and encourage physical responses to ensure that students understand.

PEER TUTORING

Encourage a fluent reader to read to an ESL student, then change places. The two might also read along together. Follow up with discussions about detail, inference, judgment and evaluation.

RECORDINGS

Record stories or other reading material, such as excerpts from content texts. Invite the student to listen to the tape and read along from the text.

CLASS LIBRARY

Gather a collection of appealing books that ESL students can take home to read.

SHARING BOOKS

Invite ESL and non-ESL students to meet in small groups to talk about the content of books they have read and share their feelings about them.

THE SCHOOL LIBRARY

Ask the librarian to help ESL students find suitable books in English, use the card catalogue, understand library procedures and find books in their first language.

READING CONFERENCES

Meet each ESL student perhaps once a week to discuss what has been read, the difficulties encountered, progress made and further reading suggestions.

The teacher's personal interest in the student's progress will encourage her to keep working at mastering reading in English.

USING LITERATURE

Good stories and poems are not necessarily difficult for the student to read. They form the background that links educated people. Do not choose badly written material because it seems easy. As the ESL student's reading ability improves, good literature can be used to demonstrate things like plot line, the universality of the story, the cultural information contained in the story, and the use of illustrations to enliven and enhance the text.

Stories can be used as springboards to other activities such as drama, rewriting the ending, writing a similar story, writing poetry and reading other stories by the same author or on the same topic.

For young children, stories containing repetitive language, such as *The Three Bears*, are effective. Many well-known fairy tales are common to many cultures.

Give children time to struggle on their own with a new piece of reading, but don't let them reach the frustration level. Either provide help that will enable them to read the material or help them select easier material.

THE COMPUTER

The computer is a great motivator. At the computer station, children can work in pairs, asking and answering questions, and reading.

INVOLVEMENT OF LIBRARIANS AND PARENTS

Students who are already literate in their first language and who are learning English have an advantage over monolingual students in that they have two pipelines for receiving and sending information. Research suggests that bilingual students may do better academically in the long run than monolingual students and that they may be more creative. To help students maintain literacy in their first language, school libraries should contain some books in the languages spoken by ESL students. Local ethnic societies will be glad to suggest suitable titles and perhaps donate books.

Parents of younger students should be encouraged to read first language books to their children. It's worth repeating that research has shown that maintaining or improving reading skills in the first language has a beneficial effect on reading skills in the second language.

Parents should also encourage their children to read to them in English, even if they don't understand everything they hear. Exposure to written English will benefit both of them.

Reading in the Content Areas

Learning to read in the content areas highlights the difference between "learning to read" and "reading to learn." Both facets of reading are necessary if the student is to progress, for they complement each other. The task of the reading teacher is to develop reading skills while the task of the subject-matter teacher is to teach functional reading skills within a particular discipline. The two should work in tandem.

Functional skills that must be taught include understanding the purpose of the parts of a book — the table of contents, preface, footnotes, bibliography, index, chapter headings, subheadings, graphs and pictures. Students should also be able to extract important information pertinent to the topic from the text by looking for key words or phrases and making notes. In addition, they should be able to recognize the way the content is structured — the schemata — and skim and scan the text for specific information.

ESL and subject-matter teachers can work together to simplify the text or the task by, for example, making the text more readable and helping students recognize where skills cross boundaries from one subject area to another. Skills related to cognitive procedures are required in all content areas and may not need to be learned separately within each discipline.

Content reading material found in textbooks is often more difficult than material used for the teaching of reading because sentences are more complex, vocabulary is more abstract and specialized, there are fewer illustrations and more graphs, charts and maps, the text is more densely packed with information, the style is less user-friendly and the text is generally more difficult than other reading material provided at the same grade level.

· · · · · · · · · · · · · ·

WRITING

W hy should children, whether they speak English as a first or second language, learn to write acceptable prose?

The most common way for children to show mastery of subject matter is through written responses — by answering, in writing, essay questions and questions on examinations or after completion of a topic.

Adherents of the whole language approach believe that growth in writing assists growth in listening, speaking and reading, and vice versa.

Besides being a mode of communication, writing is also a way of learning, providing an opportunity for children to discover what they want to say. Writing well requires children to clarify their thoughts, both before they put them on paper and during the writing process, and demands critical thinking about ideas and organization, their own and that of others.

In addition, writing provides children with the opportunity to express their inner feelings, describe their personal experiences and explore themselves. It's also a way for them to affect others through persuasion, explanation and description.

Writing is an art form. Children who master the basics of mechanics and organization can use language creatively in stories, drama and poetry, and satisfy their desire to create something of their own. Through studying good writing, students can experience the beauty and power of language.

Further, the ability to write well and easily is essential for students continuing their education.

ESL students must often overcome many hurdles on the path to becoming proficient writers. They may, for example, need to learn an entirely new writing system as some of them will be used to hieroglyphics and writing from right to left.

ESL students may have been used to organizing their material differently in compositions written in their first language. Older children may not be used to footnoting and may have different views about what constitutes plagiarism.

In addition, they may not be used to expressing their personal feelings or opinions on topics concerned with values.

Form and Content

Students must pay attention both to what they say and how they say it.

HANDWRITING

Students who are not used to the print and script used in English and other European languages will have to learn both. Some teachers introduce printing first to reinforce the type encountered in books and readers. Then they show students how to join the letters in a flowing movement. Other teachers introduce print and script simultaneously, demonstrating that, while the form is different, the meaning is the same.

Students may need basic instruction in holding a pencil or pen and forming upper- and lower-case letters. A classmate whose handwriting is good can be given the responsibility of working with an ESL student. Grade one teachers will have materials that can be adapted for older students.

SPELLING

If spelling is a problem for native speakers of English, it can be double trouble for ESL students. It will take time for students to master English spelling. They should be provided with a good speller when they are advanced enough to use it. They must learn things like how derivatives are formed from roots and that silent letters are not silent when a suffix is added. Above all, they need to be treated with patience. Spelling should not be the focus of the grading process. In the early days, *what* an ESL student says is far more important than *how* it is said.

A buddy who is a good speller can work with the ESL student for 15 minutes a day. As in so many learning tasks, regular practice works wonders.

PUNCTUATION

Periods should be taught first, then commas, question marks, quotation marks and exclamation marks. Advanced students will also need to learn how to use semi-colons and colons. Reading a passage aloud sometimes helps students become conscious of a pause that needs to be marked. Examining a piece of well-written but simple prose provides examples of how good writers use punctuation effectively.

SENTENCES

Students will need to gain some control over the various sentence patterns (described in the Syntax section of the chapter titled How Language Works), learning how to expand and combine these and which patterns to use to answer the questions "who," "what," "where," "when," "why" and "how." As they become more proficient, they will need to know how to create suspense, how to paint pictures with words, and how to produce clear, logical explanations. Learning to use sentences effectively takes years, not months. Teachers who themselves take pleasure in reading and writing good prose will be powerful, competent instructors of ESL students. We teach best what we enjoy doing ourselves.

ORGANIZATION

A paragraph usually begins with a topic sentence followed by three or four sentences that expand on this. A closing or summary sentence completes the paragraph. While experienced writers can create suspense by delaying introduction of the topic sentence, beginners should master the accepted organization before trying something new. A formal essay follows the same organization except that a paragraph takes the place of each sentence.

The ideas, events and facts in a paragraph may be organized in different ways depending on the writer's purpose. They may be ordered chronologically or spatially, by classification, for comparison or contrast, to demonstrate cause and effect, to carry out inductive or deductive reasoning, or to illustrate an analogy. Term papers and examination questions often demand that students provide proof, evidence and authority for the points they are making, and refute and rebut another's argument. These skills come with practice, but, in most cases, they have to be taught.

AUDIENCE

Students should know for whom they are writing. Often this is the teacher, but it could be classmates, a class or school newspaper, an environmental or other society, or people back home. The more important the audience is to the student, the higher the motivation to write will be — and high motivation will result in better writing.

PURPOSE

Students should be clear about their purpose in writing. Is it to describe? Explain? Persuade? Entertain? The sense of audience for and the purpose of writing will affect style.

STYLE

The style can be formal or informal. It can use the very personal first person "I," or the third person "she," "he," "they," "it" or "one." Style also affects vocabulary. For instance, should the student use "fatigued," "tired," or "bushed"? As ESL students expand their knowledge of English vocabulary, they will acquire the clichés and slang of the day that, while acceptable on the playground and in school corridors, are not acceptable in a formal paper. Some students find it helpful to try and write in the style of a well-known author, trying on the author's style themselves to see if it fits.

WRITING ACROSS THE CURRICULUM

Different subjects require different organization of material and writing styles. For example, the task of writing up a math problem about A, B, and C plowing fields is not the same as producing a critique of a piece of literature or stating reasons for the outbreak of World War II. Students need to be exposed to the models of writing that are acceptable in the various disciplines. The saying that every teacher is a teacher of English remains as true today as when it was first uttered.

TAKING NOTES

Students may need to take notes while listening to a class lecture or reading from a textbook. They will have to become skilled at recognizing phrases that indicate something important is to follow (e.g., "There are five reasons for ....").

SUMMARIZING, PARAPHRASING AND PRÉCIS WRITING

The ability to summarize or paraphrase a long prose piece so that the vital points are retained is an important thinking skill that all students must master if they are to progress academically. While précis writing (reducing a piece of prose to one-third the length of the original) may not be a particularly exciting exercise, it teaches students what to include and what to leave out, how to shorten and combine sentences, clauses and phrases, and how to make one word do the work of several.

TOPICS

Personal Topics

For some students, writing about events in their own lives may help release a trauma they have experienced. Others, however, will resent being asked to write about personal topics, viewing this is as an invasion of privacy.

Subject-Area Topics

It is important to check that students have the necessary background to tackle an assignment and that additional information is available to them. Topics related to the history, geography or culture of their homeland might be relevant and interesting to some students, while others might prefer to explore aspects of their new homeland.

ESL students often have trouble understanding the instructions for assignments. They may need to see a finished example so that they know what they are working towards.

Students will need experience in writing:

Exposition: Explanations of why things are the way they are or how things work.

Artistic Description: Descriptions of nature or whatever appeals to the artist within the student.

Scientific Description: Descriptions of what goes on in a scientific experiment or in the environment, where what happens and why is more important than how beautiful the object or process appears.

Narrative: Stories, plays or interviews.

Poetry: A variety of forms.

The Writing Process

The writing process can be broken down into a number of stages.

PRE-WRITING

During this period, students collect, sift and organize information by reading, talking, studying pictures, graphs, charts and models, or taking field trips. Brainstorming and asking questions help suggest ideas, vocabulary and sentence structures. Listing and categorizing help organize the information into a plan.

FIRST DRAFT

The first draft is simply that: the first of three or four drafts, not the finished product.

TEACHER AND PEER RESPONSE TO THE FIRST DRAFT

The teacher or a trusted group of peers or both respond to the draft by questioning the author about content and meaning and by making suggestions that the author is not bound to follow. Some major mechanical errors can be corrected at this point, but the emphasis should be on content and organization.

The student revises the first draft in light of the comments and suggestions. Review and revision continue with the help of the teacher or the peer group or both. By writing and revising with trusted peers, children appear to develop a sense of audience, voice and the power of language.

EDITING

When the text nears completion, the student goes over it carefully, catching mechanical errors, combining or expanding sentences, ensuring that ideas are soundly organized and supported, and making changes where necessary. A neat draft is prepared.

PROOFREADING

The text is carefully proofread, perhaps with the help of a peer.

FINAL DRAFT

The final text is then written or typed out. Students should understand that the production of a composition takes as much time as any other work of art. It involves preparation, criticism, review and rewriting.

First Steps in Writing

YOUNG CHILDREN

Young children's first written efforts at school often involve adding words to artwork. These can be dictated to the teacher who writes them or students may be encouraged to produce their own text.

Young English-speaking children seem to go through four stages in learning to write.

Pre-Phonetic Stage

Because children don't understand that letters correspond to sounds, pre-phonetic writing is not readable by an adult.

Semi-Phonetic Stage

Children use letters to represent words or parts of words.

Phonetic Stage

Children use letters to represent all the surface features of words.

Transitional Stage

Children depend less on the sound of words to get at spelling and more on visual representations.

Young ESL children go through roughly the same stages. It is therefore wise to avoid criticism, encouraging them to experiment and praising their efforts. The teacher's role is to provide opportunities for writing in a positive and encouraging atmosphere.

Older students who are either used to a different writing system or illiterate in their first language will need to achieve a measure of familiarity with English script. Initially, this can be accomplished by encouraging them to copy English words and sentences, then write sentences dictated by the teacher. Using the language experience approach can produce text on topics familiar to the students. This can be used for dictation or as a model for a different text created by the student.

Older students, like their younger counterparts, will need opportunities to write on a variety of topics in various genres in a positive, friendly atmosphere. Students are encouraged to try when they see their teachers writing in class and sharing the product.

Error Correction

Teachers must respond to two aspects of composition: mechanics and content.

MECHANICS

Mechanics include spelling, punctuation, sentence structure and variety, and organization. Errors in spelling, punctuation and sentence structure and variety are easy to respond to because they strike one as being un-English. Poor organization, because it is more involved, is not as easy to pin down.

In the early stages of learning English, the emphasis should be on content. Students need to be praised for content or questioned as to what they mean, not discouraged by receiving back a paper covered in red marks highlighting mechanical errors. One student said to his classmates as he carried his paper back to his desk, "Don't touch it — it's bleeding to death!" Early composition efforts should not be so badly wounded as to lead to an early death!

Spelling

Pick out a few errors and go over corrections for these. Ignore the others. No student can master English spelling in a week!

Punctuation

Read the paper aloud with the student and show how some punctuation fits in with pitch, breathing and meaning. Again, teach one or two points. Leave the rest for another day.

Sentence Structure and Variety

Again, it's better to teach one thing well than a lot of things badly! If there are a number of students making the same error, then that's the one to focus on. Use the sentence orally and draw attention to it, then provide opportunities for additional practice.

Organization

Organization is probably the hardest aspect of writing to teach because ideas can be organized in a variety of ways to produce different effects. Both audience and purpose will affect organization.

CONTENT

In the initial stages, what the student is trying to say is more important than the way it is said. Is the topic worthwhile? Has the student offered any proof or evidence to back up the proposition? Is the content interesting and important enough for the student and teacher to spend more time repairing the language?

For advanced students, comments can be put on tape to save time. Doing this tends to keep the focus on content rather than mechanics.

Students can help each other. Small groups can respond to each other's writing. The author can read his work to others or give them copies to read silently. Then the group members can question the author about content or point out places where meaning is not clear. The teacher should be careful to control those aspects of the composition that are to be commented on. After the group discussion, the author revises the paper and re-presents it at a later date.

Peer group responses create learning experiences for both the author and the critics. Poor writers should be encouraged to watch what good writers do. Most poor writers need more of everything — time, practice and encouragement.

Activities

CONTROLLED COMPOSITION

Controlled composition controls vocabulary or sentence structure or both. Key vocabulary or key sentence structures can be introduced before the exercise. The following are some controlled composition exercises:

- Copying can be useful for a student used to a different writing system.
- Filling in the blanks can help enlarge vocabulary while developing a sense of sentence structure.
- Answering questions so that the resulting sentences form a short story or expository paragraph develops a sense of paragraph organization.
- Using a model from which students can produce a similarly constructed paragraph on a slightly different topic can also develop a sense of organization.
- Taking dictation requires students to use both listening and writing skills. The material can be studied before it is dictated or dictated sight unseen. The student's work is checked for errors, which are then studied before the dictation is given again. The errors may help pinpoint the student's weaknesses.
- Rewriting a story after hearing it read aloud or reading it silently requires students to focus on key vocabulary and key sentence structures.

— Expanding and combining sentences help students master coordinate and subordinate conjunctions, which show relationships between ideas.

KEY VOCABULARY

Without words, students cannot produce language. The words they need are those that will help them *now* in their everyday life at school and in the community. The words needed will therefore differ from student to student according to age, previous life experiences, aims and ambitions, and present circumstances.

Try asking students to provide a key word — a word that is significant for them — each day. Write the word on a card and give it to the student who, in time, will build up a word bank. The student should be encouraged to use the day's word in oral and written language.

Most teachers use a variety of techniques for introducing and drilling words. They use flash cards, group words according to concepts or roots, check words in the dictionary, use visual and aural imagery, and encourage students to respond physically.

"ALL ABOUT ME" BOOKLET

Students can be asked to complete sentences that will provide information about themselves and their family. Topics covered can relate to body parts, clothing, age, weight, birthplace and the home. Pictures can be cut out of store catalogues. At the secondary school level students can create personal ID cards to be carried in a wallet, purse or backpack.

WRITING STORIES

Invite the children to draw pictures and write stories to go with them. Read them a story and suggest that they respond to it either through art or by writing a story of their own. As already noted, content is more important than form.

PICTURE STUDY

A good picture can stimulate descriptive or narrative writing. Before starting to write on their own, students should work in groups or as a class offering key vocabulary and key sentences related to objects and actions. These suggestions can remain on the chalkboard while the students write their stories.

LANGUAGE EXPERIENCE APPROACH

Students dictate a story to the teacher who writes it on the chalkboard or a sheet of newsprint. With the help of the teacher, students revise and refine the story and copy it into their books to serve as a model for future writing.

JOURNALS

Journals can deal with personal matters such as day-to-day activities and feelings, or impersonal matters such as current events. Students should write in their journals at least three times a week. An important aspect of journal-writing is personal feedback from the teacher. The journal can spark a dialogue between teacher and student as each responds to the comments and questions of the other.

CREATIVE WRITING

Creative writing can spring from picture study, listening to or reading a story, or, best of all, a personal recollection. Good creative writing occurs when students feel comfortable in an accepting and supportive atmosphere. The children should be encouraged to choose their own themes. If the piece is graded, mechanics should take second place to the quality of the story line.

LETTERS

Depending on their age, children may be interested in writing letters to family, classmates, newspaper editors, businesses or authors of books they've read. Composing letters requires students to pay attention to format and style as well as content. In some cases, students should study models that will assist them in writing their own letters.

NEWSPAPERS

ESL students often get great satisfaction from putting together their own class newspaper, which can be shared with the entire school. The first step is to study a newspaper within their ability to understand, examining the various sections, deciding which sections their newspaper will include, and then, in groups, writing, reviewing and editing each section before printing it.

WRITING REPORTS

Initially, let the ESL student work with a proficient classmate, watching the process right through to the final product. This involves gathering and sifting the data, deciding on the organization, writing, revising, rewriting, editing, proofreading, and, finally, presenting the finished product. Then invite the students to switch places, giving the ESL student an opportunity to write a report under the guidance of a competent and trusted friend.

FILLING OUT FORMS

Bring to class a variety of forms students of the age you are teaching are likely to need to fill out. Go over the terminology used (e.g., first name and surname, address, etc.). Point out the importance of printing or writing clearly and of pressing hard if more than one copy is required. Ask students to bring to class copies of forms they and their parents have been given, perhaps in the community center, at the bank or by social service workers.

SUBJECT-MATTER WRITING

No two subjects employ exactly the same kind of writing format and style. It will therefore be necessary for students to examine models of good writing in the various disciplines and use these when writing their own essays or term papers. Good examples can be gathered from top students.

NOTE-TAKING

Provide students with a sheet containing information on a topic being studied in one of the subject areas. Go through the process they are expected to follow in making notes:

— Read the information sheet.
— Underline words that are not understood but seem important and check these out.

- Circle words or phrases that indicate important facts or concepts.
- Cover up the information sheet and summarize it in three or four sentences.
- Check for accuracy.
- Consider what headings and subheadings might help condense the notes even further.

After the class has worked as a unit, provide another information sheet that they can work at as individuals.

To prevent students from copying from reference books without understanding what they've written, insist that they close the books before making their notes. This ensures that they will process the information in their own words.

SUMMARIZING

Invite students to listen to a taped item. Discuss its content, vocabulary and sentence structure. Ask them to write a condensed version of what they heard.

. . . .

LANGUAGE AND CONTENT

Because students can learn language at the same time as they learn content and vice versa, language teaching and content teaching go hand-in-hand. This can happen in three ways:

— The ESL teacher teaches content — academic subject matter — while simultaneously teaching English.
— The regular classroom teacher teaches English while simultaneously teaching academic subject matter.
— The ESL and classroom teachers work together as a team.

If ESL students are in classrooms where the emphasis is solely on language development, serious defects in their knowledge and skills in the content areas will result. On the other hand, if they are in classrooms where no attention is paid to language development, their inability to comprehend what is going on will result in not only inadequate language skills but also defects in knowledge and skills in the content areas. Barriers between ESL and classroom teachers, where they still exist, must be broken down.

The Classroom

If certain conditions are met, the classroom can provide a good environment for language learning and content learning to happen simultaneously.

- If the ESL and regular classroom teacher cooperate fully on behalf of the student. Where there is no ESL teacher, responsibility for knowing what to do and how to do it falls directly to the classroom teacher.
- If there are plenty of visual aids to make meaning comprehensible.
- If non-ESL students are shown how they can contribute to making language and content learning easier for the ESL student.
- If ESL students are actively engaged with the rest of the class in interesting, relevant and meaningful activities that use non-verbal and verbal communication.
- If ESL students feel secure enough to question the teacher and their peers as they seek help in making sense of what is going on.
- If ESL students are given time to think through their answers rather than expected to reply immediately. Formulating a sentence in another language takes much longer than formulating it in one's native language.
- If ESL students are challenged cognitively, not left to sit as if they are invisible.
- If what is learned (e.g., the names of colors or days of the week) is used to solve higher level thinking problems, not simply for recall in language drills.
- If students are expected to give answers that require more than one word or a short phrase. They will learn how to sustain a discussion only if they are able to practice using the mechanisms of taking turns, interrupting, presenting counterarguments, etc.
- If language and content learning are carefully coordinated.

Some of the language skills that ESL students need to master in order to cope effectively with content are:

- Listening to the teacher talk and lecture.
- Following oral instructions.
- Understanding other students' oral presentations.
- Taking part in group discussions.
- Answering questions orally. These should range from those requiring simple recall to those requiring reasoning, hypothesizing, etc.
- Making oral presentations.

- Reading textbooks in various disciplines.
- Interpreting maps, graphs and diagrams.
- Providing written answers to questions.
- Writing paragraphs and essays on academic topics using a standard format.
- Engaging in creative writing.
- Taking notes.
- Using reference books.
- Summarizing.
- Skimming and scanning.
- Vocabulary building.
- Knowing how to write a test.
- Knowing when and who to ask for help.

Curriculum

The subject-matter curriculum for ESL students must correlate with the mainstream curriculum appropriate to each student's age and background. The English-language curriculum must provide the students with the language they need to understand and manipulate the content of various disciplines. Some subject areas make higher language demands than others. For example, art and physical education often make fairly low demands because they use a visual, hands-on approach. Other students or the teacher or both demonstrate to ESL students what they are to do, while simultaneously providing the verbal language. History and literature, on the other hand, provide fewer visual, hands-on clues, requiring instead that ESL students listen to decontextualized language in lectures or read intensively in poorly illustrated textbooks.

It's up to the teachers in charge of drawing up ESL students' programs to decide which subjects they should begin studying and it is up to every teacher, ESL or regular, to decide on the teaching method that will enhance both English language development and content learning.

Thinking Skills

Language that is most easily understood is accompanied by non-verbal clues such as facial expressions, gestures, objects and a variety of visual aids. If language is well-supported by visual clues, teachers can move from asking simple recall questions to more challenging questions that require students to use various thinking skills.

In his book, *Language and Content*, Bernard Mohan classifies thinking skills into six categories — description, sequence, choice, classification, principles and evaluation. An activity can encompass specific thinking skills from each of the six categories, forming the main goal of a lesson and contributing to a full understanding of the topic. Students will learn the language that goes with each category.

The thinking skills and some of the language often carry over into other activities or disciplines. Each discipline includes a variety of activities that require learners to understand background knowledge and carry out actions.

For example, a series of six lessons on keeping a classroom aquarium might involve the following thinking skills:

Description: Describe the features of fish or compare and contrast fish and birds.

Sequence: Arrange in order the events in the life of a fish or plan the procedures necessary to care for the fish in an aquarium.

Choice: Decide which fish are likely to survive in a classroom aquarium or list the problems of keeping fish and propose solutions.

Classification: Classify the various types of fish suitable for an aquarium or define words used in setting up an aquarium.

Principles: Decide what a fish needs to survive or formulate, test and establish a hypothesis about keeping fish in an aquarium (e.g., What happens when the temperature of the water is increased or decreased?).

Evaluation: Evaluate the health of the fish over a period of time or set up criteria for maintaining a successful aquarium.

Each thinking skill has its own particular language but, because the thinking skills cut across all subject areas, language learned in the study of one discipline can be applied in another. The following are examples of vocabulary used when applying each skill:

Description: Large, larger, sphere, cone, made up of, different from, like, unlike, sometimes, never, far away, near, vertical, horizontal.

Sequence: First, then, next, later, finally, result, therefore, consequently, if..., then, because.

Choice: In my opinion, chose, selected, solution, answer, problem, issue, decided, concluded.

Classification: Types, definition, species, category, animal, vegetable, divide.

Principles: Hypothesize, predict, project, probability, will — would, may — might, likely that.

Evaluation: Judge, right, proper, irrelevant, unsuitable, consider, value, recommend, believe, advise.

The rationale for using these thinking skills as a basis for developing lesson plans is found in the following principles:

— Language is learned through meaningful experiences in social contexts.
— Because thinking, language and content are interdependent, thinking skills are common to all subject areas.
— Key visuals, such as diagrams, graphs and timelines, are essential to bridging the gap between thinking, content and language.
— Efficient instruction aims to meet several objectives at the same time. Efficient language instruction integrates the development of subject-matter knowledge, thinking and language skills.

Suggestions for developing lesson plans using these thinking skills are found in the chapter titled Lesson Planning.

Cognitive Academic Language Learning Approach

In an essay included in *When They Don't Speak English*, Anna Chamot and Michael O'Malley set out the cognitive academic language learning approach, which consists of three components: a content-based curriculum appropriate to the students' grade and developmental levels; academic language development activities; and instruction and practice in using learning strategies.

They recommend the phasing in of subjects in this sequence: science, mathematics, social studies, language arts (literature and composition). They begin with science because teachers can provide hands-on activities in this subject. Language arts, however, comes last because of the high level of

English and shared cultural assumptions required. The second component, academic language skills, may or may not have been developed in the first language and includes activities such as making presentations, skimming and scanning, participating in discussions, engaging in research and writing reports. For their third component, they identify three major types of learning strategies:

— Metacognitive strategies that involve planning, monitoring and evaluating one's performance.
— Cognitive strategies in which the learner interacts mentally or physically with the material to be learned (e.g., taking notes, summarizing, verifying, etc.).
— Social-affective strategies in which the learner interacts with another person to assist learning through questioning and cooperation.

. . . .

LESSON PLANNING

Lessons evolve out of curricula. For students who are native speakers of English, there is only one curriculum: that dealing with subject matter, usually laid down by a central or local authority. It is referred to here as the content curriculum.

For students who are speakers of English as a second language, there are three curricula: the subject matter or content curriculum; the English-language curriculum; and the language-and-content curriculum. Lesson plans are bite-sized pieces of whichever curriculum the teacher decides is appropriate for the students.

Content Curriculum

During the initial assessment period, the student's position in relation to the content curriculum will become clear. Some students may be ahead in some subject areas and behind in others. The teacher's task is to build bridges that will enable students to move into the content curriculum mainstream alongside their peers. This may require the school to mount an academic booster program.

English-Language Curriculum

All sorts of texts list not only the grammatical items that should be taught, but also the order in which they should be taught — in the view of the authors. For ESL students, "survival English" must come first, no matter what grammatical items or structures are involved. It is imperative that new-comers be able to state their name, address and the school they attend as well as ask for help if they are not to suffer the trauma of being lost. Teachers must determine what other survival English questions and answers the children should know. These will depend on their age and home circumstances.

Children will need to expand their vocabularies to include items inside and outside the classroom. However, naming and describing objects — using content words — is only a small part of learning a language. Students must master structures and function words — prepositions, conjunctions, articles, etc. — that show relationships and place the content words in context. Begin with short simple sentences, preferably those that can be accompanied by a meaningful activity. Provide plenty of opportunities for the students to hear and repeat the sentences in context so that meaning is clear.

Grammatical items that need to be mastered early are personal pronouns (e.g., I, you, me), action verbs that can be demonstrated (e.g., sit, walk, listen) and the present tense of the verbs "to be" and "to have," prepositions (e.g., above, under, near, far), and content words — nouns, verbs, adjectives and adverbs — that can be demonstrated (e.g., desk, stop, large, quickly).

ESL TEXTBOOKS

If you purchase a text that claims to teach English to non-English speaking children (and there are many on the market), you may prefer not to follow it page-by-page, but to use only those units the students need at a particular stage in their development. Before they are purchased, ESL texts should be evaluated according to the following criteria:

Program Goals and Objectives

What do the authors claim the text will do for the students? Do these goals and objectives match the students' needs?

Program Design

How is the text broken up? Into units? Chapters? Lessons? Are there pictures and other visual aids? Are these appropriate for the age(s) of your students? Does every unit follow the same pattern?

Entry Competencies

How much English must a student know in order to begin at page one? Must the student be literate in her own language? Must the student be conversant with the Roman alphabet? Must the student have had some years of education his own language?

Activities

What kind of activities does the text require the student to complete? Is there variety? Are they interesting? Do the activities tie in with what has gone before and with the reality of your school and community? Can the students work in pairs or in small groups?

Decision-Making

Who decides where the student starts or when she is ready to move on to a new unit or chapter — the text, the student, or the teacher?

Typical Lesson

Do the lessons fit the students' learning styles? Do the lessons meet the students' needs?

Bias

Do the pictures, stories or conversations seem to be biased in favor of or against one or more ethnic groups? Will the text provide moments of embarrassment?

Teacher Preparation

Does the text provide adequate background material? Will it be necessary for teachers to spend some hours preparing each lesson?

Assessment

Does the text provide for assessing the students' progress from time to time? If so, how? Will the assessment process provide enough information to enable the teacher to make necessary changes to the students' program?

Language-and-Content Curriculum

This is the most important curriculum, for language and content are taught together, ensuring that students who need language support get it while they simultaneously absorb aspects of the content curriculum. Teachers, both regular and ESL, must assess all the students to determine where they fit in relation to the content curriculum and what English language skills they need. Finally, they must decide whether one of them will coordinate the teaching of language and content or if it will be a joint effort.

Only teachers who work with the ESL students can draw up the language-and-content curriculum for them. No methodology text or imposed curriculum can take over what is clearly the teachers' responsibility. In addition, when planning the language-and-content curriculum, teachers must pay attention to students' educational and personal experiences.

Here are some suggestions to keep in mind when planning for a class that contains some ESL students:

— English language development in the class may range from non-existent to fluent. Every child needs to be challenged to use the English language to her maximum capability. This may mean planning for individuals, pairs or small groups, whatever seems best.

— Children's literacy levels — both in English and in their home language — may vary. They should be stimulated to read in English and encouraged to maintain and further develop literacy in their home language.

— Children's starting points may also vary according to their age, motor skills, reasoning skills, factual knowledge and knowledge of processes.

— Language and content are best learned through activities that call for interaction among students and between students and the teacher. Activities should be relevant, interesting and meaningful.

— A lesson is not cast in stone. It can be changed as circumstances dictate. The students' progress and level of interest should therefore be monitored constantly.

Lesson Plan Models

Because regular subject-matter teachers have studied the methodology relating to their own discipline and will by now be using lesson plans that fit their philosophy of learning and their teaching style, this book won't offer lesson plan models for the content curriculum.

ENGLISH-LANGUAGE CURRICULUM

Once the language objective is decided, it can be reached by following a series of steps: modeling, repetition, practice, extension and review.

Example A

Language Objective: Personal pronouns — "I," "you," "he," and "she."

Modeling: Point to yourself and say, "I am a teacher." Then point to a student and say, "You are a student." Point to other students, one at a time, and say, "He is a student," or "She is a student."

Repetition: Be careful that students do not repeat false information. For example, a student should not say, "I am a teacher." If this happens, point to yourself and say, "I am a teacher," then point to a student and ask, "What are you?" Work for the answer, "I am a student." Ask, "What am I?" and work for the answer, "You are a teacher." Go through the various pronouns until the students seem to have mastered both question and answer.

Practice: Break into groups of five or six and give each group a beanbag. Whoever has the beanbag must supply either the question or the answer. The teacher can be brought in if the students ask, "What is he?"

Extension: "I am...," "you are...," and "she is...," can be used with a variety of nouns and adjectives. Certain questions and answers — "How old are you?" "I am...," "How tall is she?" "She is...," — may need to be taught:

Review: Go back to the first questions and answers and check individuals for correct responses.

This lesson should not take more than 20 minutes. In a follow-up lesson, invite students to read and write short stories using these pronouns.

Example B

Language objective: Prepositions — "over" and "under."
Modeling: Hold a book over the desk and say, "The book is over the desk." Then hold it under the desk and say, "The book is under the desk."
Repetition: Teach the question, "Where is the book?" Encourage the children to hold a book over the desk. Ask, "Where is the book?" and listen for the correct answer. Repeat this with the book under the desk.
Practice: Invite the children to work in pairs to ask each other these questions using objects other than the book and the desk.
Extension: Extend the concept to physical education where students can hold an object over or under a piece of equipment in the gym, or to art where they can draw a picture showing objects over or under other articles.
Review: Invite pairs of students to demonstrate what they have learned.

This lesson should not take more than 15 minutes. In a follow-up lesson, invite students to write sentences using "over" and "under" to describe the position of objects in the classroom.

LANGUAGE-AND-CONTENT CURRICULUM

Because language and content are integrated in this model, lessons are structured differently. Teachers must first select a topic, then decide on the concepts (e.g., time, height, space, weight, etc.), language skills (e.g., vocabulary, structure, discourse tasks, formality or informality) and thinking skills (see the previous chapter) that will be involved in an activity. If cultural attitudes and values different from those of the students' home countries are to be introduced, these must be considered as well.

In addition, the teacher must decide what key visuals (discussed later in this chapter) and activities will be used, as well as provide for review.

Example A

Topic: Reading maps.
Concepts: Space and direction.
Language Skills: Vocabulary (e.g., street, road, on, at, address, north, south, east, west) and structures (e.g., Where do you live? What is your address? I live on..., etc.).
Thinking Skills: Description and principles.
Cultural Attitudes and Values: In many North American towns and cities, the streets and roads run at right angles to each other.
Key Visuals: A map of a town, preferably the one the students live in if the roads and streets run at right angles.
Activities: Identify the streets and roads and the directions they run, the street numbering system, important buildings and, if possible, where the students live. Encourage students to describe how they would get from one place to another, initially using their home or a central building as a base. Suggest that students work in pairs once they understand what they have to do.
Review: Ask the students to tell or write out how they would get from place A to place B. You or the students can choose these places.

This lesson should not take more than 30 minutes.

Example B

Topic: Food
Concepts: Classifying fruits and vegetables.
Language Skills: Vocabulary — names of the fruits and vegetables used as key visuals and the terms "fruit" and "vegetable" — and structures (e.g., This is a.... It belongs to the ... group).
Thinking Skills: Description and classification.
Cultural Attitudes and Values: Some fruits and vegetables may not be known to some students. Their nutritional value should be explained.
Key Visuals: A wide variety of fruits and vegetables.
Activities: Identify fruits and vegetables, classify them as fruits or vegetables, and describe their color, shape and texture.
Review: Make a vegetable and a fruit salad and identify the ingredients.

This lesson should not take more than 45 minutes. As a follow-up, students can write a recipe for a fruit or vegetable salad.

Key Visuals

A *key* visual is special. Not all visual aids are key visuals or, to put it another way, not all visual aids are used as key visuals — though they might have the potential to be key visuals. It is the way an audio-visual aid is used that determines whether it is a key visual. Computers, television, films and slides are not in themselves key visuals, but what they portray may be.

So what is a key visual? What does it do for the ESL and, in some cases, the non-ESL learner?

- Key visuals lower the language barrier. They present information in a clear and direct way.
- They simplify content and present cognitive structures visibly.
- They can be used as advanced organizers at the start of a lesson.
- They focus on the core of the content to be presented in the lesson.
- They can be used as the basis for activities.
- They help students with low attention spans focus on the core of the lesson.
- They can be reviewed, allowing processes and principles to be recalled whenever necessary.
- They provide a context for pre-teaching the vocabulary needed for a full understanding of the content to follow.

Key visuals can represent the six categories of thinking skills set out by Bernard Mohan in the preceding chapter. Here are some examples:

Description: Picture, plan, drawing, slide, map.
Sequence: Flow chart, cycle, action strip, time line, recipe.
Choice: Decision tree, flow chart.
Classification: Web, tree, table, graph, database, calendar.
Principles: Diagram, graph, table, cycle.
Evaluation: Rating chart, grid, mark book, worksheet.

Students from some cultures may not be used to drawing meaning from pictures and graphics and will need time to learn how key visuals can help them master both content and language.

Because teachers may need to create key visuals to draw together content and language learning, using them may seem time-consuming. However, by making the learning process more efficient, key visuals are, in fact, time-savers. They can be made by students as well as the teacher, providing students have been instructed in the purpose and process of constructing them. Visual (picture) dictionaries are a useful resource.

DEVELOPING A KEY VISUAL

— Survey the text to get the gist of the content and the author's conceptual structure in order to identify the sections into which the text might naturally be divided. A section may be a single paragraph or include several paragraphs or even the whole chapter.
— Read the first section and identify the key ideas students should grasp by the end of the lesson. Then identify the content vocabulary and discourse structures that will be critical for the students' understanding.
— Look again at the key ideas and identify and label the categories of thinking skills inherent in those ideas. You might find it helpful to use the discourse structures (e.g., "if..., then" for cause and effect, "first," "second," etc. for sequence) to assist you in this process.
— Look through the section and pick out aids, such as tables, diagrams or charts, and evaluate them to determine if they are suitable for transforming into key visuals.
— Work through these steps for each section of the text.
— When each section of the text has been surveyed and appropriate key visuals developed, incorporate them into a composite key visual. When incorporating the individual key visuals into a cohesive, comprehensive whole, some adjustments may be necessary.

OTHER USES FOR AUDIO-VISUAL AIDS

Audio-visual aids may also be used to develop a manual skill, provide practice with certain aspects of language, ease the teacher's burden in, for example, marking, allow the students to evaluate their performance, and provide younger students with an opportunity to engage in hands-on play as a relief from learning language. A variety of visual aids is available to teachers: looking glasses, advertisements, maps, chalkboard, calendars, newspapers, cartoons, overhead transparencies, computers, photographs, data bases, recipes, field trips, television, and so on.

. . . .

COMMUNITIES, CONFLICT
AND CLASSROOMS

W hile the classroom is itself a small community, a variety of other communities exist beyond its walls. Because these communities affect what happens in the school, they have a special relationship with teachers. Communities "out there" benefit from what teachers do, act as a resource for teachers, and can, to a degree, control what teachers do.

These communities can be classified under three headings: geo-political, common-interest and professional.

Geo-political communities, which lie within roughly defined boundaries, include neighborhoods and elected educational authorities. The most significant aspect of neighborhoods is their socio-economic and ethnic make-up. Elected educational authorities have the task of promoting the interests of people they represent.

Common-interest communities are made up of small or large groups of people united by a shared bond. In families, this bond is kinship; in minority groups, it is a historical memory and values, as well as customs and patterns of behavior; in religious groups, it is faith and liturgy; in pressure groups, it is a particular social or environmental concern.

Professional communities consist of organizations of administrators, teachers, students or parents, each of which has as its major aim the improvement of education.

What all these communities have in common is that they benefit from the work teachers do with ESL students, while at the same time acting as a resource for and maintaining some control over the educational system.

Conflict

Because schools are a microcosm of society, the prejudices held by parents and friends of students can be carried into classrooms. There are many differences among cultures. Some of these, such as differences in clothing and food, are easily observed, while others, such as learning styles or attitudes towards time, are less easy to pick out. These can cause confusion and frustration for both the teacher and students.

Teachers must encourage students to *appreciate* others who are culturally different. Mere tolerance is not enough. They must, through careful integration, encourage some students to stand astride two cultures. Often it is the ESL teacher's task both to help monolingual English-speaking children appreciate the newcomers to the school and to help ESL students integrate into both in-school and after-school activities. To provide ESL students with competent teaching and access to school activities may mean making some changes.

Classrooms

Some years ago, I was involved in helping teachers, schools and school districts change their educational systems to benefit ESL students. From that experience, I drew up a list of 20 axioms for making educational change designed, in time, to affect the classroom. Some of these axioms apply to individuals, some to organizations, some to both. You must decide who the "you" is in each axiom and which are likely to be effective in your unique situation.

1. Be quite clear in your own mind what problem needs to be addressed and what needs to be done.
2. Collect the facts and figures you need to prove your case.
3. Decide on four or five priorities. Then pick the one you think you can be reasonably sure of completing successfully and get on with it quickly.
4. Gather a few like-minded people around you.
5. Encourage outsiders to meet students in your class and see what goes on in your classroom.
6. Get to know some government officials — municipal, regional, state or provincial, and national — on a personal basis.

7. Take an active part in local politics.
8. Support your teachers' organization. Be prepared to give it some time and serve on a committee.
9. But remember that the individual is just as important as the organization. Both have a role to play in making changes.
10. Make your organization truly representative. Don't let cliques develop.
11. Advertise your organization and its cause.
12. Join hands with other community organizations that have similar interests.
13. Join hands also with state or provincial, national and international organizations.
14. Keep well-informed about what is happening in your field locally, at a provincial or state level, nationally and internationally, and, as an organization, keep members well informed.
15. Make sure you know which concerns fall under the mandate of the local government and which are handled by the provincial, state or national government.
16. Find a politician in power and another in opposition and cultivate them.
17. Show these politicians the benefits to be reaped from supporting your cause. Votes? Publicity?
18. Ask questions before making accusations.
19. Be professional in fact, not in fiction.
20. Be prepared to be hurt.

. . . .

BIBLIOGRAPHY

Learning about Students

Ashworth, M. *Blessed with Bilingual Brains: Education of Immigrant Children with English as a Second Language.* Vancouver, British Columbia: Pacific Educational Press, 1988.

Ashworth, M. and P. Wakefield. *ESL for Young Children: K-12.* Washington, D.C.: Center for Applied Linguistics, 1982.

California State Department of Education. *Beyond Language: Social and Cultural Factors in Schooling Language Minority Students.* Los Angeles, California: California State University, Evaluation, Dissemination, and Assessment Center, 1986.

Rigg, P. and V.G. Allen (Eds.) *When They Don't All Speak English: Integrating the ESL Student into the Regular Classroom.* Urbana, Illinois: National Council of Teachers of English, 1989.

How Language Works

Celce-Murcia, M. and D. Larsen-Freeman. *The Grammar Book: An ESL/EFL Teachers' Course.* Rowley, Massachusetts: Newbury House, 1983.

Fromkin, V. and R. Rodman. *An Introduction to Language.* 4th Edition. New York: Holt, Rinehart and Winston, 1988.

Leech, G. and J. Svartik. *A Communicative Grammar of English.* London: Longman Group, 1980.

O'Grady, W. and M. Dobrovolsky (Eds.) *Contemporary Linguistic Analysis: An Introduction.* Toronto, Ontario: Copp Clark Pitman, 1987.

Praninskas, J. *Rapid Review of English Grammar.* 2nd Edition. Englewood Cliffs, New Jersey: Prentice-Hall, 1975.

How a Second Language Is Acquired and Taught

Brown, H.D. *Principles of Language Learning and Teaching.* 2nd Edition. Englewood Cliffs, New Jersey: Prentice-Hall, 1987.

Cummins, J. *Bilingualism and Minority Children.* Toronto, Ontario: Ontario Institute for Studies in Education, 1981.

Dulay, H., M. Burt and S.D. Krashen. *Language Two.* New York: Oxford University Press, 1982.

Ellis, R. *Understanding Second Language Acquisition.* London: Oxford University Press, 1985.

Krashen, S.D. and T.D. Terrell. *The Natural Approach: Language Acquisition in the Classroom.* New York: Pergamon Press, 1983.

Krashen, S.D. *Principles and Practice in Second Language Acquisition.* New York: Pergamon Press, 1982.

Krashen, S.D. *Second Language Acquisition and Second Language Learning.* New York: Pergamon Press, 1981.

Larsen-Freeman, D. *Techniques and Principles in Language Teaching.* Oxford, England: Oxford University Press, 1986.

Mohan, B.A. *Language and Content.* Reading, Massachusetts: Addison-Wesley, 1986.

Naiman, N., M. Frölich, H. Stern and A. Todesco. *The Good Language Learner.* Toronto, Ontario: OISE Press, 1978.

Richards, J.C. and T.S. Rogers. *Approaches and Methods in Language Teaching: A Description and Analysis.* New York: Cambridge University Press, 1986.

Stern, H.H. *Fundamental Concepts of Language Teaching.* London: Oxford University Press, 1983.

Assessment and Programs

Ashworth, M. *Blessed with Bilingual Brains: Education of Immigrant Children with English as a Second Language.* Vancouver, British Columbia: Pacific Educational Press, 1988.

Cummins, J. *Bilingualism and Special Education: Issues in Assessment and Pedagogy.* Clevedon, Avon, England: Multilingual Matters, 1984.

Listening and Speaking

Enright, D.S. and M.L. McCloskey. "Yes, Talking! Organizing the Classroom to Promote Second Language Acquisition." In *TESOL Quarterly.* Vol.19, no. 3 (1985).

Graham, C. *Jazz Chants for Children.* New York: Oxford University Press, 1979.

Moskowitz, G. *Caring and Sharing in the Foreign Language Classroom: A Source Book on Humanistic Techniques.* Rowley, Massachusetts: Newbury House, 1978.

Savignon, S.J. *Communicative Competence: Theory and Classroom Practice.* Reading, Massachusetts: Addison-Wesley, 1983.

Reading

Adams, T.A. *Inside Textbooks: What Students Need to Know.* Reading, Massachusetts: Addison-Wesley, 1989.

Bell, J. and B. Burnaby. *A Handbook for ESL Literacy.* Toronto, Ontario: OISE Press in association with Hodder and Stoughton, 1984.

Callie, J. and S. Slater. *Literature in the Language Classroom: A Resource Book of Ideas and Activities.* Cambridge: Cambridge University Press, 1990.

Gunderson, L. *ESL Literacy Instruction.* Englewood Cliffs, New Jersey: Prentice Hall Regents, 1991.

Rathmell, G. *Bench Marks in Reading: A Guide to Reading Instruction in the Second Language Classroom.* Hayward, California: Alemany Press, 1984.

Walters, K. and L. Gunderson. "Effects of Parent Volunteers Reading First Language (L1) Books to ESL Students." In *The Reading Teacher*. Vol. 39, no. 1 (1985).

Wisconsin Department of Public Instruction. *Strategic Learning in the Content Areas*. Madison, Wisconsin: Wisconsin Department of Public Instruction, 1991.

Writing

Carruthers, C. *Open the Lights*. Reading, Massachusetts.: Addison-Wesley, 1982.

Chow, M. "Nurturing the Growth of Writing in Kindergarten and Grade One Years: How Are ESL Children Doing?" In *TESL Canada Journal*. Vol. 4, no. 1 (1986).

Sadow, S.A. *Idea Bank: Creative Activities for the Language Class*. Cambridge, Massachusetts: Newbury House, 1982.

Urzua, C. "'You Stopped Too Soon': Second Language Children Composing and Revising." In *TESOL Quarterly*. Vol. 21, no. 2 (1987).

Language and Content

British Columbia Ministry of Education. *Integrating Language and Content Instruction K-12: An ESL Resource Book*. Vol. 1. Victoria, British Columbia: British Columbia Ministry of Education, Modern Languages Branch, 1986.

Chamot, A.U. and J.M. O'Malley. "The Cognitive Academic Language Learning Approach: A Bridge to the Mainstream." In *TESOL Quarterly*. Vol. 21, no. 2 (1987).

Chamot, A.U. and J.M. O'Malley. "The Cognitive Academic Language Learning Approach." In *When They Don't All Speak English* (P. Rigg and V.G. Allen, Eds.). Urbana, Illinois. National Council of Teachers of English, 1989.

Early, M. "ESL Beginning Literacy: A Content-Based Approach." In *TESL Canada Journal*. Vol. 7, no. 2 (1990).

Filmore, L.W. 1989. "Teaching English through Content: Instructional Reform in Programs for Language Minority Students." In *Multicultural Education and Policy: ESL in the 1990s*. (J.H. Esling, Ed.). Toronto, Ontario: OISE Press, 1989.

Mohan, B.A. *Language and Content*. Reading, Massachusetts: Addison-Wesley, 1986.

Snow, M.A., M. Met and F. Genesee. "A Conceptual Framework for the Integration of Language and Content in Second/Foreign Language Instruction." In *TESOL Quarterly*. Vol. 23, no. 2 (1989).

Swain, M. "Manipulating and Complementing Content Teaching to Maximize Second Language Learning." In *TESL Canada Journal*. Vol. 6, no. 1 (1988).

Lesson Planning

British Columbia Ministry of Education. *Integrating Language and Content Instruction K-12: An ESL Resource Book*. Vol. 1. Victoria, British Columbia: British Columbia Ministry of Education, Modern Languages Branch, 1986.

Early, M., B.A. Mohan and H.R. Hooper. "The Vancouver School Board Language and Content Project." In *Multicultural Education and Policy: ESL in the 1990s*. (J.H. Esling, Ed.). Toronto, Ontario: OISE Press, 1989.

Early, M. and G.Tang. "Helping ESL Students Cope with Content-Based Texts." In *TESL Canada Journal*. Vol. 8, no. 2 (1991).

Filmore, L.W. "Teaching English through Content: Instructional Reform in Programs for Language Minority Students." In *Multicultural Education and Policy: ESL in the 1990s*. (J.H. Esling, Ed.). Toronto, Ontario: OISE Press, 1989.

Mohan, B.A. 1986. *Language and Content*. Reading, Massachusetts: Addison-Wesley, 1986.

Communities, Conflict and Classrooms

Ashworth, M. *Beyond Methodology: Second Language Teaching and the Community*. Cambridge, England: Cambridge University Press, 1985.

THE PIPPIN TEACHER'S LIBRARY

The titles in this series are designed to provide a forum for interpreting, in clear, straightforward language, current issues and trends affecting education. Teachers are invited to share — in their own voice — the insights, wisdom and knowledge they have developed out of their professional experiences.

Submissions for publication are welcomed. Manuscripts and proposals will be reviewed by members of the Pippin Teacher's Library Editorial Advisory Board, chaired by Lee Gunderson, PhD, of the University of British Columbia.

Members of the Editorial Advisory Board are:
Sally Clinton, MEd, of the University of British Columbia;
Sara E. (Sally) Lipa, PhD, of the State University of New York at Geneseo;
Richard McCallum, PhD, of St. Mary's College of California;
Marion Ralston, PhD, educational consultant;
Jon Shapiro, PhD, of the University of British Columbia.

Written submissions should be directed to:
Editorial Director
Pippin Publishing Limited
150 Telson Road
Markham, Ontario
Canada
L3R 1E5

WITHDRAWN

The Advancing South

MANPOWER PROSPECTS AND PROBLEMS

The Advancing South

MANPOWER PROSPECTS AND PROBLEMS

JAMES G. MADDOX

with

E. E. Liebhafsky

Vivian W. Henderson and

Herbert M. Hamlin

The Twentieth Century Fund · New York · 1967

Copyright © 1967 by the Twentieth Century Fund, Inc.
Printed in the United States of America
By Quinn & Boden Company, Inc., Rahway, N. J.
Library of Congress Catalog Card Number: 67-14506

Foreword

DURING THE DECADE of the nineteen sixties the American South has been undergoing rapid and fundamental changes. The old reliance on agriculture as the economic base of the region has crumbled. New industries, new technologies, new research centers and innovations in education from kindergarten to graduate school have burgeoned. The nation-wide—and indeed world-wide—drift of people away from farms and into the cities has accelerated.

What lies ahead for this growing, evolving, changing South? The Twentieth Century Fund assembled a team of experienced economists and educators, under southern leadership and based at a southern university, to make a thorough study of the region. They have spelled out both the directions and ingredients of change. Giving central attention to employment problems, they have analyzed manpower requirements and resources and made projections to 1975. Very specifically, they contrast the discriminatory pay rates still in effect for Negroes and the disproportionately high rates of Negro unemployment, and in general indicate some of the economic costs of racial discrimination in the South. The picture that emerges is one of the advancing South, a South of many hopeful prospects, but one in which grave problems remain.

The Fund is grateful to James G. Maddox, Professor of Economics at North Carolina State University at Raleigh, who ably directed the carrying out and writing of the project, and to his valued colleagues E. E. Liebhafsky, Vivian W. Henderson, and Herbert M. Hamlin, who joined him in the work at Raleigh and showed continuing interest to the end of the project. The interest and help of Philip Hammer, consulting economist, at all stages of the study deserve special note. Finally, the Fund wishes to thank three officials of North Carolina State University at Raleigh—Chancellor John T. Caldwell, C. E. Bishop, then Head of the Department of Economics, and H. Brooks James, Dean of the College of Agriculture and Life Sciences—for their unfailing courtesy and helpfulness in making this study possible.

JOHN E. BOOTH, *Acting Director*
The Twentieth Century Fund

41 East 70 Street, New York City
May 1967

Preface

IN THIS BOOK WE REPORT the major findings of a study which originated from the interest of the Twentieth Century Fund in assessing the economic implications of racial discrimination in the South. In addition to bearing the burden of discriminatory wage rates, Negroes in the South do not share in employment in proportion to their numbers. Their future role in the southern economy obviously will be closely intertwined with the growth and development of the region as a whole. Hence, a study of the nature, extent and sources of discrimination in the utilization of Negro manpower in the South necessitate an inquiry into the forces which are likely to be the principal determinants of southern economic growth in the years ahead.

These forces have both national and regional aspects. In order, therefore, to have a basis for evaluating the range of future opportunities likely to be available to southern Negroes, it was necessary not only to study the probable future course of southern employment but also to relate the growth of employment in the South to that in the nation as a whole. We have, therefore, emphasized the basic changes that are taking place in the regional economy of the South as related to the national economy, and have attempted to show how these changes are likely to affect both total employment and Negro employment during the next few years.

In many respects this report of our study, concentrating as it does on the economic aspects, is only a short step toward an evaluation of the total social costs to the nation of the South's failure to make full use of the capacities and potentials of its Negro manpower. Nevertheless, we believe that we have laid a foundation on which sound public policies for developing the human resources of the South can be built. At the same time, we have raised a number of important, complex, and unanswered questions from which students of regional economic growth can select a wide range of topics that merit more sophisticated analytical study than they have yet received.

A great many people made important contributions to this book. The Twentieth Century Fund not only financed the underlying research, but Morris B. Abram of its Board of Trustees, and members of its staff, particularly Thomas R. Carskadon and August Heckscher, gave active encouragement and sound advice at all stages of the study. Mrs. Frances Klafter, editor for the Fund, shared with me the task of organizing the final manuscript, and helped greatly to improve its readability. In the course of this work, she brought clarity to many obscure passages.

Philip Hammer aided in formulating the general plan of the study and served on an advisory panel of consultants during the early phases of the research. Other members of the panel, who read an early draft of the manuscript and made helpful suggestions for its improvement, were: C. E. Bishop, North Carolina State University, Raleigh (who has since been appointed Vice President of the Consolidated University of North Carolina); Harold C. Fleming, Potomac Institute, Washington; Howard G. Schaller, Indiana University, Bloomington; Sidney Sonenblum, National Planning Association, Washington; and Charles T. Taylor, Federal Reserve Bank, Atlanta.

Because of the intimate manner in which the authors worked together, many of the findings of the study are products of their joint efforts. There was also specialization in their research. E. E. Liebhafsky, Professor of Economics and Chairman of the Department of Economics and Finance at the University of Houston, gave primary attention to trends in employment and urbanization, as background for Chapter 2, and to projections of the southern labor force for Chapter 7. Vivian W. Henderson, formerly Chairman of the Department of Economics of Fisk University and now President of Clark College, Atlanta, focused on problems of race relations, which receive attention in several chapters, but particularly on racial discrimination in employment, to which Chapter 6 is devoted. Herbert M. Hamlin, formerly Visiting Professor at North Carolina State University and now Research Consultant in Vocational-Technical Education at the University of California at Berkeley, specialized in studying southern education, which, while of importance to several chapters, is given special consideration in Chapter 5.

As director of the project, I was responsible for the general direction of the research, for the organization of the book, for the reconciliation of divergent points of view—which appeared in the course of this study as they do in almost every study involving joint efforts of several scholars—and for the recommendations made in Chapter 9.

I owe a special debt of gratitude to C. E. Bishop, then Head of the Department of Economics, H. Brooks James, Dean of the College of Agriculture and Life Sciences, and John T. Caldwell, Chancellor, North Carolina State University, for relieving me of other duties so that I could direct the study on which this book is based, and for complete freedom in reporting our findings. They are in no way responsible for the views expressed, but without their approval and interest I could not have undertaken the project.

Milton Kelenson reviewed the statistical framework and made valuable suggestions for resolving statistical discrepancies. Among others who deserve credit are: John Nixon, Edward Yu-Ten Long, Teddy Kovac, and Virginia Gritton, for arduous statistical calculations; Marilyn Saylor, for typing the several drafts of the manuscript; and Ann Cooke, for careful checking of the galley and page proofs.

JAMES G. MADDOX

North Carolina State University
Raleigh, North Carolina

Contents

Tables, Charts, Appendices

TABLES

CHARTS

The Advancing South

MANPOWER PROSPECTS AND PROBLEMS

Chapter 1

SOUTHERN CULTURE AND
ECONOMIC UNDERDEVELOPMENT

THIS BOOK is concerned with the future of the South: its people, its institutions, and its rate of economic growth. The "South" is defined as the 11 states of the southern Confederacy—the states that seceded from the Union in 1860 and 1861—Alabama, Arkansas, Florida, Georgia, Louisiana, Mississippi, North Carolina, South Carolina, Tennessee, Texas, and Virginia, plus Oklahoma and Kentucky. It comprises approximately 28 per cent of the land area of continental United States, and in 1960 contained about 27 per cent of the U. S. population.

Although the ways in which the people of the southern states live and make a living are varied, these states have many characteristics in common. They have a long history of low income, of a high proportion of Negroes in their population, of racial discrimination, of a heavy reliance on farming, of low educational standards and achievement among large segments of the population, and of a society that has tended to concentrate power in the hands of a relatively small group in the upper strata of the social structure. The 13 states have not had all these characteristics to an equal degree, and changes of recent years are increasing the differences between them, but they still have many of these features in common and thus constitute a region quite distinct from any other equally large contiguous area of the United States.

THE FOCUS OF THE STUDY

Our study of these 13 states focuses on the factors and forces that are most likely to determine their rates of economic growth during the next decade and the effect their future economic development will have on employment, particularly on the expansion of employment opportunities for their Negro inhabitants, who are the most seriously affected by unemployment and underemployment.

Specifically, we seek answers to these questions: Approximately how many people will be employed in the South in 1975? How will they be distributed among industries and occupations? How will changes in the number and distribution of workers affect employment opportunities for Negroes in the South in the next decade?

Precise answers to these questions cannot be given. Indeed, the task of trying to reach sound judgments about the probable level and distribution of southern employment in the years ahead, particularly Negro employment, is extremely complex. The difficulties stem from at least three sources: the lack of a generally accepted theory of regional economic development on which to base a selection and weighting of factors and forces most likely to be the future determinants of employment in any large region of the country; the great paucity of statistical data and past studies of southern economic growth to serve as a foundation on which to build; and, in any case, doubt as to the extent to which past trends and past relationships are valid guides to the future, in view of the rapid changes taking place in the structure of southern society and in the organization of the southern economy.

GROWTH-GENERATING FORCES

Many of our guidelines for studying southern development were derived from studies of economic growth in both developed and underdeveloped countries. These studies, both theoretical and empirical, emphasize the importance of three forces in generating the growth of a country's total output of goods and services, its gross national product: first, increases in the supply of the traditional factors of production—natural resources, labor, and capital; second, changes in the organizational structure of the economy that increase productivity through greater specialization in the utilization of the available supplies of the factors of production; third, improvements in technology—the creation, adaptation, and introduction of new knowledge that enhances the managerial, engineering, and technical efficiency of production. In our study of the prospects for future growth in the South we put particular emphasis on the second and third of these growth-generating forces—changes in the organizational structure of the economy and improvements in technology—for several reasons:

First, they seem to have been the major factors in the rapid economic growth of Western Europe, the United States, Canada, Australia, New Zealand, and Japan, while those countries of the world that have made relatively little economic progress have experienced few changes in the organization of their societies or in technological improvements that have enhanced the productivity of labor and capital.

Second, our reading of southern history leads us to the hypothesis that the major explanations for the South's low incomes and general economic backwardness are essentially the same as those applicable to many underdeveloped national economies. That is, the South is the most underdeveloped region of the country because its social and economic structure has led to shortages of well-educated and skilled manpower, to inadequate supplies of high-quality capital, to the lack of up-to-date techniques of production, and to the paucity of innovating entrepreneurs.

Third, recent studies of rates of growth of states and regions in the United States indicate that the South's competitive position —the willingness and ability of its private firms and public agencies to bid effectively against their counterparts in other states and regions for product markets and for the growing national supplies of capital, labor, and technology—will be enhanced by raising the level of education of the general populace; by the formation of a corps of highly trained scientists with facilities and research programs for discovering and applying new knowledge; by shifts from agrarian traditions to cultural values and standards that tend to improve industrial, commercial, and urban ways of life; and by increases in the number of aggressive entrepreneurs.

In placing major emphasis on the importance of changes in the South's economic and social structure and on improvements in the quality of its human and capital resources, we recognize that the effects of such changes on the level and distribution of employment in the South are not simple and direct; they are complex and interrelated and are affected by national employment trends. In our subsequent analysis we have, therefore, attempted to keep in perspective the relationship of economic growth in the South to that in the nation as a whole.

As a background for our study of factors and forces that will be of greatest importance in shaping the future development of the region, we center attention in this chapter on a brief review of how the South developed a set of economic, social, and political institutions at variance with those of the rest of the nation and on the major effects of these peculiarly southern institutions on the economic growth of the region.

Origins of Southern Distinctiveness

It is one of the great anomalies of history that the South developed into the most poverty-stricken and backward part of the United States. Neither the early origins of southern poverty nor its continuance through subsequent decades can reasonably be attributed to inadequate natural resources or inferior markets for the region's products. Something else went wrong along the way. What was it? The immediate cause of the low incomes of the southern people has been their low productivity, which in turn has stemmed from specialization in technologically backward types of production characterized by low utilization of capital.

But why has the South for decade after decade lagged behind other regions of the country in raising its level of technology and in utilizing capital in its productive activities? The answer to this question is most likely to be found in the particular manner in which the values, aspirations, and beliefs of southern people interacted with the existing complement of natural resources and market demands to bring into being a set of economic, social, and political institutions that exerted a dominant influence on the development of the region's economy.[1]

Within a few decades after the earliest colonial settlements the southern colonies were following a course of development distinctly different from that of their northern neighbors. Virginians and Marylanders were staking their energies, hopes, and fortunes on commercial agriculture, specifically on the production of tobacco for the English market. New Englanders, New Yorkers, and Pennsylvanians, on the other hand, were involved in a more self-sufficient type of agriculture and in ocean shipping, fishing, and shipbuilding. Southerners were building an agrarian society; New Englanders were building a commercial society. These differences in production patterns continued in subsequent decades, and became focal points around which other distinctive characteristics of the two regions began to accumulate and solidify.

Although the tobacco crop of the South was one of the principal colonial exports and nearly all of it was sold in England, where proceeds from it were used to pay for imports into the colonies, the colonial South never developed a significant class of merchants and traders. In contrast, export businesses grew and flourished around Boston, Salem, Newport, New York, and Philadelphia. Southern planters found tobacco production with indentured servants and Negro slaves highly profitable, and viewed commerce and trade as occupations below the social status

[1] For a comprehensive discussion of these influences, see William H. Nicholls, *Southern Tradition and Regional Progress*, University of North Carolina Press, Chapel Hill, 1960.

to which they aspired. The seventeenth century English squire more nearly represented their ideal than did the Liverpool or London merchant.

THE PLANTATION SYSTEM

Thus, well before the Revolution large-scale, commercial farming had become a way of life in the South and had led readily to the development of the slave-based system of plantation farming. It brought into being an agrarian and pseudoaristocratic form of social organization that concentrated political and economic power in the hands of the plantation owners and their friends and associates in finance, commerce, and government. As in many underdeveloped countries of today, this form of social organization provided a profitable and agreeable way of life for the small group at the top. It seriously restricted the range of opportunities for the lower classes of society, however, and provided an environment basically hostile to technological innovation and social change.

KING COTTON

Two new but related developments in the years following the Revolution opened up such enormous potentialities in cotton production that the South, even more than during the colonial period, became wedded to an agrarian way of life, as exemplified by the plantation system and slavery. One of these developments, the application of power-driven machinery to the spinning of cotton yarn in the late 1780's, resulted from a series of inventions in England, and marked the beginnings of the factory system of production. The other, the invention of the cotton gin, was an American invention by Eli Whitney in 1793. Both developments greatly increased the profitability of cotton farming. As a consequence, "King Cotton" soon began to dominate the course of southern economic growth, rapidly overshadowing tobacco, rice, and sugar production. U. S. cotton production, most of which was exported, increased from about 3,000 bales in 1790 to over 1.3 million in 1840. This phenomenal growth in the production of cotton was a major factor in the expansion of the American economy during the first half of the past century, but it firmly fastened on southern society many of the agrarian attitudes and beliefs that had justified slavery and strengthened the influence of large landowners. At the same time it enhanced the economic efficiency of the plantation system of farming.

The first half of the nineteenth century was a period of great westward territorial expansion in which both the North and the South shared. In the Northeast and Midwest this was also a period of rapid growth of urban centers, expansion in manufacturing, progress in the agricultural arts, and dedication to the family farm as the most desirable unit in agriculture. The rapid growth of population associated with the Industrial Revolution in Europe resulted in the development of European markets as significant outlets for northern farm products—mainly grains. In the South, on the other hand, the profitability of cotton production extended the plantation system from the tidewater areas of the Southeast to Mississippi, Arkansas, and the eastern third of Texas, and led southern leaders to reject many of the new ideas that were emanating from the North and the East. The maintenance and strengthening of the slave plantation system dominated all other interests in the South.

Towns and cities were slow to develop in the South and until recent decades were few in number. Their main functions were to serve as marketing and transportation centers for the surrounding planters. Few craftsmen or artisans could find employment in this predominantly agricultural setting.

The attitudes of the powerful plantation owners toward education were particularly effective in keeping the small farmer at a competitive disadvantage. With few exceptions, education was regarded as the concern of the individual, not of the state. "It was, in truth, a privilege which marched with wealth and blood . . . the cleavage between the schooling of the favored orders and those of common clay was justified as necessary and even as desirable . . . the education of the well-heeled was thrust upon tutors and private schools while that which fell to the multitudes was left mainly to the mercy of kind hearts and charity." [2]

The Southern Economic Lag

Despite the South's mild climate and good soils for tobacco and cotton production and the more than a full century it had had to exploit its highly favorable market position for these two crops, its economy in 1840 was less efficient than that of the Northeast. In that year the 12 southern states had almost the same population (6.8 million) as the 10 states of the Northeast and an 18 per cent larger labor force, including slaves, but they produced 27 per cent less total income. Average income per capita (including slaves) in the South in 1840 was about $59. In the Northeast it was $80, and in the Midwest $46. Although the agricultural South outranked the Midwest, which at that time was as heavily dependent on agriculture as the South but had no export crop as profitable as cotton, it was far behind the commercial and industrial Northeast in per capita income.[3]

AFTERMATH OF THE CIVIL WAR

By 1880, because of the devastating effects of the Civil War, the differences in income were still greater. Average per capita income in the Northeast was $122, in the Midwest $99, and in the South $57—slightly lower than in 1840. The war had worked

[2] Adolphe E. Meyer, *An Educational History of the American People*, McGraw-Hill, New York, 1957, p. 48.

[3] The southern states for the purpose of this comparison are: Maryland, Virginia, North Carolina, South Carolina, Georgia, Florida, Kentucky, Tennessee, Alabama, Mississippi, Arkansas, Louisiana. The states of the Northeast are: New Hampshire, Vermont, Massachusetts, Rhode Island, Connecticut, New York, New Jersey, Pennsylvania, Delaware. The midwestern states included in this comparison are: Ohio, Indiana, Illinois, Michigan, Wisconsin, Iowa, and Missouri. The population, labor force, and income data are from Richard A. Easterlin, "Inter-regional Differences in Per Capita Income, Population and Total Income, 1840–1950," *Trends in the American Economy in the Nineteenth Century*, Princeton University Press, Princeton, 1960, pp. 97–104.

its havoc. A war that had been fought to maintain an agricultural system based on slavery had not only been lost by the South, but had destroyed many productive resources. Over 3.5 million slaves, most of whom were illiterate, without skills for jobs other than farming, without land, and without capital, were set free. Little was done, however, to make them productive and constructive members of society. The planters still owned the land, but they needed a labor supply to farm it. As a result, a new kind of partnership—sharecropping—was formed. The landowners supplied land and work stock and the newly freed Negroes supplied the labor to continue farm production in much the same pattern as before the war. The laborers received a share of the crop in lieu of a wage payment. The Negro, although legally a free man, was still in a state of dependency.

A few southern leaders, sensing the long-term effects of the abolition of slavery on a type of agriculture heavily dependent on a cheap, docile labor supply and seeing the superior income-generating ability of the industrial and commercial economy of the North, were promoting the "New South" movement—an attempt to shift the southern economy away from its heavy dependence on agriculture and toward the commercial and industrial system of the North. The move toward industrialization, however, met with only moderate success. As one analyst of the southern economy points out: [4]

> Having once fallen behind industrially, the South lacked the entrepreneurial talent, skilled artisans, and other external economies whose presence in the already industrially established North tended to make industrialization there self-generating. In the absence of such factors, it was the old agrarian pattern—only slightly modified by the development of such low-skill manufactures as textiles—which tended to be self-generating in the South. With scores of poor and ignorant farm workers continuing to stand in line for every new factory job, the social forces which would have favored an ever-increasing investment in the quality of the people and an ever-widening spread of the benefits of progress were kept under control in the South. In the factory as on the plantation, the general Southern

[4] Nicholls, op. cit., p. 27.

outlook continued to be conservative, paternalistic, and backward-looking.

Indeed, for more than half a century after the end of the war most of the ingenuity and energy of southern leaders was directed at reorienting southern society, which could no longer depend on slavery, so that a relatively small upper class group could still control the centers of power. One of the means of accomplishing this goal was political control of state and local government. The two-party system virtually disappeared in most areas of the South. As a result of the South's defeat in the war, the rule of the southern states by Republican forces during the period of reconstruction, and the attempt of the Federal Government to enfranchise the former slaves and their descendants by the Fourteenth and Fifteenth Amendments to the Constitution, most southern political leaders repudiated the Republican Party and became Democrats. "Few could withstand the scorn attached to the epithets 'scalawag,' 'carpetbagger,' 'nigger lover,' 'Republican.' " [5] Nevertheless, with the exception of a few years in the 1890's when the Populist movement was at its height, the dominant political forces in the South continued to represent mainly upper-class values and interests. The former Whigs simply changed their party affiliation and became the leaders of the southern Democratic Party. The change in party affiliation, however, did not represent a change in political or economic philosophy.

WHITE SUPREMACY

With only minor and sporadic variations, southern leaders continued for many years to idealize agrarian ways of life and the traditions of the past. In the two decades following Reconstruction, they deliberately set about designing ways and means of keeping the former Negro slaves and their descendants subordinate members of society. This aim became a major rallying

[5] V. O. Key, Jr., with the assistance of Alexander Heard, *Southern Politics in State and Nation*, Alfred A. Knopf, New York, 1950, p. 552.

point around which southern political leaders gained the support of family farmers, small businessmen, and laborers, though the purely economic interests of the latter group actually lay in policies and programs for diversifying the economy and enlarging and improving educational activities. The goal of "white supremacy" soon began to serve two ends. Not only was it effectively used to disfranchise Negroes, discourage them from getting an education, and relegate them to the lower rungs of the economic ladder, but it was a vehicle by which many of the economic, social, and political ideals of the pre–Civil War period were carried forward in the South.

Disfranchisement was at first accomplished through a process of force and intimidation that kept most Negroes away from the polls. After about 1890 an ingenious set of laws, state constitutional amendments, and party regulations succeeded in circumventing the Fifteenth Amendment to the Federal Constitution by such devices as the poll tax, property ownership as a suffrage qualification, the requirement that a prospective voter be able to read, understand, and explain a section of the Constitution, and the "white primary" as a mechanism for nominating Democratic candidates.

Discrimination on a wide basis became legally possible through two important Supreme Court decisions. First, a comprehensive civil rights law designed to provide equal rights for Negroes, which had been passed by the Congress in 1875, was declared unconstitutional by the Supreme Court in 1883. Then, in 1896 the Court upheld racial segregation in a transportation case in Louisiana. In that case, *Plessy vs. Ferguson,* the Jim Crow principle of "separate but equal" treatment was sanctioned, and the way was left open for the South to develop a system of statutes, regulations, and customs separating Negroes from whites from the cradle to the grave: in schools, public transportation, public facilities, hospitals, public recreation, jails and prisons, public meeting places, at drinking fountains, in rest rooms, in eating places. Thus, signs were posted and Negroes in every walk of life faced public symbols of racial separatism as constant reminders of an inferior status. Earlier, whites had tended to differentiate the treatment of Negroes according to their class and education. The new order ignored this tendency and segregation laws were applied to all Negroes alike, regardless of education, income, manners, or station in the community.

At the turn of the present century—more than a generation after the end of the Civil War—the South was still predominantly rural: 60 per cent of its income originated in agriculture and over 80 per cent of its labor force was engaged in farming.[6] Racial animosity was high: more than 100 Negroes were lynched in 1900.[7] Not for 30 or 40 years was there to be solid evidence that southern culture was breaking away from its traditional moorings.

BACKWARDNESS IN EDUCATION

A great educational awakening had swept over the North in the 1830's and 1840's, particularly in the cities. Out of it a state-supported system of public schools had arisen. But educational efforts in the South always lagged behind those in the Northeast and Midwest. Except in North Carolina and a few of the largest southern cities, the early movement toward publicly supported primary and secondary schools hardly touched the South. During the reconstruction period following the Civil War, state-supported school systems were imposed on the South; but they were strongly resented, and it was not until the early years of this century that the value of public education was generally recognized in most southern states.

Negro-White Differences

Educational opportunities for Negroes were much more seriously restricted than those for whites. In the colonial period a few Negroes had received considerable schooling, but later

---

[6] Easterlin, *op. cit.*

[7] *The World Almanac and Book of Facts for 1958*, Harry Hansen, ed., New York World-Telegram and The Sun, New York.

several of the southern states had made it illegal to teach Negroes to read or write. It is probable that when the Civil War ended 90 per cent of southern Negroes were illiterate. Soon thereafter church missionaries and philanthropic agencies from the North began to open schools for Negroes in the South, and thus provided the first significant opportunities for southern Negroes to get an education.[8]

A rough indication of the extent of the educational gap between the South and the rest of the country and between Negroes and whites can be gleaned from U. S. Census data. The Census of 1890, for instance, showed that 17 per cent of the whites and 72 per cent of the Negroes over 20 years of age in the South were illiterate, compared to 7 per cent of the whites and 40 per cent of the Negroes in the North.

STUNTED TECHNOLOGY

The Census data, however, suggest only a small part of the differences between the educational situation in the South and other regions. Until quite recently southern schools did not usually emphasize those areas of knowledge that directly encouraged growth and diversification of the economy. Southern colleges traditionally placed less emphasis on science, mathematics, engineering, and business administration than was characteristic of educational institutions in other regions. Southern leadership favored languages, law, and the humanities as areas of college study. Primary and secondary school curricula reflected these preferences.

The types of subject matter most commonly studied by the sons and daughters of the upper classes and the lack of support for a system of education that reached into the daily lives of the people not only restricted opportunities and blunted incentives

[8] Among the early schools for Negroes that either were founded by northern missionaries or received most of their early financing from northern sources and later developed into important educational centers are: Fisk University, founded in 1866; Hampton Institute, founded in 1868; Clark College, founded in 1869; and Tuskegee Normal and Industrial Institution, founded in 1881.

of many common people but also failed to stimulate technological progress—the discovery and application of new knowledge that increases the productivity of the economy. As a result the educational system of the South has always failed to produce enough inventors, engineers, mechanics, businessmen, and bankers. Moreover, the values prevailing in southern society during much of its history have discouraged migration of these specialists from other regions, partly because of the practice of slavery (and the subsequent treatment of the Negro), to which many enterprising nonsoutherners, particularly those of European extraction, objected, and partly because the places of highest status in southern society have been reserved to large landowners, military men, lawyers, politicians, orators, and writers. Thus, for many decades, the creators of technological progress in the South were few in number and low in social status.

At the same time the region had high rates of population increase and, until World War I, relatively low rates of out-migration—phenomena common to low-income, rural societies with limited educational opportunities for the people. The result was an abundance of unskilled manpower available for employment in farming, in the extraction and processing of primary products, and in low-wage manufacturing industries.

Many of the characteristics of southern culture that have, historically, set the region apart from the rest of the nation and have held back its growth and development are undergoing rapid change. Indeed, the South is in the midst of a transition from an agrarian society to an industrial, urbanized way of life.

The South, though late in starting to build an industrial and commercial economy based on modern technology and large capital investment per worker, is definitely launched on a course leading in that direction. Furthermore, the speed with which it proceeds will be greatly influenced by national policies and programs, by the existing structure of industry as the base from which change must proceed, by the educational level of the population, by the extent and nature of racial discrimination, and by the size and quality of the southern labor force. Accordingly, after a discussion of the social and economic transition through which the South is passing, it is to these factors and their bearing on regional employment that we turn our attention before attempting to project the level and distribution of southern employment to 1975.

Chapter 2

THE SOUTH IN TRANSITION

THE SOUTH is in a period of great transition. It is closing the door on one period of history and entering another. The changes it is experiencing are numerous and complex.

For more than two decades the region has been moving away from its traditional dependence on agriculture. Farming is a declining proportion of total economic activity, while manufacturing, commerce, trade, and services are expanding. Closely related to these changes in the structure of the economy is a large movement of people from rural to urban areas.

Major changes are taking place in race relations. The South has long had a dual society based on race—that is, it has had one set of standards and approved behavioral patterns for white people and another for Negroes. This has been true to a certain extent in all regions of the United States, but restrictions on the rights of Negroes have been much greater in the South than in other parts of the country. This situation is changing. The accelerated drive of the Negroes for equality, buttressed by decisions of the Supreme Court and the passage of the Civil Rights Act of 1964 and of the Voting Rights Act of 1965, has already resulted in the removal of numerous legal barriers to the attainment by southern Negroes of their full rights as citizens.

There is a growing emphasis on education. Most southern states are enlarging educational and training facilities and reorienting educational activities to reach more of the population and to meet more adequately the occupational demands of industry.

Furthermore, the political structure is changing. At various places in the once solidly Democratic South there are evidences of the growth of a two-party political system. Recent elections have shown that the balance of power within the Democratic Party no longer rests with the southern states, and the southern wing of the Democratic Party is losing some of its traditional influence in national affairs. At the same time increasing numbers of Negroes are voting, and a few are being elected to positions of influence in state and local governments.

Finally, these changes are giving rise to slow but clearly perceptible changes in many attitudes and beliefs respecting southern society. It is particularly evident in recent years that southerners are no longer idealizing agrarian ways of life, as they did only a few decades ago.

These economic, social, and political changes are interlocking and mutually re-enforcing. Hence, their total effect is greater than the sum of their individual influences. They strongly suggest that the South is breaking the bonds of agrarian traditionalism; that it is moving into an era in which science, technology, and urban ways of living play an increasingly important role; that new sets of social values and beliefs are replacing many of those of the past. Taken as a whole, the changes represent a slow-moving social revolution of significant proportions.

Some of the changes that are underway began to manifest themselves as long as 40 or 50 years ago, and their roots go even farther back in southern history, as explained in Chapter 1. Nevertheless, it is only since 1930, and largely since 1940, that the major components of the transition began to be clearly evident. The Great Depression of the 1930's and the effects of various depression-related programs and policies of the Federal Government were highly influential in paving the way for many of the changes whose outlines became clear in the 1940's. Subsequently, World War II created an unprecedented demand for labor, raised incomes, and encouraged large migrations of workers from one region to another to take advantage of war-created jobs. It thus generated new pressures for changing the traditional nature of southern society.

Historically, two of the most important forces that interacted to set the South off from the rest of the nation and to make of it the poorest and most underdeveloped region of the country were, first, the southern economy's strong orientation to farming, particularly to a type of farming—mainly tobacco and cotton production—that required large amounts of hand labor; and, second, the belief among thousands of southerners that the Negro is inherently inferior to the white man. The two have been closely interrelated. Belief in white supremacy served not only to justify enslavement of the Negro and the erection of numerous discriminatory laws and customs that came into being after the abolition of slavery, but it was also important in keeping Negroes uneducated and unskilled and thus guaranteeing the continuation of a cheap and docile labor supply for southern agriculture.

It is significant, therefore, that it is in its economic structure and in its race relations that the South is undergoing the most fundamental changes.

This chapter presents a brief review of the nature and implications of these changes, most of which are discussed in detail in subsequent chapters.

The Changing Economic Structure

The most notable change in the structure of the southern economy in recent years has been the laborsaving, technological revolution in southern agriculture, which has so raised worker productivity on the farm that farmers and farm workers have been leaving in large numbers to seek employment in non-agricultural industries. This resulted in a decrease of about 59 per cent between 1940 and 1960 in the number of persons employed in southern agriculture—from approximately 4.2 million to 1.7 million (Table 2-1).

THE AGRICULTURAL REVOLUTION

Southern farming has changed dramatically since the 1930's. It has become a capital-intensive, highly commercialized enter-

Table 2-1 **Agricultural Employment, United States,[a] Non-South, and South, 1940, 1950, 1960**

Year and region	Amount (thousands)	Per cent	Per cent of total employment	Percentage change
1940				1940–1950
United States[a]	8,475.4	100.0	18.8	−17.4
Non-South	4,240.1	50.0	12.8	−9.8
South	4,235.3	50.0	34.8	−24.9
1950				1950–1960
United States[a]	6,996.2	100.0	12.4	−38.0
Non-South	3,818.5	54.6	9.1	−31.3
South	3,177.6	45.4	22.0	−46.0
1960				1940–1960
United States[a]	4,332.0	100.0	6.7	−48.8
Non-South	2,618.4	60.4	5.5	−38.1
South	1,713.6	39.6	10.4	−59.4

Source: Appendix Table 2-1.
[a] As elsewhere throughout this book, unless otherwise noted, data exclude Alaska and Hawaii.

prise. Southern farmers purchase increasing quantities of machinery, fertilizer, and pesticides; utilize decreasing amounts of land and labor in production; and sell rising proportions of their output on the market. In other words, as agricultural output per acre and per man has risen, farming has become increasingly dependent on purchased inputs. Acreage used for crops declined from 111 million in 1940 to 81 million in 1960.[1]

The average size of farms in 1960 was twice that of 1930, while total man-hours of labor used for farm work in the South in 1960 was less than half that used in 1940.[2]

The substitution of capital and technology for labor in southern agriculture has, of course, resulted in a dramatic rise in output per man-hour.

Agriculture is a highly competitive industry in which an individual producer is unable to affect the demand for his product. In an attempt to reduce unit cost, which they could

[1] *Changes in Farm Production and Efficiency*, U. S. Department of Agriculture, Washington, rev. July 1964, p. 49, and Supplement II, pp. 5–6.
[2] *Ibid.*, p. 38.

do individually mainly by increasing total output per farm, large commercial farmers adopted laborsaving and output-increasing machinery and technology at an extremely rapid rate during the 1940's and 1950's. The scarcity of farm labor—resulting from the pull of farm workers into nonagricultural jobs during World War II—combined with high prices for farm products, had given impetus to the movement to adopt new agricultural technology, and those farmers who possessed the necessary capital and know-how hastened to do so. Following the Korean War a contrasting set of forces—declining prices of farm products accompanied by rising agricultural production costs—encouraged large farmers to further utilization of advanced technology.

The small farmer found himself being pushed out of farming by his inability to compete with the larger, more efficient operator. Since World War II, therefore, southern agriculture has tended, increasingly, to be characterized by a decline in the number of farm operators, especially operators of small farms, and a rise in investment per farm. Small farmers who were unable to make the necessary capital investment to modernize their farms and large numbers of farm laborers, mostly Negroes, for whom farm jobs were rapidly disappearing, began to leave southern farms and migrate to urban areas, both South and non-South.

EMPLOYMENT CHANGES

The shifts in the economy from rural-agricultural to urban-industrial—which began to be evident in the 1930's, took full shape in the 1940's, and continued unabated in the 1950's and 1960's—profoundly affected the distribution of employment in the South (Table 2-2).

While agricultural employment in the South decreased between 1940 and 1960, manufacturing employment almost doubled —from 1.8 million to 3.4 million—and employment in service-producing industries rose from 5.1 million to 9.2 million, an increase of almost 80 per cent. (See Tables 2-2 and 2-3 and Figure 2-1.)

Table 2-2 Employment, by Major Industry Group, United States, Non-South, and South, 1940, 1950, 1960

Year and region	All industries[a]		Agriculture		Nonagricultural goods-producing		Service-producing	
	Amount (thousands)	Per cent	Amount (thousands)	Per cent	Amount (thousands)	Per cent	Amount (thousands)	Per cent
1940								
United States	45,166.1	100.0	8,475.4	18.8	13,542.1	30.0	22,459.7	49.7
Non-South	33,009.8	100.0	4,240.1	12.9	10,894.7	33.0	17,332.4	52.5
South	12,156.3	100.0	4,235.3	34.8	2,647.4	21.8	5,127.3	42.1
1950								
United States	56,225.3	100.0	6,996.2	12.4	18,940.9	33.7	29,447.4	52.4
Non-South	41,753.4	100.0	3,818.5	9.1	15,005.7	35.9	22,318.5	53.5
South	14,471.9	100.0	3,177.6	22.0	3,935.2	27.2	7,128.9	49.3
1960								
United States	64,371.6	100.0	4,332.0	6.7	21,919.2	34.1	35,521.9	55.2
Non-South	47,932.8	100.0	2,618.4	5.5	16,971.1	35.4	26,320.0	55.0
South	16,438.8	100.0	1,713.6	10.4	4,948.1	30.1	9,201.9	56.0

Source: Appendix Table 2-1.

[a] Includes a small amount of employment which was not classified by type of industry. See Appendix Table 2-1.

Table 2-3 **Manufacturing Employment in the South, by Industry, 1940, 1950, and 1960**

Industry	Employment (thousands)			Percentage distribution			Percentage change		
	1940	1950	1960	1940	1950	1960	1940–1950	1950–1960	1940–1960
Total	1,807.2	2,563.7	3,406.8	100.0	100.0	100.0	41.9	32.9	88.5
Food and kindred products	202.4	294.8	415.6	11.2	11.5	12.2	45.7	41.0	105.3
Tobacco products	58.8	55.7	61.1	3.3	2.2	1.8	−5.3	9.7	3.9
Textile mill products	509.1	602.4	589.5	28.2	23.5	17.3	18.3	−2.1	15.8
Apparel products	86.0	154.2	305.8	4.8	6.0	9.0	79.3	98.3	255.6
Sawmills & planing mills	249.5	326.8	181.1	13.8	12.7	5.3	31.0	−44.6	−27.4
Furniture, fixtures, miscellaneous wood	95.8	126.7	168.3	5.3	4.9	4.9	32.3	32.8	75.7
Paper products	44.9	86.4	134.0	2.5	3.4	3.9	92.4	55.1	198.4
Printing & publishing	80.8	121.5	177.5	4.5	4.7	5.2	50.4	46.1	119.7
Chemicals & plastics	100.2	156.6	235.8	5.5	6.1	6.9	56.3	50.6	135.3
Petroleum & coal products	63.3	93.0	104.6	3.5	3.6	3.1	46.9	12.5	65.2
Rubber products	7.7	20.0	27.6	0.4	0.8	0.8	159.7	38.0	258.4
Leather & products	20.7	30.2	40.0	1.1	1.2	1.1	45.9	32.5	93.2
Stone, clay & glass	49.4	71.8	120.0	2.7	2.8	3.5	45.3	67.1	142.9
Metal industry	108.8	177.9	292.6	6.0	6.9	8.6	63.5	64.5	168.9
Electrical machinery	8.0	27.2	139.2	0.4	1.1	4.1	240.0	411.8	1,640.0
Nonelectrical machinery	41.8	83.2	147.3	2.3	3.2	4.3	99.0	77.0	252.4
Transportation equipment	51.5	89.9	196.2	2.8	3.5	5.8	74.6	118.2	281.0
Other manufacturing	28.5	45.4	70.6	1.6	1.8	2.1	59.3	55.5	147.7

Sources: U. S. Bureau of the Census, Washington: 1940—*Census of Population: 1940*, Vol. III, *The Labor Force*, Parts I–V, Table 17; 1950 and 1960—*Census of Population: 1960*, Series D, *Detailed Characteristics*, Table 126.

Figure 2-1 **Percentage Changes in Employment, by Major Industry Group, United States, Non-South, and South, 1940–1960**

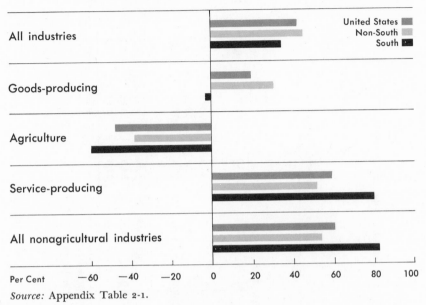

Source: Appendix Table 2-1.

These shifts in types of employment called for more skilled and better educated workers than southern agriculture had to offer. Furthermore, though employment in the southern economy was expanding, the labor force was growing too, and employment did not expand fast enough to provide jobs for all of the new entrants to the labor force plus all of the displaced agricultural workers.

As a result of these changes in the southern economy, large numbers of Negroes migrated to cities—in both the South and the non-South.

POPULATION CHANGES

In 1940 one fourth of the South's population was Negro, by 1960 only about one fifth. In this 20 years the South's share of the nation's Negro population decreased from about 70 to 52 per cent (Table 2-4). The number of Negroes living in southern rural farm areas decreased by 67 per cent, while the number living in southern urban areas rose by 81 per cent. (See Appendix Table 2-2.) By 1960, 72 per cent of the 20 million Negroes in

Table 2-4   Population, by Color,ᵃ United States, Non-South, and South, 1940, 1950, 1960, and Percentage Change, by Decade

Year	United States			Non-South			South		
	Total	White	Nonwhite	Total	White	Nonwhite	Total	White	Nonwhite
Total, thousands									
1940	131,669	118,214	13,456	94,656	90,564	4,093	37,013	27,650	9,363
1950	150,697	134,943	15,755	108,969	102,730	6,240	41,728	32,213	9,515
1960	178,464	158,459	20,006	129,662	120,053	9,610	48,802	38,406	10,396
Percentage distribution									
1940	100.0	89.8	10.2	100.0	95.7	4.3	100.0	74.7	25.3
1950	100.0	89.5	10.5	100.0	94.3	5.7	100.0	77.2	22.8
1960	100.0	88.8	11.2	100.0	92.6	7.4	100.0	78.7	21.3
Percentage change									
1940–1950	14.5	14.2	17.1	15.1	13.4	52.5	12.7	16.5	1.6
1950–1960	18.4	17.4	27.0	19.0	16.9	54.0	17.0	19.2	9.3
1940–1960	35.6	34.0	48.7	37.0	32.6	134.8	31.9	38.9	11.0

Sources: U. S. Bureau of the Census, Washington: Census of Population: 1940, 1950, and 1960.

ᵃ See footnote 3, this chapter, re interchangeable use of "nonwhite" and "Negro" in this study.

Note: Discrepancies in addition are due to rounding.

Figure 2-2 **Population Distribution by Type of Residence and by Color, Non-South and South, 1940 and 1960**

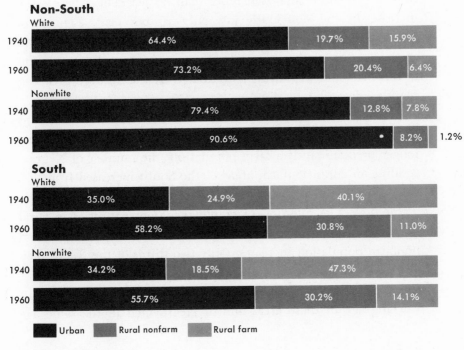

Non-South
White
1940 — 64.4% | 19.7% | 15.9%
1960 — 73.2% | 20.4% | 6.4%

Nonwhite
1940 — 79.4% | 12.8% | 7.8%
1960 — 90.6% | • | 8.2% | 1.2%

South
White
1940 — 35.0% | 24.9% | 40.1%
1960 — 58.2% | 30.8% | 11.0%

Nonwhite
1940 — 34.2% | 18.5% | 47.3%
1960 — 55.7% | 30.2% | 14.1%

■ Urban   ■ Rural nonfarm   ■ Rural farm

Source: Appendix Table 2-2.

the United States lived in urban areas and 60 per cent of these lived in cities outside of the South. Of the 10.4 million Negroes whose homes were in the South in 1960, 5.8 million or 56 per cent lived in urban areas (Figure 2-2). Thus, by 1960 in both the South and the non-South Negroes had become primarily city dwellers.[3]

[3] When dividing the population into "white" and "nonwhite," the Bureau of the Census defines "nonwhite" as persons of Negro, American Indian, Japanese, Chinese, Filipino, Korean, Asian Indian, and Malayan races. *Census of Population: 1940, General Social and Economic Characteristics, United States Summary, Final Report,* PC(1)-1C, U. S. Bureau of the Census, Washington, 1962, p. xii.

The terms "nonwhite" and "Negro" are used interchangeably in this book, although they are not strictly synonymous in U. S. statistics. In 1960, for example, Negroes accounted for about 94 per cent of the total nonwhite population in the 48 conterminous states, for about 90 per cent in the non-South, and for about 98 per cent in the South. (Percentages computed from *Statistical Abstract of the United States, 1962,* U. S. Bureau of the Census, Washington, Table 24.)

The phenomenal increase in the population of large southern cities is shown in Table 2-5. From 1940 to 1960 large-city population in the South increased more than 80 per cent, whereas the increase in the non-South was only 16 per cent. Figures in Table 2-6 reflect the economic activity in major metropolitan areas in the South that stimulated the movement of the population to the cities and was in turn stimulated by the upsurge in urban population.

It should be noted, however, that all movement from farms is not to cities. For example, the Negro rural population is no longer predominantly a farm population; the number of Negroes residing in rural nonfarm areas of the South increased from less than 2 million in 1940 to more than 3 million in 1960 (Appendix Table 2-2). The question of employment opportunities in rural nonfarm areas becomes increasingly significant as the Negro rural nonfarm population increases. Only two thirds of the Negro men of working age in southern rural nonfarm areas were in the labor force in 1960, compared with three fourths of the white men of working age in those areas and of Negro men in the same age

Table 2-5   **Population in 1940, 1950, and 1960 of Cities with 1960 Population of 100,000 or More, United States, Non-South, and South**

Year	United States	Non-South	South
Total (thousands)			
1940	40,207	34,567	5,639
1950	45,984	38,312	7,672
1960	50,450	40,121	10,330
Percentage change			
1940–1950	14.4	10.8	36.1
1950–1960	9.7	4.7	34.6
1940–1960	25.5	16.1	83.2

Source: *Statistical Abstract of the United States, 1962*, U. S. Bureau of the Census, Washington, pp. 22-23.
Note: Discrepancies in addition are due to rounding.

Table 2-6 **Some Indexes of Economic Activity in Thirty-three Major Southern Metropolitan Areas and in the United States, 1948 and 1958**

Activity and region	1948	1958	Percentage change
Number of commercial and industrial firms[a]			
United States	2,674,931	3,302,523	23.5
South	201,230	291,249	44.7
		Millions	
Retail sales			
United States	$130,520.5	$200,370.4	53.5
South	10,106.8	18,377.5	81.8
Wholesale sales			
United States	$188,688.8	$285,726.9	51.4
South	20,320.1	35,319.4	73.8
Service trade receipts			
United States	$8,578.2	$32,505.6	278.9
South	748.5	3,013.2	302.6

Source: Press Release CD63-82, Atlanta Field Office, U. S. Department of Commerce, May 28, 1963.
[a] 1949 and 1959.

group in urban areas.[4] Eighty per cent of the nation's Negro rural population lived in the South in 1960, and it is clear that lower labor force participation rates of rural nonfarm Negroes reflect limited employment opportunities for Negroes in rural communities.

THE LABOR FORCE

The South's Negro working-age population decreased from just over 6.5 million in 1940 to less than 6.4 million in 1950, and then increased to almost 6.5 million in 1960, as a result of a tapering off of Negro migration from the region during the late 1950's (Table 2-7). The southern Negro labor force decreased from just under 4 million in 1940 to less than 3.5 million in 1960.

[4] *Manpower Report of the President and Report on Manpower Requirements, Resources, Utilization and Training,* U. S. Department of Labor, Washington, March 1964, pp. 83–84 and Appendix Table G-8.

Table 2-7 **Working-Age Population and Labor Force, by Color, United States, Non-South, and South, 1940, 1950, 1960, and Percentage Change, by Decade**

| | Number (thousands) | | | | | | Percentage change | | | | | |
| | Population 14 years and older | | | Labor force | | | Population 14 years and older | | | Labor force | | |
	1940	1950	1960	1940	1950	1960	1940–1950	1950–1960	1940–1960	1940–1950	1950–1960	1940–1960
Total												
United States	101,103	111,703	125,701	52,789	59,643	69,512	10.5	12.5	24.3	13.0	16.5	31.7
Non-South	74,448	82,203	92,091	38,759	44,208	51,491	10.4	12.0	23.7	14.1	16.5	32.8
South	26,655	29,501	33,610	14,030	15,435	18,022	10.7	13.9	26.1	10.0	16.8	28.5
White												
United States	91,428	100,706	112,862	47,169	53,476	62,300	10.1	12.1	23.4	13.4	16.5	32.1
Non-South	71,295	77,572	85,736	37,134	41,560	47,771	8.8	10.5	20.3	11.9	14.9	28.6
South	20,133	23,134	27,126	10,035	11,916	14,529	14.9	17.3	34.7	18.7	21.9	44.8
Nonwhite												
United States	9,675	10,998	12,839	5,620	6,167	7,212	13.7	16.7	32.7	9.7	16.9	18.6
Non-South	3,152	4,631	6,355	1,625	2,648	3,719	46.9	37.2	101.6	63.0	40.4	128.9
South	6,522	6,367	6,484	3,995	3,519	3,493	−2.4	1.8	−0.6	−11.9	−0.7	−12.6

Sources: U. S. Bureau of the Census, Washington: Census of Population: 1940; 1950; and 1960.

Thus, while the South's Negro working-age population in 1960 was almost at its 1940 level, its Negro labor force decreased by about 500,000 persons. This change in the relationship between the size of the Negro working-age population and the size of the Negro labor force between 1940 and 1960 is attributable to the out-migration during the 1940's of large numbers of working-age Negroes and to a decline in the labor force participation rates of Negro males in the primary working-age group who remained in the South. Suffering an educational disadvantage and subjected to racial discrimination, some Negro males undoubtedly abandoned hope of finding jobs and withdrew from the labor force.

Changing Race Relations

The changes that are taking place in race relations have been resisted with much greater vigor and have been brought to national attention in much more dramatic fashion than have the shifts in the structure of the economy. Moreover, several of the most important of these changes have come quite recently, and their full effects cannot yet be evaluated. Although as early as 1910 Negroes organized the beginnings of a movement for civil rights embodying many of the same goals as their current drives for equality, the major break-throughs in race relations have come since 1940.

The Democratic white primaries were outlawed in 1944, after almost 20 years of litigation, and Negroes began to develop a new influence in southern politics. In 1932 Negroes in 12 states in the South had been so effectively disfranchised that fewer than 100,000 were able to vote in the general elections and virtually none were able to vote in the primary elections. After 1944 the situation changed; by 1947 the number of registered Negro voters in the 12 states had risen to 645,000 and by March 1965 to over 2.3 million.[5] The number was expected to increase rapidly as a

[5] *Registration and Voting Statistics*, U. S. Commission on Civil Rights, Washington, March 19, 1965.

result of the passage of the Voting Rights Act of 1965 in August 1965.

The long-standing practice of segregation and discrimination in the armed forces was ended in 1948 by executive order of the President.[6] The net effect of the order was to nullify the "separate but equal" principle governing the operation of the military through World War II. It is significant to the question of civilian manpower use that a basic consideration underlying the move to integrate the armed forces was an acknowledgment that segregation and discrimination were sources of manpower waste and contributed to inefficiency in running the military establishment.

While significant advances in race relations had been made by the late 1940's, major barriers to equality remained. Foremost among these was the southern system of compulsory segregation in schools. Public education emerged, therefore, as the area in which the next major assault on the doctrine of "separate but equal" was made. In about 1950, after more than 15 years of litigation, restrictions excluding Negroes from previously all-white, state-supported colleges and universities began to be removed. In 1954 a high point in the civil rights movement was reached. The principle of "separate but equal" in primary and secondary public schools was declared invalid by the Supreme Court in the case of *Brown vs. Board of Education.* Moreover, although the Court's decision dealt specifically with public schools, its rationale struck a blow at all laws upholding segregation. The principle that "our Constitution is color-blind and neither knows nor tolerates classes among our citizens," first enunciated in dissent by Justice Harlan when the Civil Rights Law of 1875 was declared unconstitutional in 1883, had finally become the view of a unanimous Court, three of whose members were southerners.

With the passage of the Civil Rights Act of 1964, a modern Magna Charta for Negroes was placed on the federal statute books. It established the framework for a broad public effort to eliminate discrimination in several sectors of American life. It

---

[6] Executive Order No. 9981, signed by President Truman on July 26, 1948.

set forth federal policy and administrative machinery to guarantee voting rights, relief against discrimination in places of public accommodation, desegregation of public education, nondiscrimination in federally assisted programs, and equal employment opportunity. The Voting Rights Act of 1965 was an important complement of the Civil Rights Act.

There is always a lag between passage of laws and the actual behavioral responses to them. Although many southern Negroes have already benefited from the outlawing of numerous discriminatory practices, particularly in the use of public accommodations, the full complement of rights and privileges granted Negroes by law has not yet been secured. Of great importance, however, are the facts that a legal framework has been established within which the long-sought goal of full equality of citizenship for Negroes can be pursued, and that the experiences of many southern Negroes in participating in recent civil rights demonstrations, such as mass marches in the streets, buyers' boycotts, and "sit-ins," have developed in them a new sense of confidence and independence in their relations with whites. The spirit and mood of Negroes today is one of urgent and uncompromising insistence on racial equality now. It is virtually certain that Negroes in all parts of the country, through their organizations and through greater use of the ballot, will continue vigorous efforts to eliminate all forms of racial discrimination.

Moreover, in the South as in other regions, many whites are supporting their efforts. There has long been a large body of southern opinion, particularly among urban ministers, opposed to racial segregation and discrimination on moral grounds. The speedy compliance with the public accommodations provisions of the Civil Rights Act of 1964 by thousands of southern hotel, motel, restaurant, and theater operators indicates that many of them were pleased with the passage of the act, because it relieved them of the awkward and embarrassing responsibility of deciding whether or not to serve Negroes.

Under the combined pressures from Negro organizations, Supreme Court decisions, legislative enactments, religious doctrines, and competition between business firms for Negro customers, traditional southern attitudes and practices aimed at restricting the freedom of action of Negroes are rapidly breaking down. This can be no better exemplified than in the growing political strength of southern Negroes, which has resulted in the election of Negroes to office in several southern states. For the first time since Reconstruction a Negro was elected to the Georgia State Legislature in 1963 and a Negro was elected to the Tennessee State Legislature in 1964. In 1965, 10 Negroes were elected to serve in the 1966 Georgia State Legislature, including 2 in the State Senate.

There is, to be sure, a hard core of active resistance to the Negro's drive for equality. In a few southern states, particularly Mississippi and Alabama, strong and sometimes violent actions have been taken to perpetuate segregation. Segregationist sentiment is more prevalent in rural areas than in cities, and although it is advanced strongly by some politicians and middle-class business and professional men, its most ardent advocates are low-income whites who are in direct economic competition with Negroes.

It is of much greater significance, however, that a new inter-racial environment has been established in the South. As a result white supremacy, one of the traditional pillars of southern society, is crumbling. Thus, in race relations, as in economic and political affairs, the power of the southern patrician is no longer of great significance, and with the waning of his influence southern society is rapidly moving into the urban-industrial mainstream of American life.

Chapter 3

THE SOUTH AND
THE NATIONAL ECONOMY

THE SOUTH, like other major regions of the United States, is part of a great nation within which there is a flow of knowledge and ideas, an interchange of products, and a high degree of mobility of capital and of population. Commodities produced in the South are sold in all regions of the United States and in many foreign countries. Likewise, products from all over the world are commonly found in stores in the heart of Dixie. Insurance premiums paid by southerners may finance apartment houses in New York or on the West Coast, while many southern factories and thousands of miles of southern highways have been paid for by savings accumulated in the Northeast and Midwest. Tens of thousands of people—both Negro and white—who were born and reared in the South are now living in the North and West. In brief, all regions of the United States are linked by complex economic relationships and the links are of such a nature that the growth of any one region—including the South— is heavily influenced both by the over-all growth of the national economy and by developments in other regions.

In both private and public activities the various regions of the United States are in constant competition with each other. They compete for product markets, for capital supplies, particularly in the form of new industries, for new technologies, for labor, for tourist expenditures, and for numerous types of government programs and facilities. Thus the competitive potential of the South, and hence its future rate of economic growth, will depend heavily on the ability of its private entrepreneurs to produce and sell goods and services at prices competitive with those produced in other regions and on the extent to which governments—federal, state, and local—expand public programs and facilities within the region.

In a dynamic and growing economy, such as that of the United States, competition for productive resources and for markets for goods and services results in a continuing interregional movement of capital, technology, entrepreneurship, and labor. These geographic shifts stem mainly from the desires of workers to improve their incomes and living conditions and from the desires of owners of capital to maximize returns on their investments.

The extent to which this mobility eliminates regional differences in real per capita income is influenced by several factors, among which the level of employment and the rate of growth in the national economy are especially important. Unless there are other strong counteracting forces, long periods of national full employment, coupled with rapid changes in technology, stimulate geographic movements of both capital and labor and tend to eliminate interregional differences in real per capita incomes.

Six Decades of National and Southern Growth

The close relationship between southern and national economic growth is evident from a comparison of changes in population, employment, and personal income in the South and in the nation as a whole between 1900 and 1960. During that 60-year period population in the United States increased from approximately 76 million to 178 million—a gain of 134 per cent—while southern population increased at a slightly lower rate—123 per cent—from almost 22 million to 49 million. Employment also increased more slowly in the South than in the rest of the nation, but personal income increased more rapidly (Table 3-1).

Table 3-1   Population, Employed Persons 14 Years Old and Over, and Personal Income, United States and South, by Decade, 1900–1960

Year	Population			Persons employed			Personal income		
	South	United States	South as per cent of U. S.	South	United States	South as per cent of U. S.	South	United States	South as per cent of U. S.
	Thousands			Thousands			Millions		
1900	21,913	75,995	28.8	7,646	28,283	27.0	$2,247	$15,390	14.6
1910	26,339	91,972	28.6	10,307	37,271	27.7	—	—	—
1920	29,552	105,711	28.0	10,620	41,236	25.8	11,803a	69,277a	17.0a
1930	33,772	122,775	27.5	12,517	48,595	25.8	11,129	76,780	14.5
1940	37,013	131,669	28.1	12,156	45,166	26.9	13,253	78,522	16.9
1950	41,728	150,697	27.7	14,472	56,225	25.7	44,879	225,473	19.9
1960	48,802	178,464	27.3	16,439	64,372	25.5	81,960	396,975	20.6

Sources: Population data from decennial Population Censuses are as of date of Census, which, since 1930 has been April 1. Employment data for 1900–1930 —1940: Census of Population, Vol. III, The Labor Force, Part I, U. S. Bureau of the Census, Washington; 1940–1960—decennial population censuses. Personal income data for 1900–1920—Everett S. Lee, Ann Ratner Miller, Carol P. Brainard, and Richard A. Easterlin, Population Redistribution and Economic Growth, United States, 1870–1950, American Philosophical Society, Philadelphia, 1957; 1930–1950—Personal Income by States Since 1929, A Supplement to the Survey of Current Business, 1956; 1960 data from Survey of Current Business, April 1964.

a 1919–1921 average.

In view of the great expansion in the national economy between 1900 and 1960 and the many changes that occurred in all parts of the nation, the South's shares of total population and employment, though declining slowly throughout the six decades, were remarkably stable (Table 3-1). In general, changes in southern and in national population and employment were closely correlated. The declines in the South's shares that did take place could have occurred only as a result of a large net migration of people from the South, because the natural rate of population increase—births minus deaths—has long been higher in the South than in other areas of the country. Moreover, migration from the South was made possible only by expanding job opportunities in other regions.

1900 TO 1930

During the first three decades of the present century the rates of increase in both population and employment were in general lower in the South than in the nation as a whole. The rise in southern per capita income was higher than the rise in the national average between 1900 and 1920 and the decline between 1920 and 1930 was sharper (Tables 3-1 and 3-2). Although the income estimates for 1900 and 1920 were made by different procedures and are based on less reliable data than those for later years and must, therefore, be interpreted with caution, it is reasonable to believe that they accurately reflect the directions of income changes in the South compared with those in the nation as a whole.

For example, the period between 1900 and 1920 was one of generally rising prices for farm and timber products, both of which were important to the southern economy. In addition, during the last few years of this period the manpower demands of World War I, both for the armed forces and for northern industry, provided important nonfarm employment opportunities for the expanding southern population. Net migration from the

THE SOUTH AND THE NATIONAL ECONOMY 39

South between 1910 and 1920 was almost 1.2 million people—4.6 per cent of the South's 1910 population. The combination of these two sets of forces—rising prices for farm and timber products and high demands for nonfarm labor—provided an excellent stimulus to rapid growth in southern per capita income. The South, however, started from a very low per capita income in 1900—$103, compared with $243 in the non-South—and it was still heavily burdened with a low-productivity agriculture, poor roads, and inadequate schools. Consequently, even after two decades of prosperity, average per capita income in the South in 1920 was only about 53 per cent of that in the non-South—$399 compared to $755 (Table 3-2).

In several respects the interrelationships between national and southern growth were much less favorable to the South during the 1920's than during the preceding decade. Per capita income decreased throughout the nation between 1920 and 1930 (Table 3-2), but the decline was most rapid in the South and occurred in all southern states except Florida (Table 3-3). Agriculture continued to dominate the southern economy, and the region suffered from low prices for its farm products and heavy infestations of boll weevils in many cotton-producing areas.

Table 3-2 **Per Capita Personal Income, United States, Non-South, and South, by Decade, 1900–1960**

	Per capita personal income			Per capita personal income as per cent of U. S.		
Year	United States	Non-South	South	United States	Non-South	South
1900	$203	$243	$103	100.0	119.7	50.7
1920	655	755	399	100.0	115.3	60.9
1930	625	738	329	100.0	118.1	52.6
1940	596	690	358	100.0	115.8	60.1
1950	1,496	1,657	1,075	100.0	110.8	71.9
1960	2,224	2,430	1,679	100.0	109.3	75.5

Source: Table 3-1.

Table 3-3 Per Capita Personal Income and Migration Rate, Southern States, by Decade, 1920–1960

State	Per capita income, 1920	Migration rate,[a] 1920–1930	Per capita income, 1930	Migration rate,[a] 1930–1940	Per capita income, 1940	Migration rate,[a] 1940–1950	Per capita income, 1950	Migration rate,[a] 1950–1960
South	$399	−5.2	$329	−2.8	$358	−6.1	$1,075	−2.8
Alabama	313	−7.6	266	−7.1	282	−12.1	867	−12.0
Arkansas	329	−13.2	223	−8.0	256	−21.3	805	−22.7
Florida	437	32.5	464	20.0	513	30.5	1,288	58.3
Georgia	348	−16.6	308	−5.3	340	−9.3	1,016	−6.2
Kentucky	400	−10.3	325	−4.1	320	−12.9	958	−13.2
Louisiana	426	−1.7	358	0.3	363	−6.2	1,089	−1.9
Mississippi	281	−7.1	203	−5.2	218	−19.9	729	−19.9
North Carolina	354	−0.5	293	−3.2	328	−7.2	1,009	−8.1
Oklahoma	504	−3.1	368	−12.5	373	−18.6	1,133	−9.8
South Carolina	336	−18.0	241	−7.1	307	−12.2	881	−10.5
Tennessee	361	−5.8	325	−0.7	339	−4.9	995	−8.3
Texas	539	4.9	411	−0.1	432	1.1	1,340	1.5
Virginia	420	−11.7	384	−0.2	466	6.3	1,222	0.4

Sources: Personal income data from *Personal Income by States Since 1929, A Supplement to the Survey of Current Business,* 1956 and later issues of *Survey of Current Business.* Population data from decennial Censuses of Population and C. Horace Hamilton, "The Negro Leaves the South," mimeo. (supplementary tables for a paper prepared at North Carolina State University at Raleigh and presented at the annual meeting of the American Association for the Advancement of Science, 1963).

[a] Net migration during decade as per cent of population at beginning of decade.

Figure 3-1   **Real Per Capita Personal Income, United States and South, 1929–1964**   (*1954 dollars*)

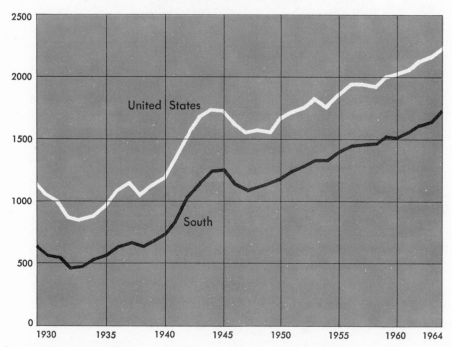

Source: Appendix Table 3-1.

1930 TO 1964

After 1930 real per capita income [1] in the South increased at a much more rapid rate than did real per capita income in the nation as a whole (Figure 3-1). Although the 1930's included the years of the Great Depression—1932–1938—a period in which both real per capita income and employment declined in virtually all parts of the nation, there was a gain in real per capita income for the decade as a whole—29 per cent in the South and 13 per cent in the non-South. This reversal of the trend of the 1920's was due largely to a higher rate of increase in the South than in the rest of the country in wage and salary payments by the Federal Government and increases in southern incomes from manufacturing, construction, and mining (Table 3-4). Labor and

[1] Personal income per capita, measured in dollars of constant purchasing power.

Table 3-4   **Civilian Income from Participation in Current Production,[a] by Industry Group, Non-South and South, Selected Years, 1929–1960**
(*Millions*)

Industry and region	1929	1940	1950	1960
Non-South				
All industries	$54,680	$51,865	$145,608	$253,103
Agriculture	4,636	3,611	10,808	9,721
Mining	1,206	966	2,319	2,460
Contract construction	3,231	1,954	8,425	16,254
Manufacturing	15,174	14,486	45,710	80,098
Wholesale & retail trade	10,476	10,811	30,437	48,872
Finance, insurance & real estate	3,315	2,524	5,854	12,969
Transportation	4,119	3,234	8,455	12,464
Communications, public utilities	1,360	1,388	3,723	7,111
Services	7,184	6,466	16,185	33,392
Government	3,869	6,309	13,262	29,007
Other	110	116	430	755
South				
All industries	$10,700	$10,986	$35,337	$64,731
Agriculture	2,623	1,992	5,212	5,134
Mining	388	401	1,248	1,879
Contract construction	439	490	2,311	4,610
Manufacturing	1,646	1,834	7,160	14,358
Wholesale & retail trade	1,891	2,109	7,489	13,224
Finance, insurance & real estate	436	368	1,177	3,221
Transportation	914	738	2,163	3,375
Communications, public utilities	198	219	826	1,788
Services	1,334	1,240	3,877	8,077
Government	760	1,538	3,737	8,804
Other	71	57	137	261

Sources: *Personal Income by States Since 1929, A Supplement to the Survey of Current Business,* 1956, pp. 207–212; and *Survey of Current Business,* August 1961, p. 19.
[a] Consists of wages and salaries, other labor income, and proprietors' income.

proprietors' income originating in these industries decreased in the non-South, but grew quite rapidly in the southern states.

The rate of decrease in income from farming was greater in the South during the 1930's than in the rest of the nation, and by 1940 almost as large a proportion of labor income in the

South came from manufacturing as from farming, while the proportion of income from wholesale and retail trade was higher than the proportion from farming. This shift in the structure of the southern economy, together with heavy disbursements by various agencies of the Federal Government, fostered an important turning point in the South's development. These two forces were significant in accounting for the more rapid rate of growth in personal income in the South than in other parts of the country during the 1930's, while the depression was important in shifting the South away from agrarian paternalism toward a more open and commercial society.

The 1940's were dominated by the exigencies of World War II, and the decade was one of rising incomes in all regions, particularly in the South. Real per capita personal income increased by 66 per cent in the South during this decade, compared to 39 per cent in the nation as a whole (Figure 3-1). Income originating in construction; manufacturing; communications and public utilities; wholesale and retail trade; and finance, insurance, and real estate rose quite rapidly in the South and at significantly higher rates than in the non-South (Table 3-4).

A major effect of the war on the southern economy was the creation of new capital investment through the building of shipyards, aircraft factories, and munition plants. In addition, the number of military personnel stationed in the South for training was larger per capita than in other regions. Military wages and salaries added to the flow of southern incomes, but because families and dependents of military men rarely accompanied them into the region, the rate of increase in population resulting from the military build-up was lower than the rate of increase in incomes. The large number of new military facilities constructed in the South also raised the demand for local goods and services, providing still an additional impetus to employment and per capita incomes.

Thus, government activities associated with World War II stimulated a large shift of workers out of southern agriculture. Because of its reservoir of underutilized manpower, the greatly expanded demand for goods and services associated with the war effort resulted in a higher rate of increase in production in the South than in most other regions.

Moreover, war-created jobs in other regions stimulated a movement of workers to other parts of the country. Indeed, out-migration of the South's population during the decade of the 1940's was unprecedentedly high—2.2 million persons (Table 3-5). This was equivalent to slightly more than 6 per cent of the number of people who were living in the South in 1940, a higher rate of out-migration than had previously been recorded. Three fourths of the migrants were Negroes, and the number of Negroes leaving the South between 1940 and 1950 was more than three and one half times as large as the number who had migrated out of the region during the depressed 1930's.

It is significant that most of the gain in the South's per capita income relative to the nation's occurred in the early 1940's (Table 3-2 and Figure 3-1). From 1940 to 1945, for instance, per capita income in the South rose from 60 per cent of the U. S. per capita to almost 73 per cent—a higher rate of gain than in any other five-year period between 1932 and 1964. The first half of the 1940's was, of course, a period in which incomes were rising rapidly throughout the economy and, as a result of the unusually strong demand for manpower in private industry and the armed forces, a higher percentage of the national labor force was employed than in any period of recent history.

The propitious trends of the 1940's did not continue into the 1950's and early 1960's. Real per capita income continued to grow more rapidly in the South than in the rest of the nation, but at a significantly lower rate than in the 1940's (Figure 3-1). Moreover, between 1960 and 1964 real per capita income in the South rose at an annual rate only slightly higher than during the 1950's. In most of the 14 years between 1950 and 1964 the national unemployment rate was considerably higher than in the 1940's. Partly as a result of this, there was again a slowing down of migration from the South, particularly among Negroes.

Table 3-5　Population and Estimated Net Migration from the South, by Decade, 1900–1960

| Decade | Population at beginning of decade (thousands) | | | Net migration during decade | | | | | | | | |
| | | | | Amount (thousands) | | | Per cent | | | Net migration rate (per cent)[a] | | |
	Total	White	Nonwhite	Total	White	Nonwhite	Total	White	Nonwhite	Total	White	Nonwhite
1900–1910	21,913	14,386	7,527	−273	−60	−213	100.0	22.0	78.0	−1.2	−0.4	−2.8
1910–1920	26,339	18,012	8,327	−1,198	−626	−572	100.0	52.3	47.7	−4.5	−3.5	−6.9
1920–1930	29,552	21,111	8,441	−1,539	−626	−913	100.0	40.7	59.4	−5.2	−3.0	−10.8
1930–1940	33,772	24,966	8,806	−955	−482	−473	100.0	50.5	49.5	−2.8	−1.9	−5.4
1940–1950	37,013	27,650	9,363	−2,242	−553	−1,689	100.0	24.7	75.3	−6.1	−2.0	−18.0
1950–1960	41,728	32,213	9,515	−1,182	330	−1,512	100.0	−27.9	127.9	−2.8	1.0	−15.9

Sources: Population data from decennial Censuses; net migration estimates from Everett S. Lee, Ann Ratner Miller, Carol P. Brainard, and Richard A. Easterlin, *Population Redistribution and Economic Growth, United States, 1870–1950*, American Philosophical Society, Philadelphia, 1957; migration data for 1940–1950 and 1950–1960 from *Current Population Reports: Population Estimates*, Series P-25, No. 247, U. S. Bureau of the Census, Washington, April 2, 1962.

[a] Net migration during decade as per cent of population at beginning of decade.

Figure 3-2   **Indexes of Employment in Nonagricultural Establishments, United States and South, 1939–1964**

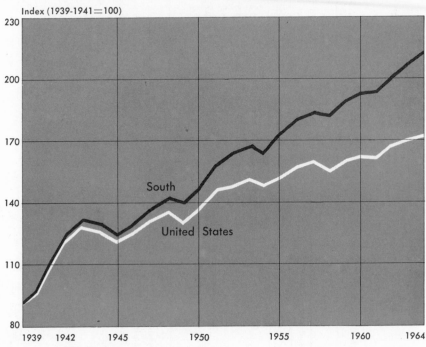

Index (1939-1941=100)

Source: Appendix Table 3-2.

Conclusions and Implications

The preceding review of relations between income, employment, and population changes in the South relative to the nation
as a whole suggests three points of significance. First, changes in
real per capita income in the South are closely linked to changes
in national income. With only minor variations, annual changes
in per capita income in the South have been closely correlated
with those in the total economy. Second, since at least 1930
southern incomes have increased at a significantly more rapid
rate than national income. Third, this higher rate of income
growth in the South has resulted mainly from a large migration
of people from the region, coupled with a shift of underemployed,
low-productivity workers out of agriculture into more productive

Figure 3-3 **Relationship Between Net Migration Rates** [a] **and Per Capita Personal Income of Southern States for Four Decades, 1920–1960**

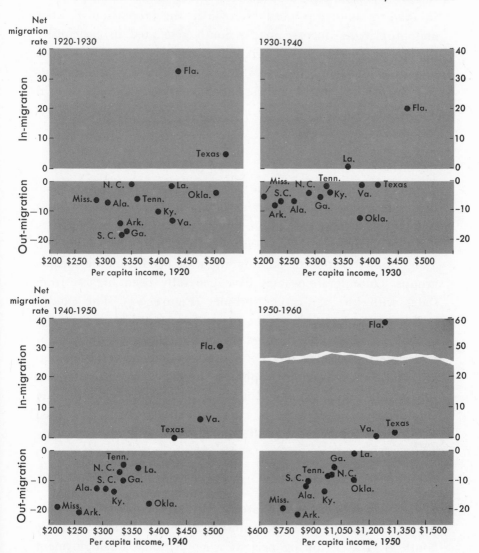

Source: Table 3-3.

[a] Net migration within a decade as per cent of the population at the beginning of that decade.

and better paid employment within the region. The extent of this shift is exemplified by the decrease from about 25 per cent in 1929 to about 8 per cent in 1960 in the proportion of labor and proprietors' income in the South generated in agriculture (Table 3-4). It is reflected in Figure 3-2, where it can be seen that the number of employees in nonagricultural establishments rose much more rapidly in the South from 1939 to 1964 than in the nation as a whole.

OUT-MIGRATION

Since about 1920 migration from the South has generally been highest during periods when employment was expanding most rapidly throughout the nation. Out-migration has contributed to a rise in southern per capita income in at least two ways. First, a high proportion of the out-migration has been from low-income groups. Out-migration rates have generally been highest from states with low per capita incomes (Figure 3-3). The exodus of low-income people from the region has tended to increase the proportion of people with relatively high incomes and in this way raise the average income. Second, had there not been out-migration, the supplies of capital, technology, and entrepreneurship within the region would not have been sufficient to provide employment and earnings at rates as high as actually prevailed for the growing labor force that remained.

CAPITAL FLOWS AND INVESTMENT

Although supporting data are woefully inadequate, it is highly probable that the flow of capital from other regions into the South is greatest during periods when national unemployment is low and improvements in technology are rapid.[2] Moreover, the southern economy itself is generating a much greater volume of

[2] For an analysis of interregional capital flows see J. Thomas Romans, *Capital Exports and Growth Among U. S. Regions,* Wesleyan University Press, Middletown, Conn., 1965.

savings and investment than it did in earlier years. For example, between 1950 and 1960 demand deposits increased almost 1.6 times as fast, savings deposits increased more than twice as fast, and the amount of life insurance in force increased almost 1.7 times as fast in the South as in the non-South.[3]

The growth in capital expenditures in the South between 1947 and 1962 is indicated by the increase in real gross investment in plant and equipment from $15.4 billion to $30.1 billion, while net investment in plant and equipment increased from $7.7 billion to $15.7 billion (Table 3-6). Moreover, the relatively steady rise in the South's share of the nation's net investment—from 18.0 per cent in 1947 to 22.1 per cent in 1962—and in its share of the nation's gross investment—from 17.3 per cent in 1947 to 21.5 per cent in 1962—is indicative of the economic growth the region has been experiencing.

It seems safe to conclude from the preceding review that full employment and high levels of activity in the national economy are important forces in raising southern incomes, providing job opportunities for southerners in other regions of the country, and hastening the shift of productive resources within the region from low-income employment, typified by traditional forms of agriculture, to enterprises with high productivity, such as manufacturing, construction, trade, and finance.

As the South's social and economic structure and its values and beliefs continue to change, and as means of transportation and communication are expanded and improved, its growth will become even more closely linked to the growth of the national economy. Indeed, the South probably has more to gain from high levels of employment and rapid rates of growth in the national economy than any other major region of the country. The consequent stimulating effect on the southern economy will result in higher living standards for the southern people, will enlarge the southern market for goods and services, and will

[3] See annual reports of the Federal Deposit Insurance Corporation, Washington; and *Statistical Abstract of the United States*, U. S. Bureau of the Census, Washington, annual.

Table 3-6   **Net and Gross Investment in Plant and Equipment, United States, Non-South, and South, 1947–1962** *(1954 dollars)*

Year	Net investment				Gross investment			
	United States	Non-South	South	South as per cent of U. S.	United States	Non-South	South	South as per cent of U. S.
	Millions					*Millions*		
1947	$42,924.6	$35,189.0	$7,735.6	18.0	$88,712.1	$73,357.4	$15,354.7	17.3
1948	47,047.1	38,452.0	8,595.1	18.3	93,044.0	76,644.3	16,399.7	17.6
1949	49,006.0	39,935.0	9,071.0	18.5	95,815.0	95,668.3	17,146.7	17.9
1950	50,481.6	41,002.9	9,478.7	18.8	98,026.2	80,267.5	17,758.7	18.1
1951	53,471.4	43,256.1	10,215.3	19.1	101,636.9	83,038.5	18,598.4	18.3
1952	56,395.6	45,361.0	11,034.6	19.6	105,522.6	85,931.6	19,591.0	18.6
1953	58,931.7	47,174.0	11,757.7	20.0	108,989.9	88,415.8	20,574.1	18.9
1954	61,465.4	49,073.1	12,392.3	20.2	111,577.7	90,102.9	21,474.8	19.2
1955	63,245.9	50,578.5	12,667.4	20.0	115,317.2	93,018.3	22,298.9	19.3
1956	67,154.0	53,505.7	13,648.3	20.3	121,708.4	97,985.5	23,722.9	19.5
1957	70,392.3	55,696.7	14,695.6	20.9	128,189.1	102,594.6	25,594.6	20.0
1958	70,943.4	55,953.2	14,990.2	21.1	132,393.4	105,639.6	26,753.8	20.2
1959	70,498.1	55,461.2	15,036.9	21.3	135,631.7	107,958.3	27,673.4	20.4
1960	70,755.8	55,570.4	15,185.4	21.5	139,140.6	110,508.5	28,632.1	20.6
1961	70,694.9	55,257.8	15,437.1	21.8	140,049.4	110,711.6	29,337.8	20.9
1962	71,106.0	55,386.2	15,719.8	22.1	139,979.0	109,912.0	30,067.0	21.5

Source: Unpublished data from U. S. Department of Commerce, Office of Business Economics, Washington.

increase the availability of investment capital. National and international markets for southern products and outside capital for industrial and urban expansion in the South can be more easily found if the output of the total national economy is expanding and the demand for labor is strong than if growth is slow nationally and unemployment is high.

Federal government policies and programs aimed at maintaining high levels of employment throughout the nation should thus have immediate and direct effects on southern economic growth. Because the South failed to fully develop the nonagricultural sectors of its economy for the first 300 years of its history, it is a late starter in the drive to industrialize. In the highly competitive race to increase the level of living and general well-being of its citizens, the essential problem facing the South is, therefore, that of finding ways and means of rapidly increasing the productivity, and, hence, the incomes of its people. Most of the following chapters are concerned with factors and forces that will be of major significance in solving this problem.

Chapter 4

INDUSTRY-MIX AND
SOUTHERN EMPLOYMENT

WE NOTED in the preceding chapter that the South has experienced a modest long-term decline in its share of total U. S. employment. In the 20-year period 1940 to 1960, U. S. employment rose by 19.2 million, from 45.2 million to 64.4 million, or 42.5 per cent, while southern employment rose from 12.1 million to 16.4 million, or 35.2 per cent (Appendix Table 4-1). In spite of the rise of southern employment, the South's share of the total decreased, because its rate of increase in employment was lower than the rate of increase of the nation as a whole. In 1940 almost 27 per cent of the people employed in the United States were in the South; by 1960, the proportion had declined to less than 26 per cent.

The lower rate of growth in employment in the South may have been attributable to two quite different causes: the region may have had a high concentration of those industries in which employment throughout the nation was declining or growing slowly; or some or all of the industries in the South may have been losing their competitive position relative to the same industries in other regions and, thus, have been forced to reduce the number of persons employed.

In this chapter we explore the changes in employment that took place in the South between 1940 and 1960 and attempt to determine the extent to which the decrease in the South's share of national employment was due to the particular mixture of industries in the region and the extent to which it was due to the competitive performance of individual southern industries. Further, we examine the probable influence of the southern industry-mix—the relative importance of different industries—on future southern employment.

Pattern of Employment Changes, 1940–1960

Although employment increased between 1940 and 1960 in 46 of the 48 states,[1] the rates at which it increased among the states varied greatly. As a result, there were significant changes in shares of total U. S. employment in the individual states. Those in which employment increased at rates lower than the national average—42.5 per cent—had declines in their shares, and those in which employment increased at rates above the national average had gains.

Nineteen states had increases in their shares of U. S. employment. Only three southern states—Florida, Texas, and Virginia—increased their shares of national employment between 1940 and 1960. The remaining ten southern states had declines. They were not alone, however, in this experience. Nineteen non-southern states and the District of Columbia also had declines in their shares of total employment. (See Appendix Table 4-1.)

The change in total employment between 1940 and 1960 in each state was generally the net result of decreases in some industries and increases in others. Moreover, there were great differences in the rates of increase in those industries in which employment expanded. An examination of changes in employment in 30 industries from 1940 to 1960 reveals that in 19 the increases in employment were at a higher rate than the U. S. average increase for all industries; in 4 employment increased, but at a rate lower than the U. S. average; and in 7 there were actual decreases in the number of persons employed (Figure 4-1 and Table 4-1).

[1] Arkansas lost slightly more than 18,000 workers, and Mississippi about 45,000.

Figure 4-1   **Changes in Number of Persons Employed, by Industry,
United States and South, 1940–1960**

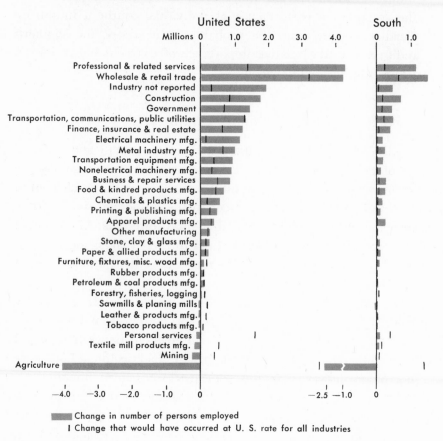

Change in number of persons employed
I Change that would have occurred at U. S. rate for all industries

Source: Table 4-1.

Among the 19 industries with higher-than-average employment
increases between 1940 and 1960, the most important numerical
gains in both the South and the nation were in: professional and
related services; wholesale and retail trade; construction; and
government—federal, state, and local. The increases in these
industries accounted for 60 per cent of the total increase of 19.2
million workers in the United States and 84 per cent of the total
increase of 4.3 million in the South.

The four industries in the United States in which employment increases were at rates lower than the U. S. average for all industries were: forestry, fisheries, and logging; petroleum and coal products manufacturing; furniture, fixtures, and miscellaneous wood manufacturing; and transportation, communications, and public utilities. The seven industries in the United States in which there were actual decreases in the number of persons employed were: agriculture; mining; textile mill products manufacturing; personal services; tobacco products manufacturing; leather and leather products manufacturing; and sawmills and planing mills.

A high proportion of the South's 1940 employment was concentrated in the 11 industries in which national employment either declined or increased at a lower rate than the U. S. average rate of increase for all industries between 1940 and 1960. For example, 62 per cent of southern employment in 1940, compared to 43 per cent in the nation as a whole, was in these 11 industries. (See Table 4-2.) Since agriculture was the industry with the largest decreases in employment both in the nation and in the South, the high proportion of total southern employment concentrated in agriculture had a particularly adverse effect on the change in the South's share of total national employment. Agriculture, however, was not the only source of the South's lowered share. The region had substantially higher proportions than the nation as a whole of its total employment in other industries whose employment declined nationally between 1940 and 1960— especially in the personal service, textile manufacturing, and sawmilling industries. Thus, the South's industry-mix in 1940 clearly was not conducive to rapid growth of total employment within the region.

INDUSTRY-MIX AND COMPETITIVE PERFORMANCE

To determine the importance of the South's industry-mix compared with the competitive performance of its individual industries as a cause of the region's decreased share of national employment, we used a method that has been used by several students

Table 4-1　Employment in 30 Industries, United States and South, 1940 and 1960

| Industry | Number of employees (thousands) | | | | Change in number of employees, 1940–1960 | | | |
| | United States | | South | | United States | | South | |
	1940	1960	1940	1960	Number (thousands)	Per cent	Number (thousands)	Per cent
Total	45,166.2	64,371.7	12,156.3	16,438.7	19,205.5	42.52	4,282.4	35.23
Below average growth[a]	19,293.3	15,994.1	7,480.3	5,705.6	−3,299.2	−17.10	−1,774.7	−23.72
Agriculture	8,372.2	4,240.5	4,179.5	1,671.7	−4,131.7	−49.35	−2,507.8	−60.00
Mining	913.0	653.0	259.0	277.9	−260.0	−28.48	18.9	7.30
Textile mill products mfg.	1,170.0	953.9	509.1	589.5	−216.1	−18.47	80.4	15.79
Personal services	4,009.3	3,839.9	1,295.8	1,399.6	−169.4	−4.23	103.8	8.01
Tobacco products mfg.	108.0	86.1	58.8	61.1	−21.9	−20.28	2.3	3.91
Leather & products mfg.	364.4	347.0	20.7	40.0	−17.4	−4.77	19.3	93.24
Sawmills & planing mills	435.6	419.7	249.5	181.1	−15.9	−3.65	−68.4	−27.41
Forestry, fisheries, logging	244.7	259.4	112.7	136.2	14.7	6.01	23.5	20.85
Petroleum & coal products mfg.	201.2	281.9	63.3	104.6	80.7	40.11	41.3	65.24
Furniture, fixtures, misc. wood mfg.	361.5	477.8	95.8	168.3	116.3	32.17	72.5	75.68
Transportation, communications, public utilities	3,113.4	4,434.9	636.1	1,075.6	1,321.5	42.45	439.5	69.09

Above average growth[b]	25,872.9	48,371.7	4,676.0	10,733.1	22,504.7	86.98	6,057.1	129.54
Professional & related services	3,317.7	7,542.9	691.7	1,760.4	4,225.2	127.36	1,068.7	154.50
Wholesale & retail trade	7,538.8	11,744.4	1,626.4	3,079.5	4,205.6	55.79	1,453.1	89.34
Industry not reported	688.8	2,599.0	146.1	575.1	1,910.2	277.32	429.0	293.63
Construction	2,056.3	3,790.8	524.5	1,169.1	1,734.5	84.35	644.6	122.90
Government	1,753.5	3,170.5	399.5	817.1	1,417.0	80.81	417.6	104.53
Finance, insurance & real estate	1,467.6	2,684.8	229.8	587.2	1,217.2	82.94	357.4	155.53
Electrical machinery mfg.	374.7	1,487.0	8.0	139.2	1,112.3	296.85	131.2	1,640.00
Metal industry mfg.	1,542.7	2,544.7	108.8	292.6	1,002.0	64.95	183.8	168.93
Transportation equipment mfg.	880.8	1,184.3	51.5	196.2	933.5	105.98	144.7	280.97
Nonelectrical machinery mfg.	697.6	1,567.7	41.8	147.3	870.1	124.73	105.5	252.39
Business & repair services	1,259.6	2,104.3	248.0	482.5	844.7	67.06	234.5	94.56
Food & kindred products mfg.	1,093.6	1,801.9	202.4	415.6	708.3	64.77	213.2	105.34
Chemicals & plastics mfg.	439.8	985.6	100.2	235.8	545.8	124.10	135.6	135.33
Printing & publishing mfg.	630.7	1,137.6	80.8	177.5	506.9	80.37	96.7	119.68
Apparel products mfg.	780.7	1,157.1	86.0	305.8	376.4	48.21	219.8	255.58
Other manufacturing	526.1	800.9	28.5	70.6	274.8	52.23	42.1	147.72
Stone, clay, & glass mfg.	336.7	599.8	49.4	120.0	263.1	78.14	70.6	142.91
Paper and allied products mfg.	328.2	578.6	44.9	134.0	250.4	76.29	89.1	198.44
Rubber products mfg.	159.0	265.7	7.7	27.6	106.7	67.11	19.9	258.44

Sources: 1940—Census of Population: 1940, Vol. III, The Labor Force, Parts I–V, Table 17 for individual states. 1950 and 1960—Census of Population: 1960, Series D, Detailed Characteristics, individual state reports, Table 126.

a Industries in which employment declined or increased at a lower rate than the U. S. average for all industries, 1940–1960.
b Industries in which employment increased at a higher rate than the U. S. average for all industries, 1940–1960.

Table 4-2   Percentage Distribution of Employment in 30 Industries, United States and South, 1940 and 1960

Industry	United States		South			
			Percentage distribution		Per cent of U. S. employment	
	1940	1960	1940	1960	1940	1960
Total	100.00	100.00	100.00	100.00	26.91	25.54
Below average growth[a]	42.72	24.85	61.53	34.71	38.77	35.67
Agriculture	18.54	6.59	34.38	10.17	49.92	39.42
Mining	2.02	1.02	2.13	1.69	28.36	42.56
Textile mill products mfg.	2.59	1.48	4.19	3.59	43.51	61.80
Personal services	8.88	5.97	10.66	8.52	32.32	36.45
Tobacco products mfg.	0.24	0.13	0.48	0.37	54.44	70.96
Leather & products mfg.	0.81	0.54	0.17	0.24	5.68	11.53
Sawmills & planing mills	0.96	0.65	2.05	1.10	57.28	43.15
Forestry, fisheries, logging	0.54	0.40	0.93	0.83	46.06	52.51
Petroleum & coal products mfg.	0.45	0.44	0.52	0.64	31.46	37.11
Furniture, fixtures, misc. wood mfg.	0.80	0.74	0.79	1.02	26.50	35.22
Transportation, communications, public utilities	6.89	6.89	5.23	6.54	20.43	24.25

Above average growth[b]	57.28	75.15	38.47	65.29	18.07	22.19
Professional & related services	7.35	11.72	5.69	10.71	20.85	23.34
Wholesale and retail trade	16.69	18.24	13.38	18.73	21.57	26.22
Industry not reported	1.53	4.04	1.20	3.50	21.24	22.13
Construction	4.55	5.89	4.32	7.11	25.51	30.84
Government	3.88	4.92	3.29	4.97	22.78	25.77
Finance, insurance, and real estate	3.25	4.17	1.89	3.57	15.66	21.87
Electrical machinery mfg.	0.83	2.31	0.07	0.85	2.14	9.36
Metal industry mfg.	3.42	3.95	0.90	1.78	7.05	11.50
Transportation equipment mfg.	1.95	2.82	0.42	1.19	5.85	10.81
Nonelectrical machinery mfg.	1.54	2.44	0.34	0.90	5.99	9.40
Business and repair services	2.79	3.27	2.04	2.93	19.69	22.93
Food and kindred products mfg.	2.42	2.80	1.67	2.53	18.51	23.06
Chemicals and plastics mfg.	0.97	1.53	0.82	1.43	22.78	23.92
Printing and publishing mfg.	1.40	1.77	0.66	1.08	12.81	15.60
Apparel products mfg.	1.73	1.80	0.71	1.86	11.02	26.43
Other manufacturing	1.16	1.24	0.23	0.43	5.42	8.82
Stone, clay and glass mfg.	0.74	0.93	0.41	0.73	14.67	20.01
Paper and allied products mfg.	0.73	0.90	0.37	0.82	13.68	23.16
Rubber products mfg.	0.35	0.41	0.06	0.17	4.84	10.39

Source: Table 4-1.

a Industries in which employment declined or increased at a lower rate than the U. S. average for all industries, 1940–1960.

b Industries in which employment increased at a higher rate than the U. S. average for all industries, 1940–1960.

of differential rates of growth between states and regions.[2] The method and its application in this study are described in detail in Appendix 4.

The method, commonly called "the shift technique," focuses attention on the comparative gains or losses of employment in each state relative to the national average increase in employment and permits the comparative gain or loss for each state to be divided into two parts—that due to the industry-mix within the state and that due to the competitive performance of the individual industries in the state.[3] As has been pointed out, employment in each of the various states between 1940 and 1960 did not increase at the national average rate of 42.5 per cent. In some, it grew at higher rates, and in others it increased at lower rates. The numerical difference between employment which actually occurred and that which would have occurred had employment changed at the national rate of 42.5 per cent is the state's "upward or downward shift" in employment. These numerical differences (which it should be noted are not actual changes in employment) are shown in the top panel of Figure 4-2 and in Column 3 of Appendix Table 4-2.

Those states with positive numerical differences had upward shifts, that is, increases in employment at rates higher than the U. S. average rate, while those with negative differences had downward shifts—increases in employment lower than the U. S. average. Thus, the former are the 19 states that increased their shares of U. S. employment and the latter are the 29 states that had decreases in their shares.

---

[2] For generalized explanations and applications of the method see: Harvey S. Perloff, Edgar S. Dunn, Jr., Eric E. Lampard, and Richard F. Muth, *Regions, Resources and Economic Growth,* Resources for the Future, Washington, 1960; Edgar S. Dunn, Jr., *Recent Southern Economic Development as Revealed by the Changing Structure of Employment,* University of Florida Monographs, *Social Sciences,* No. 14, Spring 1962; and Lowell D. Ashby, *Regional Change in a National Setting,* Staff Working Paper in Economics and Statistics, No. 7, U. S. Department of Commerce, Washington, April 1964. The method of presenting changes in employment compared to national rates of change used in Figure 4-1 was suggested by charts in the last-named publication.

[3] See Appendix 4 for a specific illustration of the application of the shift technique.

Figure 4-2 **Comparison of Effects of Competitive Performance of Industries and of Industry-Mix on Total Net Employment Shift, by State, 1940–1960** *(Thousands of Employees)*

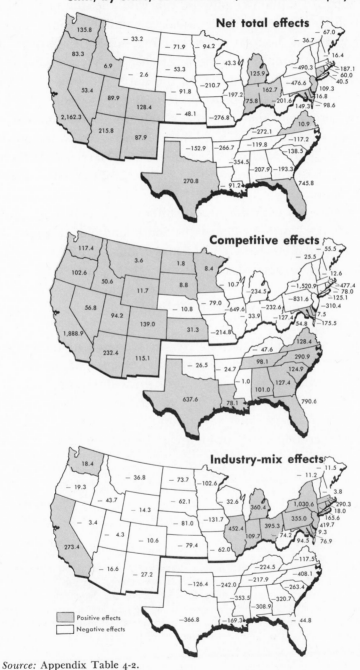

Source: Appendix Table 4-2.

When the upward shifts of the 19 states are added together, they total 4.7 million employees. Likewise, the sum of the downward shifts of the 29 states equals 4.7 million employees.[4] In other words, of the total increase of 19.2 million employees, only about 4.7 million, or 24.3 per cent changed the percentage distribution of employment among the states and thus altered the states' respective shares of total national employment.

It is clear from the top panel of Figure 4-2 that most of the states with upward shifts were in the West, but also included in this group were Michigan, Indiana, Ohio, Maryland, Delaware, and New Jersey in the North, and Florida, Texas, and Virginia in the South.

The 29 states with downward shifts were concentrated in the Midwest, the Northern Plains, the South, and New England, but also included were New York, Pennsylvania, and West Virginia. Of the total downward shift, 41 per cent occurred in the ten southern states of Kentucky, Tennessee, North Carolina, South Carolina, Georgia, Alabama, Mississippi, Louisiana, Arkansas, and Oklahoma.

When we examine the relative effects of the industry-mix in the South versus the competitive performance of southern industries as sources of the downward shifts in employment, it is quite clear that the industry-mix exerted the stronger influence. For the 13 southern states as a group the components of the total net shift (net total effects of Figure 4-2) were as follows:

	Thousands of employed workers
Shift due to industry-mix	−3,163.8
Shift due to competitive performance	+2,277.2
Total net shift	−886.6

[4] That the sum of the upward shifts is equal to the sum of the downward shifts is a result of using the U. S. average rate (42.5 per cent) of increase in employment between 1940 and 1960 as the base for calculating the hypothetical changes—Column 2, Appendix Table 4-2—from which the upward and downward shifts for each state were derived. To the extent that some states had percentage gains in employment higher than the national average, other states had to have percentage gains lower than the national average.

In each of the 13 southern states the industry-mix exerted a downward pull on increases in employment between 1940 and 1960. However, in only four of the southern states was this true of competitive performance and in these its influence was relatively minor. Moreover, in no other major region was the industry-mix as important in explaining the comparative gains and losses in employment as in the South. There were 34 states which experienced a downward pull on employment increases between 1940 and 1960 from their industry-mix. Of this number, 13 were in the South (Figure 4-2). More importantly, over three fourths of the industry-mix effect in these 34 states was exerted by the 13 states of the South.

In contrast, the competitive performance of the majority of southern industries exerted a strong offsetting influence to the downward pull of the region's industry-mix. That is, employment in most industries in the South expanded at rates higher than the national rates for the same industries. The downward pull of the industry-mix on the growth rate in employment, however, was stronger than the effect of competitive performance, and thus the rate of growth of total employment in the region was lower than in the nation as a whole. Consequently, the South had a lower share of the nation's total employment in 1960 than in 1940.

Agriculture contributed more than any other industry to the region's decreased share of total national employment. The number of persons employed in agriculture decreased in each of the 48 states except Arizona between 1940 and 1960. Because of the high proportion of the South's total employment that was in agriculture in 1940, this industry would have had an important influence on the South's share of total employment, even if the decline in agricultural employment in the region had been no more rapid than the national rate. In fact, however, agricultural employment in the South decreased more rapidly than in the nation as a whole. It, therefore, exerted a double downward pull on the South's share of total employment. (See Tables 4-1 and 4-2.)

Factors in Changing Employment Patterns

The fact that the South had an industry-mix that exerted a strong negative influence on the expansion of total employment in the region, while most of the individual industries in the South increased their employment at more rapid rates than in the nation as a whole, raises two important questions: Why did employment in some industries decline or expand quite slowly compared with other industries throughout the nation? Why did employment in most industries expand more rapidly in the South than in the country as a whole?

National declines or slower-than-average rates of job expansion in some industries could have occurred as a result of a rapid rate of adoption of laborsaving technology and machinery, or as a result of declines or slow rates of growth in the demand for the goods and services produced by these industries.

The second question—why employment in the South expanded more rapidly in most industries than in the country as a whole—suggests the need for studies of the advantages of the South compared to other regions with respect to production costs and market outlets for a wide range of individual industries. A thorough inquiry into these possibilities would have involved a commitment of time and resources far beyond the scope of our study. Until these questions have been carefully investigated, we can focus attention only on some of the more obvious factors that have been of significance in the changing industrial pattern of employment.

INDUSTRIES WITH BELOW AVERAGE EMPLOYMENT GAINS

As has been stated, the total employment change in the 11 industries that experienced declines or below average rates of expansion was dominated by the very large decline in agricultural employment. This was true both in the nation as a whole and in the South. Nationally, the decrease of over 4 million persons employed in agriculture between 1940 and 1960 was almost 6 times as large as the total decline in the other industries that experienced employment decreases. In the South only one industry other than agriculture—sawmills and planing mills—experienced an absolute decrease in employment, and the decline in agricultural employment in the South of more than 2.5 million workers far overshadowed other employment changes in the 11 below-average-growth industries (Table 4-1). The first major problem, therefore, is to find explanations for the large decline in agricultural employment throughout the nation, and for its particularly large decrease in the South.

Agriculture

During the 20 years from 1940 to 1960 the number of agricultural jobs in the South decreased by more than 4 million, or over 49 per cent. Employment in southern agriculture was affected by the same general forces as agricultural employment throughout the nation, as described in Chapter 2. Largely because of the dramatic change in cotton farming that took place in the South between 1940 and 1960, however, the rate of decline in agricultural employment was even more rapid in the South than in the rest of the nation.

Cotton production had long been the great utilizer of farm labor in South Carolina, Georgia, Alabama, Mississippi, Louisiana, Arkansas, Oklahoma, and Texas, and it was not without significance in Tennessee and North Carolina. For generations cotton had been the principal cash crop of thousands of small farmers—owners, tenants, and sharecroppers—who used horses and mules as the main source of power for preparing, planting, and cultivating the land with small, hand-guided plows that rarely made a furrow more than six to eight inches wide and three to four inches deep. Cotton chopping—thinning the small plants in the rows—with hand hoes of the type commonly used in home vegetable gardens required a tremendous amount of labor in the spring—an amount surpassed only by that required to harvest the cotton in the fall. Harvesting was done by handpicking the locks of cotton from the open bolls. By these traditional methods of farming a farm family worked an average of 20 to 30 acres of cotton on the poor upland soils of the Southeast and 8 to 12 acres on the rich, heavy soils along rivers and in the Mississippi Delta area.

The use of mechanized methods of planting, thinning, cultivating, and harvesting cotton spread rapidly in the 1940's and 1950's as a result of the invention and perfection of a workable mechanical cotton harvester in the 1930's, the shortage of farm labor that occurred during World War II, and the price competition that cotton faced from synthetic fibers. Efficient mechanization of production requires large areas of level land. As a consequence, cotton production began to shift from the small farms in the rolling upland areas of the Southeast to the irrigated lands of the Southwest—California, New Mexico, and Arizona—and production in the South tended to concentrate in the Mississippi Delta area, the Texas high plains, and in scattered level areas throughout the Southeast. Cotton acreage decreased between 1940 and 1960 in every southern state—from 25 per cent in Texas to 66 per cent in Georgia—but in California, New Mexico, and Arizona it increased 133 per cent. Yields per acre increased in every state, somewhat counterbalancing the decreased acreage, but production declined in every important cotton-producing state in the South except Mississippi, Louisiana, and Texas, where it increased 24 per cent, 11 per cent, and 35 per cent, respectively. In North Carolina production decreased 68 per cent; in South Carolina, 57 per cent; in Georgia, 50 per cent; and in Oklahoma, 43 per cent.

Because of mechanization and the resulting shifts in areas of production, there was a 66 per cent decrease during the two decades in the total number of man-hours of labor used to produce and harvest the cotton crop of the United States, although the number of bales produced declined only 5 per cent. Of the total decrease of 1.6 billion man-hours—from 2.4 billion in 1940 to 831 million in 1960—approximately 96 per cent occurred in the 13 southern states. It represented about 30 per cent of the total decrease in man-hours of labor used in southern farming between 1940 and 1960, and was the principal reason that the percentage decline in employment in southern agriculture was greater than in the rest of the nation.

Other Declining Industries

The largest decreases in national employment in nonagricultural industries between 1940 and 1960 were in mining, textile manufacturing, and personal services (Table 4-1). Mining and textiles are highly competitive industries that have a large number of small firms that in the past utilized a high proportion of low-skilled labor. But these industries followed somewhat the same path as agriculture—sharp decreases in employment occurred mainly as a result of the spread of mechanization and improved methods as ways of reducing unit costs of production.

In the mining industry the decreases were in coal mining, which experienced a technological revolution in production even more pronounced than that of agriculture. The demand for coal was under heavy competitive pressure from oil and natural gas as sources of energy. The resulting decline in market outlets, particularly for anthracite, coupled with relatively high wages to coal miners, led to new methods of mining, a greater use of machinery, and the concentration of operations in the most productive mines. Output per man-hour of labor in coal mining more than doubled between 1940 and 1960 and thousands of miners lost their jobs.

In textiles competition for markets, both from foreign and domestic sources, forced those firms that were to stay in business to adopt cost-reducing and laborsaving methods of production. Many small, inefficient textile firms that were unable or unwilling to change to more capital-intensive methods of production were forced out of business.

The decline in the number of employees performing personal services resulted from a substantial decrease in private household servants—a decrease that was not fully offset by increases in the number of workers in hotels and lodging places and in laundries and cleaning establishments. The decrease in household servants, all of which occurred in the 1940's, was mainly a reflection of the fact that thousands of such workers were able to shift to better jobs during World War II. In addition, of course, the great increase in the number of laborsaving machines and gadgets in the typical American home within the past two decades has reduced the demand for domestic servants.

Employment Growth Slow, Output Increasing

It seems clear, despite the paucity of good measures of physical output for many industries, that the physical output of goods and services expanded significantly in the industries with declines or below average increases in national employment (except coal mining and personal services). For instance, in agriculture, the industry with the outstandingly large decline in employment, the physical volume of output increased by more than 50 per cent between 1940 and 1960.[5] The Federal Reserve Board indexes of industrial production indicate that the output of textile mill products increased by almost 24 per cent during the same period, even though national employment in this industry declined by more than 18 per cent. Likewise, the output of tobacco products increased almost 32 per cent, and of lumber products 16 per cent, though national employment in both industries declined.[6]

The point of importance is that decreases or below average rates of expansion in employment do not necessarily indicate dying or declining industries in terms of their output. On the contrary, most of the industries classified as below average growth in terms of employment were vigorously increasing their productive efficiency during the two decades under review. They were turning out a significantly greater flow of goods and services per man-hour in 1960 than in 1940. As a consequence, consumers

[5] *Changes in Farm Production Efficiency*, U. S. Department of Agriculture, Washington, Statistical Bull. No. 233, rev. July 1965.
[6] *Industrial Production, 1957–59 Base*, Board of Governors of the Federal Reserve System, Washington.

were being better served and the productive efficiency of the total economy was improved. Unfortunately, the very process by which the increased efficiency was brought about—the substitution of machinery and improved technology for manpower —imposed serious problems on thousands of workers, and was a major cause of the heavy migration of rural workers to urban centers. Many of these displaced workers moved into the slum areas of large cities and augmented existing problems of unemployment, delinquency, and crime. The great decreases in agricultural employment in the South fell with heavy force on Negro farmers, most of whom were poorly prepared by education and experience to shift to other types of work and were also faced with discriminatory hiring practices in numerous industries where employment was expanding.[7]

INDUSTRIES WITH ABOVE AVERAGE EMPLOYMENT GAINS

Of the 19 industries that nationally had above average rates of gain in employment between 1940 and 1960, 5 were service-producing, 12 were manufacturing, 1 was construction, and 1 was a miscellaneous category, "industry not reported."

Service Industries

The industrial category that showed the largest gain, both in the nation and in the South, was the service-producing industries. The five industries included in this category are: professional and related services; wholesale and retail trade; government; finance, insurance, and real estate; and business and repair services. Both the absolute gains in employment and the percentage

[7] The U. S. Census of Agriculture of April 1950 reported 554,722 nonwhite farmers in the 13 southern states. The Census of Agriculture taken in October and November 1959 used a different definition of "farm" from that used in 1950. After adjustment for the change in definition, the number of nonwhite farmers in the South in 1959 comparable with the 1950 figure was approximately 295,563. Thus, there was a decline of about 259,159 nonwhite farmers in the South, or almost 47 per cent during the 1950's. In the same period the decline in the number of white farmers was approximately 554,395, or 28 per cent.

increases in the two-decade period for the United States and for the South are shown in Table 4-1. The increase of about 12 million employees in these 5 industries in the United States accounted for more than half of the total increase of over 22.5 million employees in the 19 industries with above average rates of gain. In the South, where the increase in total employment in the 19 industries was about 6 million, the gain of over 3.5 million employees in the 5 service industries represented 58 per cent of the total. Clearly the growth in employment in these five service-producing industries was a major source of the expansion in total employment both in the South and in the nation as a whole.

The factors of principal significance in contributing to the employment gains in the service industries were: first, large increases in demand for the kinds of services produced by these industries as a result of increases in total population, the movement of people into urban areas, and the rapid growth in per capita incomes; second, most of these industries were slow to mechanize and to adopt other laborsaving techniques. For example, increases in the number of employees in professional and related services (mostly school teachers and medical and health personnel) and in the number of workers in wholesale and retail trade were in types of activities that provided limited opportunities for substituting machines for human effort. It has generally been true that the service-producing industries have not been able to make extensive use of laborsaving methods, though the use of teaching machines, new kinds of record-keeping devices, and electronic computers may affect manpower requirements in these industries more in the future than they have in the past.

The Construction Industry

Employment in the construction industry increased nationally by more than 1.7 million, or 84 per cent, between 1940 and 1960 and by almost 645,000, or 123 per cent, in the South. This industry, though subject to a high degree of annual variation in activity and characterized by cyclical swings in employment, has some of the same attributes as the service industries. It is, for instance, influenced by the same demand-expansion factors—increases in population, growing urbanization, and rising incomes. Moreover, fewer laborsaving machines and methods have been introduced in the construction industry than in agriculture, mining, and several types of manufacturing. When the increase in employment in the construction industry is added to the increases in the 5 service industries, the combined gains represent 61 per cent of the total growth in employment for the nation as a whole in the 19 industries that had above average rates of increase in employment. The comparable figure for the South is 69 per cent.

Manufacturing

National employment in the 12 manufacturing industries with above average rates of gain in employment increased by about 7 million between 1940 and 1960. This was only a little more than half the combined increase in the five service-producing industries plus construction. In the South the increase in employment in these 12 manufacturing industries of 1.5 million employees was slightly less than 35 per cent of the combined increase in the 5 service-producing industries and the construction industry. Nevertheless, these manufacturing industries are of greater importance to total employment than is suggested by changes in the number of their own employees.

Employment in all types of industries is, of course, highly interdependent. Employees attached to one industry often perform much of their work for other industries. In the construction industry, for example, many employees are engaged, at any given time, in building or remodeling factories, warehouses, and facilities that are integral parts of other industries; many employees in wholesale and retail trade, government, finance, insurance, real estate, and repair activities perform services for the manufacturing, agricultural, mining, and construction industries. Because of these innumerable linkages, it is virtually impossible to single out one group of industries as being the most important determinants of employment in other industries. Nevertheless, it is quite clear that the increase in the number of employees in manufacturing brought in its wake a large proportion of the new jobs in the service-producing and construction industries, even though employment in all types of manufacturing rose from only 23 to 27 per cent of total employment in the United States between 1940 and 1960 and in the South from 15 to 21 per cent.

For the United States as a whole, the largest increases in manufacturing employment between 1940 and 1960 were in electrical machinery, the metal industry, transportation equipment, and nonelectrical machinery manufacturing. These four industries, with their emphasis on metal fabricating and machinery manufacturing, were greatly stimulated in the 1940's by the war and by heavy government purchases of armaments and, in more recent years, of materials for the exploration of outer space, as well as by the growth in size and affluence of the consuming population. In general, they are high-wage, capital-intensive industries with a high proportion of engineers, technicians, and skilled workmen among their employees. Thus, they are the kinds of industries that could make important contributions to improving the South's wage structure and income distribution. It is significant, however, that in the South these 4 manufacturing industries accounted for only 39 per cent of the increased employment in the 12 above-average-growth manufacturing industries, compared to 58 per cent for the nation as a whole, and that in 1960 only about 5 per cent of the South's total employment was in these 4 industries, compared to about 12 per cent in the nation.

The manufacturing industries that had the greatest increases in employment in the South between 1940 and 1960 were the traditionally low-wage, labor-intensive apparel and food processing industries that use a high proportion of unskilled labor (Table 4-1). Apparel manufacturing was probably attracted to the South mainly by an ample supply of cheap labor, though the growth of market outlets within the region and the nearness to textile mills that supply the apparel factories with cloth were

additional factors of some influence. Many establishments in
the food-processing industry, particularly those that add weight
and volume in the manufacturing process, such as makers of
soft drinks and bakery products, not only use a high proportion
of unskilled labor but are oriented to local markets. The growth
of cities in the South has, therefore, greatly stimulated the
expansion of this industry. The increase in dairy, livestock,
poultry, fruit, and vegetable production that took place in the
South between 1940 and 1960 also encouraged the growth of
those kinds of food-processing plants that can be most economi-
cally operated near the sources of supply of raw products.

It is significant, moreover, that the employment increases that
occurred in several of the above-average-growth, capital-intensive,
high-wage industries were not widely distributed among the
southern states. Employment gains in the metal-fabricating, transportation equipment, and chemicals and plastics manufacturing
industries, for instance, though important in adding more than
460,000 new jobs in types of manufacturing that had previously
made relatively little growth in the region, were limited mainly
to a few states. More than two thirds of the region's employment
increase in the metal-fabrication industry occurred in Texas,
Alabama, Florida, and Virginia. About the same proportion of
the increased employment in the manufacturing of transportation
equipment, mainly automobile and airplane assembly plants,
took place in Texas, Georgia, and Alabama. In the chemicals
and plastics manufacturing industry three fourths of the 136,000
increase in the number of employees occurred in Texas, Tennessee, Louisiana, Virginia, and Kentucky. These three industries
were attracted to the South partly because of a general expansion
of consumer markets associated with urbanization and higher
per capita incomes and partly because they sold their products
to other manufacturing industries, such as textile mills, food-
processing establishments, and pulp and paper mills. Some of the
industries in this latter group found an ample supply of non-
unionized labor in the South an attractive inducement to expansion, while others were drawn to the region mainly by the

economies to be gained from being near the supplies of raw materials that they needed, particularly timber, oil, and gas.

Implications for the Future

On the basis of the preceding review of the changing industrial structure of southern employment, what implications and inferences can be drawn about the influence of the region's industry-mix on future levels of employment? In considering the answer to this question it is well to recall that the South's industry-mix —specifically, the high proportion of southern employees in below-average-growth industries—was the most important single factor in the relatively slow rate of growth of southern employment between 1940 and 1960. These below-average-growth industries, such as agriculture, mining, textiles, tobacco products, and furniture manufacturing, were rapidly substituting machinery and other technological advances for manpower.

Between 1940 and 1960 the industry-mix of the South was moving toward the pattern that prevailed in the total economy, and if past trends in employment can be taken as a guide to the future, the South's industry-mix was much more favorable for future growth in employment in 1960 than it had been in 1940. In 1940, 62 per cent of the South's total employment was in the 11 below-average-growth industries and 38 per cent in the 19 above-average-growth industries. By 1960, 65 per cent of southern employment was in the 19 above-average-growth industries and 35 per cent was in the below-average-growth group (Table 4-2).

This does not mean, however, that the region's industry-mix is on a par with that of the rest of the nation. In 1960 the South still had a relatively high proportion of its total employment in the below-average-growth industries: 35 per cent compared to 25 per cent for the nation as a whole. Conversely, 65 per cent of the South's employees were in the 19 above-average-growth industries compared with 75 per cent of the nation's employees.

Moreover, at the same time that the South was experiencing

quite high rates of employment increases in the 19 above-average-growth industries, it was also increasing its share of national employment in each of the below-average-growth industries (with the important exceptions of agriculture and sawmills and planing mills). For instance, 28 per cent of total U. S. mining employment was in the South in 1940 and 43 per cent in 1960. Similarly, the South's share of total textile employment rose from 43 per cent in 1940 to 62 per cent in 1960. In the manufacture of tobacco products the South's share rose from 54 to 71 per cent, and in furniture, fixtures, and miscellaneous wood products manufacturing it rose from 27 to 35 per cent.

The evidence, thus, seems quite clear that the South still continued to be attractive to labor-intensive types of industry. If the future trend in the substitution of machinery and technology for labor continues to be in the same industries as in 1940 to 1960, the industry-mix of the South, though greatly improved over 1940, will continue to be a significant factor tending to hold future increases in southern employment below national rates of gain.

OUTLOOK FOR BELOW-AVERAGE-GROWTH INDUSTRIES

The growth of employment in three important industries in the South appears to be particularly vulnerable to the combined forces of laborsaving technological changes and a slowly expanding and inelastic demand for their products and services. They are agriculture, personal services, and textiles. There were 3.7 million employees in these three industries in the South in 1960. They represented slightly more than 22 per cent of total southern employment, compared to the 14 per cent of national employment in these three industries. In each of them there were significant national declines in the absolute numbers of persons employed between 1940 and 1960, though in the South the decline occurred only in agriculture. Pertinent questions are: Will the number of workers in southern agriculture continue to decline in the years ahead? Will the employment decreases in personal services and textile manufacturing, which manifested themselves nationally between 1940 and 1960, be extended to these industries in the South?

The answer to the first question appears to be quite clearly in the affirmative. Several studies of the probable future course of agricutural development predict substantial decreases in the number of agricultural workers, both in the nation and in the South, in the years ahead. Indeed, the decline in the number of farmers in the South is likely to be quite large, partly because of the high proportion of low-income operators throughout the region who are unable to compete with larger farmers under present methods of production, and partly because known and prospective technological advances will increase the relative advantages of those farmers who are already the most efficient producers. The extent of the exodus from agriculture, however, will be greatly influenced by the level of employment in the total economy. If a national rate of unemployment below five per cent of the labor force prevails, the movement out of farming will be significantly greater than if the unemployment rates are higher.[8]

Future employment prospects in personal services and in the textile industry are less clear than in agriculture, but there is a strong presumption that the number of workers in both industries is likely to decline in the South in the next few years. The textile industry is modernizing its production processes at a rapid rate. For the nation as a whole, there was a modest increase in the number of textile mill workers between 1940 and 1950 of approximately 57,000, but a sharp 22 per cent decrease—from 1.2 million workers to 953,900—between 1950 and 1960. The direction of change in the South was the same as in the nation, but the decline in employment between 1950 and 1960 in the South was only 2 per cent. It is probable that laborsaving methods of textile manufacturing will have greater impact on southern

[8] C. E. Bishop, "Economic Aspects of Changes in the Farm Labor Force," *Labor Mobility and Population in Agriculture,* Iowa State University Press, Ames, 1961, pp. 36–49.

employment during the next decade than in the 1950's. The directions of change in employment in personal services are particularly difficult to foresee. In 1960 approximately 8.5 per cent of the South's total employment was in the personal services industry compared to the national average of 6 per cent. If national unemployment is kept low, the proportion of persons employed in personal services in the South is likely to move closer to that of the nation.

OUTLOOK FOR ABOVE-AVERAGE-GROWTH INDUSTRIES

The relatively high proportion of southern employment that is still in industries whose employment gains are below average, particularly agriculture, textiles, and personal services, indicates that the industry-mix of the South will continue to exert some downward pull on employment expansion. However, if those industries that have a past record of above average increases in employment continue to grow, they will exert a strong counter-acting force. Much depends, therefore, on the region's competitive potential in attracting an increasing proportion of above-average-growth industries. In the future, as in the past, these are most likely to be service-producing industries, and those types of machinery, metalworking, and chemical industries that demand high proportions of professionals, technicians, and highly skilled workers.

Far too little is known about the various factors that determine plant location decisions to provide a firm basis for evaluating the South's potential in sharing in the future national growth of these kinds of industries.[9] It appears, however, that the region ranks relatively high with respect to several characteristics that seem to be important: a favorable climate; plentiful supplies of water; ample land area for low-cost factories, shopping centers, and

---

[9] For an important study pertaining to this problem, see Victor R. Fuchs, *Changes in the Location of Manufacturing in the United States Since 1929,* Yale University Press, New Haven, 1962.

parking facilities; constantly improving transportation routes; competitive power costs; abundant supplies of several types of raw materials; and growing consumer markets in and around the region's expanding cities.

Another factor that will be of increasing importance as industrialization grows in the South is expanding industrial markets for intermediate products used in manufacturing. Many industrial firms buy a significant part of the materials that they utilize in their production processes from other manufacturers. The textile industry, for instance, is a heavy user of certain kinds of chemicals that it buys from the chemical industry, and food-processing firms commonly purchase their containers from factories that specialize in the production of glass jars, tin cans, or wood and paper boxes. Thus, there is a strong tendency for one type of manufacturing to attract other industrial enterprises either as suppliers or purchasers of intermediate and complementary products. The diversity and scale of industries now existing in the South will exert this magnetlike influence on numerous other industries in the future.

THE LABOR SUPPLY

There is also the important factor of the southern "labor climate." The prospective decline of employment in agriculture and probably also in textiles, sawmilling, and personal services and the natural rates of growth in the population of working age indicate that the South will have an ample supply of labor in the years ahead available for employment in manufacturing and service-producing industries. Many of the available laborers, however, will be unskilled and inexperienced for work in these kinds of industries.

In the past the South's ample supply of nonunion labor that could be hired at low wages has been a strong attraction for those industries that used large amounts of unskilled labor or labor that could be quickly trained to perform routine jobs. Notable examples of such industries have been textile and apparel manufacturing and firms engaged primarily in assembling various kinds of components into finished products. The South will probably continue to enlarge its complement of labor-intensive industries. However, technological changes, increases in minimum wages, the growth of nationwide collective bargaining, and external economies available to many kinds of plants that locate on the periphery of large cities instead of in small towns and rural areas are factors that tend to decrease the importance of large numbers of unskilled and nonunion workers as attractions to many kinds of manufacturing enterprises.

CONCLUSIONS

It is quite clear that if the South is to develop a diversified industrial and commercial economy that will fit the needs of the future, it will have to attract an increasing proportion of capital-intensive manufacturing industries. However, the rise in the importance of professional and technical occupations in manufacturing puts in an unfavorable competitive position those workers who are inadequately trained and undereducated. A major obstacle to the South's economic development is, thus, its inadequate educational system, particularly for Negroes. The employment outlook facing the southern Negro is a discouraging one, so long as he is undereducated, lacks industrial experience, and, in addition, is subjected to racial discrimination.

The only logical solution to the economic development problem facing the South lies in a highly stepped-up rate of development of the region's human resources through education and training, so that the productive capacities of all southern workers may be efficiently utilized. There is evidence that the South is making progress in this direction, and it is to the problems and developments in the fields of education and training that we turn attention in the next chapter.

Chapter 5

EDUCATION AND SOUTHERN ECONOMIC GROWTH

IF THE SOUTH is to increase its share of the nation's expanding employment and income, its businessmen, farmers, workers, scientists, teachers, and public officials must give serious attention to developing an environment that will be attractive to new capital, risk-taking entrepreneurs, and workers with special skills and talents. This means improving the quality of the South's labor force, developing new and improved technologies of production, and encouraging greater efficiency in the organization and operation of its factories, farms, mines, and commercial establishments. The southern educational establishment has an important role in all these areas of activity.

Within the past decade there have been several studies showing positive relationships between education and earnings of individual workers and also between education and the rate of growth of total real income in the United States.[1] They emphasize the importance of an educated population to the growth and functioning of the highly complex economic system that has developed

[1] Herman P. Miller: *Rich Man, Poor Man,* Thomas Y. Crowell, New York, 1964, Chap. 8; and "Annual and Lifetime Income in Relation to Education: 1939–59," *American Economic Review,* December 1960; Theodore W. Schultz, "Education and Economic Growth," *Sixtieth Yearbook of the National Society for the Study of Education,* Chicago, 1961, Table 17; Edward F. Denison, *The Sources of Economic Growth in the United States,* Committee for Economic Development, New York, 1962, Table 32, p. 266.

in the United States. As the South's economy becomes more like that of the older commercial and manufacturing areas of the nation, southern education will be of increasing economic significance.

The educational establishment can contribute to the economic development of the South in several ways. It can increase the productivity of workers by raising their general educational level and by training them to work with the ever-growing number of new and complex machines and production processes, thus improving their opportunities to move from one job to another as technological innovations destroy existing jobs and create new ones. It can foster scientific research to help find new uses for the region's natural resources, to bring new products onto the market, and to make cost-reducing technologies available to private industry. It can be a force in instilling in individuals in all walks of life a desire to be useful to society and to achieve a higher level of living. A well-educated labor force, the presence of scientific research laboratories, and communities with good school systems and progressive-minded citizens can be important magnets to investment capital in the form of new plants and businesses.

Future Occupational Needs

In appraising the extent to which the educational establishment can be expected to contribute significantly to preparing manpower for the South's future growth, we need an indication of the types of occupations that are most likely to be in demand. The principal changes that are occurring in the structure of the southern economy, discussed in the preceding chapters, and considerations of future employment opportunities in the South, analyzed in Chapter 8, clearly indicate the growing importance of occupations that require education and specialized training and skill, such as professional, technical, clerical, sales, service, and craftsmen positions. In contrast, opportunities for farmers, farm laborers, and other unskilled workers are declining. Numerous labor-market surveys in the South reveal the same types of shifts in the demand for labor.[2]

Briefly summarized, the following occupational shifts are projected for the South between 1960 and 1975: Employment of professional, technical, and kindred workers may rise by as much as 75 per cent; demand for managers, officials, and nonfarm proprietors will probably also increase significantly. The demand for clerical and kindred workers is expected to increase by 50 per cent or more. Significant increases are expected in jobs for craftsmen, foremen, and kindred workers; service workers; and operatives. The education and skill required in these occupational groups are also likely to rise. The number of farmers, farm managers, and farm laborers is likely to decline, and the number of nonfarm laborers to increase only modestly; there will probably be a decrease of more than 20 per cent in the combined employment of these groups. (For further discussion of these projected shifts, see Chapter 8.)

Status of Southern Education

This chapter is concerned mainly with examining the present status and future prospects of education in the South to determine whether the region's educational system is likely to be able to prepare southern manpower for the types of jobs that will be in greatest demand in the years ahead.[3] Such preparation involves

[2] *Manpower Survey,* Dallas Chamber of Commerce, July 1963, p. 4; *Manpower,* Virginia Employment Commission, Richmond, 1961, p. 10; *North Carolina Study of Technical and Skilled Manpower,* Bureau of Employment Security Research, Raleigh, 1962, pp. 31–33; *North Carolina Study of Manpower and Training Needs for the Medical and Health Service Occupations,* Bureau of Employment Security Research, Raleigh, 1963, p. 6; John L. Fulmer and Robert E. Green, *Georgia Skill Study,* Georgia Department of Labor, Employment Security Agency, Atlanta, March 15, 1963, pp. 139, 140, 143.

[3] Parts of the analysis are based on a field survey of southern education made by Dr. H. M. Hamlin during 1963 and 1964. Dr. Hamlin spent 8 to 10 days in each of the 13 southern states, visiting the state departments of education, 34 colleges and universities, and 26 area schools—junior and community colleges, vocational schools, technical institutes, and two-year branches of universities—interviewing 455 southern educational leaders, and attending meetings of educators.

much more than determining the nature of the jobs available and providing specialized training for these jobs. Sound basic education and effective counseling are prerequisites to successful job training. The whole educational system—from the kindergarten through the university and including adult education—is therefore involved.

In this brief review of the status of southern educational achievements and efforts we center attention on the educational attainment of the southern population, the organization and administration of public education in the South, the qualifications and supply of public school teachers, and the financial resources that the South is putting into its educational effort. Despite the paucity of statistical information on these topics, we believe that our review provides a necessary background for appraising the extent to which the southern educational system can reasonably be expected to contribute to the growth of future employment within the region.

EDUCATIONAL ATTAINMENT OF ADULT POPULATION

In general it appears that the southern population has less schooling than the nonsouthern (Table 5-1). For instance, the median years of school completed by both whites and Negroes 25 years old and over in 1960 was lower in most southern states than in the nation as a whole. The lower level of educational attainment in the South is even more marked when we compare in the South and non-South the proportions of the population 25 years old and over with less than 5 years of elementary schooling. In the South 10.5 per cent of the whites and 33.5 per cent of the Negroes in this age group had completed less than 5 years of elementary school in 1960, compared to 5.5 per cent of the whites and 14 per cent of the Negroes in the states outside the South. The high proportion of adult southerners with less than 5 years of elementary schooling is a serious impediment to the growth of employment in the South, since the most rapidly expanding job opportunities are in service-producing industries,

Table 5-1　**Years of Schooling of Population 25 Years Old and Over, by Color, United States, Non-South, and Southern States, 1960**

Region and State	Median years of school completed		Per cent who had completed—			
			Less than 5 years of elementary school		4 or more years of high school	
	White	Nonwhite	White	Nonwhite	White	Nonwhite
United States	10.9	8.1	6.7	23.5	43.1	21.3
Non-South	—	—	5.5	14.0	44.2	28.4
South	—	—	10.5	33.5	39.6	13.8
Alabama	10.2	6.5	9.4	36.0	36.5	12.8
Arkansas	9.5	6.5	10.6	36.4	33.2	9.7
Florida	11.6	7.0	5.3	31.7	47.4	14.5
Georgia	10.3	6.1	10.3	39.7	38.8	11.5
Kentucky	8.7	8.2	13.1	23.7	28.3	18.2
Louisiana	10.5	6.0	13.5	40.9	41.0	10.4
Mississippi	11.0	6.0	7.1	39.7	42.2	7.6
North Carolina	8.9	7.0	12.2	31.9	37.1	14.7
Oklahoma	10.7	8.6	7.6	20.0	42.0	23.9
South Carolina	10.3	5.9	11.6	41.3	38.9	9.9
Tennessee	9.0	7.5	12.5	27.8	33.2	14.2
Texas	10.8	8.1	12.0	23.6	42.0	20.8
Virginia	10.8	7.2	9.3	29.5	43.0	16.3

Source: U. S. Census of Population: 1960, Series PC(1)C, Table 47, U. S. Bureau of the Census, Washington.

where educational requirements for employment are constantly rising. This is a particularly serious handicap to Negroes.

A comparison of the proportions of southerners and non-southerners who had finished high school gives the same general picture of relatively low educational levels in the South. Approximately 40 per cent of the whites and 14 per cent of the Negroes in the South over 25 years of age had completed four or more years of high school in 1960, compared to 44 per cent of the whites and 28 per cent of the Negroes in the non-South. Here the gap between the proportions of Negro high school graduates is particularly striking.

QUALITY OF SCHOOLING

It is also probable that the quality of education southerners have received at any given grade level is somewhat lower than that in many nonsouthern states. This is suggested by several types of evidence.

One of these is the fact that only about 30 per cent of the high schools in 10 southern states were accredited by the Southern Association or the North Central Association in 1963.[4] Those responsible for accreditation gave the following as usual reasons for withholding accreditation: inadequate buildings, libraries, and teaching materials; narrow and unsuitable programs; over-sized classes; overloaded teachers; teachers who did not meet certification requirements; high staff turnover; poor recruitment of staff; low salaries; inadequate funds; Negro schools below standards for white schools; poor leadership; low morale. It is generally conceded that the elementary schools are more neglected than the high schools.

Another type of evidence is the high failure rate of young southern men on the mental tests of the Selective Service system. Selective Service registrants are of the age at which most men begin their occupational careers and are recent products of the educational system. The percentage of Selective Service registrants who have been disqualified from military duty because of low scores on mental tests has been consistently higher in the South than in other regions for many years (Figure 5-1). In 1942, for instance, the failure rate in the South was 25.8 per cent, compared with 13.8 per cent in the North and 4.8 per cent in the West. Twenty years later, after the Selective Service standards had been raised throughout the nation, the failure rate was 35.8 per cent in the South, 21.6 per cent in the North, and 12.5 per cent in the West. In 1964 the failure rates were: South, 42.4 per cent; North, 20.3 per cent; and West, 15.0 per cent. The rise in failure rates in 1964 resulted mainly from the fact that the Selective

[4] No data were available for Florida, Georgia, and Virginia.

Figure 5-1   **Per Cent of Selective Service Registrants Disqualified by Mental Tests, by Region, Selected Years, 1942–1964**

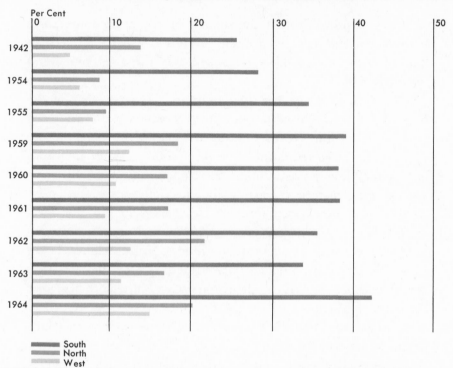

Per Cent

South
North
West

Sources: 1942 (data are for April 1942 through March 1943)—Spencer Bidwell King, Jr., *Selective Service in North Carolina in World War II*, University of North Carolina Press, Chapel Hill, 1949; other years—*Statistical Abstract of the United States*, U. S. Bureau of the Census, Washington, annual editions.

Service organization tested selectees who had finished the fifth grade or higher, whereas in several earlier years it had tested only those who had finished eight or more years of schooling. Nevertheless, the gap between the failure rate in the South and the rest of the nation was still very wide.

Negro and Rural White Schools

Census data for 1960 furnish other evidence of the low quality of schooling in the South, particularly among rural whites and Negroes, who are generally at the bottom of the educational ladder. They show that a higher proportion of youths between the ages of 8 and 17 were two or more grades below their expected grade levels in school in the South than in the North and West (Table 5-2). Moreover, the retardation rates were higher for Negroes in all age and residence categories in both the South and the non-South than for whites, but higher for southern Negroes than for Negroes in the North and West. A higher proportion of rural than of urban youth in all regions were below their expected grade level, but the gap was greatest for southern rural youth.

Though the quality of schooling in the South appears to be generally lower than in the non-South, many southern school

Table 5-2   **Per Cent of Males 8 to 17 Years Old Enrolled in School Who Were Retarded Two or More Grades in Their Age-Grade Progress,[a] by Type of Residence, Region, and Color, 1960**

Type of residence	South		North and West	
	White	Nonwhite	White	Nonwhite
8–13 Years Old				
Total	3.2	8.3	1.0	2.7
Urban	2.4	5.1	0.9	2.1
Rural nonfarm	4.1	10.3	1.3	7.1
Rural farm	4.3	15.0	0.9	8.5
14–15 Years Old				
Total	9.4	23.2	3.4	8.4
Urban	7.0	15.3	3.0	6.8
Rural nonfarm	12.7	28.1	4.6	18.3
Rural farm	10.6	35.8	3.0	24.3
16–17 Years Old				
Total	10.4	27.4	4.7	12.0
Urban	8.4	19.8	4.2	10.4
Rural nonfarm	13.4	31.9	6.2	22.7
Rural farm	11.4	40.5	4.1	22.9

Source: James G. Cowhig, *Age-Grade School Progress of Farm and Nonfarm Youth: 1960,* Economic Research Service, U. S. Department of Agriculture, Washington.

[a] The expected grades in school that were used as a basis for calculating per cents of retarded pupils in each age group were: 8 years, grades 2 to 3; 9 years, grades 3 to 4; 10 years, grades 4 to 5; 11 years, grades 5 to 6; 12 years, grades 6 to 7; 13 years, grades 7 to 8; 14 years, grades 8 to 9; 15 years, grades 9 to 10; 16 years, grades 10 to 11; 17 years, grades 11 to 12.

systems, particularly in urban centers, are apparently equal or superior to many nonsouthern systems. A statewide testing program conducted in Virginia in 1959–60 showed that on achievement tests white students in the county schools were 1 month below the national norm at the fourth grade level and 4 months below the national norm at the eighth grade level, while Negroes in the county schools were 19 months below the national norm in the fourth grade and 31 months below it in the eighth grade. Whites in the city schools were approximately at the national norm; Negroes in these schools were 12 months below it in the fourth grade and 25 months below it in the eighth grade. The average score of all white ninth grade pupils in the state on the nationally standardized School and College Ability Test (SCAT) was 6 points above the national norm, while that of their Negro counterparts was 31 points below the national norm. In the twelfth grade the gap had widened: the average score of the whites was 10 points above the national norm, that of the Negroes 37 points below.[5]

A study of Negro and white pupils in the public schools of Atlanta was made by the Educational Testing Service of Princeton, New Jersey, in the late 1950's. All of the fourth and seventh grade pupils in 66 white and 31 Negro elementary schools were tested in 1956 and retested in 1959. The Negro pupils tested considerably below their grade level in 1956, but in 3 years made gains in reading amounting to 2.5 years and gains in arithmetic amounting to 2.3 years. The white pupils tested above their grade level in 1956 and in 3 years made gains above those normally to be expected: 4.1 years in reading and 3.3 years in arithmetic. When twelfth grade pupils were tested, it was found that the white students were slightly above the national norm, while the Negro students were more than three grades below this norm.

The experience of the schools of the District of Columbia following integration is relevant to the South, since about 3,000

[5] *Summary, The Standardized Testing Program, Virginia Public Schools, 1959–60,* State Department of Public Instruction, Richmond, pp. 2–3.

pupils from the 13 southern states enter these schools each year. Initial tests, made in 1952–53, before integration, showed that the pupils in the sixth grade of the white schools were approximately at the national norm in reading ability while the pupils in the Negro schools were 1.6 years below the national norm. In 1958–59, the integrated sixth grade population was approximately at the national norm in the six tests administered. Gains in academic achievement were accompanied by decreases in delinquency rates and dropouts, both for white and nonwhite pupils.[6]

LACK OF BALANCED PROGRAMS

One of the significant characteristics of the southern educational establishment is the wide disparity in educational services for the various groups it serves. Generally the high schools of the South serve best those who plan to go on to college, and there is an increasing number of students in this category. In the fall of 1964 the number of students (295,743) who entered southern universities and colleges as beginning freshmen was 52 per cent of the number (565,456) who had graduated from high schools in the South during the 1963–64 school year, and ranged from 36 per cent in Alabama to 63 per cent in Mississippi.[7] Commonly, however, less than 10 per cent of those entering the first grade complete 4 years of college. Dropout rates reflect in part the unsuitability of many school programs to the pupils they are supposed to serve. Statewide studies in five southern states (Arkansas, Louisiana, North Carolina, Oklahoma, and South Carolina) have recently revealed average losses of 32 to 70 per cent

[6] See Carl F. Hansen, "The Scholastic Performance of Negro and White Pupils in the Integrated Public Schools of the District of Columbia," *Journal of Educational Sociology*, February 1963; and Frank H. Stallings, *Atlanta and Washington Racial Differences in Academic Achievement*, Southern Regional Council, Atlanta, 1960.

[7] Calculated from data in *Digest of Educational Statistics*, 1965 edition, U. S. Office of Education, Washington, pp. 52 and 70. The number of freshmen entering colleges and universities in the South is not strictly comparable to the number of students graduating from high schools within the region because of interstate migration of high school graduates who entered colleges.

of the pupils between the first and twelfth grades. In Kentucky the dropout rate from the ninth to the twelfth grades was 39 per cent; in New Orleans, 41 per cent. In Oklahoma the loss from the first grade through the first year of college was 73 per cent. An estimated average dropout of 60 per cent from the four-year colleges in the South reflects in part the unsuitability of many colleges to the students who enter them and in part the poor preparation of students for college-level study.

Twelve to fifteen per cent of the school population—the physically and mentally handicapped, those retarded in their school progress, speech defectives, and mentally disturbed—need attention in special classes unless they are to become social liabilities. However, no more than 3 per cent of the school population of the South was in such classes in 1963–64.

There is a large population of migrant workers whose homes are in the South but who are away from their homes for six months each year. Typically, the children of these workers are retarded in school. Few enter high school. Almost none continue beyond the ninth grade. But special schools conducted for children of migrant workers are rare.

Negroes, who constitute over 20 per cent of the population of the South, often require special attention to compensate for limited cultural backgrounds: their home and community environments are often not conducive to learning; most enter school without preschool experience; and jobs requiring extended schooling are usually not available to them.

The educational needs of adults are often as urgent as those of children and youth. Changes to which adults must adapt are coming rapidly in the South. A high percentage of southern adults received very little education when they were young and much of it was inferior in quality. Experience in many southern communities indicates that adults recognize their need for education, respond when opportunities for it are offered, and profit from it.

Many of the groups in need of special educational programs are poverty-stricken. Two fifths of the families in the United

States with less than $2,000 annual income lived in the South in 1960, although the South had only 27 per cent of the natioinal population. Lack of education perpetuates the poverty of many of these families, and at the same time their poverty is an impediment to their taking advantage of educational opportunities available to other segments of the population.

Properly balanced programs that give adequate attention to elementary, secondary, collegiate, graduate, and adult education are to be found in few, if any, southern states. The elementary schools, which are basic to all further education, are frequently neglected. The high schools, once attended by a select few, have not been adapted to the masses now attending them. The new area schools, described more fully later, are seeking their proper roles but are only here and there approaching their fulfillment. There are promising developments in some of the four-year colleges but, as a class, these are probably the least well adapted of all southern educational institutions to the new and enlarged clientele they are serving and to the changed conditions into which their graduates will go. Many lack programs for vocational specialization; others, having evolved from teachers' colleges, are still oriented to teacher training, although many of the students do not intend to become teachers.

VOCATIONAL COUNSELING AND TRAINING

The need for programs of vocational education is especially significant in the development of the southern economy and of southern human resources. Vocational education in the South has emphasized mainly agriculture and homemaking. Industrial and technical education are now receiving emphasis, but it is likely that two thirds of the people of the South are engaged in occupations for which specialized education is seldom, if ever, available.

There is also a lack of adequate occupational counseling in southern schools. Although the number of school counselors has increased rapidly since passage of the National Defense Act of

1958, which provided financial encouragement, counselors are typically preoccupied with duties other than occupational counseling, and a high percentage of school counselors are not well equipped for this specialized type of work.

In 1960–61 the enrollment in federally aided programs of vocational education per 1,000 of the population was higher than the national average in every southern state. In 1961–62 per capita expenditures on these programs of southern states from state and local funds was $1.95, compared with a national average of $1.30.[8] However, 76 per cent of the enrollment in federally aided vocational education classes in the local and area schools was in homemaking and agricultural education. Almost half of those enrolled in classes in vocational education were adults, but high school students received much more than half of the time of the teachers.

In the past the vocational education provided for Negroes was usually different and more limited than that provided for whites. Negroes received training in bricklaying, carpentry, shoe repairing, and auto mechanics, but many kinds of vocational education were denied them. With the passage of the Manpower Development and Training Act of 1962, the Vocational Education Act of 1963, the Economic Opportunity Act of 1964, and the Civil Rights Act of 1964, this situation is changing. Many new vocational training programs are being provided for both whites and Negroes that will improve their skills and enable them to meet the job requirements of the future.

Administration of Public Education

The South's approach to public education has been unique in the United States. The first state universities were established in the South. However, except in North Carolina, the South remained committed to private elementary and secondary education until after the Civil War. Most of the development of local public schools has been in this century.

---

[8] *Reports of State Boards for Vocational Education to U. S. Office of Education,* 1961 and 1962.

STATE CONTROL

In the East and the Middle West local school districts initially assumed most of the responsibility for elementary and secondary schools. The states came late, and often reluctantly, into the responsibilities they now have. In the South, on the other hand, the states took a prominent part from the beginning. Much of the control over education in the South is at the state level and in the hands of a white elite.

The constitutions and the basic laws of most of the southern states were established long before there were state systems of public education. Fundamental constitutional revisions have seldom occurred. Instead, it is common for a county legislative delegation to introduce "local and private legislation" regarding educational matters that elsewhere would be handled by a county or a municipality. The proportion of funds for educational purposes that comes from local sources is generally low, and control of funds commonly rests with county commissioners or supervisors rather than with local boards of education. One of the important consequences of the high degree of centralization of educational functions in state governments is that Negroes have had almost no influence in shaping educational policies.

The state departments of education are of great importance in the South because of their unusual influence and their many controls over the local schools. Serious difficulties have arisen in a few states in which the state superintendent, elected by popular vote, must work with an appointed or elected state board of education with views quite different from his. Generally, however, state departments of education are improving. Inspection and regulatory roles are diminishing as the state departments move toward research, in-service education of school personnel, and the better provision of information with respect to education.

LOCAL ORGANIZATION

Except in the border states a southern county usually constitutes a school district. Thus, the tiny districts common in the

East and Midwest have largely been avoided. Of 30,942 school districts in the United States in 1963, only 4,415 were in the South. Over half of these were in Texas and Oklahoma; Florida and Louisiana had only 67 each. Even in states with large districts, the attendance units are often small. Alabama had 600 schools in 1962–63 with fewer than 6 teachers. Louisiana had 648 elementary schools and 523 high schools in its 67 districts. When districts are small, attendance units tend to multiply; Oklahoma with its small districts had 1,060 public high schools, 309 of them with enrollments of 100 or less.

TEACHER QUALIFICATIONS

One of the serious problems with which the South is faced in improving educational programs, especially in elementary and secondary schools, is the short supply of qualified teachers. However, the academic training of public school teachers has improved greatly in recent years. For example, in some southern states all high school teachers now have bachelor's degrees, and in the other states most high school teachers have bachelor's degrees, as do more than 80 per cent (approximately the national average) of southern elementary school teachers. Nevertheless, many areas of the South are not getting the kinds of teachers they need. Many of the teachers are from culturally deprived homes, are narrow and provincial, and the teaching profession is not attractive to many top quality college students. Moreover, it is probable that southern teachers with bachelor's degrees, particularly from Negro colleges in the South, are not as well trained as teachers in other states with the same degree.

SHORTAGE OF TRAINED PERSONNEL

Generally, there is a shortage in the South both of classroom teachers and of special professional personnel, including administrators, business managers, supervisors, remedial teachers, counselors, curriculum specialists, visiting teachers, doctors, dentists, and nurses. There is a widely accepted standard of 50 instructional staff members for each 1,000 pupils, and in many of the best school systems in the United States the ratio is higher. In 1965–66 the average in the South was 45 to 1,000, while the national average was 48. The range in the southern states was from 39 in Alabama to 49 in Texas.[9] There is also a shortage of clerical help in southern schools, yet clerks are badly needed to assist the overloaded professional staff. North Carolina provides state aid for clerical services, but this is not a usual practice in the South. Southern schools do not attract a high proportion of men teachers; in every southern state in 1965–66 they were below the national average of 32 per cent and in South Carolina they were only 18 per cent.

The greatest shortages have been among white teachers. In fact, every southern state has commonly had a surplus of Negro teachers. In 1963–64 Negro teachers were apparently being used in predominantly white schools in only one county in one southern state. With the passage of the Civil Rights Act of 1964, this situation began to change, especially in some of the large urban centers, and we can expect an increasing number of schools to have partially integrated faculties in the future. Nevertheless, as the integration of schools takes place it is quite probable that many Negro school teachers will lose their jobs. Some of them are already moving to the North and West.

NEGRO TEACHERS

Teaching in segregated schools has been one of the best occupations open to southern Negroes. Hence, they have been more likely than whites to regard teaching as a life career, and have often been more willing than whites to invest in training beyond that required for certification. In several southern states a higher percentage of Negro than of white teachers hold master's degrees. Because Negro teachers have higher degrees and more

[9] *Estimates of School Statistics, 1965–66*, Research Report 1965-R17, National Education Association, Washington, December 1965, pp. 26 and 28.

experience in teaching, their average salaries are higher in some states than the average for white teachers. However, because of the traditionally low standards of many Negro schools in the South, from the primary grades through colleges and universities, the qualifications of Negroes preparing to enter the teaching profession may be below those of whites. This is indicated by scores on the National Teachers Examination, a test constructed by the Educational Testing Service, Princeton, New Jersey. From 1959 to 1962, 3,844 white and 2,115 Negro college seniors preparing for teaching were tested in South Carolina. The average scored by the Negro students was 163 below the white students' average score of 566, though about half of the Negro students placed in the top two groups of a four-group classification. In 1962 the examination was given to all college seniors in both North and South Carolina who were planning to teach. Students in 36 white and 15 Negro colleges were tested. The average scores in the white colleges ranged from 535 to 684, those in the Negro colleges from 413 to 488.

TEACHERS' SALARIES

One of the important reasons for the shortage of public school personnel in the South is the low salary scale for teachers. Although the salaries of instructional staff members in southern elementary and secondary schools rose by about 66 per cent between 1953 and 1963, compared to a rise of about 62 per cent in the nation as a whole, salaries are still much lower in the South than in the rest of the nation, since the percentage gains started from a much lower base in the South.

The average annual salary of classroom teachers in public schools in every one of the 13 southern states in 1965–66 was below the national average of $6,506 (Figure 5-2). Only in Florida, with an average of $6,435 was the difference minor. In the rest of the southern states the average teacher's salary ranged from $467 below the national level in Louisiana to $2,316 below in Mississippi. In six southern states it was more than $1,200 below the national average. Nationally, about 41 per cent of the

Figure 5-2 **Average Annual Salary of Classroom Teachers in Public Schools, United States and Southern States, 1965–66**

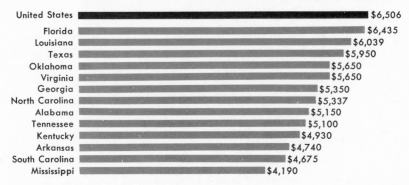

United States	$6,506
Florida	$6,435
Louisiana	$6,039
Texas	$5,950
Oklahoma	$5,650
Virginia	$5,650
Georgia	$5,350
North Carolina	$5,337
Alabama	$5,150
Tennessee	$5,100
Kentucky	$4,930
Arkansas	$4,740
South Carolina	$4,675
Mississippi	$4,190

Source: *Estimates of School Statistics, 1965–66,* National Education Association, Washington, Research Report, 1965-R17, Table 8.

classroom teachers in public schools were paid $6,500 or more in 1965–66 (Table 5-3). Among the southern states only Florida paid that much to as many as 33 per cent of its classroom teachers. In Mississippi only six tenths of one per cent of the

Table 5-3 **Percentage Distribution of Classroom Teachers in Public Schools by Salary Group, United States and Southern States, 1965–66**

State	Below $3,500	$3,500– $4,499	$4,500– $5,499	$5,500– $6,499	$6,500– $7,499	$7,500– $8,499	$8,500 and above
United States	0.9	8.6	22.7	26.5	19.5	11.9	9.9
Alabama	5.0	30.0	36.0	24.0	5.0	0.0	0.0
Arkansas	5.0	40.0	38.0	13.0	3.0	1.0	0.0
Florida	0.0	7.0	20.0	40.0	20.0	9.0	4.0
Georgia	0.0	37.0	34.0	18.0	9.0	2.0	0.0
Kentucky	3.0	41.0	42.0	12.0	2.0	0.0	0.0
Louisiana	1.0	17.0	27.0	35.0	16.5	2.0	1.5
Mississippi	10.0	63.2	23.3	2.9	0.6	0.0	0.0
North Carolina	0.2	15.0	48.0	28.0	8.0	0.8	0.0
Oklahoma	0.0	15.5	43.0	35.5	5.0	1.0	0.0
South Carolina	4.5	54.0	30.0	9.0	2.0	0.5	0.0
Tennessee	3.3	26.8	36.2	25.7	7.5	0.5	0.0
Texas	1.0	8.0	34.5	40.7	9.5	4.0	2.3
Virginia	0.5	20.0	37.0	23.0	10.0	5.0	4.5

Source: *Estimates of School Statistics, 1965–66,* National Education Association, Washington, Research Report 1965–R17, Table 8, p. 30.

public school teachers were paid $6,500 or more, and none were paid as much as $7,500. At the other end of the scale only 9.5 per cent of the teachers in the United States received an annual salary of less than $4,500 in 1965–66, but almost 75 per cent of the teachers in Mississippi received salaries below that level.[10]

FEW FRINGE BENEFITS

Low salaries are probably the single most important factor accounting for the perennial shortage of well-qualified teachers in practically all southern states. Closely related additional factors are a general lack of tenure systems, an almost total absence of provisions for sabbatical leaves of absence for study and travel, and few opportunities for teachers to attend professional meetings without loss of pay. Southern teachers have been largely deprived of the stimulation that comes from national meetings of educators, although probably as large a proportion of southern as of other teachers belong to national educational organizations. From 1954 to 1963 seven leading national educational organizations held only three national meetings in the region and these were in the "border states" of Florida and Kentucky. The principal reason that more national conventions were not held in the region is that facilities for racially integrated meetings could not be secured. Now that more facilities are integrated, more national conventions will probably be held in the South. However, significant improvements in the teacher supply situation will not only take time, but will also require substantial increases in expenditures for salaries and fringe benefits.

Financing Southern Public Schools

In the fiscal year ending June 30, 1965, the state and local governments of the South spent almost $5.3 billion on education,

[10] For an interesting analysis of teachers' salaries and segregation see Marshall R. Colberg, *Human Capital in Southern Development, 1939–1963*, University of North Carolina Press, Chapel Hill, 1965, Chap. 5.

excluding capital outlays. This was approximately 43.6 per cent of state and local expenditures for all purposes (Table 5-4). Four states—North Carolina, South Carolina, Texas, and Virginia— were well above the national average of 42.6 per cent spent for education, but the remaining nine were below the national average. Of the total current expenditures for education by state and local governments in the South, approximately $4.1 billion, or 77.2 per cent, was for elementary and secondary schools, compared with 80.8 per cent in the North and 76.3 per cent in the West. Obviously, the South ranks well both as to the propor-

Table 5-4   **Direct General Expenditures[a] of State and Local Governments for Fiscal Year Ending June 30, 1965, and Current Expenditures for School Year 1964–65**

Region and state	Total direct general expenditures (millions)	Current expenditures for education		Elementary & secondary	
		Amount (millions)	Per cent of total	Amount (millions)	Per cent of total
United States[b]	$55,686.9	$23,699.8	42.56	$18,691.8	33.57
North	30,193.5	12,555.3	41.58	10,143.4	33.59
West	13,338.1	5,847.9	43.84	4,461.1	33.45
South	12,155.3	5,296.6	43.57	4,087.3	33.63
Alabama	745.1	307.3	41.24	226.0	30.33
Arkansas	379.2	159.4	42.04	118.7	31.30
Florida	1,531.7	624.4	40.77	501.6	32.75
Georgia	991.9	418.5	42.19	335.9	33.86
Kentucky	693.6	288.3	41.57	208.8	30.10
Louisiana	1,017.6	382.4	37.58	287.4	28.24
Mississippi	485.4	203.7	41.97	145.5	29.98
North Carolina	1,006.6	488.5	48.53	373.1	37.07
Oklahoma	720.8	292.2	40.54	201.2	27.91
South Carolina	470.5	225.7	47.97	176.6	37.53
Tennessee	760.3	314.5	41.37	244.9	32.21
Texas	2,376.2	1,128.3	47.48	898.3	37.80
Virginia	976.4	463.4	47.46	369.3	37.82

Source: *Governmental Finances in 1964–65*, U. S. Bureau of the Census, Washington, June 1966, pp. 34–38.

[a] Excludes capital outlays.

[b] Excludes Alaska, Hawaii, and the District of Columbia.

tion of state and local government expenditures for educational purposes and the proportion of educational funds used for public elementary and secondary schools.

EXPENDITURE-INCOME RELATIONSHIPS

Personal income is the best available indicator of the ability of residents of the various states to support the activities of state and local governments. Appendix Table 5-1, showing comparative regional expenditures for education in relation to income in 1964–65, reveals that a higher proportion of personal income was being used for educational purposes in the South than in the nation as a whole. The South, with 21.7 per cent of the nation's personal income, made 22.3 per cent of the national expenditures for public education; the North, with almost 58 per cent of the nation's personal income, accounted for only 53.0 per cent of the nation's current expenditures for public education.[11] The West, with slightly more than 20 per cent of the income, made 25 per cent of the nation's current expenditures on education.

In relation to their ability to pay, as measured by personal income, the people of the southern states made a greater effort to support education than the citizens of several of the wealthier states of the North (Figure 5-3). There were, however, great variations among the states in the proportion of income spent by state and local governments for education. In Mississippi, for instance, the state with the lowest per capita income in 1964, about $60 of each $1,000 of personal income was used for education. In contrast, in New York and Connecticut, states with much higher per capita incomes, the comparable figures were $44 and $36, respectively, and in Florida, the southern state with the highest per capita income, the figure was slightly over $48. (See Appendix Table 5-1.)

[11] A part of the difference between the North and the South is explained by the greater prevalence of private schools in the North. In the South about 90 per cent of the pupils in elementary and secondary schools are in public schools, compared to approximately 80 per cent in the North.

Figure 5-3 **State and Local Current Expenditures for Elementary and Secondary Education Per $1,000 of Personal Income, and Per Pupil in Average Daily Attendance, by State, 1964–65**

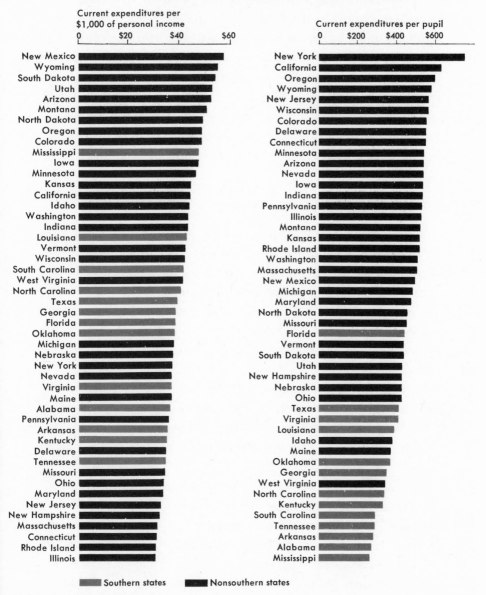

Source: Appendix Table 5-1.

Even though a higher proportion of personal income is spent for education in the South than in many of the more wealthy states of the nation, expenditures per pupil in elementary and secondary schools in the South are generally lower than in non-southern states, as shown in Figure 5-3. The extreme contrast in these two measures of expenditures within the South is Mississippi, which in 1964–65 ranked tenth among the states with respect to the proportion of personal income spent for elementary and secondary education but forty-eighth among the states with respect to expenditures per pupil in average daily attendance in public elementary and secondary schools.

LOW INCOME, LARGE SCHOOL-AGE POPULATION

This contrast points up two serious problems the South faces in attempting to improve its educational system: the low income of the people of the region, and the high proportion of the nation's school-age population residing in the South. As a result of the combination of these two factors, available funds per pupil are low, even though a relatively high proportion of the region's income is spent for public education. (See Appendix Tables 5-1 and 5-2.)

In 1964 the personal income of the South was 21.7 per cent of that for the nation, but 28.9 per cent of the nation's children between 5 and 17 years of age resided in the South. The average current expenditure per pupil attending elementary and secondary schools was $362 in 1964–65.

The personal income of the North was 58 per cent of that for the nation in 1964, but only 52.2 per cent of the nation's children between 5 and 17 years of age resided in the North. The average current expenditure per pupil in elementary and secondary schools was $553 in 1964–65.

The personal income of the West was 20 per cent of that for the nation in 1964, but only 18.9 per cent of the nation's children between 5 and 17 years of age resided in the West. The average current expenditure per pupil in elementary and secondary schools was $565 in 1964–65.

To put the same point in a different manner: total personal income per child of school age in the South was $7,466 in 1964; in the North it was $11,040; and in the West it was $10,662.

It is obvious that the South, with its low income per child of school age plus its high proportion of adults with less than five years of elementary schooling, is faced with a tremendous educational burden in relation to its income, if its labor force of the next few years is to meet the needs of the most rapidly growing industries—industries which require employees with relatively high levels of education.

On the other hand, it must be recognized that there are great differences between communities within the South in both their willingness and ability to pay for education. Furthermore, many governmental units in the South could increase their expenditures for education without burdening their citizens with heavier tax loads than are being borne in many areas of the country.

STATE VERSUS LOCAL FINANCING

As pointed out earlier, state governments in the South have much greater control over elementary and secondary schools than state governments in other regions. This is reflected in school financing. Thus, there is a conspicuous difference between the South and the rest of the country in the proportions of funds for public schools that come from state and from local sources. In 1964–65, for example, about 38 per cent of the funds received by public schools in the South came from local sources, and 56 per cent from state governments. In the non-South the corresponding percentages were 62 and 35 (Appendix Table 5-3). Local funds were as much as half the receipts of the public schools in only two southern states, Oklahoma and Virginia; and in Alabama, Georgia, Louisiana, North Carolina, and South Carolina local funds represented less than 30 per cent of public school receipts.

The significance of the high proportion of public school costs borne by the state, and the consequent control of local schools by state government officials, is difficult to evaluate. It probably has a tendency to lower local interest, initiative, and feeling of responsibility. On the other hand, every southern state has some sort of "foundation program" that either provides in each school district a minimum educational program at state expense or gives state assistance to the districts in providing programs that the state considers minimal.

Despite the limitations of some of the state "foundation programs," on the whole they have had a tremendous influence in improving the public schools of the South and in assuring state-wide minimal opportunities for education. To finance them the states have raised funds that would not otherwise have been raised, and tax burdens have been equalized to some extent. Moreover, in addition to the minimal "foundation programs," the states commonly finance a great variety of special aids to education to stimulate the enrichment of local school programs. It is quite probable that as a result of the high degree of state control over local schools, the South is in a better position to take advantage of the new federal funds provided for education and training in recent years than are some states with a high degree of local autonomy in their school systems.

UNTAPPED SOURCES OF FUNDS FOR EDUCATION

Within most of the state systems there is ample opportunity for local communities to supplement funds provided by the state. Many of the more prosperous and progressive communities are doing this.

If local funds for schools are to be increased, the property tax is likely to be a major source of additional revenue. John K. Folger, who made a survey of educational needs in the South in 1962, found that, nationally, property tax revenue is about 1.8 per cent of the estimated market value of real property. He concluded that "If every southern state collected 1.8 per cent of the current market value in property taxes . . . the region would have about a billion dollars more tax revenue from this one source each year." [12] If the entire billion-dollar increase were added to the 1964–65 current expenditures for education, it would have been an increase of slightly less than 19 per cent.

Most state governments, in contrast to local taxing units, have various untapped sources of tax revenue for educational purposes. The sales tax is heavily exploited, but seven of the southern states were deriving less than 10 per cent of state and local revenues from income taxes in 1960. In some of the states where forests and forest products have recently become important, forest land is taxed at a very low level and there is no tax on the products removed from the forests. North Carolina, the leading producer of cigarettes, has no cigarette tax. Clearly, there are various ways in which more money could be raised for educational purposes in the South if the people of the region demand better schools.

Had state and local government expenditures for educational purposes in all of the southern states been as high a proportion of personal income as they were in Mississippi in 1964, total expenditures for education in the South would have been about 19 per cent higher—about $6.3 billion, instead of almost $5.3 billion; had they been as high a proportion of personal income as they were in New Mexico—which ranked highest of all the states in this respect—they would have been more than $8.6 billion, or 62 per cent higher. Although large and increasing amounts of federal funds for education are becoming available, most southern states will also have to increase educational expenditures from state and local sources, if they are to bring the educational status of the southern population to the level of that in other regions—a task certainly important enough to warrant increased state and local government expenditures. At the same

[12] "Public School Revenues in the Southeast," *Educational Needs for the Economic Development of the South* (proceedings of a conference sponsored by the Agricultural Policy Institute, North Carolina State College in cooperation with the Southern Regional Education Board, June 1962), Agricultural Policy Institute, Raleigh, Series 7, p. 137.

time, the southern states will need to make full and effective use of all available federal funds.

INCREASED FEDERAL FUNDS

High proportions of the increased federal funds for education are being allocated among the states in ways favorable to areas with large numbers of low-income families. Consequently, the South will benefit much more than other regions, if southern school officials take the necessary steps to fully utilize the available federal funds. The most important qualifying action that southern school boards must take is the integration of pupils and faculties of heretofore all-white schools. As indicated later in this chapter, progress is being made in this direction, but much remains to be done. It is highly unlikely that any significant proportion of southern schools will refuse to integrate, and thus forgo the large amounts of federal funds that are becoming available. It will, nevertheless, probably be several years before a majority of Negro children are attending fully integrated schools in the South.

Estimates by the National Education Association of the federal funds received by public elementary and secondary schools in recent years are shown in Table 5-5. In the school year 1961–62 the public schools of the South received approximately $171 million from the Federal Government. By 1965–66, receipts from the Federal Government had increased to approximately $614 million—a rise of almost 260 per cent. The federal funds were more than 11 per cent of the revenue receipts in 1965–66, compared to 4.6 per cent in 1961–62.[13]

Most of the increases in federal funds that have recently

[13] The term "revenue receipts," as defined by the National Education Association, includes "all appropriations from general funds of federal, state, county, and local governments, receipts from taxes levied for school purposes, income from permanent school funds and endowments, income from leases of school lands, interest on bank deposits, tuition, gifts, etc." These commonly represent about 99 per cent of the total receipts of public elementary and secondary schools. The estimates of the federal funds expended by the public schools in 1965–66 were based on the assumption that in most of the states 50 to 75 per cent of the federal funds allotted under the Elementary and Secondary Education Act of 1965 would be utilized by the public schools. (See *Estimates of School Statistics, 1965–66,* p. 17.)

become available for elementary and secondary education were authorized by the Elementary and Secondary Education Act of 1965, the Vocational Education Act of 1963, and the National Defense Education Act of 1958. Moreover, it is the funds from these acts that are most likely to have direct and immediate effects on the public schools of the South, and funds allotted by the Federal Government are a better indicator than the estimated expenditures shown in Table 5-5 of the importance of the new federal sources of revenue to the public schools. The funds allotted for current expenditures of elementary and secondary schools by these three acts in the fiscal year ending June 30, 1966 were (in millions): United States, $1,491.2; North, $683.6; West, $234.8; and South, $572.8.[14] The significance of these federal funds to the South is indicated by the percentage increases they represent over the total revenues available to public elementary and secondary schools in 1961–62: United States, 8.0; North, 6.8; West, 5.5; and South, 13.4.[15]

In addition to the increased federal funds resulting from the recent acts aimed at improving elementary and secondary schools, there are substantially increased funds available for institutions of higher learning and for numerous training programs authorized by the Higher Education Act, the Manpower Development and Training Act, and the Economic Opportunity Act. Never have greater resources been available for the training and education of the nation's manpower than in the first half of the 1960's; rarely has public opinion so fully supported educational activities; and never has the South had such opportunities for improving the education, skills, and creativity of its people.

The Changing Scene in Southern Education

The southern educational situation is far from static. Indeed, it is one of the most dynamic elements in the great transition

14 Calculated from U. S. Office of Education, Washington: *Milestone in Education*, Circular Number 761, 1964; and *American Education*, November 1965.

15 Calculated from data in *Estimates of School Statistics, 1962–63*, Research Report 1962-R13, National Education Association, Washington.

Table 5-5   Estimated Revenue from Federal Government for Public Elementary and Secondary Schools, by Region and State, Selected School Years, 1960's

Region and state	Federal funds in selected school years Amount (thousands)				Percentage change, 1961–62 to —		Federal funds as per cent of revenue from all sources			
	1961–62	1963–64	1964–65	1965–66	1964–65	1965–66	1961–62	1963–64	1964–65	1965–66
United States[a]	$615,198	$723,352	$794,471	$1,869,320	29.1	203.9	3.6	3.6	3.7	7.6
North	260,724	285,699	328,972	840,227	26.2	222.3	2.8	2.6	2.7	6.3
West	183,421	210,091	210,690	415,533	14.9	126.5	4.6	4.5	4.2	7.5
South	171,053	227,562	254,809	613,560	49.0	258.7	4.6	5.2	5.4	11.2
Alabama	11,603	18,500	19,000	49,000	63.8	322.3	6.0	7.8	7.2	15.4
Arkansas	9,855	12,264	12,941	34,521	31.3	250.3	8.7	9.3	9.4	20.1
Florida	14,084	24,713	32,424	61,850	130.2	339.2	3.5	4.8	5.6	9.4
Georgia	13,429	16,894	22,358	52,000	66.5	287.2	4.8	5.1	6.1	12.0
Kentucky	7,000	14,500	15,000	40,000	114.3	471.4	3.5	6.5	6.3	14.2
Louisiana	5,779	8,596	11,871	24,119	105.4	317.4	2.0	2.6	3.3	6.0
Mississippi	7,618	12,742	16,307	41,500	114.1	444.8	5.7	8.0	9.3	20.0
North Carolina	17,000	14,000	18,298	57,000	1.8	235.3	4.9	3.6	4.6	11.8
Oklahoma	16,500	17,500	16,565	37,270	.4	125.9	8.5	8.1	7.3	14.1
South Carolina	9,169	16,398	12,033	42,000	31.2	358.1	5.9	8.2	6.0	17.3
Tennessee	9,500	10,700	13,300	40,300	40.0	324.2	4.3	4.0	4.7	11.7
Texas	29,000	34,000	36,000	86,000	24.1	196.6	3.3	3.5	3.4	7.0
Virginia	20,516	26,755	28,712	48,000	39.9	134.0	7.0	7.6	7.3	11.1
North	260,724	285,699	328,972	840,227	26.2	222.3	2.8	2.6	2.7	6.3
Connecticut	6,127	8,900	9,000	19,800	46.9	223.2	2.3	3.0	2.6	5.1
Delaware	1,600	2,200	2,250	4,500	40.6	181.3	3.1	3.3	3.2	5.7
Illinois	25,763	24,246	26,670	81,000	3.5	214.4	2.8	2.1	2.1	5.7
Indiana	16,323	16,571	21,602	38,754	32.3	137.4	3.7	3.1	3.6	5.7
Iowa	4,900	7,250	7,800	15,500	59.2	216.3	2.0	2.5	2.6	4.7
Maine	4,000	5,200	5,325	11,300	33.1	182.5	5.5	6.0	5.9	10.8

Maryland	15,700	18,279	19,389	36,139	23.5	130.2	5.6	5.2	4.5	7.3
Massachusetts	19,000	21,000	22,000	52,000	15.8	173.7	5.0	4.6	4.5	9.6
Michigan	22,305	25,000	26,400	70,000	18.4	213.8	2.6	2.7	2.6	6.1
Minnesota	10,500	12,500	10,000	35,000	−4.8	233.3	2.7	2.8	2.0	6.5
Missouri	8,359	11,875	17,017	40,888	103.6	389.1	2.5	3.1	4.0	8.5
New Hampshire	2,249	2,585	2,692	4,200	19.7	86.7	5.1	4.7	4.4	6.1
New Jersey	15,000	17,000	20,000	40,000	33.3	166.7	2.4	2.3	2.5	4.5
New York	34,000	36,000	55,000	175,000	61.8	414.7	1.8	1.5	2.2	6.0
Ohio	25,500	23,444	25,000	61,000	−2.0	139.2	2.4	2.3	2.3	5.0
Pennsylvania	30,000	32,150	34,000	98,000	13.3	226.7	3.0	2.9	2.8	7.1
Rhode Island	2,591	3,542	2,800	6,200	8.1	139.3	4.1	5.0	3.8	7.6
Vermont	900	1,210	1,267	3,946	40.8	338.4	2.9	3.3	3.0	8.3
West Virginia	5,907	4,747	6,169	12,000	4.4	103.1	4.5	3.3	4.2	7.2
Wisconsin	10,000	12,000	14,591	35,000	45.9	250.0	2.9	2.8	3.4	7.4
West	183,421	210,091	210,690	415,533	14.9	126.5	4.6	4.5	4.2	7.5
Arizona	10,895	18,000	9,341	25,000	−14.3	129.5	7.4	11.2	5.7	13.3
California	80,000	90,000	95,000	200,000	18.8	150.0	3.6	3.5	3.3	6.4
Colorado	14,200	15,700	17,000	25,000	19.7	76.1	7.0	6.5	6.6	8.9
Idaho	2,299	4,329	4,700	6,000	104.4	161.0	4.1	6.7	6.9	7.5
Kansas	9,292	10,634	12,096	25,000	30.2	169.0	4.1	4.2	4.5	8.3
Montana	4,000	4,500	4,550	8,600	13.8	115.0	5.3	5.1	4.8	8.0
Nebraska	5,000	7,300	7,900	11,000	58.0	120.0	4.4	5.5	5.4	7.2
Nevada	2,700	3,556	3,488	4,500	29.2	66.7	7.9	7.6	6.8	8.2
New Mexico	14,000	12,058	10,097	20,500	−27.9	46.4	14.3	9.3	7.6	13.6
North Dakota	3,500	3,000	3,000	6,000	−14.3	71.4	5.8	4.8	4.3	7.6
Oregon	9,200	10,500	12,000	23,200	30.4	152.2	4.3	4.2	4.5	7.9
South Dakota	5,400	6,800	7,000	15,000	29.6	177.8	9.0	9.8	9.3	17.0
Utah	5,200	5,997	5,552	13,833	6.8	166.0	4.8	4.6	4.1	9.0
Washington	16,700	16,200	17,500	28,000	4.8	67.7	4.9	4.1	4.2	8.1
Wyoming	1,035	1,517	1,466	3,900	41.6	276.8	2.7	3.4	2.8	6.3

Sources: National Education Association, Washington: *Estimates of School Statistics, 1962–63*, Research Report 1962-R13, p. 28, *Estimates of School Statistics, 1964–65*, Research Report 1964-R17, p. 28, *Estimates of School Statistics, 1965–66*, Research Report 1965-R17, pp. 31 and 32.

a Excludes Alaska, Hawaii, and the District of Columbia.

through which the region is passing. Educational standards, programs, and facilities have undergone great and rapid changes, and more are in the offing. Some changes that have occurred since 1940 are shown in Table 5-6. School terms have been lengthened, attendance at school has become more regular, the number of instructional staff members per 1,000 pupils in public schools has increased, salaries of staff members have gone up

Table 5-6   **Some Measures of Educational Progress in the South, 1940 to 1960's**

		Latest data available		
Educational standards	South, 1940	South	United States	Year
Average length of public school term (days)	164.8	177.5	179.0	1964
Average daily attendance in public schools as per cent of enrollment	83.1	89.6	89.8	1964
Instructional staff members per 1,000 pupils in public schools	31.8	45.1	47.6	1966
Average salary of instructional staff members	$826[a]	$5,517	$6,792	1966
Expenditures per pupil in average daily attendance in public schools				
Current expenses	$45.61[a]	$362	$498	1965
Capital outlay	$4.77	$78.61	$91.58	1965
Per cent of population 25 years old and over with less than 5 years of elementary schooling				
White	16.1	10.5	6.7	1960
Nonwhite	49.9	33.5	23.5	1960
Per cent of population 25 years old and over with 4 or more years of high school				
White	24.2	39.6	43.1	1960
Nonwhite	4.9	13.8	21.3	1960
Enrollment in colleges, universities, and professional schools	334,947	1,130,797	5,280,020	1965

Sources: Table 5-1 and Appendix Tables 5-1 and 5-2; *Digest of Educational Statistics, 1965* edition, U. S. Office of Education, Washington, p. 72.

[a] Median of state averages.

significantly, current expenditures per pupil in public schools in 1964–65 were almost 8 times as high as in 1940 and capital outlay per pupil was more than 16 times as high. It is particularly significant that the proportion of the population over 25 years old who had less than 5 years of schooling was significantly reduced between 1940 and 1960, while the proportion of those who had completed 4 or more years of high school was greatly increased. This is a picture of growth, of progress, and of strong public support for education.

However, as the two middle columns of Table 5-6 show, there are still significant gaps between southern education and U. S. education as a whole, particularly in the salaries of teachers in elementary and secondary schools, in total expenditures per pupil in the public schools, and in the proportion of the adult population with less than 5 years of elementary schooling.

ATTITUDES OF POLITICAL LEADERS

An extremely important change in the southern educational situation in recent years has occurred in the political arena. It has been succinctly described by James L. Miller, Jr., Associate Director for Research, of the Southern Regional Education Board: [16]

Southern political leaders have "discovered" education. Many of them have found in education a political program which appeals to nearly all of the diverse and competing segments of the electorate —urban and rural, rich and poor, white and Negro. Educational improvement appeals to those whose primary interest is in economic development because economic development can take place most easily when it is undergirded by an effective educational system. It appeals to the growing urban electorate because it satisfies one of its most pressing needs and helps to make southern cities competitive with others in the nation. It also appeals to the more

[16] "Political Responses to the South's Changing Economy," a paper presented at a conference on Manpower Requirements and Human Resource Adjustments, sponsored by the Agricultural Policy Institute of North Carolina State University, in cooperation with North Carolina A. and T. College, held at Charlotte, December 9–11, 1964. Agricultural Policy Institute, Series 15, pp. 61–62.

traditional groups in the electorate—the rural and small town voters—because it has become apparent to them also that education is essential if they and their children are to claim a slice of the good life which they see developing all around them.

And as if these factors weren't enough to make every governor conscious of education, there also has been the population explosion typified by the wave of "war babies"—the children born immediately after World War II who have come upon the schools like a tidal wave. . . .

This burden of educational support has fallen more and more heavily upon state governments. Upon assuming office most governors find that they have no choice but to underwrite a sizable increase in state appropriations for education. . . . The results have been especially beneficial in a number of southern states.

AREA SCHOOLS

One of the major ways in which this political interest in the southern educational system is being expressed is through the establishment of a new type of educational institution, which we have designated "area schools." Included in the "area school" designation are junior and community colleges, specialized vocational schools and technical institutes, and two-year branches of universities. Some of the area schools are limited institutions, others are comprehensive. The kind of institution envisioned by the leaders in the area school movement is one with four types of programs: two years of college-parallel courses; general education below college level for full-time students; specialized vocational and technical training; and adult education in a variety of fields. These institutions at their best are centers of continuing education, able to contribute—at some time during his life—to almost every individual in the areas served.

Most of the area schools are for commuters within a 50 to 60 mile radius, but dormitories are available in some that serve a large area or offer a distinctive program that is not provided by nearby schools. Many of the area schools emphasize vocational training, often as part-time evening courses for adults. Many have two-year courses for training high school graduates as technicians. Thus, the rapidly developing area schools are beginning to provide badly needed types of vocational education not hitherto available. Their usefulness is attested by the successful job placement of almost all of their graduates. Because of the shortage of skilled workers, many students in training are employed before their training can be completed. Many area schools are being used for short-term, specialized training courses financed by funds from the Manpower Development and Training Act of 1962 and the Economic Opportunity Act of 1964. These schools, though created primarily to serve young people, often have part-time enrollments of adults two or three times their enrollments of full time young students. There were 435 of these area schools in operation or authorized in the South in 1963–64 (Table 5-7).

Table 5-7   **Public and Private Area Schools Operating or Authorized in the South, 1963–64**

State	Total	Branches of public universities in operation	Public junior colleges in operation	Private junior colleges in operation	Public junior colleges authorized	Public vocational-technical schools in operation	Public vocational-technical schools authorized
Total	435	23	111	99	21	113	68
Alabama	39	0	0	6	5	13	15
Arkansas	16	1	1	4	0	2	8
Florida	34	0	28	4	1	1	0
Georgia	46	0ᵃ	9ᵃ	10	0	10	17
Kentucky	29	5	1	9	0	14	0
Louisiana	33	0	0	1	0	32	0
Mississippi	27	0	17	10	0	0	0
North Carolina	56	0	5	14	15	21	1
Oklahoma	23	7	11	4	0	0	1
South Carolina	23	6	0	7	0	7	3
Tennessee	34	0	0	7	0	4	23
Texas	46	0	33	13	0	0	0
Virginia	29	4	6	10	0	9	0

Source: Field survey by H. M. Hamlin. See footnote 3, this chapter.
ᵃ The public junior colleges in Georgia are in the University of Georgia system, but are not listed as branches.

The most rapid rate of growth in enrollment in the future is likely to be in the area schools, and in programs of adult education conducted by the local public schools, the area schools, and the colleges and universities. The area schools may eventually provide some full-time schooling for as many as two-thirds of the high school graduates and part-time schooling for a very high proportion of the adult population. No one knows how soon they will be capable of responsibilities of this order, but the area schools of the South are developing rapidly. For some time they have been growing at a faster rate than any other part of the American educational system, and the tendency has been to underestimate rather than to overestimate their potentialities. They hold particular promise for adult education, the demand for which can be expected to increase significantly in the decade ahead, not only in the South, but throughout the country.[17]

COLLEGES AND UNIVERSITIES

Another way in which education in the South is making substantial progress is in the expansion in size and number of institutions of higher learning. Furthermore, some of them are showing definite improvements in the quality of their faculties and programs of instruction. For instance, of the 34 universities in the 13 southern states that granted Ph.D. degrees in 1962, half had started awarding this degree since 1945.[18]

> The most critical areas of higher education necessary to spur economic growth are the scientific and technological fields, and these are the areas where the South traditionally has been weakest. . . . present strengths are greatest in the Humanities and the

[17] For an informative discussion of future prospects for adult education see John W. C. Johnstone, *Volunteers for Learning,* National Opinion Research Center, University of Chicago, 1964.

[18] Allan M. Cartter (Vice President of the American Council on Education and Director of its Commission on Plans and Objectives for Higher Education), "Qualitative Aspects of Southern Education," a paper presented at a conference on Education and Human Resources, sponsored by The Interuniversity Committee for Economic Research on the South, Washington, October 9–10, 1964.

Social Sciences. The South's imbalance is the reverse of that existing in other regions and special efforts will be required to bolster scientific and engineering education.

Rapid increases in college enrollments have caused serious staffing problems everywhere. In 1965 only 27.2 per cent of the new college teachers in the United States held doctor's degrees; in 1954 the percentage had been 31.4. Thirteen per cent of the new college teachers in 1965 did not even have master's degrees.[19]

The South is at a decided disadvantage in recruiting top-flight college teachers. Only about an eighth of the doctor's degrees given in the United States are given by southern institutions, and many graduates of northern universities are reluctant to go to the South. Dr. Russell Middleton of Florida State University has investigated in some depth the attitudes of doctoral candidates toward employment in southern colleges and universities. Eighteen disadvantages of working in the South were listed by graduate students in nonsouthern universities. The six most commonly named, in order, were: racial prejudice, undesirable community influences on the character and ideals of growing children (apparently linked to the first reason), lack of academic freedom, low academic standards, poor research facilities, and public schools of poor quality.[20] However valid these attitudes may be, they are deterrents in the competition for the best talent in the nation, and will continue to be handicaps to the development of institutions of higher learning in the South for many years.

THE PACE OF SCHOOL DESEGREGATION

One of the most important developments in southern education is the mounting pressure to desegregate the public schools. Many southern whites have long been unwilling to take effective and

---

[19] *Teacher Supply and Demand in Universities, Colleges, and Junior Colleges, 1963–64 and 1964–65*, National Education Association Research Report, 1965-R4, Washington, April 1965, p. 13.

[20] "Racial Problems and the Recruitment of Academic Staff at Southern Colleges and Universities," *American Sociological Review*, December 1961, pp. 960–970.

Table 5-8   **Status of Desegregation in Southern Public School Districts, by State, 1959–60, December 1964, and November 1965**

| | Negroes in school | | | | | | School districts | | | | | |
| | 1959–60 | | December 1964 | | November 1965 | | 1959–60 | | Dec. 1964 | | November 1965 | |
State	Total	In deseg-regated schools	Total	In deseg-regated schools	Total	In deseg-regated schools	Total	Deseg-regated	Total	Deseg-regated	Total	Deseg-regated
South	2,717,663	30,791	3,043,317	117,720	3,119,610	247,158	4,699	469	4,242	1,150	4,134	3,990
Alabama	271,134	0	293,426	101	295,848	1,250	113	0	118	9	119	105
Arkansas	106,731	98	114,651	931	111,952	4,900	422	9	411	24	410	400
Florida	201,091	512	247,475	6,612	256,063	25,000	67	1	67	22	67	67
Georgia	318,405	0	334,126	1,337	355,950	9,465	198	0	196	12	197	192
Kentucky	41,938	16,329	55,215	37,585	59,835	46,891	212	129	204	165	204	204
Louisiana	271,021	0	313,314	3,581	318,651	2,187	67	0	67	3	67	33
Mississippi	278,640	0	279,106	57	296,834	1,750	151	0	150	4	149	118
North Carolina	302,060	34	349,282	4,963	349,282	18,000	174	7	170	86	169	165
Oklahoma	39,405	10,246	45,000	14,000	45,750	17,500	1,323	187	1,090	211	1,048	1,044
South Carolina	257,935	0	260,667	265	263,983	3,864	108	0	108	18	107	86
Tennessee	146,700	169	173,673	9,289	176,541	28,801	154	4	152	65	151	149
Texas	279,374	3,300	344,312	27,000	349,192	60,000	1,581	126	1,379	450	1,310	1,303
Virginia	203,229	103	233,070	12,000	239,729	27,550	129	6	130	81	136	124

Source: *Statistical Summary of School Segregation-Desegregation in the Southern and Border States*, Southern Education Reporting Service, Nashville, 15th revision, December 1965.

realistic steps to improve educational and training programs and facilities for Negroes. This is one of the most serious problems the South faces today. As discussed earlier in this chapter, a high proportion of the Negro population has an extremely low level of education; most Negro schools and colleges are poorly staffed and equipped, and their standards for both faculty and students are commonly lower than the standards of schools for whites.

As a result of Supreme Court decisions, the passage of the Civil Rights Act of 1964, and several of the newer acts providing federal funds for education and training, the South is under strong pressure to desegregate its whole educational and training establishment. Progress in this direction is slowly being made. The 13 southern states had 4,134 public school districts in the fall of 1965. As of the end of November 1965, 3,990 of the 4,134 districts had received federal approval of their proposals to de-segregate (Table 5-8).

Even so, only 247,158 Negro children in the South were en-rolled in desegregated primary and secondary schools at that time. This was 7.9 per cent of the 3 million Negroes attending public schools in the southern states. (See Table 5-8 and Figure 5-4.) Slightly over 90 per cent, or 223,742, of the 247,158 Negroes who were attending schools with whites lived in seven states: Kentucky, Texas, Oklahoma, Virginia, Tennessee, North Carolina, and Florida. Of the 1.6 million Negroes in school in Alabama, Arkansas, Georgia, Louisiana, Mississippi, and South Carolina, only 23,000, or 1.4 per cent, were attending schools with whites. In the spring of 1966, with the publication of a revised set of guidelines for desegregating public schools by the Department of Health, Education and Welfare, there were strong indications that the rate of desegregation would be more rapid in the future than in the past.

Racial desegregation has moved faster in colleges and universi-ties than in elementary and secondary schools. At the time of the 1954 Supreme Court decision, only 21 colleges and universities in the South, public and private, were desegregated. But 245 of the 247 had been desegregated by 1965. Moreover, in several of

Figure 5-4   **Public School Desegregation, Southern States, 1959–1965**

Per cent of school districts desegregated

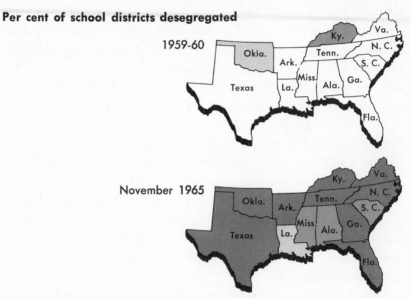

Per cent of Negro pupils attending desegregated schools

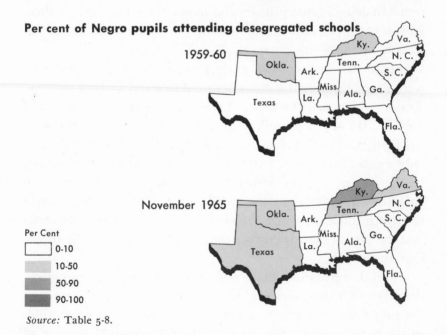

Per Cent
☐ 0-10
▨ 10-50
▧ 50-90
■ 90-100

Source: Table 5-8.

the southern states significant progress has been made in enrolling Negroes in vocational training courses authorized by the Manpower Development and Training Act of 1962, and numerous training and study programs that will be of help to Negroes are coming into being in the South as a result of the Economic Opportunity Act of 1964.

Despite the increasing use being made by Negroes of integrated institutions for graduate and professional work, predominantly Negro colleges are likely to be the principal means of providing higher education for Negroes for a good many years in the future. The plight of several of the Negro colleges in the South, particularly some of the Negro land-grant institutions, is quite serious. These colleges have not grown and developed as have the land-grant colleges for whites. Only four of them train engineers. None has a doctoral program. Federal funds for experimental research in agriculture and home economics go to the experiment stations associated with the white land-grant colleges and are seldom shared with the Negro institutions. Limited funds and limited occupational outlets for their graduates have restricted their course offerings, many of which need to be broadened and strengthened if their students are to be prepared for the kinds of jobs in which professionally trained Negroes are likely to have the greatest opportunities in the years ahead.

The Civil Rights Act of 1964 will have an important effect in speeding the rate of desegregation of public schools and training programs in the South. Title VI of that act provides that: "No person in the United States shall, on the ground of race, color, or national origin, be excluded from participation in, be denied the benefits of, or be subject to discrimination under any program or activity receiving Federal financial assistance." Since a high proportion of southern educational institutions and practically all of the new vocational training programs receive federal funds in one form or another, this provision of the act will force thousands of segregated schools in the South to integrate during the next few years.

Education and Prospects for Employment

Will the changes in educational standards, programs, and achievements growing out of the South's intensive educational effort affect the labor force enough within the next few years to significantly alter past trends in the South's share of national employment? Are the research and scientific activities of the South's institutions of higher learning likely to help to increase southern employment appreciably? Will its large supplies of poorly educated and low-skilled labor continue to make the South a mecca for labor-intensive, low-wage industries, or will the proportion of capital-intensive, high-wage industries increase as a result of its educational efforts and attainments?

Education is only one of the numerous factors that will influence the growth of employment and increases in income within the region; it will, no doubt, be of major importance over a period of one or two decades, but its short-term effects cannot be measured precisely.

We can, however, be practically certain that the southern labor force of 1975 will be better educated than that of today. If recent trends continue, the number of high school graduates in the southern population will increase from about 6.7 million in 1960 to at least 14 million in 1975, and the number of college graduates from about 1.9 million to over 3 million. In view of the heavy emphasis that the South is placing on vocational and technical training in area schools—for adults, for high school dropouts, and for high school graduates—these projections may understate the future qualifications of the South's labor force.

Employers of the future will have a large supply of qualified workers available and will also be relieved of some of the customary costs of in-plant or on-the-job training. Many of the area schools are anxious to give specialized courses for types of jobs available in both old and new plants within the area. Thus, the cost of such training is shifted from the private to the public sector, and the training service encourages the location of new plants in the area served by the school or the expansion of old ones. This, indeed, has been one of the major rationalizations for the establishment of many of the area schools.

At the same time, there is much ignorance and inertia to be overcome. Inadequate financing of education is only a manifestation of deeper and more fundamental problems that the region must resolve. Tradition, prevailing beliefs, laws, and even state constitutions are often serious impediments to rapid changes in the South's educational systems.

Although educational opportunities for Negroes in the South have greatly expanded in the past two decades, and even more rapid educational gains can be safely predicted for both whites and Negroes in the future, it is doubtful that the southern educational establishment can perform well enough within the next decade to bring the work force, the management and entrepreneurship, and the technology of the region to a competitive level with those of the more highly developed areas of the North and West.

The educational gains already made or in the offing may well be a force of considerable significance in creating jobs and in raising the occupational status of future southern workers. But in view of the growing emphasis on education in all parts of the country, it is unlikely that the South's share of total national employment during the next decade will be more than modestly affected by improvements in the educational status of the southern population. Such improvements are likely to have significant indirect influences, however, by providing opportunities for improvements in the industry-mix of the region; by reducing racial discrimination in employment; and by enhancing the qualifications of southern workers who migrate out of the region to urban centers in the North and West.

Chapter 6

RACIAL INEQUALITY
IN EMPLOYMENT

INEQUALITY OF opportunity because of race and color has been one of America's most persistent problems, and inequality in employment has been a major part of that problem. In this chapter we turn our attention to racial discrimination as a factor determining employment opportunities for Negroes in the South.

Effect on the South

While racial discrimination is national, its effects have been greater in the South than in other regions for several reasons. Over the years relationships between whites and Negroes in the South have been prescribed by law and nurtured by tradition. Likewise, racial division of the labor market into "white" and "Negro" jobs has been much more rigidly practiced in the South than elsewhere in the nation. Despite the decline since 1940 in the proportion of the nation's Negro population living in the South, the concentration of Negroes in the 13 southern states was heavier than in other sections of the country in 1960, when more than half of the nation's 20 million Negroes lived in those states.[1] Negroes made up more than a fifth of the southern population, compared to only about 7 per cent of the population in the remaining 35 states.

[1] Actually, the U. S. Negro population was 18.9 million in 1960; the nonwhite population was 20 million. See footnote 3, chapter 2, for an explanation of the use of the terms "Negro" and "nonwhite" interchangeably in this book.

LOSS OF HUMAN RESOURCES

Observers of the southern scene have long contended that traditional scuthern race relations are an impediment to economic progress, and that the southern economy will be depressed as long as the rights of Negroes are suppressed. This point was made in 1889 by Lewis Blair, a Richmond gentleman and businessman of some stature: "We must trample, or we must elevate; to maintain the *status quo* is impossible. To trample is to perpetuate and intensify the poverty and stagnation under which we groan; to elevate is to make the South rich, happy and strong." This argument is as relevant today as it was 75 years ago.[2]

As indicated in earlier chapters, southern economic, social, and political institutions have been undergoing rapid changes and the position of southern Negroes has improved significantly since pre–World War II days. However, most of the income and employment gains experienced by Negroes since the early 1940's resulted primarily from labor shortages during World War II and later years of full employment, rather than from significant efforts to lessen the economic disparity between Negroes and whites. Racial practices are still a long way from those necessary to achieve equality of opportunity for all citizens.

Segregation in housing and recreation, for example, has forced southern Negroes into subcultures divorced from the mainstream of general society. As a result, their potentialities have often gone undeveloped or underdeveloped. They have also had restricted opportunities to apply for employment: they have had meager knowledge of job openings and have not been reached by recruiting efforts of employers, who, more often than not, have ignored Negro schools and colleges and other resources in Negro communities when seeking employees. Negroes have had little or no opportunity to secure traditional apprenticeship training anywhere in the United States. In the South inferior education and

[2] Lewis Blair, *Southern Prophesy: The Prosperity of the South Dependent Upon the Elevation of the Negro,* with an introduction by C. Vann Woodward, Little, Brown, Boston, 1964 edition, p. 49.

vocational training, resulting from school segregation and inadequate financing of Negro schools, have further limited opportunities for development of skills and other means of preparing for jobs. Thus, by discrimination in education and training, the development of human resources has been impeded and the economy has been denied the potential talents of a sizable proportion of its citizens.

Moreover, the heavy migration of Negroes from the South, as a result, primarily, of their unfavorable position in the competition for jobs, has deprived the South of the services of some of its most talented, best educated, and most productive Negroes. On the other hand, the exodus of uneducated rural Negroes and other low-income groups during the 1940's and 1950's tended to raise the average per capita income of the remaining population.

In the late 1950's and early 1960's advancing technology drastically reduced the demand for unskilled labor in many of the labor markets outside of the South, causing high unemployment among Negro workers in many nonsouthern labor markets. As the pressures of segregation and discrimination in education and public accommodations are eased in the South, and technology alters employment opportunities throughout the economy, it is possible that out-migration will become less effective as a means of relieving the South of underused, low-income Negro labor, and of thus bringing per capita income in the region into line with national averages. The future rate of increase in southern per capita income is therefore likely to be influenced by the extent to which Negroes are admitted into traditionally white areas of employment.

The Status of Negro Workers

In general, movement out of the rural South has meant improvement in the economic and social situation of Negroes. Urban residence has brought them educational and social advances and better jobs in both the South and the non-South.

Despite these gains, significant racial inequality in employment persists—differences in types of industries and occupations in which Negro and white workers are employed and in income earned. The differences are more pronounced in the South than in other sections of the country, and the gap between the regions widened from 1940 to 1960.

Broadly speaking, differences between Negro and white workers in the types of industry in which they are employed are not as significant as differences in occupational categories. For example, in 1960 in the South 23 per cent of employed whites had jobs in manufacturing industries, but only 14 per cent of employed Negroes. On the other hand, 44 per cent of employed whites were in white-collar occupations, compared with 9 per cent of employed Negroes.

EMPLOYMENT, BY INDUSTRY

Between 1940 and 1960 Negro employment in the United States increased by almost 2 million, or more than 38 per cent (Table 6.1). All of the increase occurred outside of the South. Indeed, there was a decrease during the 20-year period of about 160,000 in the number of Negro workers employed in the South. In this period the South's share of national Negro employment declined from almost three fourths to less than half.

The major trend in the industrial distribution of Negro employment after 1940 was the movement out of agricultural and into nonagricultural industries (Table 6-1). This trend, established in the 1940's, continued throughout the 1950's. The number of Negroes employed in agriculture in the United States declined by about 960,000 between 1940 and 1960, but Negro employment in nonagricultural industries increased by over 2.3 million. Most of the decline in Negro employment in agriculture was in the South, where 923,000 Negroes left farm jobs; at the same time the employment of southern Negroes in nonagricultural industries increased by 660,000, or 35.6 per cent (Appendix Table 6-1). In 1940 more than a third of the Negroes working in the United States and more than two fifths of the Negroes working in the

Table 6-1　**Percentage Distribution of Employment by Major Industry Group and by Color, United States, Non-South, and South, 1940, 1950, 1960**

Industry group	White			Nonwhite		
	1940	1950	1960	1940	1950	1960
All industries	*United States*					
Number (thousands)	40,495	50,625	57,912	4,671	5,600	6,460
Per cent	100.0	100.0	100.0	100.0	100.0	100.0
Goods-producing	48.7	46.3	41.6	49.2	44.3	33.7
Agriculture, forestry, fisheries	17.1	11.6	6.4	33.5	19.8	9.4
Manufacturing	24.8	26.8	28.1	11.4	18.3	18.7
Mining	2.1	1.7	1.1	1.2	0.8	0.3
Construction	4.7	6.2	6.0	3.1	5.4	5.3
Service-producing	49.8	52.2	54.8	49.5	54.0	58.9
Transport., communic., pub. utils.	7.2	8.0	7.1	4.4	6.0	5.3
Trade	17.7	19.5	18.9	8.3	11.8	12.7
Finance, insurance, real estate	3.5	3.6	4.5	1.5	1.6	1.6
Services	17.3	16.5	19.4	34.1	31.2	34.5
Government	4.2	4.5	4.9	1.3	3.4	4.8
Industry not reported	1.6	1.5	3.7	1.3	1.7	7.4
All industries	*Non-South*					
Number (thousands)	31,684	39,426	44,659	1,325	2,327	3,274
Per cent	100.0	100.0	100.0	100.0	100.0	100.0
Goods-producing	46.6	45.7	41.7	29.1	35.5	29.9
Agriculture, forestry, fisheries	13.0	9.4	5.7	8.8	4.5	2.4
Manufacturing	26.9	28.9	29.6	14.5	24.6	22.9
Mining	2.0	1.5	0.8	1.9	1.0	0.3
Construction	4.7	5.9	5.5	3.9	5.5	4.4
Service-producing	51.8	52.9	54.6	69.3	62.7	59.8
Transport., communic., pub. utils.	7.6	8.2	7.1	6.3	7.6	5.9
Trade	18.1	19.5	18.4	13.1	13.9	13.1
Finance, insurance, real estate	3.8	3.8	4.5	3.4	2.4	2.2
Services	18.2	17.0	19.7	43.3	32.7	31.3
Government	4.1	4.5	4.7	3.2	6.0	7.4
Industry not reported	1.6	1.4	3.8	1.6	1.8	10.3
All industries	*South*					
Number (thousands)	8,811	11,199	13,253	3,346	3,273	3,186
Per cent	100.0	100.0	100.0	100.0	100.0	100.0
Goods-producing	56.4	48.7	41.2	57.1	50.5	37.5
Agriculture, forestry, fisheries	31.6	19.4	9.0	43.3	30.7	16.5
Manufacturing	17.3	19.4	23.0	10.1	13.9	14.4
Mining	2.6	2.7	2.0	0.9	0.7	0.4
Construction	4.9	7.3	7.3	2.8	5.3	6.2
Service-producing	42.4	49.7	55.5	41.7	47.9	58.0
Transport., communic., pub. utils.	5.9	7.2	7.0	3.6	4.9	4.7
Trade	16.0	19.7	20.3	6.4	10.4	12.3
Finance, insurance, real estate	2.3	2.9	4.2	0.8	0.9	1.1
Services	13.8	15.1	18.4	30.4	30.2	37.8
Government	4.3	4.8	5.7	0.5	1.5	2.1
Industry not reported	1.2	1.6	3.3	1.2	1.6	4.5

Source: Appendix Table 6-1.

Figure 6-1   **Percentage Change in Employment, by Industry Group, White and Nonwhite, Non-South and South, 1940–1960**

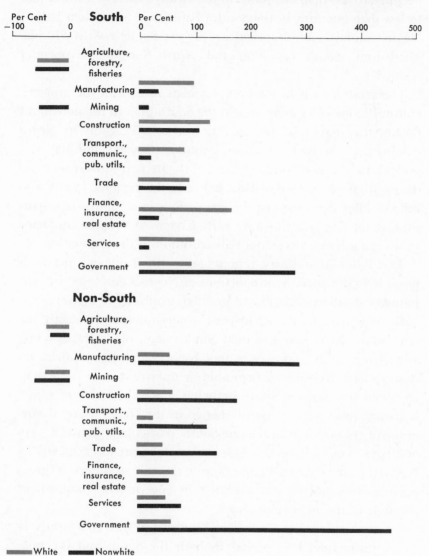

Source: Appendix Table 6-1.

South were employed in agriculture. By 1960 the proportions had declined to less than one tenth in the United States as a whole and to less than one fifth in the South (Table 6-1). More than half of Negro employment in agriculture in the South was in Florida, Mississippi, South Carolina, and North Carolina (Appendix Table 6-2).

The relative gain in total employment in each of the nonagricultural industries was greater in the South than in the non-South during the 1940–1960 period, but the relative gains in Negro employment in each of these industries (except mining) was greater in the non-South (Figure 6-1). In part this reflects redistribution of the population between the regions, but it also reflects differences between the two regions in employment opportunities for Negroes, which, in turn, have been a significant factor in bringing about a regional redistribution of the population.

The index of industry representation in Table 6-2 makes it possible to compare the proportions of Negroes employed in each industry at different times and in different places. In a given year, if the Negro share of employment in any industry is exactly the same as the Negro share of total employment, the index of representation for that industry is 100. Negro employment in an industry can be considered favorable or unfavorable by the extent to which the index is above or below 100. The index of representation reflects a significant change in the Negro share of government employment in the non-South, particularly between 1940 and 1950. Some gain in government employment was achieved by Negroes in the South also, but despite the gain, southern Negroes continued to be underrepresented in government employment throughout the 1940's and 1950's.

Negro employment in service industries was comparatively heavy throughout this period in both the South and the non-South; the index of representation moved upward in the South after 1950, but declined sharply in the non-South throughout the period. In both regions Negro representation in finance, insurance, and real estate tended to decline. The index for trade showed increased representation of Negroes in the South after 1940, while

Table 6-2 **Nonwhite Shares of Employment, by Major Industry Group, United States, Non-South, and South, 1940, 1950, 1960**

Industry group	Per cent			Index of industry representation[a]		
	1940	1950	1960	1940	1950	1960
United States						
All industries	10.3	10.0	10.0	100.0	100.0	100.0
Goods-producing	10.4	9.6	8.3	101.0	96.0	83.0
Agriculture, forestry, fisheries	18.5	15.8	14.0	179.6	158.0	140.0
Manufacturing	5.0	7.0	6.9	48.5	70.0	69.0
Mining	5.9	4.8	3.3	57.3	48.0	33.0
Construction	7.1	8.7	9.0	68.9	87.0	90.0
Service-producing	10.3	10.3	10.7	100.0	103.0	107.0
Transport., communic., pub. utils.	6.6	7.8	7.7	64.1	78.0	77.0
Trade	5.1	6.3	7.0	49.5	63.0	70.0
Finance, insurance, real estate	4.8	4.5	4.0	46.6	45.0	40.0
Service	18.5	17.3	16.5	179.6	173.0	165.0
Government	3.5	7.6	9.8	34.0	76.0	98.0
Industry not reported	8.9	11.2	18.5	86.4	112.0	185.0
Non-South						
All industries	4.0	5.6	6.8	100.0	100.0	100.0
Goods-producing	2.5	4.4	5.0	62.5	78.6	73.5
Agriculture, forestry, fisheries	2.7	2.7	3.0	67.5	48.2	44.1
Manufacturing	2.2	4.8	5.4	55.0	85.7	79.4
Mining	3.9	3.7	2.3	97.5	66.1	33.8
Construction	3.4	5.2	5.5	85.0	92.9	80.9
Service-producing	5.3	6.5	7.4	132.5	116.1	108.8
Transport., communic., pub. utils.	3.4	5.2	5.7	85.0	92.9	83.8
Trade	2.9	4.0	4.9	72.5	71.4	72.1
Finance, insurance, real estate	3.6	3.6	3.4	90.0	64.3	50.0
Services	9.0	10.2	10.4	225.0	182.1	152.9
Government	3.2	7.4	10.3	80.0	132.1	151.5
Industry not reported	3.9	6.9	16.6	97.5	123.2	244.1
South						
All industries	27.5	22.6	19.4	100.0	100.0	100.0
Goods-producing	27.8	23.3	17.9	101.1	103.1	92.3
Agriculture, forestry, fisheries	34.2	31.6	30.8	124.4	139.8	158.8
Manufacturing	18.2	17.3	13.1	66.2	76.5	67.5
Mining	11.0	7.0	4.7	40.0	31.0	24.2
Construction	18.0	17.5	16.8	65.4	77.4	86.6
Service-producing	27.2	22.0	20.1	98.9	97.3	103.6
Transport., communic., pub. utils.	19.0	16.6	13.8	69.1	73.5	71.1
Trade	13.1	13.4	12.7	47.6	59.3	65.5
Finance, insurance, real estate	11.2	8.6	6.0	40.7	38.1	30.9
Services	45.5	36.9	33.1	165.5	163.4	170.6
Government	4.5	8.3	8.4	16.4	36.7	43.3
Industry not reported	27.2	22.4	24.8	98.9	99.1	127.8

Source: Appendix Table 6-1.   [a] See text.

there was little change in the index in the non-South. The index of industry representation in manufacturing in both the South and the non-South increased in the 1940's and then declined in the 1950's. It is noteworthy that in spite of the dramatic decline in agricultural employment among Negroes the index of representation in agriculture in the South increased during the 20-year period from 124.4 to 158.8, clearly indicating that Negroes continue to depend on agriculture for a substantial proportion of their employment.

EMPLOYMENT, BY OCCUPATION

Job security and income are closely related to occupation. Irrespective of the industries in which people work, the kinds of jobs they hold and the extent to which they have mobility between occupations are important measures of their employment status.

Undoubtedly, the occupational position of Negro workers, South and non-South, was better in 1960 than in 1940, but inequality in employment still persisted. The proportion of white-collar workers among Negroes increased during this period in both the South and the non-South and the relative gains in white-collar occupations were greater for Negroes than for whites. Moreover, the relative gains of Negroes in white-collar occupations in the South were greater than in the non-South. However, the actual number of Negroes in white-collar occupations in the South in 1960 was less than half the number in the non-South, although total employment of Negroes in the two regions was not greatly different. (See Appendix Table 6-3.)

Even though increasing proportions of Negroes in both the South and the non-South have been moving into white-collar occupations since 1940, Negro employment in 1960 was still much more heavily weighted on the side of agricultural and service jobs than was white employment. The imbalance was more striking in the South than in the non-South.

The continued concentration of Negroes in low-status jobs, particularly in the South, can be seen in Table 6-3. While Negroes

Table 6-3 **Nonwhite Shares of Employment, by Major Occupational Group, Non-South and South, 1940, 1950, 1960**

Occupational group	Per cent			Index of occupational representation [a]		
	1940	1950	1960	1940	1950	1960
	Non-South					
All occupations	4.0	5.6	6.8	100.0	100.0	100.0
White-collar	1.2	2.1	3.2	30.0	37.5	47.1
Professional & technical	1.6	2.1	3.4	40.0	37.5	50.0
Nonfarm proprietors	1.2	1.6	1.8	30.0	28.6	26.5
Clerical	1.0	2.8	4.5	25.0	50.0	66.2
Sales	1.0	1.4	1.9	25.0	25.0	27.9
Manual	3.6	6.3	7.2	90.0	112.5	105.9
Craftsmen & foremen	1.4	2.5	3.5	35.0	44.6	51.5
Operatives	3.3	6.5	8.1	82.5	116.1	119.1
Nonfarm	8.9	15.2	15.4	222.5	271.4	226.5
Service	15.1	18.5	17.8	377.5	330.4	261.8
General service	10.5	13.7	14.2	262.5	244.6	208.8
Private household	25.0	38.0	32.9	625.0	678.6	483.8
Agricultural	2.7	2.6	2.8	67.5	46.4	41.2
Farmers & farm managers	1.4	1.3	1.4	35.0	23.2	20.6
Farm laborers & foremen	4.9	5.0	5.5	122.5	89.3	80.9
Occupation not reported	3.4	7.4	15.4	85.0	132.1	226.5
	South					
All occupations	27.5	22.6	19.4	100.0	100.0	100.0
White-collar	5.0	5.1	4.7	18.2	22.6	24.2
Professional & technical	12.1	10.6	9.2	44.0	46.9	47.4
Nonfarm proprietors	3.3	4.0	2.8	12.0	17.7	14.4
Clerical	2.0	3.0	3.5	7.3	13.3	18.0
Sales	2.8	3.2	2.6	10.2	14.2	13.4
Manual	23.0	21.7	19.2	83.6	96.0	99.0
Craftsmen & foremen	8.7	8.2	8.1	31.6	36.3	41.8
Operatives	16.1	18.9	17.6	58.5	83.6	90.7
Nonfarm	51.4	50.9	48.4	186.9	225.2	249.5
Service	60.5	57.3	52.9	220.0	253.5	272.7
General service	35.4	40.2	37.1	128.7	177.9	191.2
Private household	83.1	85.5	80.6	302.2	378.3	415.5
Agricultural	34.2	31.7	30.8	124.4	140.3	158.8
Farmers & farm managers	26.6	25.3	18.5	96.7	111.9	95.4
Farm laborers & foremen	45.8	42.6	48.4	166.5	188.5	249.5
Occupation not reported	21.1	21.9	22.6	76.7	96.9	116.5

Source: Appendix Table 6-3.   [a] See text.

made up about one fifth of all employed persons in the South in 1960, they made up over four fifths of all household servants, about one half of all nonfarm laborers as well as of all farm laborers, but less than one twentieth of all white-collar workers. The index of occupational representation in this table, comparing the Negro share of jobs in each occupational group with the Negro share of all jobs, suggests that Negroes in the non-South are moving more rapidly than Negroes in the South toward achieving a proportion of high-status jobs equal to their representation in the work force. (For a clarification of the meaning of the index, see the explanation of the "index of industry representation" in the preceding section.)

OCCUPATIONAL STATUS AND EDUCATION

The figures in Table 6-4 showing the educational gap between Negro and white workers indicate that education is much less effective in raising the occupational status of Negroes than of whites, particularly in the South.[3]

For instance, among high school male graduates 25 years of age and over in the South the proportion of whites (46.3 per cent) employed in white-collar occupations in 1960 was almost three times that of Negroes (16.3 per cent). (See Table 6-4.) In the non-South the difference was much less—38.9 per cent for whites, compared to 23.6 per cent for Negroes.

Occupational inequality was not as significant between whites and Negroes with four years of college as between whites and Negroes with one to three years of college. Moreover, college graduation is apparently more effective in raising the occupational level of Negroes in the South than in the non-South, since a higher

[3] What appears to be racial discrimination in filling jobs may, in some cases, be the result of inadequate education of Negroes. Jobs with high educational requirements may be filled by white applicants because Negro applicants do not qualify or because no Negroes apply. Because of the history of racial discrimination in employment practices, many Negroes have come to believe that certain jobs are not available to them; they therefore do not apply for them. One of the important economic aims of the Negro protest and civil rights movement is to place Negroes in jobs above traditional levels in adequate numbers to make open employment opportunities evident.

proportion of Negroes with four years of college was in white-collar occupations in the South than in the non-South. In fact, there was almost as high a proportion of Negro college graduates as of white college graduates in white-collar occupations in the South, where teaching in segregated public schools has been a major source of employment for Negro college graduates who stay in the region. More than one fifth of all Negro college graduates in the United States in clerical occupations were postal clerks and mail carriers, compared to one twentieth of white college graduates who were in clerical occupations.

Racial Discrimination and Income

While the importance of racial discrimination as a factor in Negro and white income differences cannot be precisely determined, patterns of income, education, age, and occupational relationships offer meaningful indicators that leave little room for doubt that racial discrimination plays a major role.

Earnings of Negro workers have improved greatly since 1939, and the gap in earnings between white and Negro workers was reduced during the period of full employment associated with the Korean War. Since then, however, there has been a tendency for the relative size of Negro and white incomes to remain virtually stable. In 1939 the average annual earnings of Negro male workers in the United States were $460, or 41 per cent of the $1,112 earned by white male workers. By 1952 the average annual earnings of Negro male workers were $2,038, or 58 per cent of the $3,507 of white male workers. By 1964 the average earnings of Negro male workers ($3,426) were still about 58 per cent of average earnings of white males ($5,853).[4]

Differences in earnings between white and Negro workers are more pronounced in the South [5] than in other regions (Table 6-5).

[4] *Current Population Reports: Consumer Income,* U. S. Bureau of the Census, Washington, Series P-60, various dates.

[5] Unless otherwise specified, "the South," as used in this section, conforms to the U. S. Bureau of the Census definition, that is, it includes Delaware, Maryland, West Virginia, and the District of Columbia, in addition to the 13 states defined as the South in this study.

Table 6-4 Males with Earnings, 25–64 Years of Age, by Color and Occupation and by Years of Schooling, Non-South and South, 1959

Color and occupation	Total	Elementary school (years) 1-7	8	High school (years) 1-3	4	College (years) 1-3	4	5 or more
White					Non-South			
Number (thousands)	24,344	2,984	4,329	5,156	6,497	2,457	1,562	1,360
Per cent	100.0	100.0	100.0	100.0	100.0	100.0	100.0	100.0
Professional & technical	11.8	0.8	1.3	3.1	7.0	20.3	42.9	73.9
Nonfarm proprietors & managers	12.0	4.8	7.0	9.6	13.9	21.6	24.3	11.9
Clerical	6.8	2.9	4.3	6.8	9.7	10.8	6.5	3.2
Sales	6.6	2.3	3.4	5.6	8.3	13.0	12.8	3.9
Craftsmen & foremen	22.5	23.1	26.8	28.8	25.6	14.7	5.6	2.3
Operatives	20.1	30.8	27.9	26.6	17.8	7.8	1.8	0.8
Nonfarm laborers	5.2	12.6	8.0	5.6	3.3	1.4	0.4	0.2
Service	5.1	8.1	6.4	5.8	4.9	3.5	1.0	0.6
Farmers & farm managers	4.7	5.3	9.2	3.3	5.0	2.6	1.4	0.4
Farm laborers & foremen	1.3	4.3	1.9	0.9	0.6	0.4	0.2	0.1
Nonwhite								
Number (thousands)	1,646	500	251	386	315	111	41	43
Per cent	100.0	100.0	100.0	100.0	100.0	100.0	100.0	100.0
Professional & technical	4.9	0.4	0.7	1.3	3.5	12.6	42.3	71.4
Nonfarm proprietors & managers	3.3	2.1	2.6	2.6	4.2	6.3	9.6	6.9
Clerical	7.1	2.0	3.8	6.9	13.1	19.2	14.1	6.5
Sales	1.7	0.7	1.1	1.5	2.8	3.9	4.5	1.6
Craftsmen & foremen	12.6	11.0	13.7	13.8	15.1	12.4	6.0	1.9
Operatives	25.7	27.4	29.5	29.8	24.2	16.6	5.4	1.6
Nonfarm laborers	16.1	23.5	18.6	15.8	10.2	5.2	2.4	0.7
Service	14.8	16.5	16.2	15.4	14.0	12.4	5.9	2.1
Farmers & farm managers	1.0	0.9	1.1	0.8	1.7	1.0	0.8	0.2
Farm laborers & foremen	2.1	4.3	2.1	1.1	1.0	0.7	0.1	0.2

White

Number (thousands)	8,413	2,128	1,079	1,646	1,833	789	527	412
Per cent	100.0	100.0	100.0	100.0	100.0	100.0	100.0	100.0
Professional & technical	10.5	0.8	1.6	3.0	7.2	18.2	41.6	73.7
Nonfarm proprietors & managers	13.8	5.6	9.1	13.3	18.5	25.8	25.3	12.0
Clerical	6.1	1.9	3.8	5.8	10.3	11.8	7.5	3.8
Sales	7.1	2.6	4.6	7.0	10.2	13.8	12.1	4.3
Craftsmen & foremen	22.8	25.0	29.2	29.6	24.0	13.4	5.6	2.0
Operatives	19.1	29.0	26.3	22.7	14.9	6.5	1.4	0.6
Nonfarm laborers	4.6	10.3	5.8	3.5	2.0	1.0	0.3	0.2
Service	3.8	4.8	4.8	4.5	3.7	2.4	0.6	0.4
Farmers & farm managers	6.6	10.8	9.5	5.8	4.8	3.1	2.1	0.6
Farm laborers & foremen	2.1	5.8	2.0	1.1	0.6	0.3	0.2	0.1

Nonwhite

Number (thousands)	1,703	1,008	181	258	150	52	31	24
Per cent	100.0	100.0	100.0	100.0	100.0	100.0	100.0	100.0
Professional & technical	3.2	0.3	1.0	1.2	2.7	12.1	55.3	81.0
Nonfarm proprietors & managers	1.6	1.1	1.3	1.6	2.7	4.1	5.1	4.4
Clerical	3.1	1.1	2.1	4.7	9.2	15.7	11.8	4.0
Sales	0.8	0.5	0.7	1.0	1.7	2.5	2.6	0.6
Craftsmen & foremen	10.0	8.9	11.6	12.4	12.6	12.6	3.8	1.1
Operatives	23.8	23.8	27.5	27.5	24.5	14.7	4.5	1.4
Nonfarm laborers	24.4	28.4	24.0	21.8	15.8	10.6	3.3	0.8
Service	12.3	10.0	14.8	16.2	19.1	17.7	6.9	1.6
Farmers & farm managers	6.3	8.8	4.7	2.7	1.4	1.5	1.0	0.3
Farm laborers & foremen	8.7	12.5	5.6	3.3	1.9	0.7	0.5	0.2

Source: Appendix Table 6-4.

Table 6-5　Median Earnings of Males 18–64 Years of Age with Earnings in the Experienced Labor Force, 1959, by Years of Schooling, United States, Non-South, and South[a]

Age and education	United States			Non-South			South[a]		
	White	Non-white	Nonwhite as per cent of white	White	Non-white	Nonwhite as per cent of white	White	Non-white	Nonwhite as per cent of white
25 to 64 years of age									
All levels of education	$5,278	$3,037	57.5	$5,471	$4,017	73.4	$4,565	$2,238	49.0
Less than 8 years	3,757	2,348	62.5	4,286	3,553	82.9	2,974	1,873	63.0
8 years	4,578	3,205	70.0	4,731	3,802	80.4	3,857	2,437	63.2
1 to 3 years high school	5,180	3,430	66.2	5,341	4,042	75.7	4,556	2,587	56.8
4 years high school	5,624	3,925	69.8	5,714	4,397	77.0	5,269	2,886	54.8
1 to 3 years college	6,236	4,280	68.6	6,342	4,674	73.7	5,894	3,360	57.0
4 or more years college	7,792	5,023	64.5	7,917	5,537	69.9	7,372	4,308	58.4
18 to 24 years of age									
All levels of education	2,604	1,584	60.8	2,769	2,275	82.2	2,242	1,227	54.7
Less than 8 years	1,837	1,161	63.2	2,218	2,184	98.5	1,553	1,017	65.5
8 years	2,400	1,472	61.3	2,650	2,252	85.0	1,984	1,171	59.0
1 to 3 years high school	2,431	1,581	65.0	2,588	2,139	82.7	2,132	1,256	58.9
4 years high school	3,019	1,988	65.8	3,117	2,473	79.3	2,724	1,519	55.8
1 to 3 years college	2,146	1,796	83.7	2,196	2,101	95.7	1,989	1,256	63.1
4 or more years college	3,140	2,543	81.0	3,200	2,664	83.2	2,956	2,405	81.4
25 to 34 years of age									
All levels of education	5,102	3,004	58.9	5,285	3,904	73.9	4,500	2,280	50.7
Less than 8 years	3,379	2,151	63.7	3,893	3,324	85.4	2,875	1,827	63.5
8 years	4,263	2,844	66.7	4,459	3,546	79.5	3,654	2,295	62.8
1 to 3 years high school	4,865	3,136	64.5	5,049	3,777	74.8	4,305	2,445	56.8

1 to 3 years college	$5,363	$4,078	73.5	$5,671	$4,462	78.7	$5,233	$3,255	82.2
4 or more years college	6,356	4,439	69.8	6,428	5,004	77.8	6,125	3,753	61.3
35 to 44 years of age									
All levels of education	5,657	3,322	58.7	5,842	4,281	73.3	5,016	2,424	48.3
Less than 8 years	3,817	2,444	64.0	4,381	3,670	83.8	3,227	2,024	62.7
8 years	4,685	3,362	71.8	4,826	3,924	81.3	4,139	2,597	62.7
1 to 3 years high school	5,371	3,740	69.6	5,509	4,289	77.9	4,839	2,826	58.4
4 years high school	5,906	4,266	72.2	5,992	4,692	78.3	5,568	3,163	56.8
1 to 3 years college	6,779	4,623	68.2	6,880	5,003	72.7	6,450	3,703	57.4
4 or more years college	8,797	5,479	62.3	8,893	6,086	68.4	8,485	4,672	55.1
45 to 54 years of age									
All levels of education	5,317	2,966	55.8	5,535	3,998	72.2	4,465	2,190	49.0
Less than 8 years	3,872	2,436	62.9	4,431	3,633	82.0	3,000	1,922	64.1
8 years	4,722	3,396	71.9	4,869	3,945	81.0	3,937	2,512	63.8
1 to 3 years high school	5,335	3,591	67.3	5,504	4,169	75.7	4,623	2,669	57.7
4 years high school	5,829	4,017	68.9	5,901	4,431	75.1	5,531	3,045	55.1
1 to 3 years college	6,765	4,312	63.7	6,841	4,799	70.2	6,505	3,200	49.2
4 or more years college	9,233	5,482	59.4	9,349	5,986	64.0	8,810	4,978	56.5
55 to 64 years of age									
All levels of education	4,802	2,678	55.8	5,014	3,709	74.0	3,859	1,831	47.4
Less than 8 years	3,826	2,284	59.7	4,259	3,479	81.7	2,722	1,646	60.5
8 years	4,516	3,211	71.1	4,649	3,730	80.2	3,613	2,320	64.2
1 to 3 years high school	5,086	3,397	66.8	5,246	3,914	74.6	4,341	2,382	54.9
4 years high school	5,545	3,780	68.2	5,621	4,128	73.4	5,232	2,679	51.2
1 to 3 years college	6,322	3,998	63.2	6,396	4,340	67.9	6,059	2,998	49.5
4 or more years college	8,691	5,108	58.8	8,835	5,555	62.9	8,148	4,254	52.2

Source: U. S. Census of Population: 1960, Occupation by Earnings and Education, PC(2)7B, U. S. Bureau of the Census, Washington.

a Includes, in addition to the 13 states included in the South in this study, Delaware, Maryland, West Virginia, and the District of Columbia.

In 1959 the average annual earnings of Negro male workers 25 to 64 years of age in the experienced labor force were 49 per cent of those of white male workers in the South and 73.4 per cent of those of white male workers in the non-South.

INCOME AND EDUCATIONAL ATTAINMENT

Various studies [6] have shown a rather close relationship between occupation and level of education, and a high correlation between education and income. Though we use educational level as an index of earnings potential, we recognize that it is not a precise measure of productive ability, since quality of schooling varies and the effectiveness of a year of school differs with individuals. A year in a "Negro school" in a southern city, for example, may not produce the same results as a year in a "white school" in the same city. Nevertheless, educational level provides a rough index of earning capacity, particularly when there is a difference of several years in schooling completed. For instance, there is little question that 16 years of schooling yield higher productive capacity, greater employment mobility, and higher incomes than 8 years of schooling, if there are no other offsetting factors.

Income patterns indicate, however, that the income accruing to Negroes from higher educational attainment has been much less than to whites (Table 6-5). Male Negro college graduates 25 to 64 years of age in the South had average earnings in 1959 of only $4,308, compared with an average of $5,269 for white male high school graduates in the same age group. Negro high school graduates had lower average earnings than whites with less than eight years of schooling. Furthermore, the average Negro male college graduate in the South in 1959 had annual earnings only $1,871 higher than the Negro elementary school graduate, whereas

6 Herman P. Miller, "Annual and Lifetime Income in Relation to Education: 1939–1959," *American Economic Review,* December 1960; H. S. Houthakker, "Education and Income," *Review of Economics and Statistics,* February 1959; Theodore W. Schultz, "Rise in the Capital Stock Represented by Education in the United States, 1900–57," *Economics and Higher Education,* U. S. Office of Education, Washington, 1962.

the difference for whites with comparable years of schooling was $3,515, or almost twice that for Negroes.

Instead of diminishing with increases in education, differences in earnings of Negroes and whites tend to grow larger. The difference in the South in 1959 ranged from $1,420 for those with eight years of school, to $2,383 for high school graduates, and to $3,064 for college graduates; in the non-South the range in the difference was from $929 to $1,317 to $2,380 for the respective educational levels. The average earnings of Negro males with eight years of school were 63.2 per cent of the average earnings of whites with the same years of schooling in the South, and 80.4 per cent in the non-South. The ratio of Negro to white earnings of college graduates, on the other hand, was 58.4 per cent in the South and 69.9 per cent in the non-South (Table 6-5).

The relationships between age and income follow the same general patterns for both whites and Negroes in all regions of the country, when differences in education are not taken into account (Table 6-5). Income tends to rise with advances in age for most workers between 18 and 45 years old. By the time workers in many occupations reach 45 years of age their incomes may have reached a peak or even have begun to taper off. However, at higher educational levels, Negroes tend to reach their maximum income at an earlier age than whites (Figure 6-2). In the United States as a whole the 1959 median income of white male college graduates continued to rise markedly with successive age groups until it reached a peak with the group 45 to 54 years old. On the other hand, the median income of Negro male college graduates beyond the age group of 35 to 44 years rose only slightly. Moreover, their peak median income was little more than that of white male high school graduates in the age group 25 to 34 years, who had been in the labor force from 10 to 20 years less than the Negro college graduates. Negro high school graduates 35 to 44 years of age had a median income about the same as white males 25 to 34 years of age with only 8 years of schooling (Figure 6-2).

The basic differences in the age, income, and educational patterns not only indicate a more limited ability of Negroes than

Figure 6-2 **Median Earnings of Males, by Age Group, Color, and Years of Schooling, United States, Non-South, and South, 1959**

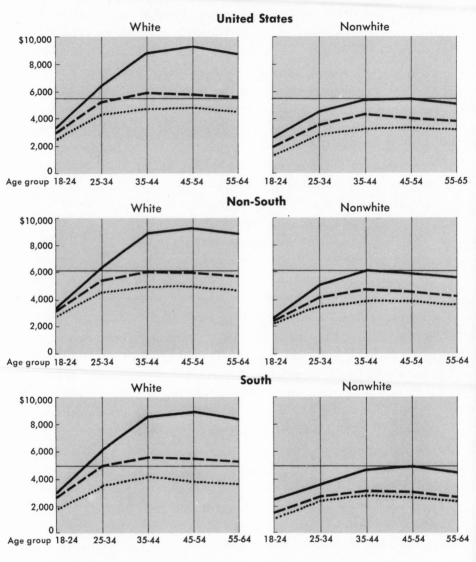

——— Peak median earnings of Negroes with 4 or more years of college
━━━ 4 or more years college
━ ━ 4 years high school
•••••••• 8 years elementary school

Source: Table 6-5.

of whites to exploit the advantages of education as they advance in age but also demonstrate the early point in their working lives at which inequalities between Negro and white workers become apparent.

INCOME, EDUCATION, AND OCCUPATION

Even when Negroes are in the same occupational groups as whites and have had the same number of years of schooling, their earnings are usually less (Figure 6-3). Two characteristics of Negro employment account for this. One is that Negroes who have penetrated white-collar and skilled occupations are not often employed

Figure 6-3 **Median Earnings of Males 25–64 Years of Age in the Experienced Labor Force,[a] by Years of Schooling, Major Occupational Group, and Color, Non-South and South, 1959**

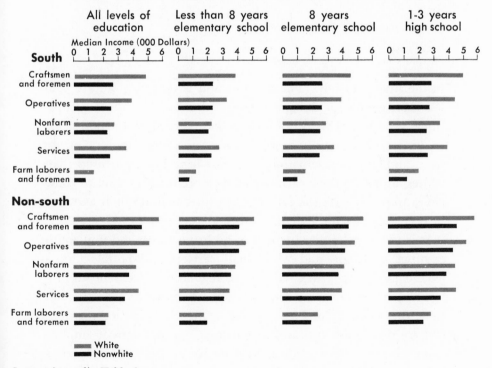

Source: Appendix Table 6-4.
a Excludes males with no earnings.

Figure 6-4   **Median Earnings of Nonwhite Males 25–64 Years of Age in the Experienced Labor Force as Per Cent of Those of White Males,**[a] **Selected Occupations, Non-South and South, 1959**

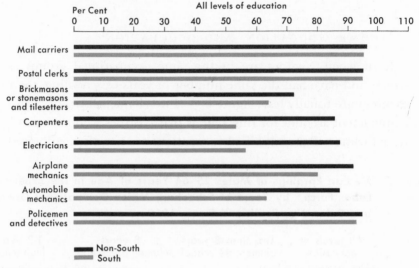

Per Cent   All levels of education

Mail carriers
Postal clerks
Brickmasons or stonemasons and tilesetters
Carpenters
Electricians
Airplane mechanics
Automobile mechanics
Policemen and detectives

■ Non-South
▬ South

Source: Appendix Table 6-5.
a Excludes males with no earnings.

in the high-paid jobs. The other reason is that Negroes are paid less than whites for doing the same work. Even in those occupational groups in which education is not likely to be a major factor in determining earning power, such as unskilled laborers, operatives, and service occupations, Negroes have lower earnings than whites, although their earnings in such occupations tend to come closer to parity with the earnings of whites than do their earnings in occupations with a higher status.

It is noteworthy that in 1959 in both the South and non-South earnings of Negro and white mail carriers and postal clerks— federal jobs subject to Civil Service regulations that tend to promote equal employment opportunities—were nearer equality than were the earnings of Negroes and whites in other occupations (Figure 6-4). This indicates that in many occupations if employment discrimination against Negroes were removed, differences in earnings between white and Negro workers would disappear.

Economic Consequences of Discrimination

The preceding review of employment practices presents overwhelming evidence of the disadvantaged position of Negroes in competing with whites for jobs and incomes. Regardless of their education or ability, Negroes are viewed by employers as less desirable employees than whites. Thus, employment opportunities for Negroes are restricted to certain types of jobs and occupations and to segregated areas of the economy.

Both the scope and the intensity of employment discrimination against Negroes are more pronounced in the South than in other regions. This is particularly obvious with respect to employment of well-educated Negroes in white-collar occupations. The South's share of national Negro employment in white-collar jobs declined from 50 per cent to 30 per cent between 1940 and 1960, even though white-collar employment was the most rapidly growing occupational category in the South. Although employment opportunities and earnings of Negroes improved significantly between 1940 and 1960, as stated earlier in this chapter, most of the gains resulted from labor shortages and full employment associated with World War II and the Korean conflict, rather than from conscious attempts to lessen racial inequalities.

The Council of Economic Advisers, in its 1966 annual report, summarized the effect of discrimination on Negro income: [7]

> . . . In 1964, the average income of nonwhite families was only 56 per cent of the average income of white families. . . .
> Three important and distinct types of discrimination help to explain the difference between white and nonwhite incomes.
> Discrimination results in lower wages for Negroes (who comprise 90 per cent of the nonwhite group) even when they are doing the same kind of work as whites. Available data show that Negroes receive less income in every industry, in every occupation, and at every level of education.
> Discrimination also excludes many Negroes from higher-paying

[7] *Economic Report of the President, Together With the Annual Report of the Council of Economic Advisers,* Washington, January 1966, p. 107.

jobs that would fully utilize their talents or training. Negroes are frequently forced to hold jobs that whites with the same experience and training would not ordinarily hold; and Negroes suffer from higher unemployment rates within all skill categories.

Finally, part of the income difference is explained by past discrimination which has lowered the potential productivity of Negroes by providing less investment in human resources for them than for their white contemporaries. This type of discrimination is manifested by lower expenditures for schools and health facilities in Negro neighborhoods.

The many results of racial discrimination are impossible to measure. It is clear, however, that Negroes are disadvantaged in competing with whites for a livelihood; that national income is distributed in ways that are more favorable to whites than to Negroes; that the costs to taxpayers of welfare and public assistance programs are increased as a result of structural unemployment that is in part the result of racial discrimination; and that the productive efficiency of the economy is reduced by the failure to fully utilize the skills of Negro workers and to fully develop their potential abilities.

Possibly the most disastrous result of racial discrimination in employment in the long run is the stifling of the desire of many Negroes to improve their economic position. Because occupational advancement of Negroes is restricted and the monetary return from education is much more limited than for whites, incentives for self-improvement are often weak. As a result, Negroes are commonly accused of being lazy and lacking in ambition. A somewhat similar consequence of racial discrimination in employment is that many Negro youths tend to develop attitudes toward future job opportunities that lead to disappointments and frustrations in later life.

In a study [8] of 1,245 white and 777 Negro junior and senior high school students in a southern city, for example, it was found

[8] Lewis Wade Jones, "The Social Unreadiness of Negro Youth," *Saturday Review*, October 20, 1962, pp. 81–83. (Based on Paul Geisel, *I.Q. Performance, Education and Occupational Aspirations of Youth in a Southern City: A Racial Comparison*, unpublished Ph.D. Thesis, Vanderbilt University, 1962.)

that 70 per cent of the Negro students confined their occupational aspirations to 7 occupations, all in the professional category: teacher, doctor, lawyer, social worker, minister, mortician, and nurse; the white students, on the other hand, listed 210 occupations. Obviously, the Negro youths had come to think of opportunities for Negroes only in the segregated sector of the economy, and aspired to what they saw in the Negro community as "success" models and "status" occupations. Because of the limited number of such jobs and the costs of schooling required to qualify for them, most of the Negro youths will almost surely fall far short of achieving the kinds of jobs to which they aspire. Moreover, they will be poorly trained and psychologically unprepared to compete effectively with whites for the more numerous jobs in occupations of lower status.

LOSS IN NEGRO EARNINGS

Although the totality of psychic, social, and economic costs emanating from racial discrimination is not measurable, it is possible to make a rough estimate of the economic gain to the nation—that is, the amount by which the gross national product (GNP) would increase—if Negroes were able to utilize their present skills and abilities as fully as whites.

To make such an estimate, it is necessary to assume that the contribution made by an individual to the GNP is indicated by his earnings and that present skills and abilities of both whites and Negroes can be measured by their years of schooling. The significant points underlying these assumptions are that the income of Negroes is lower than that of whites with the same number of years of schooling, primarily because discrimination in employment restricts Negroes to positions of lower productivity, and that such discrimination, by restricting Negroes from moving from low-productivity to high-productivity occupations, restricts the growth in GNP.

The method of measuring the difference in earnings of white and Negro (nonwhite) males in the experienced labor force who

Table 6-6   **Earnings of Males, 18–64 Years of Age, with Earnings in the Experienced Civilian Labor Force in the United States, by Years of Schooling and by Age Group, 1959**

Years of school completed and age group	White Number (thousands)	White Mean earnings	White Total earnings (thousands)	Nonwhite Number (thousands)	Nonwhite Mean earnings	Nonwhite Total earnings (thousands) Actual	Nonwhite Total earnings (thousands) At level of mean earnings for whites
Total	37,178		$212,938,862	3,895		$11,956,900	$18,676,920
18–24 years of age	4,418		12,523,158	545		1,029,133	1,452,461
Less than 8 years	308	$2,131	656,348	119	$1,475	175,525	253,589
8 years schooling	328	2,589	849,192	56	1,745	97,720	144,984
1–3 years high school	1,130	2,662	3,008,060	186	1,860	345,960	495,132
4 years high school	1,752	3,105	5,439,960	145	2,216	321,320	450,225
1–3 years college	691	2,641	1,824,931	33	2,168	71,544	87,153
4 or more years college	209	3,563	744,667	6	2,844	17,064	21,378
25–64 years of age	32,760		200,415,704	3,350		10,927,767	17,224,459
Less than 8 years	5,113	3,983	20,365,079	1,508	2,562	3,863,496	6,006,364
8 years schooling	5,408	4,837	26,158,496	432	3,318	1,433,376	2,089,584
1–3 years high school	6,803	5,555	37,790,665	643	3,522	2,264,646	3,571,865
4 years high school	8,330	6,250	52,062,500	466	4,021	1,873,786	2,912,500
1–3 years college	3,246	7,554	24,520,284	163	4,355	709,865	1,231,302
4 or more years college	3,860	10,238	39,518,680	138	5,671	782,598	1,412,844

Source: *United States Census of Population: 1960*, PC(2)78, *Occupation by Earnings and Education*, Tables 1 and 4, U. S. Bureau of the Census, Washington.

were employed and had earnings in 1959 is shown in Table 6-6. The results show that the total earnings of employed Negro males 18 to 64 years of age were approximately $12 billion in 1959, whereas they would have been about $18.7 billion had the average earnings of the Negroes been the same as those of whites with equal years of schooling. The difference between these two figures —$6.7 billion—represents the approximate loss in earnings of the Negro males as a result of discrimination in employment. Analogous calculations for employed Negro females 18 to 64 years of age indicate that their loss in earnings as a result of discriminatory employment practices was approximately $1.3 billion,[9] bringing to a total of $8 billion the estimated 1959 loss of earnings resulting from failure to utilize the skills and abilities of Negroes as fully as those of whites. This loss in earnings equaled about 1.7 per cent of GNP in 1959.

This estimate does not take into account the differences in unemployment rates between Negroes and whites in 1959. Since the rates of unemployment in each of the educational and age groups were probably higher for Negroes than for whites, the loss in GNP as a result of discriminatory employment practices was probably higher than this estimate suggests. Also, it is reasonable to believe that the shifting of Negroes to types of work performed by whites would result in the creation of new capital, the income from which should be added to the estimated loss of $8 billion in labor earnings.[10] Neither factor was taken into account in our calculations, because adequate data were not available.

Moreover, the failure to utilize the existing skills and abilities of Negroes as fully as those of whites is only one of the ways in which racial discrimination reduces the total output of the economy. Most Negroes have had fewer years of schooling than whites.

[9] The estimated earnings of nonwhite females were calculated from data in the *U. S. Census of Population: 1960, Detailed Characteristics,* PC(1)1D. In making the estimates it was assumed that the ratio of mean to median earnings of females in each "year of schooling" group was the same as for males; and that the ratio of females 18–24 years of age to those 25–64 years old was the same as for males.

[10] This belief is based on the assumption that employed whites in 1959 were utilizing more capital per worker than were Negroes.

This is in large part the result of past discrimination in educational practices, and is an important factor in limiting their employment opportunities. Thus, it is relevant to estimate the loss in GNP resulting not only from underutilization of the present productive capacities of Negroes compared to whites, but also the loss that results from past inequalities in educational practices.

Had the percentage distribution by years of school completed of the 3.9 million Negro males in the experienced civilian labor force been the same as the percentage distribution of the white males (Table 6-6), and had the average annual earnings of the Negroes been the same as those of whites, total Negro earnings would have been $22 billion, compared to their actual earnings of $12 billion. The difference of $10 billion represents their approximate loss in earnings resulting from the combination of lower levels of education and the failure to utilize their existing skills and abilities as fully as those of whites. Analogous calculations for females indicate that their loss of earnings due to these two factors was $2.9 billion. Thus, the total estimated loss in Negro earnings resulting from discriminatory practices in employment and inequalities in educational opportunities was $13 billion.[11] This equaled approximately 2.7 per cent of GNP in 1959.

Though we believe that our estimates of the loss in GNP resulting from racial discrimination in employment and education in 1959 are valid, it is important to keep several points in mind in evaluating them. First, they pertain to only a one-year period.

---

[11] Of the estimated $13 billion, $8 billion arose from a failure to utilize existing skills and abilities of Negroes as fully as those of whites and the remaining $5 billion was a result of the lower educational level of the Negroes. The first factor is almost certainly overweighted because of our assumption that a given number of "years of school completed" resulted in the same level of skills and abilities for both whites and Negroes. As was pointed out in the preceding chapter, there is strong evidence that predominantly Negro schools are generally inferior to white schools, particularly in the South, where discrimination both in employment practices and in education are most pronounced. Although we have no statistical evidence to substantiate it, we strongly suspect that the relative weights of the two factors should be reversed; in other words, that the long-standing discrimination in education is a far more important factor in explaining the lower earnings of Negroes compared to whites than our calculations suggest.

Second, they are rough measures of only the economic costs to the nation, when such costs are defined as "the amount of output forgone." Third, the gains resulting from eliminating racial discrimination in employment and in education will accrue to the nation only over a relatively long period of time, as the upgrading of the nonwhite segment of the labor force takes place and as the occupational distribution of jobs held by Negroes improves. Fourth, an estimate of the loss to GNP as a result of racial discrimination that occurs in a one-year period is almost surely too low to apply to longer periods, because of the interlocking and self-reinforcing nature of job discrimination and educational attainment. For example, the elimination of occupational discrimination based on race would raise the incentives of Negroes to improve both the quantity and quality of their education. Finally, the elimination of racial discrimination would lower some of the social costs of crime, poor health, and the maintenance of separate public facilities for Negroes and whites, which would have little, if any, effect on GNP but would represent gains in national welfare.

A much larger estimate of the economic loss resulting from discrimination was made by the Council of Economic Advisers in its 1966 annual report: [12]

> If economic and social policies could be specifically designed to lower Negro unemployment to the current unemployment level of whites, the resulting gain in GNP would be $5 billion. Part of this gain would be in wages of the new Negro employees, and part would accrue as other forms of income. A further gain would result if all Negroes were able to obtain jobs which would better utilize their abilities and training.
>
> National output can be further expanded by improving the average level of productivity of each individual. Education and training are two of the most important means to this end. If the average productivity of the Negro and white labor force were equalized at the white level, total production would expand by $22 billion. If both unemployment rates and productivity levels

---

[12] *Economic Report of the President, Together With the Annual Report of the Council of Economic Advisers,* Washington, January 1966, p. 110.

were equalized, the total output of the economy would rise by about $27 billion—4 percent of GNP. This is a measure of the annual economic loss as a result of discrimination. . . .

The Negro Protest Movement

Negroes themselves have, of course, been the primary victims of racial discrimination. But for a long time the position of the Negro in the South was so hopeless that there was no effectual organized protest against discriminatory policies and practices. As the economic position of the South, and of the southern Negro to a more limited degree, improved, southern Negroes began to organize. As a result, since the late 1950's the Negro's discontent with his unequal status and limited opportunity for improving his situation has been expressed in picket lines, boycotts, street demonstrations, and other forms of protest.[13]

In the North demonstrations have been directed mainly against *de facto* school segregation, which is the result of segregated housing patterns; in the South they have been directed against deprivation of voting rights and segregation and discrimination in education and in the use of public accommodations, including health and recreational facilities. In both the North and the South, however, dissatisfaction with restricted employment opportunities and economic inequality has permeated the Negro protest movement, and the removal of racial barriers to employment has been, and without doubt will continue to be, a major target in the drive for equality.[14] Of all the forms of inequality suffered by Negroes, employment discrimination is the most widespread, the most consistent, and the most acutely felt.[15]

[13] *Civil Rights: Year-End Summary*, Southern Regional Council, Atlanta, December 31, 1963.

[14] It is noteworthy that when 250,000 Negroes marched on Washington on August 28, 1963, the official title given the march was "March on Washington for Jobs and Freedom." Of the 10 "demands" expressed by the marchers, 4 were explicitly directed toward relief from discrimination in employment and economic inequality. *Crisis*, October 1963.

[15] Paul H. Norgreen and Samuel E. Hill, *Toward Fair Employment*, Columbia University Press, New York, 1964, p. 4.

A major step toward removing several types of inequality between Negroes and whites was achieved with the passage of the Civil Rights Act of 1964. For the first time since 1883, when a bill similar in intent was declared unconstitutional, the promotion of equal status in public life and equality of opportunity in employment for Negroes is stated national policy. Moreover, the various programs inaugurated under the Economic Opportunity Act of 1964 and increased federal funds for training and education will help to prepare thousands of Negroes for types of work for which they have not been qualified in the past. The full effects of these new policies and programs cannot now be clearly foreseen. It will take many years for Negroes to overcome the handicaps resulting from discriminatory treatment so long suffered, even if they achieve full equality of opportunity in fact as well as in law. President Johnson recognized this fact when he said, at Howard University in June 1965, ". . . it is not enough just to open the gates of opportunity. All our citizens must have the ability to walk through those gates. . . . We seek . . . equality as a fact and equality as a result."

Prospects for the Future

Acceleration of the Negro's drive for equality has brought to national attention the urgency of eliminating racial discrimination in employment and of improving education and training to make it possible for larger numbers of Negroes to meet changing manpower demands. As a result, there is evidence of some forward movement in breaking traditional employment patterns in the South. A few break-throughs by Negroes have already occurred in sales jobs in retail establishments, in professional and technical jobs in manufacturing, and in clerical jobs in southern state and local government offices and in offices of the Federal Government located in the South. By and large, however, changes have been few and scattered. The 1963 Report of the President's Committee on Equal Employment Opportunity showed, for example, that in 7 southern labor-market areas where employers with government contracts employed 10,000 or more workers, only 360 Negroes were in white-collar jobs in 1963—only 44 more than in 1962. Most of the increase occurred in Birmingham alone.

Racial employment practices in the South are likely to improve. The equal employment opportunity program included in Title VII of the Civil Rights Act of 1964 should be of value in educating employers and combating discrimination. This section of the act went into effect in July 1965 for employers with 100 or more employees; after 3 years it will extend to employers with 25 or more employees.

In effect Title VII of the act establishes a new national civil right—equal opportunity in employment. However, the act has several weaknesses: the machinery for redress in employment discrimination is completely complaint-oriented, providing for investigations and hearings, conferences and conciliations, referrals to state and local agencies, and civil court actions; it includes various exemptions; and there are few real penalties for violations. Change can be expected to be slow and piecemeal. Resistance, either by outright noncompliance or subterfuge, is apt to create turmoil and tension, in view of the fundamental importance of expanded employment opportunities for Negroes. Nonetheless, it represents real progress in national attitudes toward the basic right of every man to a job, without discrimination because of race, color, religion, sex, or national origin. Though the effectiveness of the act as its coverage expands in the years ahead cannot be predicted with certainty, its impact is likely to be significant. Coupled with efforts to create more jobs and to increase the training of Negroes to help them to qualify for better jobs, the new act could hit at the heart of job discrimination.

A few southern state governments have also taken steps to promote better employment opportunities for Negroes. Kentucky in 1963 was the first southern state to adopt a fair employment practices code to combat discrimination in employment by the state government and by firms holding state government contracts. In the same year the governor of North Carolina established a

Good Neighbor Council for the express purpose of promoting equal employment opportunities for Negroes, and a statewide Human Relations Commission with similar aims was established in Tennessee.

The increase in efforts by industry recruiters to attract graduates of Negro colleges in the South has been another important recent development. Few, if any, recruiters visited Negro colleges in search of talent in 1960. By 1964 recruiters from important business firms North and South were reported to be quite successful in reaching previously untapped sources of promising personnel on Negro college campuses.[16]

In and of themselves, the factors that are tending to break down racial discrimination are unlikely to result in really significant improvements in the Negro job situation. In other words, it will not be enough for artificial barriers to employment of Negro workers to be broken, as important as this is. Negro youth entering the labor force during the next decade will face manpower problems increasingly different from those of a few years past. Technology has significantly decreased the demand for unskilled labor and has increased the demand for manpower of high quality. The occupational and educational structure of the Negro work force does not lend itself to ready adaptation to such changes. Indeed, unless the demand for unskilled labor increases, many poorly educated Negroes may face even greater difficulties in finding jobs in the future than in the past. Past improvements in Negro employment have come primarily during periods of tight labor markets, when Negro labor was used to fill gaps resulting from an inadequate supply of white labor, despite the fact that the job market was dominated by racial discrimination. Continued full employment is still essential to attainment of equality of opportunity in employment for Negroes, but because of structural changes in the economy, even full employment may have little meaning to large numbers of Negro workers.

In the 1940's there were unskilled jobs available, but the

16 "Industry Rushes for Negro Youth," *Business Week*, April 25, 1964, p. 78.

number of such jobs has been steadily decreasing. Many Negroes trapped in low-skilled occupations, or just migrating out of agriculture, find little, if any, demand for their services. Large-scale expansion in training and retraining programs to increase the employability of the many workers who do not have the skills to adjust to technological change are essential in order to alter this situation.

As the number of unskilled jobs diminishes and traditional "Negro jobs" disappear, southern Negroes will be largely in competition with white job seekers. Negroes will be in a position to compete more favorably in nondiscriminatory labor markets, as the disparity in levels of school attainment of whites and Negroes narrows. At best, however, improvements in job opportunities for Negroes can do little more than parallel those for whites. Thus, substantial reduction in inequality in employment in the South is not likely in the near future. To the extent that traditional employment practices persist, southern Negroes with qualifications and training are likely to continue to look to other regions for jobs to match their abilities. And to the extent that Negroes with limited skills and training are excluded by discriminatory practices from jobs where their abilities could be profitably used, they will continue to impede the progress of southern growth by placing on urban centers the burden of supporting an unproductive labor force.

Chapter 7

THE SOUTH'S FUTURE
LABOR FORCE

THE SIZE AND quality of the labor force will be a decisive factor in the economic development of the South during the next decade. As emphasized in earlier chapters, the South's status as the most underdeveloped region of the United States is attributable, in large measure, to past forms of social and economic organization that stifled development of its manpower. We have also shown that the South is going through a period of transition—is being transformed from an agricultural economy, requiring a large reservoir of docile, unskilled labor, to an urban, industrial economy, demanding a trained and educated work force. The economic changes have been accompanied by the beginnings of change in traditional attitudes toward Negroes, making it possible for them to share to some extent in new opportunities for education and training and better jobs.

The South's future manpower will be better educated than ever before. If recent trends described in Chapter 5 continue, the number of southern high school graduates will increase from almost 7 million in 1960 to at least 14 million in 1975, and the number of college graduates, from about 2 million to more than 3 million. Increased efforts to provide vocational and technical training for adults, for high school graduates, and for high school dropouts will significantly improve the quality of the manpower that will become available to southern employers during the next decade.

The higher level of education and greater skill of the southern population will not, however, be the only characteristics of the region's manpower supply that will influence future employment opportunities in the South. The number of persons of working age, their distribution by age, sex, and color, and the proportion of each group participating in the labor force will also be of significance. The major purposes of this chapter are to describe past trends in these characteristics of the South's labor force, to discuss factors that will influence them in the future, and to project the number of persons by age, sex, and color who are likely to be active participants in southern job markets in 1975.

Developments in the southern economy closely follow national economic trends, as shown in Chapter 3. Future manpower developments in the South will, therefore, depend not only on the demands of the southern economy and on the size and composition of the southern labor force, but also on national economic trends, including the size and composition of the nation's labor force.

The U. S. Labor Force in 1975

The size of the nation's labor force in 1975 will be determined by the number of persons of working age—14 years of age and over—in the population willing and able to work for pay or profit. The labor force consists of those persons of working age who are working or seeking work.[1] Its size is a measure of the economic activity of the population. Persons of working age not in the labor force include housewives working in their own homes, full-time

[1] Gertrude Bancroft, *The American Labor Force: Its Growth and Changing Composition,* John Wiley, New York, 1958, p. 186. Subsequent to the completion of this study, new definitions for employment and unemployment, which went into effect in January 1967, were adopted by the U. S. Bureau of Labor Statistics for use in the *Monthly Report of the Labor Force.* The new definitions do not, of course, apply to figures used in this study, but in any case they do not affect over-all unemployment rates by more than from one tenth to one fifth of a percentage point in either direction. (See U. S. Department of Labor, "New Definitions for Employment and Unemployment," News Release 7996, Washington, November 22, 1966.)

students, persons suffering long-term physical or mental illness, the voluntarily idle, and seasonal workers who are in an "off" season and who, therefore, are not reported as looking for work.[2]

PERSONS OF WORKING AGE

The number of persons in the United States who will be 14 years of age and over in 1975 can be estimated with a rather high degree of accuracy, for the youngest of them were born in 1961. According to projections of the U. S. Bureau of the Census, there will be approximately 162 million people in this age group by 1975, compared with 127 million in 1960 (Appendix Table 7-1). This represents an increase of about 2.3 million persons per year compared with an average annual increase of about 1.4 million persons in this age group between 1950 and 1960. The projected annual increase in the number of persons of working age is, in large part, a result of the baby boom in the years following World War II. Of the projected increase of 35 million, almost half—16.6 million—is expected in the age group 14 to 24 years old, including about 8.6 million in the age group 14 to 19. The projections also indicate a gain of about 33 per cent in the number of women 55 years old and over.[3]

LABOR FORCE PARTICIPATION RATES

The percentages of people in the various age groups in the working-age population who are employed or are looking for work (the labor force participation rates) in 1975 will be the final determinants of both the size and the composition of the labor

[2] *Concepts and Methods Used in Household Statistics on Employment and Unemployment from the Current Population Survey*, a joint publication of U. S. Bureau of Labor Statistics (Report No. 279) and U. S. Bureau of the Census (*Current Population Reports*, Series P-23, No. 13), Washington, 1964, p. 3.

[3] Sophia Cooper and Denis F. Johnston, "Labor Force Projections for 1970–1980," *Monthly Labor Review*, February 1965, p. 130. All figures in these projections include Alaska and Hawaii as well as the armed forces, in contrast to projections made in connection with the present study, shown in Appendix Table 7-2.

Table 7-1   Civilian Working-Age Population, Labor Force, and Labor Force Participation Rates, United States,[a] 1960, and Projections for 1975

Age group and sex	Working-age population (thousands)			Labor force (thousands)			Participation rate (per cent)		
	Total	White	Nonwhite	Total	White	Nonwhite	Total	White	Nonwhite
				1960					
Both sexes, 14 years and over	122,364	109,829	12,535	70,306	62,957	7,349	57.5	57.3	58.6
Male, 14 years and over	58,563	52,660	5,903	46,812	42,422	4,390	79.9	80.6	74.4
14–24 years	12,252	10,770	1,482	6,889	6,131	759	56.2	56.9	51.2
25–54 years	31,688	28,501	3,187	31,199	28,268	2,931	98.5	99.2	92.0
55 years and over	14,623	13,389	1,234	8,724	8,024	700	59.7	59.9	56.7
Female, 14 years and over	63,801	57,169	6,632	23,494	20,535	2,959	36.8	35.9	44.6
14–24 years	13,191	11,566	1,625	4,567	4,065	502	34.6	35.1	30.9
25–54 years	33,840	30,184	3,656	14,966	12,903	2,062	44.2	42.7	56.4
55 years and over	16,770	15,419	1,351	3,961	3,566	395	23.6	23.1	29.2
				Projections for 1975					
Both sexes, 14 years and over	160,003	142,368	17,635	90,457	80,202	10,255	56.5	56.3	58.2
Male, 14 years and over	76,336	67,983	8,353	57,736	51,687	6,049	75.6	76.0	72.4
14–24 years	20,592	17,713	2,879	11,664	10,150	1,514	56.6	57.3	52.6
25–54 years	36,890	32,982	3,908	35,655	31,930	3,725	96.7	96.8	95.3
55 years and over	18,855	17,289	1,566	10,417	9,607	810	55.2	55.6	51.2
Female, 14 years and over	83,667	74,385	9,282	32,721	28,515	4,206	39.1	38.3	45.3
14–24 years	21,448	18,458	2,990	7,735	6,727	1,008	36.1	36.4	33.7
25–54 years	38,945	34,576	4,369	19,208	16,597	2,611	49.3	48.0	59.8
55 years and over	23,274	21,351	1,923	5,778	5,191	587	24.8	24.3	30.5

Source: Appendix Table 7-2.

[a] Excludes Alaska and Hawaii.

force. Numerous factors, such as the availability of jobs, the rate of urbanization, the length of time teenagers remain in school, the kinds of jobs available to middle-aged and elderly women, and the age at which people retire, influence labor force participation rates. Though the long-run effects of many of these factors on the size and composition of the labor force cannot be precisely predicted, studies of past trends in labor force participation rates among various population groups, and of factors that influence such trends, provide important bases for labor force projections.

On the basis of such studies, the U. S. Bureau of Labor Statistics has projected a 1975 U. S. labor force of approximately 93.6 million persons (Appendix Table 7-1).[4] Not all of the members of the 1975 labor force will be in the civilian job market; some will be in the armed forces. Little is to be gained by speculating about the manpower requirements of the armed forces in 1975. Our projection is based on the assumption that the size of the armed forces in 1975 will be the same as in 1960—2.7 million. This means that there will be about 90.9 million persons in the U. S. civilian labor force in 1975, about 90.5 million of whom will be in the 48 conterminous states. This represents an increase of 20.2 million over the 1960 labor force of about 70.3 million (Table 7-1).

From this brief review of the projected U. S. labor force, two points are especially significant: both the population of working age and the total labor force are expected to increase at unusually rapid rates during the next decade; and a high proportion of the increase will be due to the entrance of young persons with little or no work experience into the labor market. Young Negroes, particularly, will constitute a significantly higher proportion of the labor force in 1975 than in 1960 (Figure 7-1). Since unemployment rates for the past several years have been much higher among young workers, both white and Negro, than among older workers, increased representation of youth in the labor force in the years ahead has important implications for future employment problems and policies.

[4] See *ibid.*, pp. 134–140, for a full description of the method and assumptions on which the BLS projections are based.

Figure 7-1   **U. S. Civilian Labor Force, by Age Group and Color, 1950, 1960, 1975**

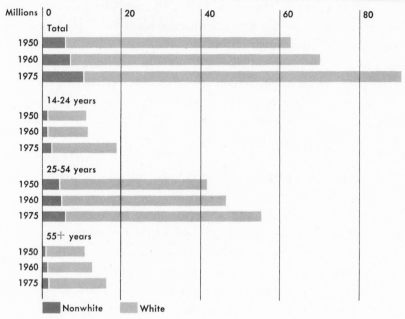

Source: Appendix Table 7-2.

Southern Labor Force Projections [5]

The projected increase of 20.2 million persons in the civilian labor force of the 48 conterminous states between 1960 and 1975 will be shared by all major regions of the country, South and non-South, and in general the changes in the southern labor force will follow national trends. The extent, however, to which the South will share in the future labor force of the nation will depend upon, first, the number of people of working age in the region, and, second, the proportion of these who participate in the labor force.

[5] See source note to Appendix Table 7-2 for methods and sources used in making the projections of the U. S. and southern working-age population and labor force, by age, sex, and color, as well as estimates for 1950 and 1960.

WORKING-AGE POPULATION

The number of persons of working age will be directly affected by patterns of net interstate migration. In past decades the natural increase of population in the South was so high and employment opportunities within the region were so limited that large numbers of southerners—many of working age—left to seek jobs in other parts of the country. In spite of this, as shown in Chapter 3, the total population of the region continued to increase. Between 1950 and 1960, for example, the population of the South rose from approximately 41.7 million to 48.8 million —an increase of 7.1 million persons (Table 3-1). Had there been no migration into or out of the region, the gain in population during the 1950's would have been about 8.3 million. In other words, approximately 1.2 million more people moved out of the South than moved into it during the 1950's. Migration patterns of whites and Negroes were vastly different. There was a net out-migration of slightly over 1.5 million Negroes, but a net in-migration of about 330,000 whites (Table 3-5).

Numerous factors will affect future decisions of southerners to move out of the South and of persons in other parts of the country to move into it. The shift of the southern economy away from its traditional dependence on agriculture, the growing urbanization of the region, the increased education and skill of southern workers will tend to increase the mobility of the southern population. Likewise, the number and kinds of jobs available in the South compared to those in other regions will affect net migration rates, especially of persons of working age, in the South as well as in other regions in the years ahead. Thus, if job opportunities in the South expand faster than in other regions, out-migration from the South will tend to slow down.

However, the relationship between the availability of jobs and the size and characteristics of the southern labor supply is a two-way street. Historically, the quantity and quality of the

Table 7-2   Southern Civilian Working-Age Population, Labor Force, and Labor Force Participation Rates, 1960, and Projections for 1975

Age group and sex	Working-age population (thousands)			Labor force (thousands)			Participation rate (per cent)		
	Total	White	Nonwhite	Total	White	Nonwhite	Total	White	Nonwhite
				1960					
Both sexes, 14 years and over	32,428	26,087	6,341	17,912	14,344	3,568	55.2	55.0	56.3
Male, 14 years and over	15,386	12,424	2,963	11,846	9,722	2,124	77.0	78.3	71.7
14–24 years	3,642	2,800	842	1,948	1,521	428	53.5	54.3	50.8
25–54 years	8,139	6,681	1,458	7,878	6,540	1,338	96.8	97.9	91.8
55 years and over	3,605	2,943	663	2,019	1,662	358	56.0	56.5	54.0
Female, 14 years and over	17,042	13,663	3,378	6,066	4,621	1,444	35.6	33.8	42.7
14–24 years	3,892	3,008	884	1,149	904	246	29.5	30.1	27.8
25–54 years	8,973	7,241	1,732	4,035	3,045	990	45.0	42.1	57.2
55 years and over	4,177	3,414	762	882	673	209	21.1	19.7	27.4
				Projections for 1975					
Both sexes, 14 years and over	41,710	34,585	7,126	22,631	18,737	3,894	54.3	54.2	54.6
Male, 14 years and over	19,404	16,172	3,232	14,137	11,907	2,230	77.0	78.3	69.0
14–24 years	5,256	4,117	1,139	2,856	2,264	592	54.3	55.0	52.0
25–54 years	9,198	7,835	1,363	8,832	7,537	1,295	96.0	96.2	95.0
55 years and over	4,951	4,221	730	2,449	2,106	343	49.5	49.9	47.0
Female, 14 years and over	22,306	18,413	3,894	8,494	6,830	1,664	38.1	37.1	42.7
14–24 years	5,564	4,320	1,243	1,800	1,426	374	32.4	33.0	30.1
25–54 years	10,529	8,818	1,711	5,260	4,233	1,027	50.0	48.0	60.6
55 years and over	6,214	5,274	940	1,434	1,171	263	23.1	22.2	28.0

Source: Appendix Table 7-2.

southern labor force have been important factors affecting the number and kinds of jobs that became available within the region, and, as is shown in Chapters 3 and 4, employment expanded less rapidly in the South than in the nation as a whole in each decade between 1940 and 1960. Since the cost of labor is the largest item of expense in practically all types of production, the availability and productivity of southern workers will continue to be important factors determining the ability of southern firms to compete with their counterparts in other regions.

Our projections of the South's 1975 working-age population are therefore based on the assumption that net interstate migration rates for each age group, of both sexes, white and nonwhite, will be the same as in the 1950's. On the basis of this assumption, the South's working-age population is expected to increase from approximately 32.4 million persons in 1960 to 41.7 million in 1975 (Table 7-2), representing a projected average annual increase of almost 619,000, compared with the actual annual increase of 374,000 during the 1950's. The projected annual increase of about 219,000 in the age group 14 to 24 is almost 6 times the annual increase that occurred during the 1950's. The age group 25 to 54 is expected to increase at a rate of 174,000 per year, compared with 131,000 per year during the 1950's; while the annual increase in the number of people 55 years and older is expected to be about 226,000, compared with the 205,000 of the 1950's. (See Appendix Table 7-2.)

From these figures it can be seen that in the South, as in the nation as a whole, the largest increases are expected among persons 14 to 24 years of age and those 55 years and older. However, persons in the prime working ages (25 to 54 years) will still furnish the bulk of the South's labor supply. In 1960 they represented more than half of the people of working age in the region; they are expected to account for almost half in 1975.

Whites will predominate in all age groups in the 1975 working-age population. Indeed, though the number of Negroes of working age is expected to increase from approximately 6.3 million in 1960 to about 7.1 million in 1975, Negro migration from the region is expected to result in a continuation of the downward trend in the Negro share of the South's working-age population— from about 22 per cent in 1950, to almost 20 per cent in 1960, to 17 per cent in 1975 (Appendix Table 7-2).

Estimated state population changes from 1960 to 1965 indicate that net out-migration from the South was less during the first half of the 1960's than during the 1950's.[6] If this trend continues, the projection of 41.7 million persons of working age in the South in 1975 may prove to be low. Had we assumed that net interstate migration rates of each age, sex, and color group would gradually decrease to zero by 1980, the projected working-age population of the South in 1975 would have been 42.5 million persons instead of 41.7. If the national unemployment rate continues to be about 4 per cent of the labor force during the next few years, a projected southern civilian working-age population in the neighborhood of 42 million persons in 1975 is not unreasonable.

LABOR FORCE PARTICIPATION RATES

The southern population of working age represents the reservoir from which the labor supply of the region will be drawn, but the future southern labor force will, of course, be smaller than the future southern population of working age. Some of the persons 14 years of age and older will be enrolled in school. Some will be keeping house, retired, or disabled. Others will be voluntarily idle, and still others will be neither working nor seeking work, because they will have abandoned hope of finding employment.

If labor force participation rates remained constant, labor force growth would occur solely as a result of an increase in the number of persons of working age. Labor force growth, however, is the result of changes in labor force participation rates of different groups in the population in response to social and economic changes, such as rural to urban shifts in population, changes in the educational level of persons of working age, and rises in educational requirements for employment.

[6] See *Americans at Mid-Decade*, U. S. Bureau of the Census, Washington, Series P-23, No. 16, January 1966.

Furthermore, as the economy of the South becomes more like that of the rest of the country, it is likely to respond with increasing sensitivity to changes in the national level of economic activity. Future southern labor force participation rates and, consequently, the size and structure of the southern labor force will, therefore, be increasingly affected by the level of employment in the national economy.

Urbanization

Of the major factors affecting the size and structure of the South's future labor force, the effect of urbanization is, perhaps, least subject to independent analysis. With urbanization come increased employment opportunity and increased opportunity for education. Furthermore, educational requirements for employment are usually higher in urban areas, enforcement of compulsory school attendance and child labor laws is more rigid, and the influence of traditions against the employment of women is weaker.

Urban mothers of school-age children, for example, find many opportunities for employment, especially in clerical, sales, and service occupations. At the same time, because of the technological revolution in housekeeping—laborsaving household appliances, ease of food preparation, and the availability of many types of household services—care of the home is generally less time-consuming in urban than in rural areas. Urbanization therefore increases the availability of women for participation in the labor force.

In contrast, urbanization contributes to a lowering of the labor force participation rates of some groups. For young boys, for example, work opportunities are more limited in urban than in rural areas, where many boys work on farms as unpaid family workers. Men who have passed the prime working years tend to work on farms as long as they are physically able to do so, but they find age to be a barrier to employment in urban jobs. In addition, men who have been employed for long periods in urban jobs are more likely than farm workers to be eligible for private retirement benefits to supplement Social Security benefits, and thus to be financially able to withdraw from the labor force.

Education

Education, like urbanization, operates through the forces of both supply and demand to affect labor force participation rates. For example, because women have, in the past, attained a higher average level of education than men, unemployed men in the oldest working-age groups are at a disadvantage in job competition with women in the same age groups. The women are considered to have a better retraining potential, since they have more education, and they are willing to work at lower wages. Education has also given women an advantage over untrained young male workers. In hiring workers in clerical, sales, and numerous service occupations, employers have tended to prefer easily trained, mature women to young men who are high school dropouts or high school graduates seeking their first jobs.

Undoubtedly, this decrease in the demand for the services of young men has encouraged many of them to remain in school in order to gain educational qualifications for a subsequent successful entry into the labor market. At the same time, contributions of women to family incomes have permitted young males to defer their entrance to the labor force. Even discounting the effect of increased employment of women on the participation rates of young males, there is little doubt that increased public awareness of changing qualifications necessary to compete for jobs and increased emphasis on the cultural and social value of education have caused young men to stay in school longer and have thus kept labor force participation rates of young males at a lower level than they would otherwise have been.

Job Vacancies

The number and kind of job vacancies are important influences on labor force participation rates, especially among Negroes and workers in the oldest and youngest age groups. In general, increases in the number of unfilled jobs tend to produce increases in labor force participation rates, but the effects are uneven among different groups of potential workers and there are other important offsetting influences.

The available jobs may not be suitable to the education, skills, and social characteristics of workers who might otherwise enter the labor force. Young persons may choose to continue their education, older persons may choose to retire or may not have the necessary education or skills to qualify for available jobs, Negroes may find that employers refuse to consider them for employment, and well-educated, middle-class wives may find that available jobs fail to offer the noneconomic satisfactions they seek through participation in the labor force.

Though the degree of urbanization, the level of education, and the availability of jobs are important factors in the decision to seek employment, their effects on labor force participation rates are modified by the kinds of jobs available, discriminatory practices of employers with respect to age, sex, or color of potential workers, and the qualifications required to fill available jobs. Thus, there is a need to analyze the interaction of a variety of economic and social forces in order to project labor force participation rates of the southern population of working age.

LABOR FORCE PARTICIPATION RATES, 1950–1960

During the 1950's more than 3.6 million white persons and 90,000 Negroes were added to the South's working-age population, resulting in increases of about 16.3 per cent and 1.4 per cent, respectively, in the white and Negro population in this age group. (See Appendix Table 7-2.) However, the number of whites in the South's civilian labor force increased by 2 million, or about 16 per cent, while the number of Negro labor force participants decreased by 196,000, or about 5 per cent. In contrast, about 4.5 million whites and almost 1 million Negroes were added to the non-South's labor force during this period, resulting in an increase of about 10 per cent in the white labor force and 34 per cent in the Negro labor force. Thus, the white labor force increased at a

Figure 7-2   **Southern Civilian Labor Force, by Age Group and Color, 1950, 1960, 1975**

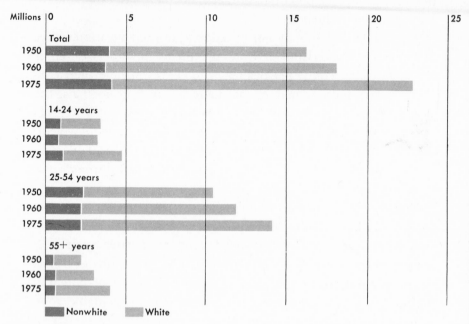

Source: Appendix Table 7-2.

more rapid rate in the South than in the non-South, while the Negro labor force declined in the South and increased substantially in the non-South. (See Figures 7-1 and 7-2.)

One of the significant manpower developments of the 1950's was a decline in the labor force participation rates of young workers (Appendix Table 7-2). In the age group 14 to 24 years old the participation rate increased only among white females in the South, while the rate of decline for young Negro males was about 4 times greater in the South than in the non-South.

The decrease in the participation rate of young white males reflected mainly an increased emphasis on education. For young Negro males, however, much of the decrease was due to their lack of employment opportunities in the 1950's, which resulted in their withdrawal from or failure to enter the labor force.

Males in the prime working ages, 25 to 54, have little choice but to engage in economic activity, and their participation rates, consequently, remained relatively stable at a high level. The rise in the participation rate of female workers in the same age group was largely a result of increased employment opportunity. Although noneconomic factors played a role in inducing white women to enter the labor market, the increased rate among southern Negro women was probably attributable primarily to increased job opportunities in urban centers. While relatively little change occurred in the number of unmarried women in the labor force, the number of married women workers increased from 7.5 million to 14.8 million fom 1947 to 1962.[7]

The participation rates of males 55 years and over declined for all groups. Increased availability of retirement benefits contributed to these changes, but the large decline in rates for southern Negro males in the oldest working-age group offers evidence of the role of discouragement in causing withdrawal from the labor force. The trend in participation rates of female workers in this age group was the opposite from that of males, though participation rates rose less for southern Negro women than for other women 55 and over. To some extent the increased labor market activity of elderly white women reflected an increasing tendency for them to compete for jobs—for example, in cafeterias, restaurants, hotels, and a few other service establishments—that were formerly held almost exclusively by Negro males. Elderly Negro women apparently found it increasingly necessary to seek jobs in order to supplement family income.

LABOR FORCE PARTICIPATION RATES, 1975

The projected labor force participation rates, shown in Table 7-2, reflect trends that were evident in the 1950's. They are also based on an analysis of the probable effects of further urbanization; improvements in educational opportunities, particularly for Negroes in the South; and the availability of jobs in 1975, when

[7] *Manpower Report of the President and Report on Manpower Requirements, Resources, Utilization, and Training,* U. S. Department of Labor, Washington, 1963, p. 12.

it is assumed that the national level of unemployment will be 4 per cent of the labor force.[8]

By 1975 many young southerners born in the early 1950's will have reached their early twenties, will have completed school, and will have entered the labor force. Most of them will have better education and training than their parents and grandparents had. Many will be able to work a full 40-hour week and continue their education in community colleges and technical schools, the number of which will continue to increase. Expanding educational opportunities and growing recognition of the value of attending school will probably further reduce the participation rates of young people who have not finished high school. By 1975, however, high school dropouts will constitute a smaller proportion of the population 14 to 24 years old than in recent years.

We have, therefore, projected modest increases from 1960 to 1975 in the participation rates of all groups 14 to 24 years of age in both the South and the non-South. The participation rates of young southern women are likely to rise the most rapidly, as opportunities for employment in white-collar jobs in urban areas increase.

The participation rates of white males in the prime working ages (25–54 years) are expected to remain high, though slightly lower in the South than in the rest of the country.[9] Better education and training, together with civil rights legislation and fair employment practices, are expected to contribute to a rise in participation rates of Negroes in this age group by 1975.

The participation rates of both Negro and white females 25 to 54 years of age are expected to continue to rise, because opportunities for their employment are growing in service-producing industries, and the requirements of housekeeping are becoming less time-consuming. Moreover, the proportion of southern Negro women working or seeking work will probably increase because of their growing desire to contribute to family incomes.

8 See the source note to Appendix Table 7-2 for more detail as to sources and methods of making the projections.

9 See note to Appendix Table 7-2 regarding estimated participation rates of white males in this age group in 1950 and 1960.

The participation rates of white and Negro men 55 years of age and older are expected to decline slightly, partly because of the greater availability of retirement benefits and partly because many of them are likely to be unsuccessful in finding work. The participation rates of southern white and Negro women in this age group are expected to continue to rise, however, largely because there will be more jobs for which they are qualified in the full-employment economy of 1975.

THE SOUTHERN CIVILIAN LABOR FORCE, 1975

Projections of the future southern labor force, by age, color, and sex, as summarized in Table 7-2 and shown in detail in Appendix Table 7-2, are based on the projections of labor force participation rates and of the working-age population, discussed in preceding sections.

According to our projections, the southern civilian labor force —the number of persons working or looking for work—will increase from 17.9 million in 1960 to 22.6 million in 1975, a gain of 4.7 million or 26.3 per cent. Approximately 18.7 million members of the South's 1975 labor force will be white and 3.9 million will be Negro.

Despite the fact that the South's labor force is expected to increase, its share of the nation's labor force is projected to decrease slightly during this period from 25.5 per cent to 25.0 per cent. The slower rate of growth of the South's labor force compared to the non-South's is explained primarily by the projected decrease in the number of southern Negro males. The South's share of the nation's white labor force is expected to increase from 22.8 per cent in 1960 to 23.4 per cent in 1975, but its share of the nation's Negro labor force is projected to decrease from 48.6 per cent to 38.0 per cent.

Of the 4.7 million increase in the number of persons in the southern labor force between 1960 and 1975, approximately 1.5 million will be 14 to 24 years of age. This will raise the proportion of workers in this young age group in the region from 17 to 21 per cent. There will also be an increase of approximately 2.2 million persons in the prime working-age group—from 25 to 54 years of age, but there will be a decline in their proportion of the region's labor force from almost 67 to 62 per cent. The number of workers 55 years and over will increase by almost 1 million—from 2.9 million to approximately 3.9 million. Their proportion of the total labor force in the region will increase from 16 per cent to 17 per cent.

Of the projected 22.6 million persons in the southern labor force in 1975, approximately 14.1 million will be males and 8.5 million will be females. This is an increase from 1960 of 19 per cent in the number of males and 40 per cent in the number of females. The proportion of males in the southern labor force will decrease from 66 per cent in 1960 to 62 per cent in 1975, while the proportion of females will increase from 34 per cent in 1960 to 38 per cent in 1975.

If our assumptions with respect to future net interstate migration rates and future participation rates prove to be reasonably accurate, the southern labor force in 1975 will be predominantly white, and white workers in the South will have little reason to fear competition from Negroes for most high-paying jobs. There will be increases, during the next decade, in both the number and proportion of workers in the youngest and oldest age groups. However, the number of workers 25 to 54 years of age will still represent approximately 62 per cent of the region's labor force in 1975. Although the number of women in the southern labor force will increase significantly, women will still represent less than 40 per cent of the total in 1975.

The projected 26.3 per cent increase in the southern labor force between 1960 and 1975 will clearly be large enough to permit a substantial expansion of employment in the South in the years ahead. The extent to which the South is likely to offer employment opportunities sufficiently attractive to permit full utilization of its available manpower is a problem to which we turn in the next chapter.

Chapter 8

EMPLOYMENT PROSPECTS AND PROJECTIONS

IN CHAPTER 1 we indicated that our inquiry would focus on three questions: Approximately, how many people are likely to be employed in the South in 1975? How will they be distributed among industries and occupations? How are employment opportunities for Negroes likely to change in the South during the next 10 years? In this chapter we summarize our answers to these questions.

In preceding chapters we have examined factors that will significantly influence southern employment in the years ahead. Most of these factors are interrelated. Several of them will not only affect the number of persons who will be employed in the South, but also the kinds of jobs that will be available.

The level of employment and the rate of growth in the national economy will have a significant influence on the number of persons employed in the South. As the population and labor force of the nation grow, and as the demand for goods and services expands, the South will share in the resulting increase in national employment. The maintenance of a low unemployment rate throughout the nation will tend to expand job opportunities in the South and at the same time encourage migration from the South, especially from farms and rural areas, where employment opportunities will be limited. Thus, though full employment and rapid growth in the national economy will

almost surely be important contributors to expanding employment in the South and to raising southern incomes by hastening
the shift of employment from low-wage to high-wage industries
and occupations, these factors may have little effect on the South's
share of national employment.

Changes in the political, social, and economic structure of the
South, along with the increasing efforts of many southern leaders
to diversify the southern economy by encouraging the growth of
manufacturing and commercial enterprises, will clearly change
the future job-mix of the region. Moreover, diversification of jobs
in the South will be facilitated by an increased supply of educated
and skilled workers, resulting from improvements in the South's
educational establishment. All of these changes, however, will
also tend to increase the ability and willingness of many workers
to move out of the South to take advantage of attractive opportunities in other areas of the country. Their principal net result
may well be to raise the per capita income of southern people,
but they may have little effect on the South's share of national
employment.

The future industry-mix of the region will continue to be an
important factor influencing the growth of employment in the
South relative to that in other areas of the country. The combination of industries that has characterized the southern economy
in the past has been a major impediment to the rapid growth
of employment within the region, because the South has had a
heavy concentration of industries in which national employment
was either declining or expanding quite slowly. Though the
industry-mix improved greatly between 1940 and 1960, it will
still tend to hold the South's rate of growth in employment below
the national average and thus reduce the region's share of national
employment. This tendency will be especially strong in those
states and areas which are heavily dependent on farming.

As pointed out above, the southern labor supply is likely to be
considerably more conducive to the growth of a diversified regional
economy in the future than in the past. Nevertheless, the future
size and composition of the South's labor force, and the number

of persons of working age who can readily be drawn into the labor force if job opportunities are available, indicate that the region as a whole will continue, for at least the next decade, to have an abundant labor supply. Thus, many areas of the South, particularly those with a high proportion of rural population, will continue to invite an expansion of employment in labor-intensive, low-wage industries.

Although racial discrimination in employment is diminishing in the South, and educational opportunities are improving, Negroes will continue to be at a disadvantage in the competitive struggle for available jobs. A high proportion of southern Negroes is still employed in agriculture and in domestic service—fields in which employment in the future will almost surely decline. Many others are too old, too poorly educated, and too firmly accustomed to rural ways of making a living to profit significantly from the new training programs and new kinds of jobs that are of growing importance within the region. Unemployment and underemployment among Negroes in the South can be expected, therefore, to remain higher than among whites. Many educated Negroes will continue to find their best employment opportunities outside of the South.

The combined net effects of these various factors on the future employment situation in the South are difficult to measure quantitatively. Nevertheless, three general conclusions are warranted. First, the South is presently in a much stronger position than at any time in the past century to increase its total output of goods and services, to raise its productivity per man-hour, and to improve the occupational status and income of its workers. Second, as national employment expands, the South will share in this growth. Third, the decline in the South's share of national employment that occurred between 1940 and 1950 and again between 1950 and 1960 [1] may be virtually halted by 1975, but there is no indication that the South's share of total U. S. employment will change significantly within the next decade.

[1] The South's share of national employment declined from 26.9 per cent in 1940 to 25.7 per cent in 1950 and 25.5 per cent in 1960. (See Table 3-1.)

Projections of National Employment

Because future employment in the South will be greatly influenced both by the level of employment in the total economy and by variations in the rates at which employment will change in different industries, it was necessary to examine the prospects of attaining full employment in the national economy and probable employment changes in the major industries of the country in the next few years as a basis for projecting the growth in southern employment.

LEVEL OF NATIONAL EMPLOYMENT

In the preceding chapter we project a national civilian labor force in the conterminous United States of about 90.5 million persons in 1975. Assuming "frictional" unemployment of 4 per cent of this labor force, the number of persons employed will be about 86.8 million, compared with 66.4 million in 1960. Achievement of this increase will necessitate a rise in the number of employed workers of about 1.4 million per year.

The problems involved in achieving such an expansion in employment are suggested by comparing it with the 1947–1965 average annual increase of slightly less than 800,000 in the number of civilians employed. In only 5 years during that period did the economy generate a net increase in civilian employment of as many as 1.4 million workers. The problems of maintaining the projected high level of employment are further complicated by gains in productivity per man-hour and by shifts that will occur in the industrial, occupational, and geographical distribution of jobs during the next decade.

Productivity, as measured by output per man-hour in the private economy, has increased at an average annual rate of slightly over 3 per cent since World War II, but at a somewhat higher rate since 1960. An annual increase in productivity of approximately 3 per cent is assumed to be consistent with the expected 20.4 million increase in employment. However, a productivity gain of 3.2 to 3.5 per cent annually during the next decade would not be an unreasonable assumption.

New capital investments and related technological changes have stimulated, and will continue to stimulate, important gains in productivity, simultaneously creating new jobs and eliminating old ones. The long-run effect of increases in productivity on the number of available jobs is therefore difficult to evaluate. It is evident, however, that increases in productivity raise the capacity of the economy. If this increased capacity is to be utilized to the extent necessary to achieve an unemployment rate of no higher than 4 per cent of the civilian labor force, and if the length of the work week does not decrease significantly, more than a 4 per cent annual rate of growth in real gross national product will probably be necessary for the next several years. This compares with the postwar annual growth rate of about 3.8 per cent.

Important industrial, occupational, and regional shifts in employment will take place in the next decade. Such shifts will arise from uneven rates of adoption of technological changes and of capital investment by industries, changes in consumer tastes and buying power, changes in the industrial and geographical distribution of, and volume of, government expenditures, exhaustion of minerals and other raw materials in some areas and discoveries of new sources of raw materials in others, and the development and utilization of new products and of new methods of producing old products. The human adjustments that such shifts necessitate will add to the difficulties of maintaining a high rate of employment, since new jobs must be created not only to provide for the projected 20.4 million net increase in employment, but to replace many of the old jobs eliminated by shifts in the industrial, occupational, and regional shifts in employment.

INDUSTRIAL SHIFTS IN EMPLOYMENT

The nature and extent of industrial, occupational, and geographical shifts in employment that will take place cannot be predicted

Table 8-1   Estimate of U. S. Civilian Employment, by Industry, 1950, 1960, and Projections for 1975

Industry	Number (thousands)			Change per year (thousands)		Percentage distribution		
	1950	1960	1975	1950–1960	1960–1975	1950	1960	1975
All industries	59,748	66,392	86,839	664.4	1,363.1	100.00	100.00	100.00
Agriculture	7,419	4,553	3,150	−286.6	−93.5	12.42	6.86	3.63
Forestry, fisheries, logging	315	279	250	−3.7	−1.9	0.53	0.42	0.29
Mining	1,003	701	450	−30.2	−16.7	1.68	1.06	0.52
Construction	3,712	4,073	5,800	36.1	115.1	6.21	6.13	6.68
Transportation, communications, utilities	4,780	4,767	5,000	−1.3	15.5	8.00	7.18	5.76
Wholesale and retail trade	11,295	12,622	17,500	132.7	325.2	18.90	19.01	20.15
Finance, insurance, real estate	2,066	2,886	4,500	82.0	107.6	3.46	4.35	5.18
Services	10,845	14,494	21,800	364.9	487.1	18.15	21.83	25.10
Personal	3,725	4,124	4,800	39.9	45.1	6.23	6.21	5.53
Professional and related	5,185	8,108	14,000	292.4	392.8	8.68	12.21	16.12
Business, recreation, and repair	1,935	2,262	3,000	32.6	49.2	3.24	3.41	3.45
Government	2,685	3,407	4,800	72.3	92.8	4.49	5.13	5.53
Manufacturing	15,628	18,610	23,589	298.2	331.9	26.16	28.03	27.16
Food and kindred products	1,582	1,937	2,600	35.5	44.2	2.65	2.92	2.99
Tobacco products	101	92	82	−0.9	−0.7	0.17	0.14	0.09
Textile mill products	1,324	1,023	820	−30.2	−13.5	2.22	1.54	0.95
Apparel products	1,151	1,244	1,600	9.3	23.7	1.93	1.87	1.84
Sawmills and planing mills	634	451	400	−18.4	−3.4	1.06	0.68	0.46
Furniture, fixture, misc. wood	470	513	650	4.3	9.1	0.79	0.77	0.75
Paper products	501	622	850	12.1	15.2	0.84	0.94	0.98
Printing and publishing	929	1,224	1,550	29.6	21.7	1.55	1.84	1.79

Chemicals and plastics	756	1,059	1,200	30.3	9.4	1.27	1.60	1.38
Petroleum and coal products	301	302	350	0.1	3.2	0.50	0.46	0.40
Rubber products	256	286	350	3.0	4.3	0.43	0.43	0.40
Leather and products	418	373	360	−4.5	−0.9	0.70	0.56	0.42
Stone, clay, and glass	507	645	800	13.7	10.4	0.85	0.97	0.92
Metal industry	2,229	2,738	3,600	50.9	57.5	3.73	4.12	4.15
Electrical machinery	929	1,600	2,600	67.1	66.7	1.55	2.41	2.99
Nonelectrical machinery	1,352	1,687	2,200	33.5	34.2	2.26	2.54	2.53
Transportation equipment	1,445	1,952	2,500	50.8	36.5	2.42	2.94	2.88
Other	743	862	1,077	12.0	14.3	1.24	1.30	1.24

Sources: U. S. totals, 1950 and 1960, as published in *Economic Report of the President, Together with the Annual Report of the Council of Economic Advisers,* Washington, 1966, p. 232. These totals (which exclude Alaska and Hawaii) are from the U. S. Bureau of Labor Statistics, *Monthly Report of the Labor Force* (MRLF). The distribution by industry, not estimated by the BLS, was obtained by applying to the MRLF totals the industrial distribution of employment as reported in the decennial Censuses of Population in 1950 and 1960. 1975 projections are staff judgments, based on 1950–1960 employment trends and evaluation of the effects on employment during the next few years of such factors as changes in productivity, taste, income, population, technology, and availability of jobs in 1975, as explained in text.

Note: Employment figures in this and subsequent tables in Chapter 8 disagree with employment figures in tables in Chapters 2, 3, 4, and 6, in which decennial Census figures were used, whereas employment figures in this chapter are based on BLS, *Monthly Report of the Labor Force* U. S. totals, as explained above.

with accuracy, but past employment trends provide important clues to the types of changes that are likely to occur. As has been pointed out in earlier chapters, two dominant trends have characterized industrial shifts in employment for more than two decades: a decline in the percentage of total employment in the goods-producing industries and an increase in the percentage of total employment in the service-producing industries.

These trends are likely to continue, and were taken into account in projecting 1975 employment among industries as shown in Table 8-1. In addition, attention was given to changes in productivity, and to changes in demand for industrial output as a result of changing tastes, income, population, and labor force. The projections are based on several assumptions: that the nation will not be involved in a large war or great social upheaval that will change the basic organization of our society; that national full employment (96 per cent of the civilian labor force) will be maintained; that labor force growth and increasing capital investment and the consequent improvements in technology will result in an annual increment to total output of goods and services (GNP) of something over 4 per cent; that the major effects of the introduction of technological improvements in an industry can be forecasted on the basis of the current research and development work being carried out; and that the effects of most of the new techniques that are apt to be significant by 1975 are to a large extent embodied in the trends of the past decade.[2]

The projected increase of 20.4 million employees in the United States between 1960 and 1975 will be the net result of decreases totaling almost 2 million in 7 industries (agriculture; forestry,

[2] In order to gain insight into changing patterns of national and southern employment, we contracted with the National Planning Association (NPA), Washington, an agency that has specialized in making national economic projections, to make a special study of the distribution of employment by industrial and occupational category and by state and region in 1950 and 1960, and to supplement their findings by a set of employment projections for 1975. The NPA's findings were reported in *Occupational Employment, by Industry, State and Region, 1950, 1960, 1975,* an unpublished report prepared for the Agricultural Policy Institute, North Carolina State University at Raleigh, September 1963. Although our projections differ from those made by the NPA, the latter were of significant value to us in arriving at the 1975 projections shown in Table 8-1.

fisheries, and logging; mining; textile manufacturing; tobacco manufacturers; sawmills and planing mills; and leather products manufacturing) and increases amounting to 22.4 million in the remaining 22 industries shown in Table 8-1. Of the decrease of 2 million workers in the 7 industries, approximately 1.4 million are expected to be in agriculture. Of the projected 22.4 million increase in the remaining industries, the 7 with the largest projected gains (in millions) are: professional and related services, 5.9; wholesale and retail trade, 4.9; manufacturing (excluding textiles, sawmills and planing mills, tobacco, and leather products), 5.3; construction, 1.7; finance, insurance, real estate, 1.6; government (federal, state, and local), 1.4; and business, recreational, and repair services, 0.7.

Though unforeseeable developments may prove our projections to be wide of the mark, since, like all human judgments, they may be in error, we feel that the projections are of value in analyzing future prospects for the growth of employment in the South.[3]

Projections of Southern Employment

Of the projected U. S. employment in 1975 of 86.8 million persons, how many are likely to be employed in the South? To what extent, in other words, will the South share in the nation's employment growth? Has the competitive position of the southern economy altered enough in recent years that its share of national employment in 1975 will have increased significantly over 1960? The fundamental problem in answering these questions is to determine the extent to which past trends are valid in projecting future employment in the South.

One of the important limitations on using past employment trends in the South as an indicator of the probable future level

[3] Further refinement of procedures for projecting employment, procedures that would make possible a narrower breakdown of industry groups and that would rely less heavily than we have done on past trends, are clearly needed. For an illuminating discussion of methods of making projections, see W. Lee Hansen, "Labor Force and Occupational Projections," a paper presented at meetings of the Industrial Relations Research Association, New York, December, 1965.

Table 8-2   Estimate of Southern Civilian Employment, by Industry, 1950, 1960, and Projections for 1975

Industry	Number (thousands)			Change per year (thousands)		Percentage distribution		
	1950	1960	1975	1950–1960	1960–1975	1950	1960	1975
All industries	15,379	16,955	21,865	157.6	327.3	100.00	100.00	100.00
Agriculture	3,370	1,787	1,100	−158.3	−45.8	21.91	10.54	5.03
Forestry, fisheries, logging	142	146	150	0.3	0.3	0.92	0.86	0.69
Mining	345	297	250	−4.9	−3.1	2.24	1.75	1.14
Construction	1,073	1,249	1,600	17.6	23.4	6.98	7.37	7.32
Transportation, communications, utilities	1,062	1,150	1,300	8.8	10.0	6.91	6.78	5.95
Wholesale & retail trade	2,728	3,291	4,160	56.4	57.9	17.74	19.41	19.02
Finance, insurance, real estate	385	628	1,050	24.3	28.1	2.50	3.70	4.80
Services	2,870	3,893	5,750	102.3	123.8	18.66	22.96	26.30
Personal	1,263	1,496	1,550	23.3	3.6	8.21	8.82	7.09
Professional and related	1,181	1,881	3,500	70.1	107.9	7.68	11.10	16.01
Business, recreation, and repair	426	516	700	8.9	12.3	2.77	3.04	3.20
Government	636	873	1,250	23.8	25.1	4.14	5.15	5.72

Manufacturing	2,768	3,641	5,255	87.3	107.6	18.00	21.48	24.03
Food and kindred products	318	444	700	12.6	17.1	2.07	2.62	3.20
Tobacco products	60	65	60	0.5	−0.4	0.39	0.38	.27
Textile mill products	651	630	550	−2.0	−5.3	4.23	3.72	2.52
Apparel products	167	327	530	16.0	13.5	1.09	1.93	2.42
Sawmills and planing mills	353	194	150	−16.0	−2.9	2.30	1.14	.69
Furniture, fixture, misc. wood	137	180	270	4.3	6.0	0.89	1.06	1.24
Paper products	93	143	220	5.0	5.1	0.60	0.84	1.01
Printing and publishing	131	190	270	5.8	5.3	0.85	1.12	1.24
Chemicals and plastics	169	252	350	8.3	6.5	1.10	1.49	1.60
Petroleum and coal products	100	112	120	1.1	0.6	0.65	0.66	0.55
Rubber products	21	29	40	0.8	0.7	0.14	0.17	0.18
Leather and products	33	43	55	1.0	0.8	0.21	0.25	0.25
Stone, clay, and glass	78	128	200	5.1	4.8	0.51	0.76	0.91
Metal industry	192	313	650	12.1	22.5	1.25	1.85	2.97
Electrical machinery	29	149	300	11.9	10.1	0.19	0.88	1.37
Nonelectrical machinery	90	157	290	6.8	8.9	0.58	0.93	1.33
Transportation equipment	97	210	390	11.3	12.0	0.63	1.24	1.78
Other	49	75	110	2.7	2.3	0.32	0.44	0.50

Sources: 1950 and 1960—Total southern employment was obtained by applying to the U. S. totals shown in Table 8-1 the percentage of U. S. employment in the 13 southern states, as shown in the decennial Census reports. The industrial distribution is likewise based on the decennial Census reports. 1975 projections are staff estimates reflecting analysis of past trends, prospective technological development, and competitive potentials of southern industries.

of employment is that the region's poor performance in increasing its share of national employment in the past may be the very factor that will generate the necessary changes in attitudes, behavior and policies—public and private, federal, state, and local—to improve its performance in the future.

Accordingly, the projection of southern civilian employment, by industry, of almost 21.9 million workers in 1975, reflects not only an analysis of past trends and the expected rapid rise of the national labor force, discussed in Chapter 7, but also our evaluation of prospective technological developments and competitive potentials of each of 29 industries in the southern states (Table 8-2). Nevertheless, projections of this nature are more accurate indicators of directions and patterns of change in employment than of the precise number of persons likely to be employed in each industry. The projected increase of 4.9 million employees in 1960–1975 represents a significantly greater average annual increase than occurred in the 1950's, but it indicates that the South's share of national employment in 1975 may be little different than it was in 1960—25.2 per cent compared with 25.5 per cent in 1960. This small decrease projected in the South's share of national employment will be the result of projected continued downward trends in employment in agriculture, mining, textiles, and sawmilling, without sufficient offsetting increases in other industries.

Industry-Mix

Although the projections indicate little change in the South's share of total U. S. employment, they do indicate significant changes in the industry-mix of the region (Figure 8-1). This is evident in the projected shift in employment between goods-producing and service-producing industries shown in Table 8-3. In 1950 employment in the five goods-producing industries (agriculture; forestry, fisheries, and logging; mining; construction; and manufacturing) represented about 50 per cent of total employment in the South. By 1960 the proportion of southern employ-

Figure 8-1 **Percentage Changes in Employment, by Industry Group, United States and South, 1960–1975**

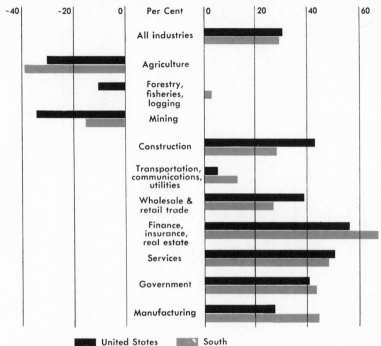

Sources: Tables 8-1 and 8-2.

ment in the goods-producing industries had declined to 42 per cent and is projected to decline to 38.2 per cent by 1975.

The very large decline in agricultural employment in the South between 1950 and 1960 was the major factor accounting for the decrease in employment in the goods-producing industries, but there were also modest declines in employment in textiles, mining, sawmills and planing mills. Further declines in these industries and in tobacco products are expected by 1975 (Table 8-2).

In contrast, employment in all other industries in the South is expected to increase—quite significantly in professional services; wholesale and retail trade; finance, insurance, and real estate; and most manufacturing industries. As a result of the changes in the industry-mix of the region between 1950 and 1960, the balance between goods-producing and service-producing industries in the

Table 8-3　**Estimates of Civilian Employment, by Goods-Producing and Service-Producing Industries, United States, Non-South, and South, 1950, 1960, and Projections for 1975ᵃ**

Type of Industry	United States		Non-South		South	
	Number (thousands)	Percentage distribution	Number (thousands)	Percentage distribution	Number (thousands)	Percentage distribution
1950						
Total	59,748	100.0	44,369	100.0	15,379	100.0
Goods-producing	28,077	47.0	20,378	45.9	7,699	50.1
Service-producing	31,671	53.0	23,991	54.1	7,680	49.9
1960						
Total	66,392	100.0	49,437	100.0	16,955	100.0
Goods-producing	28,215	42.5	21,095	42.7	7,120	42.0
Service-producing	38,177	57.5	28,342	57.3	9,835	58.0
1975						
Total	86,839	100.0	64,974	100.0	21,865	100.0
Goods-producing	33,239	38.3	24,884	38.3	8,355	38.2
Service-producing	53,600	61.7	40,090	61.7	13,510	61.8

Source: Table 8-2.

ᵃThe goods-producing industries are: agriculture; forestry, fisheries, and logging; mining; construction; and manufacturing. The other industries shown in Table 8-2 are service-producing.

South in 1960 was virtually the same as in the rest of the nation. Indeed, the industry-mix of the region has become so nearly like the national average that future changes in total employment in the South will depend more on the ability of individual southern industries to compete with the same industries in other regions than at any time in recent decades.

Occupational Distribution

Expected changes in the distribution of southern workers by occupation are of interest from several viewpoints. (See Table 8-4.) Increases in the proportion of workers in professional, administrative, managerial, and clerical occupations are indicators of the rates of economic growth and of changes in per capita income. The occupational distribution of workers is related to the quality of the labor force—its education, skill, training, and experience. Prospective changes in the occupational distribution, therefore, indicate educational and training activities needed to encourage the future growth and development of the region.

Two interrelated factors have been important in determining the occupational distribution of southern workers: the industry-mix of the region and the degree of specialization and level of skill required within a given industry. Future changes in the occupational distribution of southern workers will be influenced by both factors.

The mobility between industries of a worker in a given occupation tends to be higher than his mobility between occupations in the same industry.[4] Generally, the greater the specialization required in a specific occupation, the less is the mobility of workers into it. The unskilled or semiskilled worker who loses his job because of contracting employment in his industry or because technological changes have caused the upgrading of his job to a higher skill level, must therefore acquire new skills or run the risk of joining the ranks of the hard-core unemployed.

For more than two decades the proportion of southern workers

[4] Workers in agricultural occupations (farmers and farm managers; farm laborers and foremen), however, have virtually no interindustry mobility in those occupations.

employed in occupations requiring neither special abilities nor training has decreased, and the proportion employed as professional, managerial, clerical, craftsmen, and sales workers has increased. In addition to changes in the occupational structure of employment in specific industries, the changing industry-mix has resulted in more rapidly expanding employment opportunities in white-collar than in unskilled or semiskilled occupations.

These types of changes in the occupational status of southern workers during the 1950's are evident in Table 8-4. The number of service-type occupations—professional, technical, managerial, and administrative workers; clerical and kindred workers; service workers; and sales workers—increased rapidly. With the growth of manufacturing, the number of craftsmen and operatives also rose. In contrast, the number of farmers and farm managers and farm and nonfarm laborers decreased. This general pattern of change is expected to continue during 1960–1975.

Our projections indicate that in 1975, as in the past, operatives and kindred workers will be the largest occupational group in the South, but their proportion of total employees will be little different from what it was in 1950. The second largest occupational group is expected to be clerical and kindred workers, who will represent almost 15 per cent of the total number of southern workers in 1975, compared to 9 per cent in 1950. The number and proportion of service workers, craftsmen, and nonfarm foremen is also expected to increase significantly between 1960 and 1975 (Table 8-4).

The projected changes in the occupational distribution of southern employees have important implications. The generally upward shift of workers into the service-type occupations will tend to raise the per capita income of the region. Because many of the jobs in the service-type occupations require a higher level of classroom education than jobs in the goods-producing occupations, the demand for educated people will be strong and investments in education will pay high returns. The changes in the occupational distribution of employment will not increase job opportunities for Negroes, unless there are significant changes in the

Table 8-4   Estimates of Southern Civilian Employment, by Occupation, 1950, 1960, and Projections for 1975

Occupation	Number (thousands)			Change per year (thousands)		Percentage distribution		
	1950	1960	1975	1950–1960	1960–1975	1950	1960	1975
All occupations	15,379	16,955	21,865	157.6	327.3	100.00	100.00	100.00
Professional, technical, and kindred	1,118	1,702	2,950	58.4	83.2	7.27	10.04	13.49
Nonfarm managers, officials, and proprietors	1,251	1,505	2,000	25.5	33.0	8.13	8.88	9.15
Clerical and kindred	1,387	2,082	3,200	69.5	74.5	9.02	12.28	14.64
Sales	995	1,222	1,550	22.7	21.9	6.47	7.21	7.09
General service and private household	1,700	2,269	3,180	56.9	60.7	11.05	13.38	14.54
Craftsmen, foremen, and kindred	1,804	2,217	3,040	41.4	54.9	11.73	13.08	13.90
Operatives and kindred	2,744	3,261	3,950	51.7	45.9	17.84	19.23	18.07
Nonfarm laborers	1,089	1,033	985	−5.6	−3.2	7.08	6.09	4.50
Farmers and farm managers	2,088	974	560	−111.4	−27.6	13.58	5.74	2.56
Farm laborers and foremen	1,205	691	450	−51.5	−16.1	7.84	4.07	2.06

Sources: 1950, 1960, and 1975 southern employment totals are from Table 8-2. The occupational distribution for 1950 and 1960 was obtained by applying to these totals the occupational distribution shown in the decennial Census reports for the southern states. The 1975 projections are staff estimates, based primarily on past trends, analysis of the expected industry-mix of the region, the educational level of the labor force, and the skills required by individual industries.

educational qualifications of Negroes and in the attitudes of many southern whites. The projected decreases in the number of farmers and in farm and nonfarm laborers mean that Negro job opportunities will shrink in occupations in which Negro employment is high. On the other hand, in the rapidly growing service-type occupations, Negroes face two quite different kinds of barriers: an educational barrier, since relatively few Negroes are qualified for jobs in the professional, technical, and managerial occupations; and a racial barrier, since many of the white-collar, clerical, sales, and other service jobs require close physical and face-to-face relations between fellow workers and between workers and their customers or clients. These are the types of jobs in which discrimination against Negroes has traditionally been most pronounced in the South.

State Distribution

Employment in all southern states is projected to increase between 1960 and 1975, as shown in Table 8-5. Large differences between the states in the number of persons employed in 1975 and in the rates of growth in employment between 1960 and 1975 will occur because of changes in the industry-mix of the states, differences in levels of education of available workers, the differing effects of the interstate highway system, variations in rates of growth of large urban centers, the nature and intensity of state action to attract industries from other areas, and the distribution of federal expenditures for defense, explorations of outer space, and the development of federal facilities for other activities.

Because precise changes in many of these factors cannot be foreseen, long-term projections of employment for individual states are subject to larger errors than those for the southern region as a whole. Nevertheless, by relying primarily on past trends in employment in major industries, we have projected total employment in each southern state as shown in Table 8-5.

Only Florida is likely to significantly increase its share of national employment—from about 2.7 per cent in 1960 to 3.2 in 1975. Texas, Florida, Virginia, Georgia, Tennessee, Louisiana,

Table 8-5 Estimates of Civilian Employment, by Region and Southern State, 1950, 1960, and Projections for 1975

Region and state	Number (thousands)			Change per year (thousands)		Percentage distribution		
	1950	1960	1975	1950–1960	1960–1975	1950	1960	1975
United States	59,748	66,392	86,839	664.4	1363.1	100.00	100.00	100.00
Non-South	44,369	49,437	64,974	506.8	1035.8	74.26	74.46	74.82
South	15,379	16,955	21,865	157.6	327.3	25.74	25.54	25.18
Alabama	1,093	1,102	1,290	0.9	12.5	1.83	1.66	1.49
Arkansas	657	584	643	−7.3	3.9	1.10	0.88	0.74
Florida	1,069	1,772	2,746	70.3	64.9	1.79	2.67	3.16
Georgia	1,332	1,427	1,830	9.5	26.8	2.23	2.15	2.11
Kentucky	1,016	963	1,242	−5.3	18.6	1.70	1.45	1.43
Louisiana	932	1,042	1,426	11.0	25.6	1.56	1.57	1.64
Mississippi	759	704	759	−5.5	3.7	1.27	1.06	0.87
North Carolina	1,553	1,653	1,977	10.0	21.6	2.60	2.49	2.28
Oklahoma	801	810	1,008	0.9	13.2	1.34	1.22	1.16
South Carolina	801	830	890	2.9	4.0	1.34	1.25	1.02
Tennessee	1,207	1,261	1,646	5.4	25.7	2.02	1.90	1.90
Texas	2,934	3,426	4,576	49.2	76.7	4.91	5.16	5.27
Virginia	1,225	1,381	1,832	15.6	30.1	2.05	2.08	2.11

Sources: 1950, 1960, and 1975 U. S. and southern employment totals are from Tables 8-1 and 8-2. The 1950 and 1960 state distribution was obtained by applying to these totals the state distribution shown in the decennial Census reports. The 1975 projections are staff estimates, based on analysis of past trends and expected future changes in the industry-mix, the levels of education, and the general economic environment of the southern states.

and North Carolina are expected to experience the largest gains in numbers of workers employed. Of the 4.9 million increase in total employment projected for the South in 1960–1975, about 83 per cent will probably take place in these 7 states (Table 8-5).

Prospects for Negro Employment

For generations Negroes in the South have been denied the full range of opportunities available to whites. Today, however, southern Negroes have both the legal rights and greater opportunities than ever before in the nation's history to vote, to hold public office, to obtain an education, and to be employed in a wide range of jobs.

How these new rights and opportunities will affect Negro employment is difficult to predict. Most of the relevant laws and court decisions are quite recent and are only beginning to be implemented. The response of Negroes to their expanded opportunities is also uncertain. The determination and speed with which government acts to enforce the new statutes will affect this response. The manner and vigor with which Negroes continue their drive for equality will, in turn, affect governmental actions at all levels to bring about full and complete enforcement.

Many Negroes are still trapped in low-skilled occupations, particularly in agriculture. As pointed out earlier, employment in agriculture will almost surely continue to decline in the South, and this will mean further loss of jobs for Negroes. As a result, Negroes will continue to move to urban centers, and problems of Negro employment will increasingly become urban problems. The Negro population is already highly urbanized. In 1960, for example, 72.5 per cent of all Negroes in the United States and 56 per cent of southern Negroes lived in urban areas; an additional 20 per cent of the Negroes in the United States, and 30 per cent of the Negroes in the South, lived in rural nonfarm areas. The urbanization of the Negro population is dramatically illustrated by U. S. Census data showing that in 1960 the Negro population of only three southern states—Texas, North Carolina, and Georgia —was larger than that of New York City.

PROJECTIONS OF NEGRO EMPLOYMENT

We do not expect the new laws, court decisions, and expanding employment opportunities to have revolutionary effects on Negro employment in the South during the next decade, as indicated in Chapter 6.

Negro employment declined in the South between 1950 and 1960 by 225,000 workers (Table 8-6). This was the net result of decreases totaling 547,000 in agriculture, mining, and transportation, and increases amounting to 322,000 in the other 6 industries shown in Table 8-6. The major decrease, totaling 522,000, was in agriculture, forestry, fisheries, and logging, in which there was a decline of 48 per cent.

Negro employment in the non-South increased by 713,000 workers, or 29 per cent, between 1950 and 1960. Approximately 83 per cent of this increase resulted from gains in three industries —services, trade, and manufacturing.

We have projected Negro civilian employment, as shown in Table 8-6 and Figure 8-2, largely on the basis of past trends in the South and non-South, the probable effects of Title VII of the Civil Rights Act of 1964, the growing voting power of southern Negroes and their increased educational opportunities, and a desire on the part of an increasing number of southern employers not to be accused of discriminatory employment practices. It seems reasonable to believe that between 1960 and 1975 the Negro share of employment in the South will continue to rise in all major industry groups, except agriculture, mining, and transportation, and that there will be a large decline in the Negro share only in agriculture.

According to these projections, about 9.6 million Negroes will be employed in civilian occupations in the United States in 1975. They will constitute almost 11 per cent of total employment. This

Table 8-6   **Estimates of Nonwhite Civilian Employment, by Major Industry Group, United States, Non-South, and South, 1950, 1960, and Projections for 1975**

Industry	United States			Non-South			South		
	1950	1960	1975	1950	1960	1975	1950	1960	1975
	Number (thousands)								
All industries	5,939	6,427	9,553	2,462	3,175	5,915	3,477	3,252	3,638
Agriculture, forestry, fisheries, logging	1,196	651	320	111	88	80	1,085	563	240
Mining	49	24	19	25	10	7	24	14	12
Construction	325	366	589	138	156	295	187	210	294
Transportation, communications, utilities	365	365	437	191	206	270	174	159	167
Wholesale and retail trade	715	881	1,346	349	463	844	366	418	502
Finance, insurance, real estate	94	113	168	62	76	124	32	37	44
Services	1,886	2,395	3,761	820	1,108	2,152	1,066	1,287	1,609
Government	204	335	839	151	262	699	53	73	140
Manufacturing	1,105	1,297	2,074	615	806	1,444	490	491	630
	Percentage distribution								
All industries	100.00	100.00	100.00	100.00	100.00	100.00	100.00	100.00	100.00
Agriculture, forestry, fisheries, logging	20.14	10.13	3.34	4.51	2.77	1.35	31.21	17.31	6.59
Mining	0.83	0.37	0.20	1.02	0.32	0.12	0.69	0.43	0.33
Construction	5.47	5.69	6.17	5.60	4.91	4.99	5.38	6.46	8.08
Transportation, communications, utilities	6.14	5.68	4.57	7.76	6.49	4.56	5.00	4.89	4.59
Wholesale and retail trade	12.04	13.71	14.09	14.17	14.58	14.27	10.53	12.85	13.80
Finance, insurance, real estate	1.58	1.76	1.77	2.52	2.39	2.10	0.92	1.14	1.21
Services	31.76	37.27	39.37	33.31	34.90	36.38	30.66	39.58	44.23
Government	3.43	5.21	8.78	6.13	8.25	11.82	1.52	2.24	3.85
Manufacturing	18.61	20.18	21.71	24.98	25.39	24.41	14.09	15.10	17.32

Sources: 1950 and 1960—Total nonwhite employment for the United States, the South, and the non-South was obtained by applying to the totals shown in Tables 8-1 and 8-2 the racial distribution of employment shown in the decennial Census reports. The industrial distribution is likewise based on that of the decennial Census reports. The 1975 projections are staff estimates, based on analysis of past trends and the changing educational level and political and economic status of Negroes in the United States and in the South.

Figure 8-2   **Trends in White and Nonwhite Employment, United States and South, 1950, 1960, and 1975**

Millions

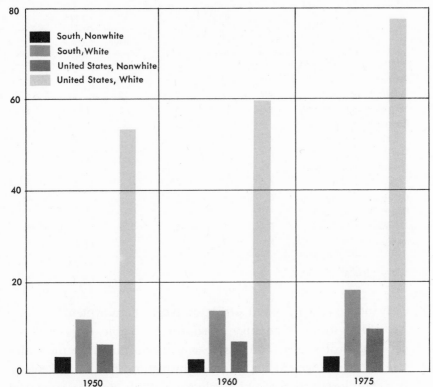

Legend:
- South, Nonwhite
- South, White
- United States, Nonwhite
- United States, White

Sources: Tables 8-5 and 8-6.

will mean a rise in Negro employment of slightly more than 3 million, or about 49 per cent, between 1960 and 1975. The projections also indicate that Negro employment in the South in 1975 will be about 3.6 million—a rise of approximately 386,000 workers, or about 12 per cent, above the 1960 level. About 38 per cent of the nation's Negro employment will probably be in the South in 1975, compared to about 51 per cent in 1960, and 62 per cent in the non-South, compared to about 49 per cent in 1960.

To obtain a picture of the projected shifts in the relative importance of the various industries as sources of employment for Negroes, we ranked industries according to Negro employment in

Table 8-7   **Industries Ranked According to the Estimated Number of Nonwhite Persons Employed in Each Industry, 1960 and Projections for 1975**

Industry	1960			1975		
	United States	Non-South	South	United States	Non-South	South
Services	1	1	1	1	1	1
Manufacturing	2	2	3	2	2	2
Wholesale and retail trade	3	3	4	3	3	3
Agriculture, forestry, fisheries, and logging	4	7	2	7	8	5
Government	7	4	7	4	4	7
Transportation, communications and utilities	6	5	6	6	6	6
Construction	5	6	5	5	5	4
Finance, insurance, real estate	8	8	8	8	7	8
Mining	9	9	9	9	9	9

Source: Table 8-6.

each industry in 1960 and projected Negro employment in 1975. According to this ranking, as shown in Table 8-7, services—personal, professional, and business—will continue to be the major source of employment for Negroes throughout the United States. In 1960 there were approximately 2.4 million Negroes employed in services in the United States as a whole and almost 1.3 million in the South. These included: teachers; lawyers; hospital and medical personnel; radio, television, and automobile repairmen; workers in hotels, restaurants, and recreation services; and domestic workers. The demand for services will increase with urbanization and growth in population. According to our projections, the number of Negroes employed in services will increase to almost 3.8 million in the United States and to 1.6 million in the South by 1975.

Manufacturing is expected to be the second largest source of employment for Negroes in the United States as a whole, and to rise from third place in the South in 1960 to second in 1975.

Negro employment in the manufacturing industries, which was approximately 1.3 million in the United States in 1960, is expected to rise to about 2.1 million in 1975. In the South it is expected to rise from 491,000 in 1960 to 630,000 in 1975.

Wholesale and retail trade was the fourth largest employer of Negroes in the South and the third largest in the non-South in 1960. By 1975 this industry group is expected to rank third as a source of employment for Negroes in both the non-South and the South. As with other service-producing industries, the importance of trade increases as the population expands and becomes more urbanized. As the purchasing power of Negro consumers is strengthened, both by improvement in their economic status and their concentration in urban areas, their employment in retail outlets will be increased. According to our projections, the number of Negroes working in wholesale and retail trade in the South will increase from 418,000 in 1960 to 502,000 in 1975. Their gain in this industry, however, is likely to be much more significant outside the South.

Two of the most striking projected changes in the industrial distribution of Negro employment in the South are in agriculture and government. In 1960 Negro agricultural employment in the South was 563,000; by 1975 we expect it to decline by 57 per cent to 240,000. Large numbers of small-scale, low-income Negro farmers will be forced out of farming by competition from larger and better financed white farmers. Maturing Negro youth will have extreme difficulties obtaining land and capital to become operators of profitable farms. The 1975 Negro employment in agriculture may well be even lower than we have projected. Clearly, employment adjustment problems for southern Negroes leaving agriculture will be serious during the next few years.

On the other hand, Negro government employment in the South—federal, state, and local—is expected almost to double between 1960 and 1975: from 73,000 in 1960 to 140,000 in 1975. Enforcement of various laws and regulations and pressures from civil rights groups will inevitably result in large increases in Negro employment in the lower echelons of public administration, with the result, we believe, of significant increases in the number of Negroes employed in government. Although the actual number of Negroes who are expected to obtain jobs in government in the South is small compared to the large decline in agricultural employment, the projected gain is of great significance in setting a new pattern of nondiscriminatory employment of Negroes.

Summary

In this chapter we have attempted to answer the major questions about the future employment outlook for the South—on which our study has focused. The highlights of our findings are:

Employment in the South is projected to increase from almost 17 million workers in 1960 to almost 22 million in 1975—a gain of about 29 per cent. This projection assumes national unemployment of 4 per cent of the labor force in 1975. The projected southern employment of 21.9 million and the projected southern civilian labor force of about 22.6 million indicate that the unemployment rate in the South will be 3.4 per cent (Table 8-8).

The South's share of total U. S. employment is projected to decline slightly between 1960 and 1975, mainly because there are likely to be important decreases in the number and proportion of southern workers employed in farming. At the same time, the South's share of employment in manufacturing and service-producing industries is projected to increase significantly. The increase in manufacturing employment in the South, for example, is projected to rise from approximately 3.6 million workers in 1960 to almost 5.3 million in 1975—a gain of more than 44 per cent, compared to about 27 per cent in the nation as a whole. The shifts that are taking place in southern employment will clearly result in increased productivity and higher incomes per worker.

Total Negro employment in the South is projected to increase from approximately 3.3 million workers in 1960 to 3.6 million in 1975. The projected increase of almost 400,000 employed Negro workers in the South between 1960 and 1975 compares with the decrease of over 200,000 which occurred in the 1950's, when

Table 8-8   **Estimates of Number of Persons in the Civilian Labor Force, Employed and Unemployed, 1950, 1960, and Projections for 1975**

Year, civilian labor force, and employment	Total			White			Non-White		
	United States	Non-South	South	United States	Non-South	South	United States	Non-South	South
1950									
Civilian labor force	63,099	46,977	16,122	56,508	44,151	12,357	6,591	2,826	3,764
Employed	59,748	44,369	15,379	53,809	41,907	11,902	5,939	2,462	3,477
Unemployed	3,351	2,608	743	2,699	2,244	455	652	364	287
Per cent unemployed	5.3	5.6	4.6	4.8	5.1	3.7	9.9	12.9	7.6
1960									
Civilian labor force	70,306	52,394	17,912	62,957	48,613	14,344	7,349	3,781	3,568
Employed	66,392	49,437	16,955	59,965	46,262	13,703	6,427	3,175	3,252
Unemployed	3,914	2,957	957	2,992	2,351	641	922	606	316
Per cent unemployed	5.6	5.6	5.3	4.8	4.8	4.5	12.6	16.0	8.9
Projected 1975									
Civilian labor force	90,457	67,826	22,631	80,202	61,465	18,737	10,255	6,361	3,894
Employed	86,839	64,974	21,865	77,286	59,059	18,227	9,553	5,915	3,638
Unemployed	3,618	2,852	766	2,916	2,406	510	702	446	256
Per cent unemployed	4.0	4.2	3.4	3.6	3.9	2.7	6.9	7.0	6.6

Sources: Tables 7-1 and 7-2; Appendix Tables 7-2, 8-1, 8-2, 8-5, and 8-6.

unemployment among Negroes was extremely high. It indicates, however, that unemployment among Negroes in the South, though slightly lower than in the non-South, may still be more than double that of southern whites in 1975 (Table 8-8).

We have projected Negro employment to increase much more rapidly between 1960 and 1975 outside of the South (about 86 per cent) than within the South (12 per cent), mainly because we believe that a relatively high proportion of southern Negro boys and girls who enter the labor force during the next decade, plus many Negro workers between 25 and 45 years of age who leave southern farms, will seek employment in urban centers of the North and West. Far too little is known about factors affecting labor force participation rates and migration patterns of Negroes to warrant a claim of a high degree of precision for our projections of 1975 Negro employment. Nevertheless, it is quite clear that the outlook for Negro employment is far from satisfactory. Neither the South nor the nation is likely to be making full and efficient use of its Negro manpower by 1975, unless there are substantial changes in both public and private policies within the near future. In the next chapter we discuss the policy changes needed and programs necessary to implement them.

Chapter 9

POLICIES FOR
SOUTHERN DEVELOPMENT

IN PRECEDING chapters we have reached generally optimistic conclusions about the future of the South: that southern incomes will rise, as the balance in the industry-mix continues to shift from low-wage to high-wage industries; that the rising new industries will attract other industries as buyers or suppliers of manufactured goods; that the quality of the labor force will continue to improve; and that with national full employment southern employment is likely to rise much more rapidly between 1960 and 1975 than in the 1950's.

We have shown that the southern economic structure and social attitudes have changed, as the economy has evolved from rural-agrarian to urban-industrial, and that while these changes have brought new industrial development to the South, they have also created new problems. The greatest of these is a large, unskilled, poorly educated agricultural work force that is no longer needed to till the land and is insufficiently trained to meet the requirements of the expanding manufacturing and service-producing industries. The South has the essential natural resources to continue to attract new industries. Its greatest handicaps in competition with other regions for rapid-growth, high-wage industries are the shortage of a trained work force and the remnants of values and traditions that attach too little importance to developing the full potentials of the region's human resources.

It is entirely possible for southern policy makers—in government and in industry—to adopt policies and programs that will accelerate southern economic development beyond the range of our projections. In order to do so, they must have a clear understanding of development goals. There must also be a wide consensus among southern people with respect to these goals and the policies and programs designed to achieve them.

Development Goals

The wide variety of policies commonly suggested to foster southern economic growth is not surprising, in view of the varied concepts of the goal of regional development. These fall into three broad categories—increasing aggregate income, increasing per capita productivity, and increasing the efficiency of the distribution of production among regions.[1]

INCREASING AGGREGATE INCOME

One of the most widely held of the three concepts, common among many civic leaders, government officials, and local businessmen, is that, in effect, regional development means increasing aggregate regional income, either by raising the average income per worker without increasing the number of jobs, or by increasing the number of jobs without increasing the average income per worker, that is, without increasing wages. The latter method is often favored by employers, who constitute an important segment of those who consider regional development synonymous with increasing aggregate income. In their opinion, raising regional income without raising wages represents the best of all possible worlds, particularly if they operate businesses whose costs per unit

[1] These concepts and the interest groups associated with them are described by Charles L. Leven in "Theories of Regional Growth," a paper presented at a workshop held in Asheville, North Carolina, on *Problems of Chronically Depressed Rural Areas*, April 26–28, 1965, under the joint sponsorship of the Agricultural Policy Institute of North Carolina State University, Raleigh, and the Tennessee Valley Authority. (The workshop papers were issued in mimeographed form under the above title by the sponsoring organizations in November 1965.)

of product decrease as output increases (public utilities, banks, newspapers, and retail stores, for example). Those who adhere to this concept are also apt to consider that regional growth is largely dependent on expansion of external markets for regional products, and to think that owners of many southern farms and food-processing and manufacturing firms who have a low-cost area in which to produce goods and services and high-income areas in which to market them have an ideal situation.

INCREASING PER CAPITA PRODUCTIVITY

A second concept is that the goal of economic development should be to raise the level of living of the people within a given region by increasing their productivity and thus their per capita income. This view, held by many economists and other social scientists, is shared by many teachers and other professional people, some government officials, businessmen, labor leaders, and civil rights workers. They argue that the ability of southern industry to compete in external markets and even in markets within the region is limited mainly by the low productivity of southern labor and capital; that therefore, in order to raise per capita incomes, the South must: increase investment, not only in plants and equipment and in research facilities to develop new technologies, but also in education, health, and related services to improve the productivity of the people; eliminate or reorganize institutional arrangements that inhibit the development of members of minority groups; and, where accumulated effects of imbalances in society exist, broaden the expectations, incentives, and opportunities of the underprivileged.[2]

2 Some people who agree that the level of per capita income is the proper indicator of regional development, recommend increasing the amount of capital investment but fail to recommend steps to improve human resources. Thus, they unwittingly slip into the aggregate income concept of regional development, and sometimes into that version of the concept that emphasizes an increase in total employment without an increase in wages.

IMPROVING THE DISTRIBUTION OF PRODUCTION AMONG REGIONS

A third concept is that the goal of regional development should be to increase the efficiency of the distribution of production among regions. Significant regional differences in wages in comparable industries and occupations, except those that reflect differences in the cost of living, are accepted by adherents to this concept of regional growth, mainly economists, as being prima-facie evidence of inefficient allocation of production among regions.

Those who favor this concept would be likely to hold that the main cause of low returns to labor in the South is insufficient past investments, either in plant and equipment or in human beings. Historically, they have been prone to put more emphasis on the importance of investment in plant and equipment. Their most common explanations for the insufficiency of past investments are that past returns on investments have been low (and that there are thus grounds for believing that the region should be allowed to decline as a production area, though they would be more apt to apply this to small southern areas or subregions than to the South as a whole), and that interregional markets for labor and capital are inefficient. They often advocate policies aimed at removing restrictions on the free flow of capital and labor between regions; they emphasize the lack of wisdom in trade-union restrictions and in minimum wage laws; and they point to the need for improved information about job and investment opportunities throughout the country.

APPLICABILITY TO THE SOUTH

Which of the foregoing concepts offers the most promising goals on which to base development policies for the South? Though the development goals associated with the three concepts are not always in conflict, rarely are they complementary, and policy makers concerned with regional development are thus forced to choose from among them. Aggregate income can be raised by increasing both wage rates and the number of jobs, but the cause of southern development could not be served by policies that would increase the number of jobs without increasing wage rates —that is, that would encourage the proliferation of low-wage, low-productivity industries. Efficient distribution of production among the regions of the country is a proper matter of concern to policy makers. Clearly, not every community, county, or small subregion of the South can have a sizable manufacturing plant—for which so many such areas are frantically searching—without impairing the efficiency of the total economy. Assurance of good jobs for everybody in the places where they now live would therefore be an unwise policy goal.

We believe that the most effective development policies for enhancing the efficiency of the southern economy and contributing to the welfare of the southern people will be those associated with the goal of increasing per capita productivity. This concept of regional growth traces low southern productivity to insufficient past investments—in physical capital, in research to engender technological advance, and in the education of the people—and to institutional arrangements that for generation after generation have limited the incentives, the opportunities— and, hence, the abilities—of thousands of southerners to develop fully their potentialities.

Significantly increasing per capita income by raising the productivity of southern people would remove a major weakness in the southern economy. For decades poverty has been passed from one generation of southerners to another as a social, economic, political, and cultural disease. If the South fails to take advantage of the opportunity to break the cycle of poverty, while the region is in a period of social and economic transition, it will be following the worst possible course of action. In other words, if the manufacturing and service-producing industries now rising so rapidly in the South are to be based on inefficient, low-wage labor, nothing more than the landscape of the region will be changed. The major development problem will shift from a rural to an urban setting, but southern people and southern institutions will continue to be the poorest of the nation, and the southern intellectual and cultural environment the most backward. Surely these should not be the goals of southern development policies.

If the leaders of the nation, particularly southern leaders, will be guided in the formulation of policies and programs by the development goal of significantly increasing the per capita productivity of southern people and at the same time encouraging an efficient distribution of production within the South as well as among the other regions of the country, the future development of the South can proceed at an even faster rate than either the trends of recent decades or our projections suggest.

Policies to Achieve Development Goals

What, then, are the policies and programs most urgently needed to increase the productivity and incomes of southern people, and, at the same time, to contribute to an efficient distribution of productive activity throughout the nation? They are of three principal kinds: first, those that will contribute to the rapid growth and the maintenance of full employment in the national economy; second, those that will increase the productive abilities of the southern population; and, third, those that will help to expand opportunities for the large number of underprivileged people in the South.

NATIONAL FULL EMPLOYMENT

The rate of expansion in southern employment and the level of per capita income in the South is closely related to the level of employment and the rate of growth in the national economy, as is evident from the relationships summarized in Chapter 3. The South makes its greatest gains in employment, in improving the occupational status of its workers, and in raising per capita incomes during periods of national full employment—when unemployment is at or below 4 per cent of the national labor force. These are also the periods during which opportunities for Negroes and other minority groups expand most rapidly. Therefore, for the southern economy to grow and develop most rapidly, the first requirement is that the productive capacity of the total economy constantly expand, and that this capacity be fully utilized.

It is outside the scope of this study to attempt to set forth the policies necessary to maintain national full employment, except as these national policies have a direct bearing on the economic development of the South. It goes without saying that it is as important for the South as for the rest of the nation that the Federal Government adopt fiscal and monetary policies that will help to maintain demand for goods and services at a high level, so that available supplies of labor, capital, and national resources will be fully utilized.

High levels of aggregate demand, however, are not sufficient. In addition, workers must be qualified to fill the available jobs. It is particularly important for the South that the Federal Government expand its policy of promoting and contributing to the financing of programs for educating and training new entrants into the labor force and experienced workers thrown out of work because of automation and other shifts in employment patterns.

In order to have qualified workers in the right place at the right time, federal policy should also encompass programs for increasing mobility of workers. A national integrated network of interviewing, testing, counseling, and job referral services is needed, so that an unemployed worker in any area of the country can be quickly informed of employment opportunities and job requirements in all parts of the country. This would probably necessitate bringing under full federal control employment services now federally financed but administered by the states. In addition, it would also be necessary to provide for financing the costs of moving the unemployed worker and his family to an area where employment is available.

Finally, federal policy must provide for well-planned public employment programs that can be put into operation quickly to offset seasonal and more prolonged periods of slack in private employment and make jobs available at all times for all persons who are able and willing to work.

There is nothing novel about these recommendations. Most of them are, to some extent, already established federal policy. The scope and timing of the actions which they involve, however, can be greatly improved. This will require more careful planning and a greater degree of cooperation between federal and state governments than heretofore. The basic objective of these proposals is to assure both rapid growth and continuing full employment in the national economy.[3]

DEVELOPING HUMAN RESOURCES

Given national full employment, no type of public or private action holds greater promise for speeding southern development than action aimed at upgrading the quality of the South's human resources. The shortages of skilled workers, of technicians, of scientists, of managerial ability among small businessmen, and of risk-taking entrepreneurs are serious stumbling blocks to further industrialization and technological development of the South. Education and training that sufficed for the southern agricultural labor force are not adequate to meet the demands of today's manpower market and certainly will not be adequate in the years to come in the industries of the South and elsewhere in the nation.

With a few exceptions, the children of the South have long been receiving education inferior to that received by children in most other regions. (See Chapter 5.) Although great progress has been made in the South in recent years in improving educational facilities and raising the quality of instruction, there are still important barriers to the development of an educational system that will prepare southern children—particularly Negro children, who have always been the most disadvantaged—for the occupations,

[3] For more specific recommendations aimed at the same general objective see: *Technology and the American Economy*, Report of the National Commission on Technology, Automation and Economic Progress, Vol. 1, Washington, February 1966; and *White House Conference "To Fulfill These Rights,"* Council's Report and Recommendations to the Conference, Washington, June 1–2, 1966.

duties, and responsibilities of an industrialized, urban society. Among the most important of these barriers are low incomes, narrow parochial views of what constitutes a good education, traditional values of middle-class whites toward Negroes and "poor white trash," and abstract doctrines of states' rights.

Equalization of the Quality of Schooling

Steps should be taken to raise the level of all U. S. public schools to that of the best public schools in the country. This means equalization of financial resources to improve facilities and the quality of instruction in southern schools, particularly rural and predominantly Negro schools. It should be a matter of national policy that neither place of residence nor color of skin will be a determinant of the quality of schooling that a child receives.

This means greatly expanded public expenditures for education by state and local governments, and federal aid and federal action on a much more massive scale than at present. The Elementary and Secondary Education Act of 1965 was a step in the right direction, but much more federal aid is needed. Average current operating expenditure per pupil in public primary and secondary schools in the United States in the year 1964–65 was $491. The highest per-pupil expenditure was New York's $737, and the lowest was Mississippi's $274. (See Appendix Table 5-1.) To have raised the per-pupil expenditure in all states to New York's $737 would have required an added expenditure (above the $18.7 billion which was spent by state and local governments) of approximately $9.3 billion—about $4.2 billion of which would have been required in the 13 southern states. This would not have included, of course, the necessary investment in facilities, equipment, and teacher training to have brought equality of education to all the nation's children. It would, however, have more than doubled the current operating expenditure by state and local governments for elementary and secondary schools in the South in 1964–65.

Increased funds for backward schools must be supplemented by other important changes. In most areas of the South, but especially in small towns and farming communities, primary and secondary schools should be much larger than at present; the number of pupils per teacher should be greatly reduced; the school term should be lengthened; the curriculum should be flexible, so that it will fit the needs of individual children, according to their abilities, desires, and plans for future study and work; much retraining of teachers and administrative personnel, including short courses and educational tours for school board members, is in order; and schools should become important contributors to, and participants in, a wide spectrum of life within the communities in which they are situated.

Particularly important at the present stage of the South's development is early and continuing orientation of children and youth toward useful work. This should begin in the elementary schools and continue through junior and senior high schools. Training programs in the practical arts should be introduced early in high school, along with counseling programs aimed at guiding some students into specialized vocational and technical schools and others into colleges and universities. In addition, widespread continuing programs of adult education are needed in the South to combat the plague of illiteracy and to help adults improve their skills.

School Integration

Southern and national leaders—including members of school boards, teachers, school administrators, government employees and officials—and all concerned citizens, white and Negro, will need to work together in a creative and rational way to assure that integration of southern schools will strengthen the quality of education in the South rather than weaken it. The day is past for emotional debates about the wisdom of integrating schools. Segregated schools, both white and Negro, have already failed, and will continue to fail, to prepare children to live and function effectively in our rapidly changing, multiracial society.

It is thus evident that racial integration of southern schools merits more careful and continuous planning and action than the problem is now receiving, if southern children of all races are to receive as good an education as children in most regions of the United States are receiving.

The present so-called "freedom of choice" procedures, by which a few Negro children in various grades are added to predominantly white schools each year, impose heavy burdens and risks on the Negro children and their parents. Except for the occasional star athlete who plays on a football or a basketball team, the Negro children are usually isolated by their white classmates from school-connected social and extracurricular activities, and their parents are subject to loss of jobs, harassment by profane telephone calls and threats—even the terror of having their homes shot into or bombed.

On the other hand, the rapid transfer of large numbers of Negro pupils to white schools and of white pupils to Negro schools is likely to cause increased violence in some southern communities, and, in the absence of careful preparation, will result in lowering the quality of education now being received by a large proportion of the white children. Because of differences in home and community environments, and in the quality of elementary schooling —differences that stem from long years of discrimination against Negroes—the gap in achievement levels between white and Negro pupils appears in the early elementary grades. Most areas of the South have, in fact, long had separate standards for their white and Negro school systems. The achievement levels of large numbers of Negro children graduated from southern high schools are at about the level of eighth or ninth grade pupils in white high schools in the same communities.

Emphasis on Nursery Schools and Elementary Grades

The major thrust of integrating the public schools of the South should start in the elementary grades. Moreover, both learning and integration in these grades will be accelerated if children have previously attended well-operated, integrated nursery schools and kindergartens. An important step, therefore, would be for the Federal Government to establish and operate a comprehensive regionwide system of racially integrated training and child care centers for preschool children. The services of such centers, including transportation, should be available to all preschool children without cost to their parents. The physical facilities should be designed to serve the needs of small children, and the staffs should be well-trained and interracial. The Federal Government could either construct and operate the centers, as it does post offices, or it could contract with qualified private individuals or groups to construct, maintain, and operate them. The experience of Project Head Start for preschool children, operated on a small scale by the Office of Economic Opportunity in cooperation with local boards of education, and confined to children from poor families, will no doubt be valuable in planning such a program.

The need, however, is for integrated training and child care centers that are operated throughout the year, and are available to all children. If such centers properly served the nutritional, health, recreational, and educational needs of the children for 8 to 10 hours each day, they would not only provide an environment for the growth and development of young children far superior to that now available to thousands of youngsters in low-income homes and communities, but they would also serve the needs of children of middle-class families whose mothers are employed in jobs outside of the home. For all children they would provide at an early age interracial experiences that would greatly ease the strain of integration in regular public schools.

The cost of establishing and operating a regionwide system of child care and training centers for all preschool children would be much too great to be borne by state and local governments of the South at the same time that they were attempting to greatly increase the quality of education in the public school systems. For financial reasons alone, therefore, most of these centers would have to be established and operated with federal funds. Moreover, they could much more easily operate on a racially integrated basis if they were administered by the Federal Government than if they were "tacked on" to the existing educational establishments.

Within the public school systems substantial improvement

could be made by immediate integration of the first three elementary grades. These grades should be housed in separate school buildings or parts of existing buildings, and should be taught by specially trained, interracial staffs. They should have only 10 to 15 pupils per teacher. Greatly increased federal aid should be made available to school districts that adopt this procedure.

Specialized Services

By suggesting that emphasis be placed on integrated child care centers and on the immediate integration of the first three elementary grades, we do not imply that other steps should not be taken to integrate all grade levels as rapidly as this can be done without encouraging violence or lowering the quality of the educational system.

Specialized school services of several kinds will be needed for successful integration. Some of these are already in effect on an experimental basis under Office of Economic Opportunity, U. S. Office of Education, and other programs. They include: tutoring and a wide range of courses during summer months for children who need intensive training to maintain the customary grade levels for their ages; libraries with resources for placing appropriate books and magazines in the homes of low-income families; supervised study centers in congested neighborhoods where homes afford few opportunities for children to read and study during evening hours; and home counseling with parents whose children are having difficulties in school.

Teacher Training

Special programs are needed to train teachers, both white and Negro, for teaching and counseling in integrated schools. This problem merits the attention of highly competent experts in the behavioral sciences. In addition to special training courses with integrated faculties in institutions of higher learning to prepare new teachers for elementary and secondary schools, summer short courses and training institutes are needed for teachers and school administrators who are presently employed in southern schools.

Programs for upgrading the quality of instruction in many of the predominantly Negro colleges and universities are also needed.

Integrating southern schools and at the same time improving the quality of education for all children in the South cannot be accomplished by simple and inexpensive methods. The task is enormous in scope and exceedingly complex. It calls for actions that presently are not only beyond the desires of both whites and Negroes in many school districts of the South, but are beyond the financial resources of nearly all such districts. It is only with very large amounts of federal funds, much wider and more rational participation of imaginative local leaders, and an end to the tug of war between state and federal officials over the minutiae of regulations and guidelines that the goal can be achieved within the foreseeable future.

EXPANDING OPPORTUNITIES FOR THE UNDERPRIVILEGED

Although the maintenance of national full employment and the various steps to upgrade the human resources of the South that we have suggested would undoubtedly raise the productivity and thus the incomes of southern people, further actions are needed to enlarge the opportunities of the underprivileged, including most southern Negroes and both white and Negro poorly educated, inefficient farm operators and hired farm laborers. The productivity of many persons in these groups is so low that they and their families are economic and social burdens on the southern economy. Before significantly greater opportunities will be available to persons in these groups and before they will be motivated to take advantage of enlarged opportunities, it will be necessary for the South to improve its social, economic, and political institutions, including many of its laws and customs.

The accumulated results of long years of discrimination against Negroes cannot easily and quickly be erased. More jobs and better education are prerequisites, but much can be accomplished if the following steps are taken immediately: local civic, religious, and social organizations of both races establish better lines of communication; labor unions cease to discriminate against Negroes; employers, both public and private, provide equal employment opportunities for Negroes; towns, cities, and counties enact zoning laws and building regulations to inhibit the spread of segregated residential patterns and the growth of Negro ghettos in southern cities of the kind that characterize so many of the large cities of the North; and local law enforcement agencies provide real equality of justice for Negroes.

These actions would not accomplish the necessary goals, however, if educated and responsible southern leaders—both white and Negro—failed to assume peaceful and constructive leadership roles in the continuing drive for Negro equality. In view of the numerous reprehensible acts of violence—murders, bombings of homes and churches, and personal assaults—inflicted by whites on many southern Negroes in recent years, the entire nation must be grateful for and recognize the wisdom of the nonviolent nature of the civil rights movement in the South. Nevertheless, the road to full equality is still a long one, and to travel it successfully southern leaders of both races will need to show patience and creativity in securing full equality of opportunity for Negroes and in encouraging southern Negroes to take full and constructive advantage of the expanded opportunities that are already available to them.

Means must also be found for raising the productivity and incomes of the many small, inefficient, and poorly educated southern farm operators, a majority of whom are white. A large proportion of them will be forced out of farming during the next few years, and few are equipped to assume new and productive roles in nonfarm occupations. The younger ones will be able to find jobs in a full-employment economy, provided they can receive specialized training plus guidance and counseling from a comprehensive and efficiently functioning national employment service, recommended earlier in this chapter. Their situation would be greatly improved, however, if more nonfarm businesses would locate in rural areas. Much is already being done by local, state, and federal agencies to encourage the growth of manufacturing and service in-

dustries in the South. However, there is need for further research
to guide the various agencies engaged in what is rapidly becoming
a large and expensive effort to influence the location of private
business firms.

Many of the older farmers whose prospects in agriculture are
poor will also find it virtually impossible to transfer to other kinds
of productive employment. Serious consideration should be given
to lowering the age at which those without assets can become eligible for Social Security and Medicare benefits, to making available
direct federal grants for improving their housing conditions, and
to instituting a system of income payments to supplement their
meager farm earnings.

Among the most disadvantaged and underprivileged people in
the South are hired farm workers, particularly the migrant farm
laborers who harvest the fruit and vegetable crops. To improve
the living conditions and incomes of this group of workers, there
is urgent need for federal rural housing and health programs,
minimum wage legislation, special educational programs in home
management, and literacy and vocational training programs.

In Conclusion

In this chapter, in which we have suggested the areas of action
that we consider most fruitful for new or expanded public programs to increase southern productivity, incomes, and employment, we have centered attention on maintaining full employment
in the national economy, developing human resources in the
South, and expanding opportunities for grossly underprivileged
groups in southern society.

Throughout the chapter, and indeed throughout preceding
chapters, we have emphasized the importance of increasing the
productivity of the southern economy. We do not believe that it
would be sound policy to continue indefinitely large income trans-
fers to the South. Nevertheless, large public investments, both
from within and from without the region, will be needed for some
time, if the South is to make its full contribution to national

progress. Public investments of the kinds that we have suggested will yield returns to the nation as a whole and to the South much higher than those commonly earned in many private endeavors. We can only hope that the traditional values and beliefs of southern people have changed sufficiently in recent years to permit them and their political leaders to join wholeheartedly in such large and continuing national efforts to develop the South's full potentials.

Appendix Table 2-1

Employment, by Major Industry Group, United States,[a] Non-South, and South, 1940, 1950, and 1960, and Percentage Change, by Decade

Year and region	All industries	Goods-producing			Service-producing	All nonagricultural	Industry not reported
		Total	Agriculture	Nonagricultural			
			Thousands				
1940							
United States[a]	45,166.1	22,017.5	8,475.4	13,542.1	22,459.7	36,001.8	688.8
Non-South	33,009.8	15,134.8	4,240.1	10,894.7	17,332.4	28,227.1	542.6
South	12,156.3	6,882.8	4,235.3	2,647.4	5,127.3	7,774.7	146.3
1950							
United States[a]	56,225.3	25,937.1	6,996.2	18,940.9	29,447.4	48,388.3	840.9
Non-South	41,753.4	18,824.3	3,818.5	15,005.7	22,318.5	37,324.2	610.6
South	14,471.9	7,112.8	3,177.6	3,935.2	7,128.9	11,064.0	230.3
1960							
United States[a]	64,371.6	26,251.2	4,332.0	21,919.2	35,521.9	57,441.1	2,598.6
Non-South	47,932.8	19,589.5	2,618.4	16,971.1	26,320.0	43,291.2	2,023.2
South	16,438.8	6,661.6	1,713.6	4,948.1	9,201.9	14,149.8	575.4
			Percentage Distribution				
1940							
United States[a]	100.0	48.8	18.8	30.0	49.7	79.7	1.5
Non-South	100.0	45.8	12.8	33.0	52.5	85.5	1.6
South	100.0	56.6	34.8	21.8	42.2	64.0	1.2
1950							
United States[a]	100.0	46.1	12.4	33.7	52.4	86.1	1.5
Non-South	100.0	45.1	9.1	35.9	53.5	89.4	1.5
South	100.0	49.1	22.0	27.2	49.3	76.5	1.6

(Continued on following page)

Appendix Table 2-1 (continued)

Year and region	All industries	Goods-producing			Service-producing	All nonagricultural	Industry not reported
		Total	Agriculture	Nonagricultural			
Percentage Distribution (cont.)							
1960							
United States[a]	100.0	40.8	6.7	34.1	55.2	89.2	4.0
Non-South	100.0	40.9	5.5	35.4	54.9	90.3	4.2
South	100.0	40.5	10.4	30.1	56.0	86.1	3.5
Percentage Change							
1940–1950							
United States[a]	24.5	17.8	−17.4	39.9	31.1	34.4	22.1
Non-South	26.5	24.4	−9.8	37.7	28.8	32.2	12.5
South	19.0	3.3	−24.9	48.6	39.0	42.3	57.4
1950–1960							
United States[a]	14.5	1.2	−38.0	15.7	20.6	18.7	209.0
Non-South	14.8	4.1	−31.3	13.1	17.9	16.0	231.3
South	13.6	−6.2	−46.0	25.7	29.1	27.9	149.9
1940–1960							
United States[a]	42.5	19.2	−48.8	61.9	58.2	59.6	277.2
Non-South	45.2	29.4	−38.1	55.8	51.9	53.4	272.9
South	35.2	−3.1	−59.4	86.9	79.5	82.0	293.4

Sources: U. S. Bureau of the Census, Washington: *Census of Population: 1940*, Vol. III, *The Labor Force*, Tables 13 and 62; *Census of Population: 1950*, Vol. II, Part I, Tables 76 and 77; *Census of Population: 1960*, Series C, Table 58.

[a] As elsewhere throughout this book, unless otherwise noted, data exclude Alaska and Hawaii.

Note: Discrepancies in addition are due to rounding.

Appendix Table 2-2

Population, by Type of Residence and Color, United States, Non-South, and South, 1940, 1950, 1960, and Percentage Change, by Decade

Residence and year	United States			Non-South			South		
	Total	White	Nonwhite	Total	White	Nonwhite	Total	White	Nonwhite
				Thousands					
Urban									
1940	74,424	67,973	6,451	61,551	58,302	3,249	12,873	9,671	3,202
1950	96,467	86,756	9,711	76,821	71,402	5,419	19,646	15,354	4,292
1960	124,710	110,212	14,498	96,570	87,864	8,706	28,140	22,348	5,792
Rural nonfarm									
1940	27,030	24,779	2,251	18,413	17,890	523	8,616	6,888	1,728
1950	31,181	28,470	2,711	20,365	19,765	600	10,816	8,705	2,111
1960	40,320	36,395	3,925	25,339	24,555	784	14,981	11,840	3,141
Rural farm									
1940	30,216	25,463	4,753	14,693	14,372	321	15,524	11,092	4,432
1950	23,048	19,715	3,333	11,782	11,562	220	11,266	8,153	3,113
1960	13,431	11,848	1,583	7,761	7,642	119	5,670	4,206	1,464
				Percentage Distribution					
Urban									
1940	56.4	57.5	47.9	65.0	64.4	79.4	34.8	35.0	34.2
1950	64.0	64.3	61.6	70.5	69.5	86.9	47.1	47.7	45.1
1960	69.9	69.6	72.5	74.5	73.2	90.6	57.7	58.2	55.7
Rural nonfarm									
1940	20.5	21.0	16.7	19.5	19.8	12.8	23.3	24.9	18.5
1950	20.7	21.1	17.2	18.7	19.2	9.6	25.9	27.0	22.2
1960	22.6	22.9	19.6	19.5	20.4	8.2	30.7	30.8	30.2

(Continued on following page)

Appendix 2-2 (continued)

Residence and year	United States			Non-South			South		
	Total	White	Nonwhite	Total	White	Nonwhite	Total	White	Nonwhite
				Percentage Distribution (cont.)					
Rural farm									
1940	22.9	21.5	35.3	15.5	15.9	7.8	41.9	40.1	47.3
1950	15.3	14.6	21.2	10.8	11.3	3.5	27.0	25.3	32.7
1960	7.5	7.5	7.9	6.0	6.4	1.2	11.6	11.0	14.1
				Percentage Change					
Urban									
1940–1950	29.6	27.6	50.5	24.8	22.5	66.8	52.6	58.8	34.0
1950–1960	29.3	27.0	49.3	25.7	23.1	60.7	43.2	45.6	34.9
1940–1960	67.6	62.1	124.7	56.9	50.7	167.9	118.6	131.1	80.9
Rural nonfarm									
1940–1950	15.4	14.9	20.4	10.6	10.5	14.7	25.5	26.4	22.2
1950–1960	29.3	27.8	44.8	24.4	24.2	30.7	38.5	36.0	48.8
1940–1960	49.2	46.9	74.4	37.6	37.3	49.9	73.9	71.9	81.8
Rural farm									
1940–1950	−23.7	−22.6	−29.9	−19.8	−19.6	−31.5	−27.4	−26.5	−29.8
1950–1960	−41.7	−39.9	−52.5	−34.1	−33.9	−45.9	−49.7	−48.4	−53.0
1940–1960	−55.6	−53.5	−66.7	−47.2	−46.8	−62.9	−63.5	−62.1	−67.0

Sources: U. S. Bureau of the Census, Washington: Census of Population: 1940; 1950; and 1960.

Appendix Table 3-1

Personal Income and Population, United States and South, 1929-1964[a]

Year	Population (thousands) United States	South	Personal income (millions) Current dollars United States	South	1954 dollars United States	South	Implicit price deflator
1929	121,770	33,569	$85,661	$13,025	$139,060	$21,144	61.6
1930	123,077	33,824	76,780	11,129	130,136	18,863	59.0
1931	124,040	34,033	65,597	9,642	124,709	18,331	52.6
1932	124,840	34,273	50,022	7,282	107,574	15,660	46.5
1933	125,579	34,557	47,122	7,375	105,183	16,462	44.8
1934	126,374	34,863	53,482	8,594	112,357	18,055	47.6
1935	127,250	35,133	60,104	9,604	123,671	19,761	48.6
1936	128,053	35,377	68,363	11,001	139,232	22,405	49.1
1937	128,825	35,694	73,803	12,105	149,097	23,782	50.9
1938	129,825	36,147	68,433	11,478	137,416	23,048	49.8
1939	130,880	36,668	72,753	12,207	147,872	24,811	49.2
1940	131,954	37,120	78,522	13,253	157,992	26,666	49.7
1941	133,417	37,992	95,953	17,001	180,702	32,017	53.1
1942	134,670	38,761	122,417	23,545	205,743	39,571	59.5
1943	134,697	39,184	148,409	29,741	228,322	45,755	65.0
1944	134,075	38,505	160,118	33,137	233,408	48,305	68.6
1945	133,387	37,960	164,549	33,988	231,759	47,870	71.0
1946	140,638	39,253	175,701	34,682	229,675	45,336	76.5
1947	143,665	39,804	189,077	36,978	223,495	43,709	84.6
1948	146,093	40,091	207,414	40,470	231,747	45,218	89.5
1949	148,665	40,601	205,452	41,103	231,625	46,339	88.7
1950	151,234	41,839	225,473	44,879	250,804	49,921	89.9
1951	153,384	42,839	252,960	51,093	263,500	53,222	96.0
1952	155,761	43,356	269,050	54,760	274,541	55,878	98.0
1953	158,313	43,602	283,140	56,780	286,000	57,354	99.0
1954	161,164	43,516	285,339	57,287	285,339	57,287	100.0
1955	164,308	44,429	306,598	62,289	305,376	62,041	100.4
1956	167,305	45,317	330,380	67,087	323,585	65,707	102.1
1957	170,372	46,383	348,724	70,994	331,802	67,549	105.1
1958	173,320	47,109	357,498	74,235	333,176	69,185	107.3
1959	176,289	47,954	381,326	79,120	351,453	72,922	108.5
1960	179,113	49,023	396,975	81,960	360,559	74,441	110.1
1961	182,148	50,085	413,033	86,398	372,102	77,836	111.0
1962	184,887	51,014	437,729	91,810	391,179	82,046	111.9
1963	187,686	51,842	459,299	97,221	405,026	85,733	113.4
1964	190,383[b]	52,725[b]	488,418	104,223	425,081	90,708	114.9

(Sources and notes on following pages)

Appendix Table 3-2

Employees in Nonagricultural Establishments, United States, Non-South, and

			South					
Year	United States	Non-South	Total	Alabama	Arkansas	Florida	Georgia	Kentucky
1939	30,516.9	24,655.9	5,861.0	405.3	198.0	390.5	526.7	382.5
1940	32,221.8	26,062.6	6,159.2	427.6	201.3	424.4	553.5	401.7
1941	36,422.3	29,404.7	7,017.6	500.7	230.7	474.6	637.3	441.9
1942	39,994.6	32,101.9	7,892.7	608.4	280.9	516.8	701.9	477.7
1943	42,417.1	33,996.3	8,420.8	632.7	280.8	583.1	760.1	481.1
1944	41,734.9	33,474.1	8,260.8	618.4	267.8	582.5	753.3	475.2
1945	40,037.6	32,061.8	7,975.8	579.1	273.1	562.2	725.4	466.4
1946	41,176.9	33,011.0	8,165.9	561.8	270.5	593.4	732.1	487.6
1947	43,435.5	34,749.1	8,686.4	610.4	286.1	641.4	759.4	529.6
1948	44,586.5	35,553.0	9,033.5	629.0	294.3	657.9	779.3	556.7
1949	43,384.4	34,497.6	8,886.8	604.5	288.0	657.3	769.6	536.7
1950	44,942.4	35,663.9	9,278.5	619.6	298.3	704.4	806.6	556.6
1951	47,654.6	37,665.1	9,989.5	662.8	319.0	759.7	872.3	598.9
1952	48,664.5	38,298.8	10,365.7	681.4	323.2	808.8	905.0	619.6
1953	49,920.2	39,356.2	10,564.0	692.7	319.6	848.8	929.7	631.2
1954	48,636.6	38,210.6	10,426.0	678.0	311.3	882.7	915.0	598.7
1955	50,230.9	39,356.3	10,874.6	702.9	321.0	965.9	959.5	620.2
1956	51,944.7	40,577.8	11,366.9	734.7	333.1	1060.0	994.2	649.0
1957	52,583.8	40,973.5	11,610.3	754.8	337.4	1152.7	997.4	656.7
1958	51,223.5	39,668.1	11,555.4	742.3	343.7	1185.6	989.1	634.9
1959	52,905.7	40,921.5	11,984.2	764.4	359.4	1273.0	1030.1	647.3
1960	53,790.3	41,593.5	12,196.8	776.4	367.2	1320.6	1051.1	653.6
1961	53,684.9	41,415.8	12,269.1	774.6	376.0	1333.9	1053.3	648.0
1962	55,221.2	42,506.3	12,714.9	791.8	396.8	1387.8	1101.1	674.4
1963	56,240.2	43,132.4	13,107.8	804.8	416.4	1438.8	1147.2	701.6
1964	57,245.7	43,798.0	13,447.7	818.2	427.2	1497.6	1177.0	713.4

Sources: 1939–1959—Employment and Earnings Statistics for States and Areas, 1939–62, U. S. Bureau of Labor Statistics, Washington, Bulletin No. 1370, 1963; 1960–1964—Manpower Report of the

Sources to Appendix Table 3-1

Personal income and population 1929–1953 from *Personal Income by States Since 1929, A Supplement to the Survey of Current Business*, 1956; Personal income 1954–1964 from *Survey of Current Business*, July 1965; Population 1954–1962 from *Statistical Abstract of the United States*, U. S. Bureau of the Census, Washington, 1964; 1963–1964 from *Current Population Reports*, Series P-25, No. 301, U. S. Bureau of the Census, Washington, Feb. 26, 1965; implicit price deflator (for personal consumption expenditures) from *Economic Report of the President, Together with the Annual Report of the Council of Economic Advisers*, Washington, January 1965, p. 196.

South, by State, 1939–1964 (Thousands)

| | | | | South (continued) | | | | |
Louisiana	Mississippi	North Carolina	Oklahoma	South Carolina	Tennessee	Texas	Virginia	Year
410.1	203.0	622.7	326.2	310.0	475.3	1070.7	539.9	1939
434.4	213.2	653.6	332.4	328.7	494.1	1120.5	573.8	1940
489.2	245.8	736.3	358.0	387.5	568.8	1269.5	677.3	1941
531.8	276.7	783.5	411.4	416.5	626.6	1475.2	785.3	1942
579.4	286.5	812.7	447.0	428.5	683.1	1657.8	788.0	1943
571.8	279.4	779.4	435.8	408.6	708.0	1631.7	748.9	1944
540.6	268.1	759.2	424.0	396.0	682.0	1571.4	728.3	1945
543.5	280.3	827.8	412.0	411.6	676.4	1623.4	745.5	1946
592.4	291.2	879.6	437.3	436.1	716.8	1734.0	772.1	1947
617.9	302.6	895.0	462.7	456.4	753.8	1842.0	785.9	1948
623.1	296.7	868.2	466.0	443.1	722.1	1836.1	775.4	1949
636.2	311.6	927.8	476.9	461.4	759.3	1914.4	805.4	1950
669.5	333.7	987.2	504.3	505.8	805.9	2101.0	869.4	1951
684.4	339.6	1006.5	526.6	544.3	826.5	2201.6	898.2	1952
711.4	344.1	1023.7	535.3	543.8	852.6	2227.9	903.2	1953
708.8	339.5	1012.0	531.3	519.7	842.2	2206.6	880.2	1954
725.5	354.0	1059.4	550.9	533.0	867.6	2302.7	912.0	1955
771.5	364.4	1099.3	563.4	542.9	886.7	2412.2	955.5	1956
802.6	366.9	1101.3	564.5	545.0	886.8	2472.2	972.0	1957
782.6	381.3	1108.8	557.1	545.9	875.1	2441.8	967.2	1958
789.1	397.2	1163.7	573.2	566.8	906.5	2513.0	1000.5	1959
789.8	404.0	1195.5	581.6	582.5	925.2	2531.7	1017.6	1960
780.6	408.7	1209.1	586.7	587.0	932.3	2544.1	1034.8	1961
794.9	425.7	1258.5	601.6	609.3	966.4	2624.8	1081.8	1962
809.2	442.3	1298.6	612.4	626.5	998.7	2687.5	1123.8	1963
826.1	451.0	1337.6	621.8	640.8	1034.3	2747.9	1154.8	1964

President and A Report on Manpower Requirements, Resources, Utilization, and Training, U. S. Department of Labor, Washington, March 1965.

Notes to Appendix Table 3-1
[a]For all years, except 1941–1947, figures are the midyear estimates of the Bureau of the Census; for 1941–1947 figures are the sum of civilian population as measured by midyear estimates of the Bureau of the Census and military personnel stationed in the United States, as derived from monthly or quarterly information supplied by the military services. Therefore, the figures differ from those shown in Table 3-1, which are from the decennial Population Censuses.
[b]Preliminary.

Appendix 4

METHOD OF DETERMINING
EFFECT OF INDUSTRY-MIX
ON EMPLOYMENT CHANGES

THIS APPENDIX describes the method used in determining to what extent the decrease in the South's share of national employment between 1940 and 1960 was due to its industry-mix and to what extent it was due to the competitive performance of its industries.

The method can be illustrated by referring to the changes in employment that took place in North Carolina between 1940 and 1960.

In 1940 there were 1,208,700 persons employed in North Carolina. By 1960 the number had risen to 1,605,500—a gain of 396,800, or 32.8 per cent. In the nation as a whole the increase in employment between 1940 and 1960 was 42.5 per cent. Since national employment increased at a more rapid rate than did North Carolina employment during this period, North Carolina's share of national employment dropped from 2.68 per cent in 1940 to 2.49 per cent in 1960. Had the increase in employment in North Carolina been 42.5 per cent, the same as the national increase, its share of national employment would have been the same in 1960 as in 1940, and its increase in employment would have been 514,000 instead of the actual increase of 396,800. The difference between these two figures, that is 117,200 employed workers, indicates the extent to which employment in the state in 1960 was below the level that it would have been had North Carolina's employment increased at the national rate between 1940 and 1960. (See Appendix Tables 4-1 and 4-2.)

The difference between the actual change in employment and the hypothetical change that would have occurred at the U. S. rate is called the "net shift" in employment. For the 48 states combined it was zero, because some states had increases in employment at higher than the national rate while others had increases at lower than the national rate and the two sets of changes offset each other. In North Carolina, even though employment increased, its rate of gain was enough below the national rate to result in a net downward shift of 117,200 employees. (See Appendix Table 4.2.)

We are interested in knowing to what extent this difference of 117,200 workers was a result of (1) the industry-mix within the state and (2) the competitive performance of the state's individual industries. In other words, did it result mainly from the high proportion of industries in the state in which employment was declining or expanding slowly throughout the nation, or was it the result of the inability of North Carolina's individual industries to compete effectively with the same industries in other states and regions? To arrive at an answer to this question we divided total employment in the state into the 30 industrial categories shown in text Figure 4-1 and proceeded as follows:

First, we computed the hypothetical change in employment in each industry—the number of persons who would have been employed in each of the 30 industries in North Carolina in 1960 if employment within the state in each of these industries had changed (increased or decreased) at the national rate for the respective industry.

Second, the hypothetical change in state employment in each of the 30 industries was then subtracted from the actual change in state employment that occurred in each industry between 1940 and 1960, to determine the extent to which each industry in North Carolina either fell short of or increased its employment relative to the change that would have occurred at the national rate for that industry. The difference between the actual and the hypothetical change in employment in each industry is a measure of its competitive performance in North Carolina compared to its national performance, as indicated by growth in employment.

Third, these differences between the actual and hypothetical changes in employment for the 30 industries in the state were totaled to obtain a measure for the state as a whole of how employment changes between 1940 and 1960 compared to national rates of change in the same industries. The sum of these differences is a measure of the competitive performance of all industries within the state when the influence of the industry-mix is eliminated from consideration. (See Column 4, Appendix Table 4-2.)

On the basis of competitive performance alone, North Carolina would have increased its share of national employment by 290,900 workers instead of having decreased its share by 117,200 workers. The difference between these two figures—a negative 117,200 and a positive

290,900—is a negative 408,100, and is a measure of the industry-mix effect.

The calculations and results for North Carolina can be summarized as follows:

Persons
employed

Employment in 1940	1,208,700
Employment in 1960	1,605,500
Actual increase in employment	396,800
Hypothetical increase (increase at U. S. rate of 42.5 per cent)	514,000
Total net shift (difference between actual and hypothetical increase)	−117,200
Competitive performance effects (sum of differences between actual and hypothetical changes in employment in 30 industries)	290,900
Industry-mix effects (total net shift minus the competitive performance effects)	−408,100

Similar calculations were made for each of the 48 conterminous states and the District of Columbia. The results are shown in text Figure 4-2 and Appendix Table 4-2.

Appendix Table 4-1

Total Employment, Changes in Employment, and Percentage Distribution, by State and Region, 1940 and 1960

Region and state	Persons employed (thousands)		Change in employment, 1940–1960		Per cent of U. S. employment	
	1940	1960	Number (thousands)	Per cent	1940	1960
United States	45,166.2	64,371.7	19,205.5	42.52	100.00	100.00
New England	3,060.1	4,034.6	974.5	31.85	6.78	6.27
Maine	279.0	330.6	51.6	18.49	0.62	0.51
New Hampshire	176.0	234.4	58.4	33.18	0.39	0.36
Vermont	125.1	141.6	16.5	13.19	0.28	0.22
Massachusetts	1,534.8	2,000.3	465.5	30.33	3.39	3.11
Rhode Island	264.7	317.3	52.6	19.87	0.59	0.49
Connecticut	680.5	1,010.4	329.9	48.48	1.51	1.58
Mideast	11,395.2	15,249.0	3,853.8	33.82	25.23	23.68
New York	4,974.5	6,599.5	1,625.0	32.67	11.02	10.25
New Jersey	1,569.0	2,345.5	776.5	49.49	3.47	3.64
Pennsylvania	3,230.2	4,127.2	897.0	27.77	7.15	6.41
Delaware	102.6	163.0	60.4	58.87	0.23	0.25
Maryland	690.9	1,134.0	443.1	64.13	1.53	1.76
District of Columbia	308.9	341.6	32.7	10.59	0.68	0.53
West Virginia	519.1	538.2	19.1	3.68	1.15	0.84
Great Lakes	9,256.9	13,317.1	4,060.2	43.86	20.50	20.69
Michigan	1,825.0	2,726.9	901.9	49.42	4.04	4.24
Ohio	2,345.0	3,504.9	1,159.9	49.46	5.19	5.44
Indiana	1,151.7	1,717.2	565.5	49.10	2.55	2.67
Illinois	2,874.4	3,899.5	1,025.1	35.66	6.37	6.06
Wisconsin	1,060.8	1,468.6	407.8	38.44	2.35	2.28
Plains	4,513.5	5,586.0	1,072.5	23.76	9.99	8.68
Minnesota	931.5	1,233.4	301.9	32.41	2.06	1.92
Iowa	862.8	1,019.0	156.2	18.10	1.91	1.58
Missouri	1,297.1	1,571.9	274.8	21.19	2.88	2.44
North Dakota	200.4	213.7	13.3	6.64	0.44	0.33
South Dakota	204.5	238.2	33.7	16.48	0.45	0.37
Nebraska	433.4	525.9	92.5	21.34	0.96	0.82
Kansas	583.8	783.9	200.1	34.28	1.29	1.22
South	12,156.3	16,438.7	4,282.4	35.23	26.91	25.54
Virginia	933.1	1,340.8	407.7	43.69	2.07	2.08
Kentucky	847.6	935.9	88.3	10.42	1.88	1.45
Tennessee	941.7	1,222.3	280.6	29.80	2.08	1.90

Appendix Table 4-1 (continued)

Region and state	Persons employed (thousands)		Change in employment, 1940–1960		Per cent of U. S. employment	
	1940	1960	Number (thousands)	Per cent	1940	1960
South (cont.)						
North Carolina	1,208.7	1,605.5	396.8	32.83	2.68	2.49
South Carolina	661.1	803.7	142.6	21.57	1.46	1.25
Georgia	1,107.4	1,385.0	277.6	25.07	2.45	2.15
Florida	683.3	1,719.6	1,036.3	151.66	1.51	2.67
Alabama	893.8	1,065.9	172.1	19.25	1.98	1.66
Mississippi	727.5	682.3	−45.2	−6.21	1.61	1.06
Louisiana	771.1	1,007.8	236.7	30.70	1.71	1.57
Arkansas	583.9	565.5	−18.4	−3.15	1.29	0.88
Oklahoma	658.7	785.9	127.2	19.31	1.46	1.22
Texas	2,138.4	3,318.5	1,180.1	55.19	4.73	5.16
Rocky Mountain	1,219.9	2,231.7	1,011.8	82.94	2.70	3.47
Montana	185.6	231.3	45.7	24.62	0.41	0.36
Idaho	158.6	232.9	74.3	46.85	0.35	0.36
Wyoming	86.6	120.8	34.2	39.49	0.19	0.19
Colorado	349.7	626.8	277.1	79.24	0.78	0.97
Utah	148.9	302.1	153.2	102.89	0.33	0.47
New Mexico	140.3	287.9	147.6	105.20	0.31	0.45
Arizona	150.2	429.9	279.7	186.22	0.33	0.67
Far West	3,564.3	7,514.6	3,950.3	110.83	7.89	11.67
Washington	607.7	1,001.9	394.2	64.87	1.35	1.56
Oregon	389.8	638.8	249.0	63.90	0.86	0.99
Nevada	41.5	112.5	71.0	171.08	0.09	0.17
California	2,525.3	5,761.4	3,236.1	128.15	5.59	8.95

Sources: 1940—Census of Population: 1940, Vol. III, The Labor Force, Parts I–V, Table 17 for individual states; 1950 and 1960—Census of Population: 1960, Series D, Detailed Characteristics, individual state reports, Table 126.

Appendix Table 4-2

Actual and Hypothetical[a] Changes in Employment in 30 Industries, by Region and State, 1940–1960

(Millions)

Region and state	Actual change (1)	Hypothetical change[a] (2)	Difference between actual and hypothetical[a] change (upward or downward shift)		
			Total[b] (3)	Due to competitive performance[c] (4)	Due to industry-mix[d] (5)
United States	19,205.5	19,205.5	0.0	—	—
New England	974.5	1,301.2	−326.7	−774.1	447.4
Maine	51.6	118.6	−67.0	−55.5	−11.5
New Hampshire	58.4	74.8	−16.4	−12.6	−3.8
Vermont	16.5	53.2	−36.7	−25.5	−11.2
Massachusetts	465.5	652.6	−187.1	−477.4	290.3
Rhode Island	52.6	112.6	−60.0	−78.0	18.0
Connecticut	329.9	289.4	40.5	−125.1	165.6
Mideast	3,853.8	4,845.5	−991.7	−2,903.5	1,911.8
New York	1,625.0	2,115.3	−490.3	−1,520.9	1,030.6
New Jersey	776.5	667.2	109.3	−310.4	419.7
Pennsylvania	897.0	1,373.6	−476.6	−831.6	355.0
Delaware	60.4	43.6	16.8	7.5	9.3
Maryland	443.1	293.8	149.3	54.8	94.5
District of Columbia	32.7	131.3	−98.6	−175.5	76.9
West Virginia	19.1	220.7	−201.6	−127.4	−74.2
Great Lakes	4,060.2	3,936.3	123.9	−1,161.3	1,285.2
Michigan	901.9	776.0	125.9	−234.5	360.4
Ohio	1,159.9	997.2	162.7	−232.6	395.3
Indiana	565.5	489.7	75.8	−33.9	109.7
Illinois	1,025.1	1,222.3	−197.2	−649.6	452.4
Wisconsin	407.8	451.1	−43.3	−10.7	−32.6
Plains	1,072.5	1,919.3	−846.8	−254.3	−592.5
Minnesota	301.9	396.1	−94.2	8.4	−102.6
Iowa	156.2	366.9	−210.7	−79.0	−131.7
Missouri	274.8	551.6	−276.8	−214.8	−62.0
North Dakota	13.3	85.2	−71.9	1.8	−73.7
South Dakota	33.7	87.0	−53.3	8.8	−62.1
Nebraska	92.5	184.3	−91.8	−10.8	−81.0
Kansas	200.1	248.2	−48.1	31.3	−79.4
South	4,282.4	5,169.0	−886.6	2,277.2	−3,163.8
Virginia	407.7	396.8	10.9	128.4	−117.5
Kentucky	88.3	360.4	−272.1	−47.6	−224.5

Appendix Table 4-2 (continued)

Region and state	Actual change (1)	Hypothetical change[a] (2)	Difference between actual and hypothetical[a] change (upward or downward shift)		
			Total[b] (3)	Due to competitive performance[c] (4)	Due to industry-mix[d] (5)
South (cont.)					
Tennessee	280.6	400.4	−119.8	98.1	−217.9
North Carolina	396.8	514.0	−117.2	290.9	−408.1
South Carolina	142.6	281.1	−138.5	124.9	−263.4
Georgia	277.6	470.9	−193.3	127.4	−320.7
Florida	1,036.3	290.5	745.8	790.6	−44.8
Alabama	172.1	380.0	−207.9	101.0	−308.9
Mississippi	−45.2	309.3	−354.5	−1.0	−353.5
Louisiana	236.7	327.9	−91.2	78.1	−169.3
Arkansas	−18.4	248.3	−266.7	−24.7	−242.0
Oklahoma	127.2	280.1	−152.9	−26.5	−126.4
Texas	1,180.1	909.3	270.8	637.6	−366.8
Rocky Mountain	1,011.8	518.7	493.1	646.6	−153.5
Montana	45.7	78.9	−33.2	3.6	−36.8
Idaho	74.3	67.4	6.9	50.6	−43.7
Wyoming	34.2	36.8	−2.6	11.7	−14.3
Colorado	277.1	148.7	128.4	139.0	−10.6
Utah	153.2	63.3	89.9	94.2	−4.3
New Mexico	147.6	59.7	87.9	115.1	−27.2
Arizona	279.7	63.9	215.8	232.4	−16.6
Far West	3,950.3	1,515.5	2,434.8	2,165.7	269.1
Washington	394.2	258.4	135.8	117.4	18.4
Oregon	249.0	165.7	83.3	102.6	−19.3
Nevada	71.0	17.6	53.4	56.8	−3.4
California	3,236.1	1,073.8	2,162.3	1,888.9	273.4

Sources: 1940—Census of Population: 1940, Vol. III, Parts I–V, The Labor Force, Table 17 for individual states; 1950 and 1960—Census of Population: 1960, Series D, Detailed Characteristics, individual state reports, Table 126.

[a]Change that would have occurred if employment in the state or region had changed at the average rate of change for the nation as a whole (42.52 per cent).

[b]This difference between the actual and the hypothetical change (Col. 1 minus Col. 2) is the "net shift."

[c]The difference between the sum of the actual changes in employment in the 30 industries in the state and the sum of the hypothetical changes (the changes that would have occurred if state employment in each industry had changed at the national rate in that industry).

[d]Total net shift (Col. 3) minus the competitive performance effect (Col. 4).

Note: Discrepancies in addition are due to rounding.

Appendix Table 5-1

Current Expenditures of State and Local Governments for Educational Purposes in 1964–65 in Relation to Personal Income in 1964, and per Pupil in Average Daily Attendance, 1964–65, by State

Region and state	Personal income		Pupils in average daily attendance in public elementary and secondary schools	Current expenditures for education				
	Total (millions)	Per cent		Total (millions)	Elementary and secondary schools (millions)	Per $1,000 of personal income		Per pupil in average daily attendance
						Total	Elementary and secondary schools	
United States[a]	$487,903	100.00	38,031,086	$23,699.8	$18,691.8	$48.57	$38.31	$491.49
South	105,965	21.72	11,276,860	5,296.6	4,087.3	49.98	38.57	362.45
Alabama	6,098	1.25	785,706	307.3	226.0	50.39	37.06	287.64
Arkansas	3,374	0.69	404,874	159.4	118.7	47.24	35.18	293.18
Florida	12,920	2.65	1,121,461	624.4	501.6	48.33	38.82	447.27
Georgia	8,626	1.77	952,691	418.5	335.9	48.52	38.94	352.58
Kentucky	5,968	1.22	618,500	288.3	208.8	48.31	34.99	337.59
Louisiana	6,762	1.39	726,545	382.4	287.4	56.55	42.50	395.57
Mississippi	3,422	0.70	530,883	203.7	145.5	59.53	48.15	274.07
North Carolina	9,321	1.91	1,100,132	488.5	373.1	52.41	40.00	339.14
Oklahoma	5,196	1.06	541,367	292.2	201.2	56.24	38.72	371.65
South Carolina	4,287	0.88	588,220	225.7	176.6	52.65	41.19	300.23
Tennessee	7,130	1.46	821,192	314.5	244.9	44.11	34.35	298.23
Texas	22,966	4.71	2,185,334	1,128.3	898.3	49.13	39.11	411.06
Virginia	9,895	2.03	899,955	463.4	369.3	46.83	37.32	410.35
North	282,857	57.97	18,858,276	12,555.3	10,143.4	44.39	35.86	537.88
Connecticut	9,004	1.85	514,100	327.5	279.1	36.37	31.00	542.89
Delaware	1,542	0.32	97,500	71.6	53.0	46.43	34.37	543.59
Illinois	32,136	6.59	1,846,012	1,220.7	974.3	37.99	30.32	527.79
Indiana	12,556	2.57	1,010,917	726.9	535.2	57.89	42.62	529.42
Iowa	6,608	1.35	590,500	420.7	313.8	63.67	47.49	531.41
Maine	2,088	0.43	208,000	99.4	77.9	47.61	37.31	374.52

Maryland	9,734	1.99	677,893	408.7	328.1	41.99	33.71	484.00
Massachusetts	15,383	3.15	948,000	540.3	478.1	35.12	31.08	504.32
Michigan	22,626	4.64	1,764,423	1,191.2	863.2	52.65	38.15	489.23
Minnesota	8,610	1.76	749,500	531.0	402.8	61.67	46.78	537.42
Missouri	10,988	2.25	822,800	459.3	377.1	41.80	34.32	458.21
New Hampshire	1,600	0.33	117,311	68.3	51.1	42.69	31.94	435.59
New Jersey	20,501	4.20	1,157,000	747.1	656.0	36.44	32.00	566.98
New York	55,946	11.47	2,859,000	2,488.1	2,107.8	44.47	37.68	737.25
Ohio	26,736	5.48	2,087,842	1,105.3	901.7	41.35	33.73	431.88
Pennsylvania	29,770	6.10	2,021,436	1,246.3	1,067.8	41.86	35.87	528.24
Rhode Island	2,344	0.48	138,877	95.1	72.1	40.57	30.76	519.16
Vermont	850	0.17	79,980	54.2	35.4	63.76	41.65	442.61
West Virginia	3,447	0.71	408,535	183.4	139.5	53.21	40.47	341.46
Wisconsin	10,388	2.13	758,650	570.0	429.4	54.87	41.35	566.01
West	99,081	20.31	7,895,950	5,847.9	4,461.1	59.02	45.02	564.99
Arizona	3,520	0.72	343,422	249.0	183.6	70.74	52.16	534.62
California	56,404	11.56	3,950,000	3,099.5	2,465.2	54.95	43.71	624.10
Colorado	4,967	1.02	442,906	340.4	241.0	68.53	48.52	544.13
Idaho	1,464	0.30	164,076	83.4	63.6	56.97	43.44	387.63
Kansas	5,565	1.14	472,000	331.7	245.4	59.60	44.10	519.92
Montana	1,585	0.32	152,000	105.9	79.7	66.81	50.28	524.34
Nebraska	3,506	0.72	308,000	176.7	133.2	50.40	37.99	432.47
Nevada	1,351	0.28	94,701	62.3	50.5	46.11	37.38	533.26
New Mexico	2,107	0.43	242,661	170.9	121.5	81.11	57.66	500.70
North Dakota	1,294	0.27	137,016	90.5	63.2	69.94	48.84	461.26
Oregon	4,904	1.01	406,858	329.2	238.0	67.13	48.53	584.97
South Dakota	1,314	.27	161,000	96.0	70.8	73.06	53.88	439.75
Utah	2,216	.45	264,346	170.0	116.2	76.71	52.44	439.58
Washington	8,063	1.65	679,000	480.5	344.5	59.59	42.73	507.36
Wyoming	821	.17	77,964	61.9	44.7	75.40	54.45	573.34

Sources: *Governmental Finance in 1964–65*, U. S. Bureau of the Census, Washington, Series GF-No. 6, June 1966; and *Estimates of School Statistics, 1965-66*, Research Division, National Education Association, Washington, December 1965.

ª Excludes Alaska, Hawaii, and the District of Columbia.

Appendix Table 5-2

School-Age Population, Enrollment, Teachers in Public Elementary and Secondary Schools, 1964–65

Region and state	Population 5–17 years old, July 1, 1964 (thousands)	Total enrollment		Number of classroom teachers	Enrolled pupils per teacher
		Number	Per cent of population 5–17 years old		
United States[a]	49,108	40,983,541	83.5	1,623,396	25
South	14,193	12,178,850	85.8	461,911	26
Alabama	959	820,739	85.6	29,430	28
Arkansas	509	448,384	88.1	16,483	27
Florida	1,385	1,184,360	85.5	46,054	26
Georgia	1,175	1,041,981	88.7	38,548	27
Kentucky	846	663,433	78.4	25,464	26
Louisiana	1,001	786,237	78.5	31,251	25
Mississippi	673	578,854	86.0	19,841	29
North Carolina	1,327	1,178,134	88.8	43,197	27
Oklahoma	616	594,589	96.5	22,334	27
South Carolina	734	632,608	86.2	22,754	28
Tennessee	999	864,431	86.5	30,613	28
Texas	2,820	2,416,000	85.7	97,054	25
Virginia	1,149	969,100	84.3	38,888	25
North	25,622	20,425,669	79.7	833,307	25
Connecticut	689	555,894	80.7	24,450	23
Delaware	132	104,659	79.3	4,417	24
Illinois	2,630	2,043,343	77.7	86,090	24
Indiana	1,285	1,099,380	85.6	42,319	26
Iowa	720	620,431	86.2	24,726	25
Maine	255	218,146	85.5	9,278	24
Maryland	914	735,242	80.4	29,168	25
Massachusetts	1,285	1,008,575	78.5	42,100	24
Michigan	2,249	1,917,851	85.3	69,958	27
Minnesota	957	788,022	82.3	33,519	24
Missouri	1,104	934,116	84.6	35,657	26
New Hampshire	166	125,370	75.5	5,086	25
New Jersey	1,618	1,254,625	77.5	56,686	22
New York	4,164	3,121,717	75.0	140,890	22
Ohio	2,707	2,230,124	82.4	83,920	27
Pennsylvania	2,838	2,168,145	76.4	83,612	26
Rhode Island	217	150,701	69.4	6,328	24
Vermont	105	81,962	78.1	3,431	24
West Virginia	491	435,951	88.8	14,935	29
Wisconsin	1,096	831,415	75.9	36,737	23

Appendix Table 5-2 (continued)

Region and state	Population 5–17 years old, July 1, 1964 (thousands)	Total enrollment		Number of classroom teachers	Enrolled pupils per teacher
		Number	Per cent of population 5–17 years old		
West	9,293	8,379,022	90.2	328,178	26
Arizona	434	391,759	90.3	15,435	25
California	4,553	4,140,400	90.9	148,000	28
Colorado	518	475,928	91.9	20,655	23
Idaho	196	172,505	88.0	6,974	25
Kansas	576	507,272	88.1	23,622	21
Montana	195	164,943	84.6	7,535	22
Nebraska	378	318,746	84.3	14,800	22
Nevada	109	105,952	97.2	4,129	26
New Mexico	306	260,252	85.0	10,040	26
North Dakota	182	147,627	81.1	7,007	21
Oregon	489	440,871	90.2	19,120	23
South Dakota	194	164,045	84.6	8,480	19
Utah	294	282,631	96.1	10,436	27
Washington	776	718,574	92.6	27,883	26
Wyoming	93	87,517	94.1	4,062	22

Source: *Estimates of School Statistics, 1965–66*, Research Division, National Education Association, Washington, December 1965, pp. 24 and 27.

a Excludes Alaska, Hawaii, and the District of Columbia.

Appendix Table 5-3

Sources of Public School Revenues, by Region and State, 1964–65

Region and State	Local Thousands	Local Per cent	State Thousands	State Per cent	Federal Thousands	Federal Per cent
United States[a]	$12,301,910	56.6	$8,647,007	39.8	$794,471	3.7
Non-South	10,508,834	61.6	5,999,649	35.2	539,662	3.2
South	1,793,076	38.2	2,647,358	56.4	254,809	5.4
Alabama	75,000	28.4	170,000	64.4	19,000	7.2
Arkansas	61,101	44.6	63,000	46.0	12,941	9.4
Florida	232,848	40.2	314,653	54.3	32,424	5.6
Georgia	102,463	27.8	243,345	66.1	22,358	6.1
Kentucky	90,000	37.5	135,000	56.3	15,000	6.3
Louisiana	89,070	24.8	258,880	71.9	11,871	3.3
Mississippi	58,402	33.2	101,409	57.6	16,307	9.3
North Carolina	99,000	24.7	282,783	70.7	18,298	4.6
Oklahoma	146,000	64.8	62,859	27.9	16,565	7.3
South Carolina	55,000	27.6	132,500	66.4	12,033	6.0
Tennessee	118,900	41.7	153,100	53.7	13,300	4.7
Texas	460,000	43.2	569,000	53.4	36,000	3.4
Virginia	205,292	52.0	160,829	40.7	28,712	7.3
North	7,567,469	63.1	4,095,382	34.2	328,972	2.7
Connecticut	231,944	66.1	110,000	31.3	9,000	2.6
Delaware	13,500	19.1	55,000	77.7	2,250	3.2
Illinois	963,204	75.1	292,293	22.8	26,670	2.1
Indiana	370,003	61.2	212,825	35.2	21,602	3.6
Iowa	260,000	87.0	31,000	10.4	7,800	2.6
Maine	59,175	65.0	26,500	29.1	5,325	5.9
Maryland	261,010	60.3	152,688	35.3	19,389	4.5
Massachusetts	350,000	72.2	113,000	23.3	22,000	4.5
Michigan	550,000	53.9	444,000	43.5	26,400	2.6
Minnesota	286,000	58.0	197,000	40.0	10,000	2.0
Missouri	268,700	63.6	137,050	32.4	17,017	4.0
New Hampshire	51,096	84.3	6,831	11.3	2,692	4.4
New Jersey	615,000	75.4	181,000	22.2	20,000	2.5
New York	1,390,000	54.8	1,090,000	43.0	55,000	2.2
Ohio	788,000	70.9	298,000	26.8	25,000	2.3
Pennsylvania	657,054	53.6	534,795	43.6	34,000	2.8
Rhode Island	46,400	63.7	23,630	32.4	2,800	3.8
Vermont	29,600	70.2	11,320	26.8	1,267	3.0
West Virginia	66,783	45.0	75,308	50.8	6,169	4.2
Wisconsin	310,000	72.5	103,142	24.1	14,591	3.4
West	2,941,365	58.2	1,904,267	37.7	210,690	4.2
Arizona	88,164	54.0	65,773	40.3	9,341	5.7
California	1,625,000	57.1	1,125,000	39.5	95,000	3.3
Colorado	193,789	72.6	56,000	21.0	17,000	6.4
Idaho	42,100	61.6	21,500	31.5	4,700	6.9
Kansas	202,165	75.0	55,234	20.5	12,096	4.5
Montana	63,500	67.5	26,000	27.6	4,550	4.8
Nebraska	130,000	88.8	8,500	5.8	7,900	5.4

Appendix Table 5-3 (continued)

Region and State	Local		State		Federal	
	Thousands	Per cent	Thousands	Per cent	Thousands	Per cent
West (cont.)						
Nevada	$19,099	37.4	$28,528	55.8	$3,488	6.8
New Mexico	27,926	21.0	94,713	71.4	10,097	7.6
North Dakota	51,375	74.1	15,000	21.6	3,000	4.3
Oregon	187,700	70.1	68,000	25.4	12,000	4.5
South Dakota	60,900	80.8	7,500	9.9	7,000	9.3
Utah	61,647	45.3	68,819	50.6	5,552	4.1
Washington	160,000	38.2	241,700	57.7	17,500	4.2
Wyoming	28,000	54.4	22,000	42.7	1,466	2.8

Source: *Estimates of School Statistics, 1965–66,* National Education Association, Washington, December 1965, p. 31.
ᵃ Excludes Alaska, Hawaii, and the District of Columbia.

Appendix Table 6-1

Employment by Major Industry Group, White and Nonwhite, United States, Non-South, and South, 1940, 1950, 1960
(Thousands)

Industry group	1940			1950			1960		
	Total	White	Nonwhite	Total	White	Nonwhite	Total	White	Nonwhite
United States									
All industries	45,166	40,495	4,671	56,225	50,625	5,600	64,372	57,912	6,460
Goods-producing	22,018	19,721	2,297	25,937	23,457	2,480	26,251	24,077	2,174
Agriculture, forestry, fisheries	8,475	6,909	1,566	6,996	5,887	1,109	4,332	3,726	606
Manufacturing	10,573	10,042	531	14,571	13,546	1,025	17,475	16,268	1,207
Mining	913	859	54	929	885	45	653	631	22
Construction	2,056	1,911	146	3,441	3,140	301	3,791	3,451	340
Service-producing	22,460	20,147	2,313	29,447	26,421	3,027	35,522	31,716	3,806
Transport., communic., pub. utils.	3,113	2,909	204	4,369	4,030	339	4,435	4,095	340
Trade	7,539	7,152	387	10,550	9,887	663	11,744	10,926	819
Finance, insurance, real estate	1,468	1,397	70	1,915	1,828	87	2,685	2,579	106
Services	8,586	6,996	1,591	10,124	8,376	1,749	13,487	11,258	2,229
Government	1,753	1,693	61	2,489	2,300	189	3,170	2,859	311
Industry not reported	689	628	61	841	747	94	2,599	2,119	480
Non-South									
All industries	33,010	31,684	1,325	41,753	39,426	2,327	47,933	44,659	3,274
Goods-producing	15,135	14,749	385	18,824	17,999	826	19,590	18,611	979
Agriculture, forestry, fisheries	4,240	4,124	116	3,819	3,714	104	2,618	2,540	78
Manufacturing	8,709	8,517	192	11,949	11,377	572	13,974	13,226	748
Mining	654	628	26	610	587	22	375	366	9
Construction	1,532	1,480	52	2,447	2,320	127	2,622	2,478	144

Service-producing	17,332	16,414	918	22,318	20,859	1,459	26,320	24,362	1,958
Transport., communic., pub. utils.	2,477	2,394	84	3,399	3,222	178	3,359	3,168	192
Trade	5,912	5,739	174	8,009	7,686	324	8,665	8,237	428
Finance, insurance, real estate	1,238	1,193	45	1,559	1,503	56	2,098	2,027	71
Services	6,351	5,777	574	7,451	6,689	761	9,845	8,820	1,025
Government	1,354	1,311	43	1,900	1,760	140	2,353	2,110	243
Industry not reported	543	521	21	611	568	42	2,023	1,686	337
					South				
All industries	12,156	8,811	3,346	14,472	11,199	3,273	16,439	13,253	3,186
Goods-producing	6,883	4,971	1,911	7,113	5,459	1,654	6,662	5,466	1,196
Agriculture, forestry, fisheries	4,235	2,785	1,450	3,178	2,173	1,005	1,714	1,186	527
Manufacturing	1,864	1,525	339	2,622	2,168	454	3,501	3,042	459
Mining	259	230	29	320	297	22	278	265	13
Construction	524	420	94	994	820	173	1,169	973	196
Service-producing	5,127	3,733	1,395	7,129	5,562	1,567	9,202	7,354	1,848
Transport., communic., pub. utils.	636	515	121	969	809	161	1,075	927	149
Trade	1,626	1,413	213	2,541	2,201	339	3,079	2,688	391
Finance, insurance, real estate	230	204	26	356	326	30	587	552	35
Services	2,235	1,218	1,017	2,674	1,686	987	3,642	2,438	1,204
Government	400	382	18	589	540	49	817	749	68
Industry not reported	146	107	40	230	179	52	575	432	143

Sources: *Census of Population: 1940, 1950, and 1960,* U. S. Bureau of the Census, Washington.

Appendix Table 6-2

Percentage Distribution by State of Nonwhite Employment in the South, by Major Industry Group, 1940, 1950, 1960

Industry group	Alabama			Arkansas			Florida			Georgia		
	1940	1950	1960	1940	1950	1960	1940	1950	1960	1940	1950	1960
All industries	10.1	9.9	8.9	4.8	4.0	3.2	6.6	7.7	10.5	12.3	11.9	11.4
Goods-producing	11.2	10.7	9.5	5.9	4.8	3.9	4.8	6.3	9.4	11.8	11.9	11.3
Agriculture, forestry, fisheries	10.6	9.6	7.8	6.7	5.8	4.9	4.0	6.1	10.3	11.8	11.3	9.9
Manufacturing	12.0	12.9	12.0	4.3	3.8	3.5	6.4	5.2	6.0	12.4	13.7	13.2
Mining	45.7	43.7	23.0	1.1	1.5	1.4	4.5	6.8	14.9	5.1	7.4	12.0
Construction	7.1	7.7	7.4	2.4	2.4	2.1	10.1	10.5	14.6	12.3	10.8	10.8
Service-producing	8.7	9.1	8.9	3.3	3.0	2.8	9.0	9.1	10.7	12.9	11.9	11.6
Transport., communic., pub. utils.	8.6	8.9	7.9	4.0	3.3	2.7	10.3	9.9	11.6	11.8	11.0	11.0
Trade	7.7	8.2	7.5	3.2	3.1	2.8	10.1	9.4	11.2	11.9	11.1	11.1
Finance, insurance, real estate	8.0	9.7	9.7	2.4	2.0	2.1	10.2	9.0	11.2	12.6	12.4	11.9
Services	8.9	9.5	9.4	3.2	3.0	2.9	8.7	8.9	10.4	13.2	12.5	11.8
Government	6.4	7.3	9.0	1.9	1.9	1.2	7.6	9.3	10.1	16.7	10.2	12.5
Industry not reported	8.5	8.8	4.6	5.2	4.8	1.9	7.2	7.1	16.7	11.5	9.2	8.0

Industry group	Kentucky			Louisiana			Mississippi			North Carolina		
	1940	1950	1960	1940	1950	1960	1940	1950	1960	1940	1950	1960
All industries	2.3	2.3	2.2	8.8	8.4	9.0	11.8	9.7	7.9	10.1	11.2	10.9
Goods-producing	1.5	1.6	1.6	8.8	7.9	7.9	15.8	13.2	11.0	10.5	12.7	13.1
Agriculture, forestry, fisheries	1.1	1.1	1.3	9.0	7.4	6.8	18.6	17.6	16.8	9.8	13.2	14.7
Manufacturing	1.3	1.6	1.5	8.6	8.4	8.2	7.4	6.9	6.6	13.8	13.1	12.7
Mining	20.5	14.1	8.6	2.0	3.7	8.5	0.9	1.3	2.7	2.6	2.5	3.6
Construction	3.4	2.3	1.8	9.7	9.8	10.1	7.3	5.5	5.9	11.0	10.6	10.3
Service-producing	3.3	3.1	2.5	8.8	8.9	9.7	6.3	6.0	6.3	9.5	9.5	9.6
Transport., communic., pub. utils.	2.9	3.1	2.3	11.0	11.5	12.5	5.7	5.2	5.6	7.1	7.8	8.1
Trade	33.2	2.8	2.4	10.1	10.1	10.9	6.3	6.4	6.3	8.8	8.3	8.7
Finance, insurance, real estate	5.0	4.2	3.4	9.1	9.3	10.3	2.9	3.3	3.3	7.6	8.0	7.9
Services	3.3	3.1	2.5	8.4	8.1	9.2	6.6	6.2	6.6	10.0	10.4	10.3
Government	3.8	3.5	3.2	5.3	6.3	6.3	3.9	2.7	2.7	9.3	7.4	7.0
Industry not reported	3.7	3.6	3.3	5.9	9.1	8.6	7.6	8.5	3.6	13.0	11.6	8.5

	Oklahoma			South Carolina			Tennessee			Texas		
	1940	1950	1960	1940	1950	1960	1940	1950	1960	1940	1950	1960
All industries	1.7	1.7	1.7	7.6	8.3	8.6	5.9	6.0	5.8	12.6	11.2	10.2
Goods-producing	1.2	1.1	1.2	9.5	10.2	10.2	5.0	4.7	4.4	8.8	7.7	7.5
Agriculture, forestry, fisheries	1.4	1.3	0.8	11.0	11.7	11.0	4.2	3.8	3.7	6.2	6.2	7.6
Manufacturing	0.7	0.8	0.9	8.0	8.1	8.3	6.0	6.0	6.5	7.0	8.8	10.2
Mining	1.2	1.9	3.7	2.8	2.5	4.4	2.8	2.8	3.5	3.2	4.8	9.1
Construction	1.5	2.1	1.8	8.4	8.1	8.9	7.0	7.0	7.8	10.1	14.3	12.7
Service-producing	2.2	2.2	2.0	6.5	6.3	6.4	7.7	7.3	6.5	13.7	14.8	14.7
Transport., communic., pub. utils.	1.2	1.7	1.8	5.2	5.2	5.2	7.8	7.6	7.2	13.8	14.7	15.0
Trade	2.5	2.3	2.2	5.5	5.2	5.6	8.6	7.8	6.3	14.4	16.7	17.0
Finance, insurance, real estate	3.1	2.2	1.9	2.6	3.1	3.2	10.3	9.4	8.3	16.1	16.4	16.8
Services	2.2	2.1	1.8	7.0	7.1	7.0	7.4	7.1	6.5	13.5	14.1	13.9
Government	4.6	4.5	5.2	4.9	3.9	4.0	7.7	6.1	5.6	10.1	13.5	12.7
Industry not reported	3.5	2.5	3.7	6.5	8.1	6.4	6.6	6.5	6.3	12.2	11.9	18.2

	Virginia		
	1940	1950	1960
All industries	7.0	7.9	8.2
Goods-producing	6.2	6.9	8.0
Agriculture, forestry, fisheries	4.8	4.9	5.4
Manufacturing	11.7	10.6	10.9
Mining	6.8	7.2	5.2
Construction	8.8	8.9	8.3
Service-producing	8.0	8.8	8.3
Transport., communic., pub. utils.	10.6	10.0	9.2
Trade	7.7	8.6	8.0
Finance, insurance, real estate	10.1	11.0	10.1
Services	7.5	7.9	7.5
Government	18.1	23.4	20.5
Industry not reported	8.6	8.2	9.1

Sources: United States Census of Population: 1940, 1950, and 1960, U. S. Bureau of the Census, Washington.

Appendix Table 6-3

Employment by Major Occupational Group, by Color, United States, Non-South, and South, 1940, 1950, 1960

(Thousands)

Occupational group	1940			1950			1960		
	Total	White	Nonwhite	Total	White	Nonwhite	Total	White	Nonwhite
					United States				
All occupations	45,166	40,495	4,671	56,225	50,625	5,600	64,372	57,912	6,460
White-collar	14,612	14,332	280	20,748	20,178	569	26,473	25,531	942
Professional & technical	3,345	3,220	125	4,909	4,717	192	7,198	6,862	336
Nonfarm proprietors & managers	3,749	3,686	63	5,017	4,908	109	5,385	5,275	110
Clerical	4,612	4,559	53	6,894	6,699	196	9,267	8,868	399
Sales	2,905	2,866	39	3,927	3,854	72	4,622	4,526	96
Manual	16,372	15,098	1,275	22,336	20,122	2,214	23,653	21,217	2,436
Craftsmen & foremen	5,056	4,918	137	7,773	7,480	293	8,699	8,303	397
Operatives	8,252	7,764	488	11,146	10,103	1,044	11,862	10,613	1,250
Nonfarm	3,064	2,415	649	3,417	2,540	877	3,091	2,302	789
Service	5,570	4,005	1,564	5,695	4,028	1,667	7,138	5,137	2,001
General service	3,458	2,909	549	4,288	3,439	848	5,419	4,345	1,074
Private household	2,111	1,096	1,015	1,407	589	818	1,719	792	927
Agricultural	8,234	6,710	1,524	6,706	5,642	1,064	3,937	3,394	542
Farmers & farm managers	5,144	4,443	701	4,306	3,783	524	2,502	2,312	190
Farm laborers & foremen	3,090	2,267	823	2,400	1,859	541	1,435	1,082	352
Occupation not reported	379	351	28	741	654	86	3,172	2,632	540
					Non-South				
All occupations	33,010	31,684	1,325	41,753	39,426	2,327	47,933	44,659	3,274
White-collar	11,796	11,655	141	16,344	15,998	346	20,419	19,760	659
Professional & technical	2,668	2,625	43	3,872	3,790	82	5,617	5,426	191
Nonfarm proprietors & managers	2,927	2,891	36	3,853	3,790	63	3,983	3,913	70
Clerical	3,885	3,847	39	5,614	5,457	157	7,334	7,002	332
Sales	2,315	2,292	23	3,004	2,961	43	3,485	3,419	66

Manual	12,843	12,380	464	17,119	16,035	1,084	17,630	16,352	1,277
Craftsmen & foremen	4,113	4,057	56	6,009	5,944	155	6,639	6,409	230
Operatives	6,551	6,337	213	8,609	8,046	563	8,850	8,132	718
Nonfarm	2,180	1,985	195	2,411	2,046	366	2,141	1,811	329
Service	3,980	3,378	602	4,119	3,356	763	5,050	4,154	896
General service	2,706	2,423	283	3,308	2,853	455	4,087	3,508	580
Private household	1,274	955	319	811	503	309	963	646	317
Agricultural	4,098	3,989	109	3,646	3,550	95	2,393	2,326	66
Farmers & farm managers	2,649	2,612	38	2,365	2,333	32	1,597	1,574	23
Farm laborers & foremen	1,448	1,377	71	1,281	1,217	63	796	752	44
Occupation not reported	293	283	10	526	487	39	2,441	2,066	375
South									
All occupations	12,156	8,811	3,346	14,472	11,199	3,273	16,439	13,253	3,186
White-collar	2,816	2,677	140	4,404	4,180	223	6,053	5,771	283
Professional & technical	677	595	82	1,037	928	109	1,581	1,436	145
Nonfarm proprietors & managers	822	795	27	1,164	1,118	46	1,402	1,362	40
Clerical	727	713	14	1,280	1,242	38	1,933	1,866	68
Sales	590	574	16	923	893	29	1,137	1,107	30
Manual	3,529	2,718	811	5,217	4,087	1,130	6,023	4,865	1,158
Craftsmen & foremen	943	861	82	1,674	1,536	138	2,060	1,893	167
Operatives	1,702	1,427	275	2,537	2,057	480	3,012	2,481	531
Nonfarm	884	430	454	1,006	494	512	950	490	460
Service	1,589	627	962	1,576	672	904	2,087	983	1,104
General service	752	486	266	980	586	394	1,331	837	494
Private household	837	141	696	596	86	510	756	146	610
Agricultural	4,136	2,721	1,415	3,060	2,092	969	1,544	1,068	476
Farmers & farm managers	2,494	1,831	663	1,942	1,450	492	905	738	167
Farm laborers & foremen	1,642	889	752	1,119	642	477	639	330	309
Occupation not reported	86	68	18	215	168	47	731	566	165

Sources: United States Census of Population: 1940, 1950, and 1960, U. S. Bureau of the Census, Washington.

Appendix Table 6-4

Number of and Median Earnings of Males 25–64 Years of Age with Earnings in the Experienced Labor Force, by Educational Level and Major Occupational Group, and by Color, Non-South and South,[a] 1959

Non-South

Educational level and occupational group	Males with earnings			Median earnings		
	Total (thousands)	Nonwhite Number (thousands)	Nonwhite Per cent of total	White	Nonwhite	Nonwhite as per cent of white
Total, all levels of education	25,991	1,647	6.3	$5,471	$4,017	73.4
Professional & technical	2,949	81	2.7	7,247	5,520	76.2
Nonfarm proprietors & managers	2,976	53	1.8	7,258	4,656	64.1
Clerical	1,783	118	6.6	5,339	4,564	85.5
Sales	1,638	28	1.7	6,014	4,201	69.9
Craftsmen & foremen	5,686	206	3.6	5,737	4,514	78.7
Operatives	5,308	424	8.0	5,036	4,217	83.7
Nonfarm laborers	1,536	263	17.1	4,194	3,678	87.7
Service	1,494	244	16.3	4,290	3,327	77.6
Farmers & farm managers	1,157	17	1.5	2,880	3,826	132.8
Farm laborers & foremen	346	35	10.1	2,247	2,056	91.5
Less than 8 years of school	3,482	501	14.4	4,286	3,553	82.9
Professional & technical	34			5,467	—	—
Nonfarm proprietors & managers	154	10	6.5	5,241	3,182	60.7
Clerical	98	10	10.2	4,668	3,915	83.9
Sales	72	3	4.2	4,216	3,053	72.4
Craftsmen & foremen	744	55	7.4	5,045	4,083	80.9
Operatives	1,059	137	12.9	4,521	4,013	88.8
Nonfarm laborers	494	118	23.9	3,807	3,512	92.3
Service	325	81	24.9	3,437	3,075	89.5
Farmers & farm managers	164	4	2.4	2,247	2,341	104.2
Farm laborers & foremen	150	22	14.7	1,754	1,959	111.7

8 years of school	4,578	251	5.5	4,731	3,802	80.4
Professional & technical	57	7	—	5,807	—	—
Nonfarm proprietors & managers	311	8	2.3	5,779	3,787	65.5
Clerical	195	1	4.1	4,975	4,068	81.8
Sales	148	35	.7	4,838	3,777	78.1
Craftsmen & foremen	1,197	73	2.9	5,371	4,360	81.2
Operatives	1,281	47	5.7	4,844	4,131	85.3
Nonfarm laborers	391	41	12.0	4,109	3,655	89.0
Service	319		12.9	3,879	3,211	82.8
Farmers & farm managers	398	5	—	2,607	—	—
Farm laborers & foremen	87		5.7	2,285	1,852	81.1
1 to 3 years high school	5,542	387	7.0	5,341	4,042	75.7
Professional & technical	160	4	2.5	6,374	4,080	64.0
Nonfarm proprietors & managers	510	11	2.2	6,478	4,515	69.7
Clerical	378	26	6.9	5,242	4,415	84.2
Sales	293	4	1.4	5,509	4,146	75.3
Craftsmen & foremen	1,535	54	3.5	5,767	4,550	78.9
Operatives	1,488	114	7.7	5,184	4,272	82.4
Nonfarm laborers	350	62	17.7	4,410	3,793	86.0
Service	358	60	16.8	4,457	3,409	76.5
Farmers & farm managers	173	1	.6	2,984	4,000	134.0
Farm laborers & foremen	48	4	8.3	2,749	2,253	82.0
4 years high school	6,813	315	4.6	5,714	4,397	77.0
Professional & technical	466	11	2.4	6,629	5,128	77.4
Nonfarm proprietors & managers	918	13	1.4	6,961	5,204	74.8
Clerical	670	40	6.0	5,420	4,684	86.4
Sales	546	9	1.6	5,979	4,435	74.2
Craftsmen & foremen	1,714	47	2.7	6,068	4,904	80.8
Operatives	1,230	76	6.2	5,368	4,459	83.1
Nonfarm laborers	249	32	12.9	4,616	4,060	88.0
Services	360	45	12.5	4,986	3,640	73.0
Farmers & farm managers	328			3,274	—	—
Farm laborers & foremen	42	3	7.1	2,946	2,941	99.8

(Continued on following page)

Appendix Table 6-4 (continued)

Educational level and occupational group	Males with earnings			Median earnings		
	Total (thousands)	Nonwhite Number (thousands)	Nonwhite Per cent of total	White	Nonwhite	Nonwhite as per cent of white
			Non-South (cont.)			
1 to 3 years college	2,558	109	4.2	$6,342	$4,674	73.7
Professional & technical	515	13	2.5	6,839	5,339	78.1
Nonfarm proprietors & managers	537	6	1.1	8,092	5,366	66.3
Clerical	288	22	7.6	5,487	4,812	87.7
Sales	323	4	1.2	6,632	4,745	71.5
Craftsmen & foremen	375	15	4.0	6,338	5,114	80.7
Operatives	211	20	9.5	5,399	4,669	86.5
Nonfarm laborers	40	5	12.5	4,484	3,902	87.0
Service	101	13	12.9	5,149	3,882	75.4
Farmers & farm managers	65	—	—	3,795	—	—
Farm laborers & foremen	9			3,350		—
4 or more years college	3,005	83	2.8	7,917	5,537	69.9
Professional & technical	1,724	49	2.8	7,931	5,990	75.5
Nonfarm proprietors & managers	549	7	1.3	9,695	5,931	61.2
Clerical	154	6	3.9	5,940	5,251	88.4
Sales	256	1	0.4	7,649	5,248	68.6
Craftsmen & foremen	124	3	2.4	7,849	5,454	69.5
Operatives	42	3	7.1	5,538	4,546	82.1
Nonfarm laborers	10	—	—	4,474	—	—
Service	26	2	7.7	5,205	4,058	78.0
Farmers & farm managers	28	—	—	4,326	—	—
Farm laborers & foremen	2	—	—	4,087	—	—
5 or more years college	1,403	—	—	—	—	—
Professional & technical	1,036	—	—	—	—	—
Nonfarm proprietors & managers	165	—	—	—	—	—
Clerical	46	—	—	—	—	—

	(1)	(2)	(3)	(4)	(5)	(6)
Sales	54	—	—	—	—	—
Craftsmen & foremen	33	—	—	—	—	—
Operatives	12	—	—	—	—	—
Nonfarm laborers	1	—	—	—	—	—
Service	9	—	—	—	—	—
Farmers & farm managers	5	—	—	—	—	—
South						
Total, all levels of education	10,116	1,703	16.8	4,565	2,238	49.0
Professional & technical	936	54	5.8	6,653	3,992	60.0
Nonfarm proprietors & managers	1,190	26	2.2	6,181	2,764	44.7
Clerical	568	54	9.5	5,035	3,921	77.9
Sales	608	11	1.8	5,107	2,570	50.3
Craftsmen & foremen	2,085	171	8.2	4,769	2,616	54.9
Operatives	2,014	405	20.1	3,902	2,507	64.2
Nonfarm laborers	804	416	51.7	2,639	2,204	83.5
Service	528	210	39.8	3,502	2,310	66.0
Farmers & farm managers	661	107	16.2	1,902	752	39.5
Farm laborers & foremen	324	149	46.0	1,364	846	62.0
Less than 8 years of school	3,137	1,008	32.1	2,974	1,873	63.0
Professional & technical	18	3	16.7	3,985	2,138	53.7
Nonfarm proprietors & managers	130	11	8.5	3,938	1,934	49.1
Clerical	52	11	21.2	3,977	2,858	71.9
Sales	60	3	5.0	3,204	1,927	60.1
Craftsmen & foremen	662	89	14.3	3,826	2,381	62.2
Operatives	857	240	28.0	3,276	2,339	71.4
Nonfarm laborers	508	286	56.3	2,251	2,062	91.6
Service	202	99	49.0	2,699	2,117	78.4
Farmers & farm managers	317	87	27.4	1,377	733	53.2
Farm laborers & foremen	249	126	50.6	1,180	819	69.4
8 years of school	1,261	181	14.4	3,857	2,437	63.2
Professional & technical	18	—	—	4,640	—	—
Nonfarm proprietors & managers	101	—	—	4,804	—	—
Clerical	44	3	6.8	4,387	3,455	78.8
Sales	51	—	—	3,899	—	—
Craftsmen & foremen	335	21	6.3	4,462	2,693	60.4
Operatives	333	49	14.7	$3,895	$2,657	68.2

(Continued on following page)

Appendix Table 6-4 (continued)

Educational level and occupational group	Males with earnings			Median earnings		
	Total (thousands)	Nonwhite		White	Nonwhite	Nonwhite as per cent of white
		Number (thousands)	Per cent of total			
South (cont.)						
8 years of school (cont.)						
Nonfarm laborers	107	44	41.1	$2,853	$2,478	86.9
Service	77	28	36.4	3,303	2,399	72.6
Farmers & farm managers	112	8	7.1	1,803	851	47.2
Farm laborers & foremen	31	9	29.0	1,562	979	62.7
1 to 3 years high school	1,905	258	13.5	4,556	2,587	56.8
Professional & technical	52	3	5.8	5,534	2,692	48.6
Nonfarm proprietors & managers	223	4	1.8	5,422	2,996	55.3
Clerical	109	11	10.1	4,820	3,837	79.6
Sales	117	1	.9	4,555	2,601	57.1
Craftsmen & foremen	517	30	5.8	4,984	2,852	57.2
Operatives	445	71	16.0	4,296	2,746	63.9
Nonfarm laborers	114	56	49.0	3,264	2,428	74.4
Service	116	42	36.2	3,803	2,442	64.2
Farmers & farm managers	100	7	7.0	2,421	820	33.7
Farm laborers & foremen	26	8	30.8	1,935	1,117	57.7
4 years high school	1,982	148	7.5	5,269	2,886	54.8
Professional & technical	135	4	3.0	6,125	3,189	52.1
Nonfarm proprietors & managers	342	3	.9	6,228	3,387	54.4
Clerical	203	13	6.4	5,116	4,172	81.5
Sales	189	2	1.1	5,228	3,430	65.6
Craftsmen & foremen	459	19	4.1	5,476	3,139	57.3
Operatives	310	37	11.9	4,789	2,894	60.4
Nonfarm laborers	62	23	37.1	3,745	2,688	71.8
Service	95	28	29.5	4,348	2,547	58.6
Farmers & farm managers	90	1	1.1	3,024	852	28.2
Farm laborers & foremen	14	2	14.3	2,463	1,064	43.2

1 to 3 years college	840	53	6.3	$5,894	$3,360	57.0
Professional & technical	150	6	4.0	6,338	3,583	56.5
Nonfarm proprietors & managers	207	—	—	7,208	—	—
Clerical	102	6	5.9	5,280	4,563	86.4
Sales	109	—	—	5,955	—	—
Craftsmen & foremen	112	6	5.4	5,734	3,201	55.8
Operatives	59	8	13.6	5,034	3,081	61.2
Nonfarm laborers	15	5	33.3	4,106	3,078	75.0
Service	27	8	29.6	4,330	2,792	64.5
Farmers & farm managers	23	—	—	3,993	—	—
Farm laborers & foremen	1	—	—	—	—	—
4 or more years college	993	54	5.4	7,372	4,308	58.4
Professional and technical	559	37	6.6	7,397	4,469	60.4
Nonfarm proprietors & managers	187	—	—	9,066	—	—
Clerical	61	4	6.6	5,912	4,844	81.9
Sales	81	—	—	6,903	—	—
Craftsmen & foremen	41	—	—	6,989	—	—
Operatives	12	—	—	5,345	—	—
Nonfarm laborers	3	—	—	4,781	—	—
Service	9	1	11.1	4,732	2,775	58.0
Farmers & farm managers	15	—	—	—	—	—
Farm laborers & foremen	—	—	—	—	—	—
5 or more years college	436	24	5.5	—	—	—
Professional & technical	324	19	5.9	—	—	—
Nonfarm proprietors & managers	50	1	2.0	—	—	—
Clerical	17	1	5.9	—	—	—
Sales	18	—	—	—	—	—
Craftsmen & foremen	9	—	—	—	—	—
Operatives	1	—	—	—	—	—
Nonfarm laborers	—	—	—	—	—	—
Service	—	—	—	—	—	—
Farmers & farm managers	—	—	—	—	—	—
Farm laborers & foremen	—	—	—	—	—	—

Source: *United States Census of Population: 1960*, PC(2)7B, *Occupation by Earnings and Education*, U. S. Bureau of the Census, Washington, Tables 2 and 3.
a South includes, in addition to the states covered by this study, Delaware, Maryland, West Virginia, and the District of Columbia.

Appendix Table 6-5

Median Earnings of Males 25–64 Years of Age with Earnings in the Experienced Labor Force, by Educational Level and Occupation, and by Color, Non-South and South, 1959

Occupation	All educational levels		Elementary school graduates		High school graduates		Nonwhite as per cent of white, all educational levels
	White	Nonwhite	White	Nonwhite	White	Nonwhite	
			Non-South				
Clerical and kindred workers							
Mail carriers	$5,374	$5,183	$5,307	a	$5,391	$5,195	96.4
Postal clerks	5,486	5,185	5,430	a	5,516	5,192	94.5
Shipping & receiving clerks	4,749	3,856	4,658	$3,630	4,871	3,793	81.2
All other	5,407	4,320	4,964	3,976	5,488	4,427	79.9
Craftsmen, foremen & kindred workers							
Brick & stonemasons & tilesetters	5,601	4,073	5,295	4,685	6,118	4,182	72.7
Carpenters	5,041	4,323	4,678	4,337	5,444	4,828	85.8
Cement & concrete finishers	5,516	3,994	5,485	a	5,891	a	72.4
Electricians	6,347	5,572	6,139	a	6,483	5,695	87.8
Foremen[b]	6,975	5,370	6,535	5,454	7,202	5,837	77.0
Machinists	5,698	4,854	5,489	4,497	5,915	5,240	85.2
Mechanics & repairmen[b]	5,234	4,354	4,933	4,220	5,517	4,717	83.2
Airplane mechanics	6,250	5,704	5,860	a	6,395	5,712	91.3
Automobile mechanics	4,954	4,309	4,764	4,145	5,176	4,765	87.0
Radio & television repairmen	5,018	4,498	4,103	a	5,283	4,411	89.6
Painters, construction, & maintenance	4,518	3,493	4,372	3,440	4,990	3,911	77.3
Plasterers	5,604	3,958	5,138	3,807	6,179	a	70.6
Plumbers & pipefitters	6,093	4,847	5,760	a	6,408	5,177	79.6
Other construction craftsmen[b]	5,372	4,578	5,150	3,983	5,707	4,805	85.2
Other metal craftsmen[b]	5,787	4,681	5,588	4,560	6,127	5,036	80.9
All other	5,598	4,601	5,225	4,524	5,789	4,820	82.2

Operatives and kindred workers							
Bus drivers	4,913	5,211	4,704	4,585	5,245	5,236	106.1
Mine operatives & laborers[b]	4,480	3,797	4,291	a	5,056	a	84.8
Truck and tractor drivers	5,138	4,034	4,947	4,103	5,398	4,417	78.5
Operatives & kindred workers[b]	5,000	4,342	4,848	4,271	5,353	4,510	86.8
All other	5,075	4,098	4,838	3,965	5,392	4,328	80.7
Service workers, including private household							
Barbers	4,331	3,231	4,228	a	4,653	3,862	74.6
Protective service workers[b]	5,336	4,755	4,729	3,807	5,570	5,108	89.1
Firemen & fire protection	5,742	5,452	5,428	a	5,841	a	94.9
Policemen & detectives	5,569	5,271	5,068	a	5,581	5,339	94.6
All other	3,647	3,235	3,571	3,192	4,108	3,424	88.7
South							
Clerical and kindred workers							
Mail carriers	5,355	5,097	5,167	5,058	5,396	5,096	95.2
Postal clerks	5,425	5,134	5,423	4,150	5,406	5,109	94.6
Shipping & receiving clerks	4,052	3,016	3,978	a	4,310	2,990	74.4
All other	5,047	3,571	4,301	3,355	5,106	3,874	70.8
Craftsmen, foremen & kindred workers							
Brick & stonemasons & tilesetters	4,469	2,830	4,142	2,875	5,131	3,538	63.3
Carpenters	3,349	1,769	3,369	1,714	4,203	2,542	52.8
Cement & concrete finishers	3,856	2,698	4,127	2,718	a	a	70.0
Electricians	5,586	3,167	5,380	a	5,795	a	56.7
Foremen[b]	5,943	3,895	5,491	a	6,411	a	65.5
Machinists	5,325	3,436	5,183	a	5,588	a	64.5
Mechanics & repairmen[b]	4,491	2,657	4,279	2,670	5,074	3,006	59.2
Airplane mechanics	5,740	4,539	5,516	a	5,870	a	79.1
Automobile mechanics	3,923	2,460	3,872	2,550	4,342	2,849	62.7
Radio & television repairmen	4,173	2,209	3,293	a	4,456	a	52.9
Painters, construction & maintenance	3,243	1,991	4,328	2,170	4,055	2,304	61.4
Plasterers	4,799	2,591	4,906	a	6,198	a	54.0
Plumbers and pipefitters	5,109	2,480		a	5,715	a	48.5

(Continued on following page)

Appendix Table 6-5 (continued)

Occupation	All educational levels		Elementary school graduates		High school graduates		Nonwhite as per cent of white, all educational levels
	White	Nonwhite	White	Nonwhite	White	Nonwhite	
South (cont.)							
Craftsmen, foremen & kindred workers (cont.)							
Other construction craftsmen[b]	$4,040	$2,686	$4,027	$3,087	$4,810	a	66.5
Other metal craftsmen[b]	5,227	3,452	4,975	a	5,683	a	66.0
All other	4,877	2,936	4,524	2,929	5,371	$2,919	60.2
Operatives and kindred workers							
Bus drivers	3,645	1,804	3,431	1,766	4,646	a	49.5
Mine operatives & laborers[b]	4,431	3,333	4,298	3,353	5,562	3,907	75.2
Truck & tractor drivers	3,548	2,399	3,658	2,591	4,320	2,865	67.6
Operatives & kindred workers[b]	3,965	2,650	4,010	2,802	5,003	3,122	66.8
All other	3,964	2,446	3,869	2,571	4,630	2,710	61.7
Service workers, including private household							
Barbers	3,660	2,129	3,647	2,006	4,086	2,473	58.2
Protective service workers[b]	4,277	3,693	3,855	3,411	4,696	4,355	86.3
Firemen & fire protection	4,895	a	4,776	a	4,926	a	—
Policemen & detectives	4,518	4,184	4,094	a	4,650	a	92.6
All other	2,674	2,284	2,710	2,391	3,441	2,486	85.4

Source: Special tabulations of the U. S. Bureau of the Census, Washington.
a Less than 1,000 persons reported income.
b Not elsewhere classified.

Appendix Table 7-1

U. S. Working-Age Population and Labor Force, by Age and Sex, 1960, and Projections for 1975[a]

Age group and sex	Working-age population					Labor force				
	1960		1975		Percentage change, 1960 –1975	1960		1975		Percentage change, 1960 –1975
	Number (thousands)	Per cent	Number (thousands)	Per cent		Number (thousands)	Per cent	Number (thousands)	Per cent	
Both sexes, 14 years and over	127,327	100.0	162,046	100.0	27.3	73,081	100.0	93,646	100.0	28.1
14 to 24 years	27,283	21.4	43,857	27.1	60.8	13,697	18.7	22,524	24.0	64.4
25 to 54 years	67,764	53.2	77,172	47.6	13.9	46,596	63.8	55,209	59.0	18.5
55 years and over	32,279	25.4	41,016	25.3	27.1	12,788	17.5	15,913	17.0	24.4
Male, 14 years and over	62,216	48.9	78,408	48.4	26.0	49,563	67.8	60,281	64.4	21.6
14 to 24 years	13,747	10.8	22,192	13.7	61.4	8,731	12.0	13,920	14.9	59.4
25 to 54 years	33,373	26.2	38,004	23.4	13.9	31,962	43.7	36,479	38.9	14.1
55 years and over	15,094	11.9	18,210	11.2	20.6	8,870	12.1	9,882	10.6	11.4
Female, 14 years and over	65,111	51.1	83,638	51.6	28.5	23,518	32.2	33,365	35.6	41.9
14 to 24 years	13,536	10.6	21,665	13.4	60.1	4,966	6.8	8,604	9.2	73.3
25 to 54 years	34,391	27.0	39,168	24.2	13.9	14,634	20.0	18,730	20.0	28.0
55 years and over	17,185	13.5	22,806	14.1	32.7	3,918	5.4	6,031	6.4	53.9

Source: Sophia Cooper and Denis F. Johnston, "Labor Force Projections for 1970-80," Monthly Labor Review, February 1965, p. 130.

[a] Includes Alaska and Hawaii; also includes armed forces.

Note: Discrepancies in addition are due to rounding.

Appendix Table 7-2

Civilian Working-Age Population, Labor Force, and Labor Force Participation Rate, 1950 and 1960, and Projections for 1975, by Age, Sex, and Color, United States, Non-South, and South

Sex, color, and region	Working-age population (thousands)			Labor force (thousands)			Participation rate (per cent)		
	1950	1960	1975	1950	1960	1975	1950	1960	1975
				14 Years and Over					
Both sexes									
Total									
United States	109,279	122,364	160,003	63,099	70,306	90,457	57.7	57.5	56.5
Non-South	80,594	89,936	118,293	46,977	52,394	67,826	58.3	58.3	57.3
South	28,685	32,428	41,710	16,122	17,912	22,631	56.2	55.2	54.3
White									
United States	98,491	109,829	142,368	56,508	62,957	80,202	57.4	57.3	56.3
Non-South	76,057	83,742	107,784	44,151	48,613	61,465	58.0	58.0	57.0
South	22,434	26,087	34,585	12,357	14,344	18,737	55.2	55.0	54.2
Nonwhite									
United States	10,788	12,535	17,635	6,591	7,349	10,255	61.1	58.6	58.2
Non-South	4,537	6,194	10,509	2,826	3,781	6,361	61.8	61.0	60.5
South	6,251	6,341	7,126	3,764	3,568	3,894	60.2	56.3	54.6
Males									
Total									
United States	52,899	58,563	76,336	44,442	46,812	57,736	84.0	79.9	75.6
Non-South	39,086	43,177	56,932	32,929	34,966	43,599	84.2	81.0	76.6
South	13,813	15,386	19,404	11,513	11,846	14,137	83.3	77.0	72.9
White									
United States	47,737	52,660	67,983	40,232	42,422	51,687	84.3	80.6	76.0
Non-South	36,878	40,236	51,811	31,155	32,700	39,780	84.5	81.3	76.8
South	10,859	12,424	16,172	9,077	9,722	11,907	83.6	78.3	73.6

Nonwhite

United States	5,162	5,903	8,353	4,210	4,390	6,049	81.6	74.4	72.4
Non-South	2,207	2,940	5,121	1,774	2,266	3,819	80.4	77.1	74.6
South	2,955	2,963	3,232	2,436	2,124	2,230	82.4	71.7	69.0

Females

Total

United States	56,380	63,801	83,667	18,657	23,494	32,721	33.1	36.8	39.1
Non-South	41,508	46,759	61,361	14,048	17,428	24,227	33.8	37.3	39.5
South	14,872	17,042	22,306	4,609	6,066	8,494	31.0	35.6	38.1

White

United States	50,754	57,169	74,385	16,277	20,535	28,515	32.1	35.9	38.3
Non-South	39,179	43,506	55,973	12,996	15,913	21,685	33.2	36.6	38.7
South	11,575	13,663	18,413	3,280	4,621	6,830	28.3	33.8	37.1

Nonwhite

United States	5,626	6,632	9,282	2,380	2,959	4,206	42.3	44.6	45.3
Non-South	2,330	3,254	5,388	1,052	1,514	2,542	45.2	46.5	47.2
South	3,296	3,378	3,894	1,328	1,444	1,664	40.3	42.7	42.7

14-24 Years

Both sexes

Total

United States	23,382	25,443	42,040	11,390	11,456	19,399	48.7	45.0	46.1
Non-South	16,226	17,909	31,220	8,110	8,358	14,743	50.0	46.7	47.2
South	7,156	7,534	10,820	3,280	3,098	4,656	45.8	41.1	43.0

White

United States	20,604	22,336	36,171	10,102	10,196	16,877	49.0	45.6	46.7
Non-South	15,202	16,528	27,733	7,656	7,772	13,187	50.4	47.0	47.5
South	5,402	5,808	8,437	2,446	2,424	3,690	45.3	41.7	43.7

Nonwhite

United States	2,778	3,107	5,869	1,289	1,260	2,522	46.4	40.6	43.0
Non-South	1,024	1,381	3,487	454	587	1,556	44.3	42.5	44.6
South	1,754	1,726	2,382	835	674	966	47.6	39.0	40.6

(Continued on following page)

Appendix Table 7-2 (continued)

Sex, color, and region	Working-age population (thousands)			Labor force (thousands)			Participation rate (per cent)		
	1950	1960	1975	1950	1960	1975	1950	1960	1975
				14-24 Years (cont.)					
Males									
Total									
United States	11,294	12,252	20,592	6,912	6,889	11,664	61.2	56.2	56.6
Non-South	7,852	8,610	15,336	4,731	4,941	8,803	60.3	57.4	57.4
South	3,442	3,642	5,256	2,181	1,948	2,856	63.4	53.5	54.3
White									
United States	9,995	10,770	17,713	6,098	6,131	10,150	61.0	56.9	57.3
Non-South	7,379	7,970	13,596	4,471	4,610	7,886	60.6	57.8	58.0
South	2,616	2,800	4,117	1,627	1,521	2,264	62.2	54.3	55.0
Nonwhite									
United States	1,299	1,482	2,879	813	759	1,514	62.6	51.2	52.6
Non-South	473	640	1,740	260	331	922	55.0	51.7	53.0
South	826	842	1,139	553	428	592	66.9	50.8	52.0
Females									
Total									
United States	12,088	13,191	21,448	4,479	4,567	7,735	37.1	34.6	36.1
Non-South	8,374	9,299	15,884	3,379	3,418	5,935	40.4	36.8	37.4
South	3,714	3,892	5,564	1,100	1,149	1,800	29.6	29.5	32.4
White									
United States	10,609	11,566	18,458	4,003	4,065	6,727	37.7	35.1	36.4
Non-South	7,823	8,558	14,137	3,185	3,162	5,301	40.7	36.9	37.5
South	2,786	3,008	4,320	818	904	1,426	29.4	30.1	33.0
Nonwhite									
United States	1,479	1,625	2,990	475	502	1,008	32.1	30.9	33.7
Non-South	551	741	1,747	194	256	634	35.2	34.5	36.3
South	928	884	1,243	282	246	374	30.4	27.8	30.1

25-54 Years

Both sexes								
Total								
United States	60,807	65,528	75,835	41,133	46,165	54,863	67.6	70.4	72.3
Non-South	45,007	48,416	56,108	30,610	34,252	40,771	68.0	70.7	72.7
South	15,800	17,112	19,727	10,523	11,913	14,092	66.6	69.6	71.4
White								
United States	54,620	58,685	67,558	36,663	41,171	48,527	67.1	70.2	71.8
Non-South	42,183	44,763	50,905	28,555	31,587	36,757	67.7	70.6	72.2
South	12,437	13,922	16,653	8,109	9,585	11,770	65.2	68.8	70.7
Nonwhite								
United States	6,187	6,843	8,277	4,470	4,993	6,336	72.2	73.0	76.5
Non-South	2,824	3,653	5,203	2,055	2,665	4,014	72.8	73.0	77.1
South	3,363	3,190	3,074	2,415	2,328	2,322	71.8	73.0	75.5
Males								
Total								
United States	29,510	31,688	36,890	29,279	31,199	35,655	99.2	98.5	96.7
Non-South	21,902	23,549	27,692	21,795	23,321	26,823	99.5	99.0	96.9
South	7,608	8,139	9,198	7,484	7,878	8,832	98.4	96.8	96.0
White								
United States	26,558	28,501	32,982	26,494	28,268	31,930	99.8	99.2	96.8
Non-South	20,520	21,820	25,147	20,515	21,728	24,393	99.9	99.6	97.0
South	6,038	6,681	7,835	5,979	6,540	7,537	99.0	97.9	96.2
Nonwhite								
United States	2,952	3,187	3,908	2,785	2,931	3,725	94.3	92.0	95.3
Non-South	1,382	1,729	2,545	1,281	1,593	2,430	92.7	92.1	95.5
South	1,570	1,458	1,363	1,504	1,338	1,295	95.8	91.8	95.0
Females								
Total								
United States	31,297	33,840	38,945	11,854	14,966	19,208	37.9	44.2	49.3
Non-South	23,105	24,867	28,416	8,814	10,931	13,948	38.1	44.0	49.1
South	8,192	8,973	10,529	3,039	4,035	5,260	37.1	45.0	50.0

(Continued on following page)

Appendix Table 7-2 (continued)

Sex, color, and region	Working-age population (thousands)			Labor force (thousands)			Participation rate (per cent)		
	1950	1960	1975	1950	1960	1975	1950	1960	1975
Females (cont.)									
25-54 years (cont.)									
White									
United States	28,062	30,184	34,576	10,169	12,903	16,597	36.2	42.7	48.0
Non-South	21,663	22,943	25,758	8,040	9,859	12,364	37.1	43.0	48.0
South	6,399	7,241	8,818	2,129	3,045	4,233	33.3	42.1	48.0
Nonwhite									
United States	3,235	3,656	4,369	1,684	2,062	2,611	52.1	56.4	59.8
Non-South	1,442	1,924	2,658	774	1,072	1,584	53.7	55.7	59.6
South	1,793	1,732	1,711	910	990	1,027	50.8	57.2	60.6
55 Years and Over									
Both sexes									
Total									
United States	25,090	31,393	42,129	10,576	12,685	16,195	42.2	40.4	38.4
Non-South	19,361	23,611	30,964	8,257	9,784	12,312	42.6	41.4	39.8
South	5,729	7,782	11,165	2,318	2,901	3,883	40.5	37.3	34.8
White									
United States	23,267	28,808	38,640	9,743	11,590	14,798	41.9	40.2	38.3
Non-South	18,672	22,451	29,145	7,940	9,255	11,521	42.5	41.2	39.5
South	4,595	6,357	9,495	1,803	2,335	3,277	39.2	36.7	34.5
Nonwhite									
United States	1,823	2,585	3,489	833	1,095	1,397	45.7	42.4	40.0
Non-South	689	1,160	1,819	317	529	791	46.0	45.6	43.5
South	1,134	1,425	1,670	515	567	606	45.4	39.8	36.3

Males

Total									
United States	12,095	14,623	18,855	8,251	8,724	10,417	68.2	59.7	55.2
Non-South	9,332	11,018	13,904	6,402	6,705	7,968	68.6	60.9	57.3
South	2,763	3,605	4,951	1,849	2,019	2,449	66.9	56.0	49.5
White									
United States	11,184	13,389	17,289	7,640	8,024	9,607	68.3	59.9	55.6
Non-South	8,979	10,446	13,068	6,169	6,362	7,501	68.7	60.9	57.4
South	2,205	2,943	4,221	1,470	1,662	2,106	66.7	56.5	49.9
Nonwhite									
United States	911	1,234	1,566	612	700	810	67.2	56.7	51.7
Non-South	352	571	836	233	342	467	66.2	59.9	55.9
South	559	663	730	379	358	343	67.8	54.0	47.0

Females

Total									
United States	12,995	16,770	23,274	2,325	3,961	5,778	17.9	23.6	24.8
Non-South	10,029	12,593	17,060	1,855	3,079	4,344	18.5	24.4	25.5
South	2,966	4,177	6,214	469	882	1,434	15.8	21.1	23.1
White									
United States	12,083	15,419	21,351	2,104	3,566	5,191	17.4	23.1	24.3
Non-South	9,693	12,005	16,077	1,771	2,893	4,020	18.3	24.1	25.0
South	2,390	3,414	5,274	333	673	1,171	13.9	19.7	22.2
Nonwhite									
United States	912	1,351	1,923	221	395	587	24.2	29.2	30.5
Non-South	337	589	983	84	187	324	24.9	31.7	33.0
South	575	762	940	136	209	263	23.7	27.4	28.0

Sources: U. S. totals, 1950 and 1960, as published in *Economic Report of the President, Together with the Annual Report of the Council of Economic Advisers,* Washington, 1966, p. 232. These totals (which exclude Alaska and Hawaii) are annual estimates from the U. S. Bureau of Labor Statistics, *Monthly Report of the Labor Force* (MRLF). The distribution by age, sex, and color and by South and non-South, not estimated by the BLS, was obtained, with

Appendix Table 7-2 (continued)

the exception explained below, by applying to the MRLF totals the percentage distribution of these items as reported in the decennial Censuses of Population in 1950 and 1960.

Since Census figures are as of April 1 of the Census year and MRLF figures are annual averages based on a monthly sample survey, the Census and MRLF U. S. totals for the working-age population and the labor force differ. Because of these differences, the application of the Census percentage distribution by sex to the MRLF labor force totals resulted in male labor force estimates—particularly of the age group 25 to 54 years old, the largest single group in the labor force—that were unreasonably high. Hence, the Census distribution by sex was disregarded and the sex distribution shown in *Manpower Report of the President and A Report on Manpower Requirements, Resources, Utilization, and Training* U. S. Department of Labor, Washington, March 1966, Table A-3, p. 155, was applied to the MRLF totals. Even after this adjustment, the resulting participation rates for white males 25 to 54 years of age are unreasonably high. (See, for example, the 1966 Manpower report cited above, Table A-4, p. 157.)

The projections of the civilian population of working age for 1975 are special projections of the population, by state, made by the U. S. Bureau of the Census for use in this study in 1963. These projections are based on the assumptions that the death rate for each age-sex group in each state in 1960 to 1975 will be the same as for the corresponding group for the United States as a whole, as projected in "Interim Revised Projections of the Population of the United States: 1960 to 1980," *Current Population Reports,* U. S. Bureau of the Census, Series P-25, No. 251, and that the rate of net civilian migration for each age-sex-color group for each state for this period will be the same as for 1950 to 1960.

The 1975 projections of the labor force were made by estimating the participation rate for each age-sex-color group in 1975 and multiplying it by the projected working-age population in the same group. The estimates of the 1975 participation rates were based on: trends that prevailed between 1950 and 1960; extrapolation to 1975 of the projected participation rates to 1970 published in the 1963 *Manpower Report of the President;* and evaluation of the influence during the next few years of such factors as continuing urbanization, increasing educational attainments and opportunities, declines in employment discrimination, and availability of jobs in 1975. In consideration of all of these factors, it was assumed that the national rate of unemployment in 1975 would be 4 per cent of the labor force.

Note: Discrepancies in addition are due to rounding.

Index

N

O

P